HEART WATERS

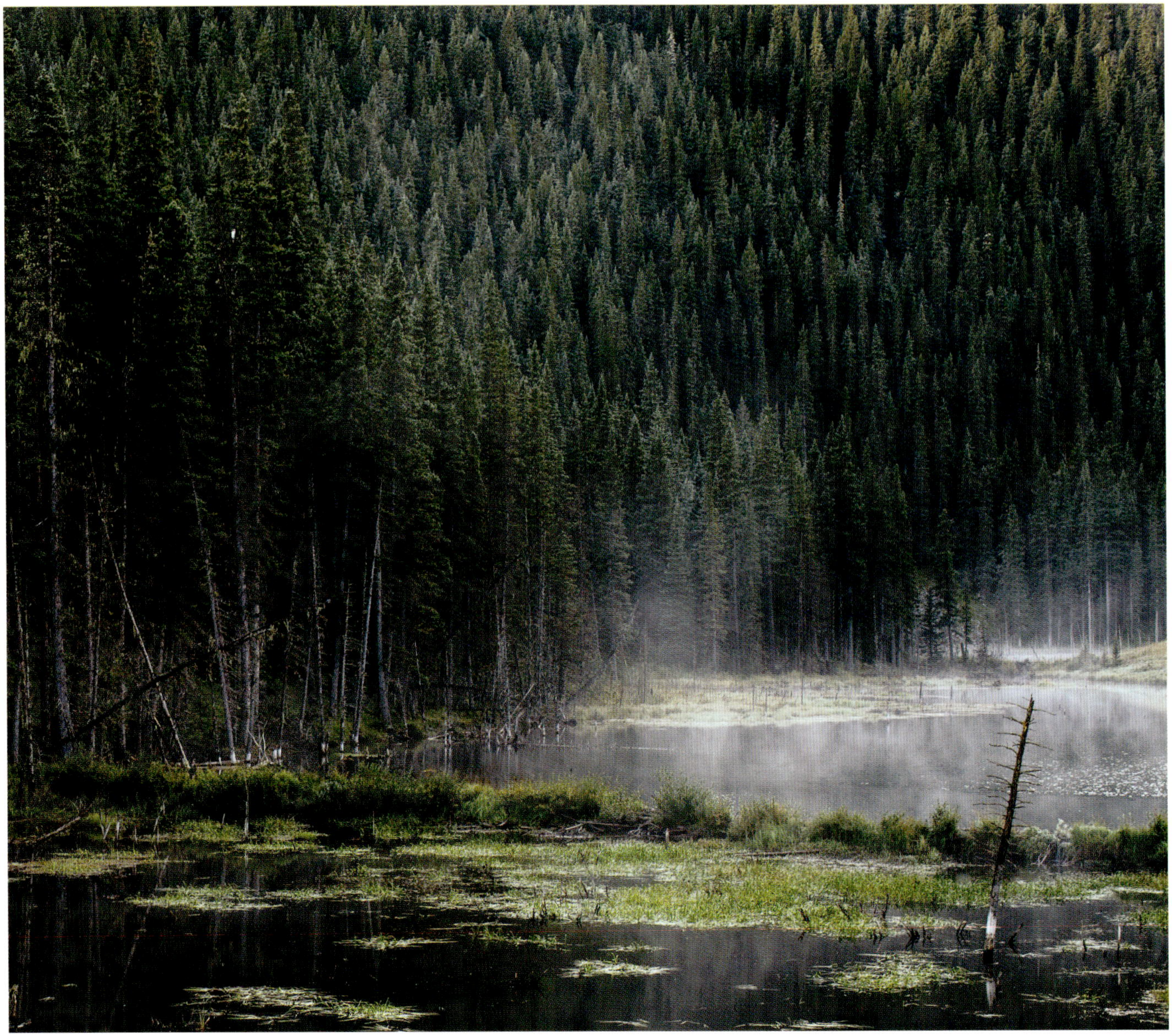

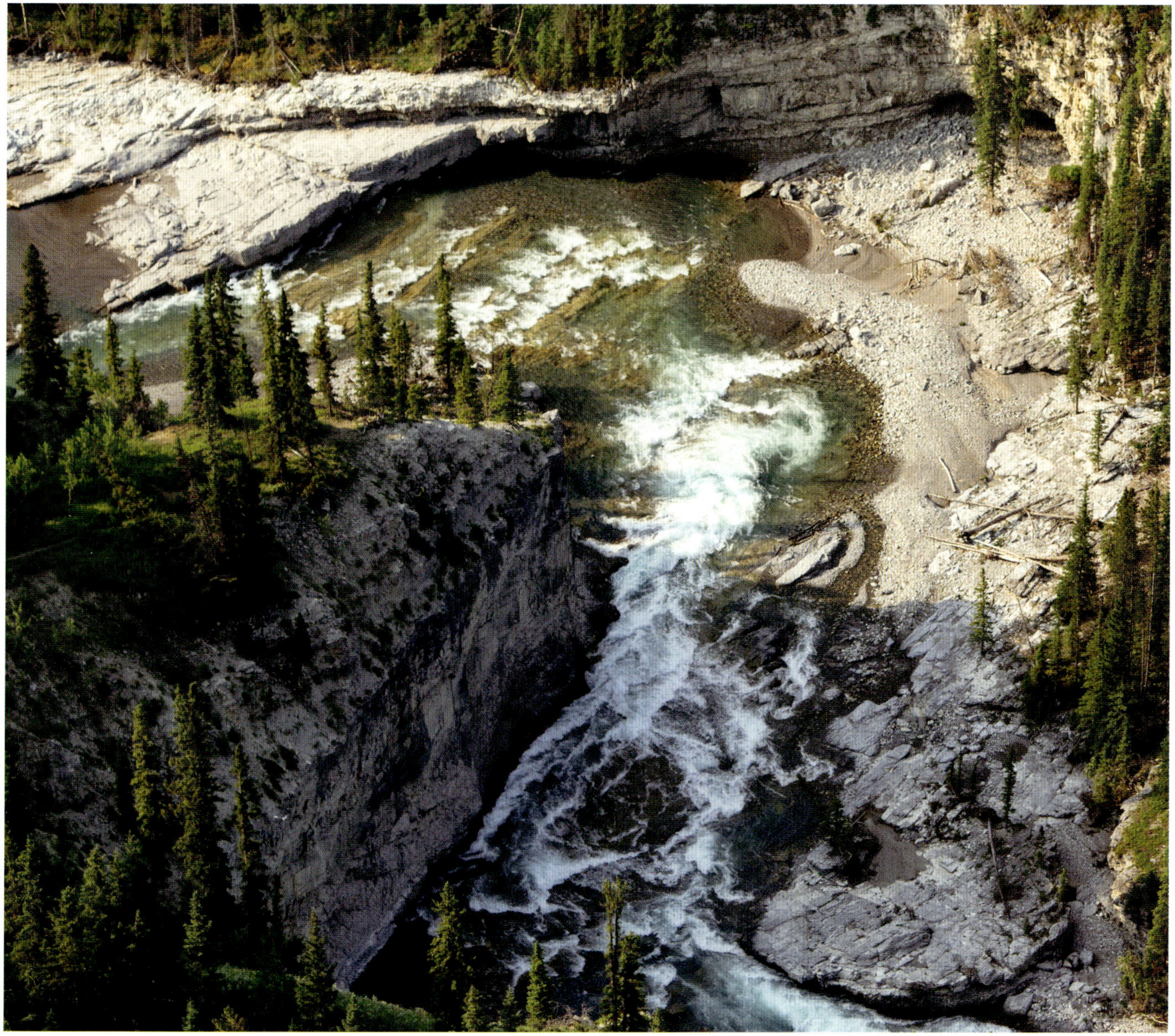

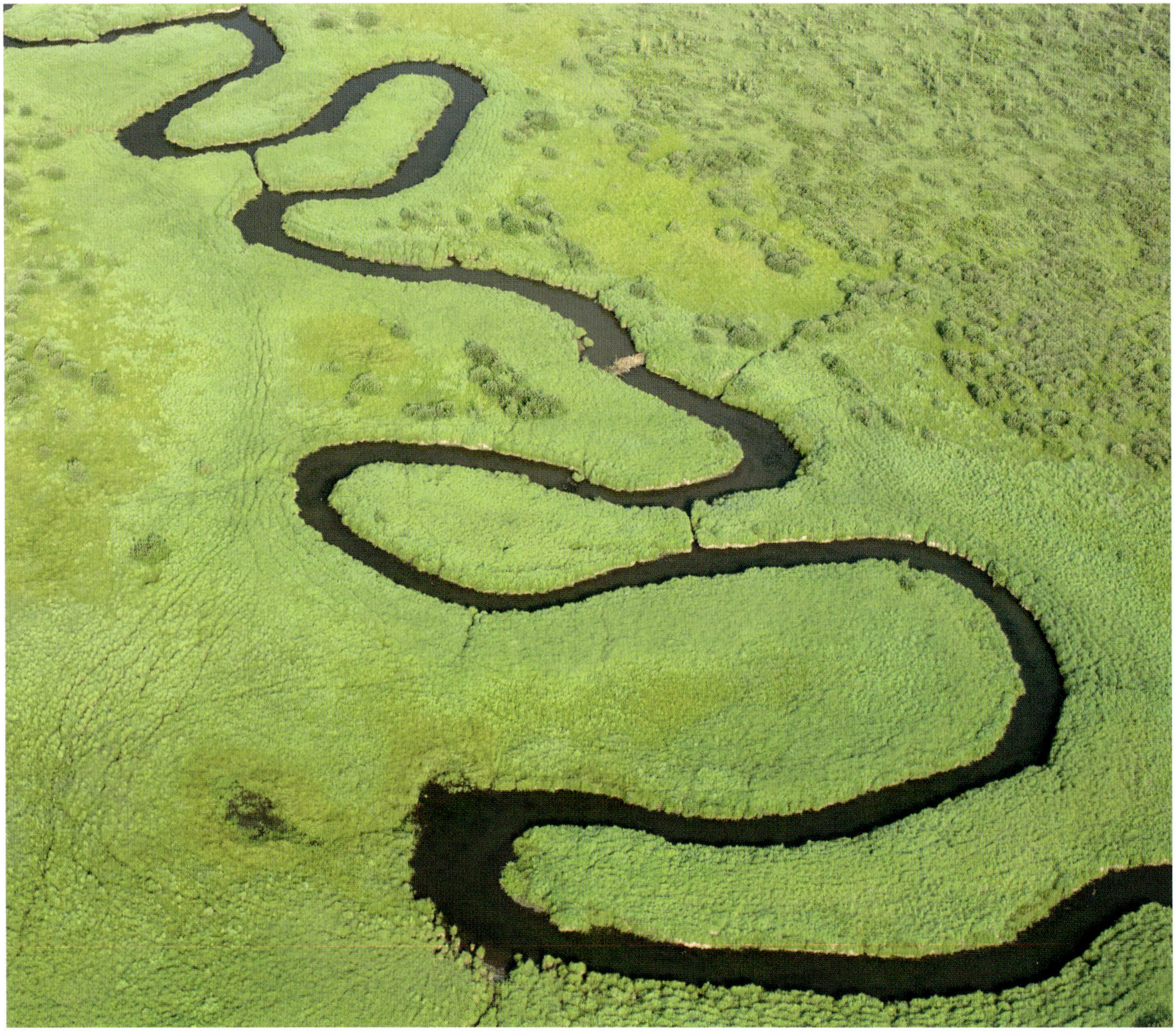

HEART WATERS

Sources of the Bow River

Kevin Van Tighem / *Text*

Brian Van Tighem / *Photography*

RMB

1st Edition

RMB | Rocky Mountain Books Ltd.

rmbooks.com
@rmbooks
facebook.com/rmbooks

Cataloguing data available from Library and Archives Canada

ISBN 978-1-77160-139-9 (hardcover)

Also available in electronic formats

Images on pp. 56, 83, and 150 by Kevin Van Tighem. Bull trout image on pp. 68 by Joel Sartore, National Geographic with Wade Fredenberg. Bull trout images on pp. 74 and 77 by Frank Wood. Image on pp. 109 by Gail Van Tighem. Beaver images on pp. 112 and 118 by Mike Kelly. Map on pp. 95 by Jonathan Ball. Maps on pp. 230-246 by Bow River Basin Council.

Printed and bound in China by 1010 Printing International Ltd.

Distributed in Canada by Heritage Group Distribution and in the U.S. by Publishers Group West

For information on purchasing bulk quantities of this book, or to obtain media excerpts or invite the author to speak at an event, please visit rmbooks.com and select the "Contact Us" tab.

RMB | Rocky Mountain Books is dedicated to the environment and committed to reducing the destruction of old-growth forests. Our books are produced with respect for the future and consideration for the past.

We acknowledge the financial support of the Government of Canada through the Canada Book Fund and the Canada Council for the Arts, and of the province of British Columbia through the British Columbia Arts Council and the Book Publishing Tax Credit.

Nous reconnaissons l'aide financière du gouvernement du Canada par l'entremise du Fonds du livre du Canada et le Conseil des arts du Canada, et de la province de la Colombie-Britannique par le Conseil des arts de la Colombie-Britannique et le Crédit d'impôt pour l'édition de livres.

Canada | Canada Council for the Arts | Conseil des Arts du Canada | British Columbia Arts Council

He thought his happiness was complete when, as he meandered aimlessly along, suddenly he stood by the edge of a full-fed river. Never in his life had he seen a river before – this sleek, sinuous, full-bodied animal, chasing and chuckling, gripping things with a gurgle and leaving them with a laugh, to fling itself on fresh play-mates that shook themselves free, and were caught and held again. All as a-shake and a-shiver – glints and gleams and sparkles, rustle and swirl, chatter and bubble. The Mole was bewitched, entranced, fascinated. By the side of the river he trotted as one trots, when very small, by the side of a man who holds one spellbound by exciting stories; and when tired at last, he sat on the bank, while the river still chattered on to him, a babbling procession of the best stories in the world, sent from the heart of the earth to be told at last to the insatiable sea.

— Kenneth Grahame, *The Wind in the Willows*

CONTENTS

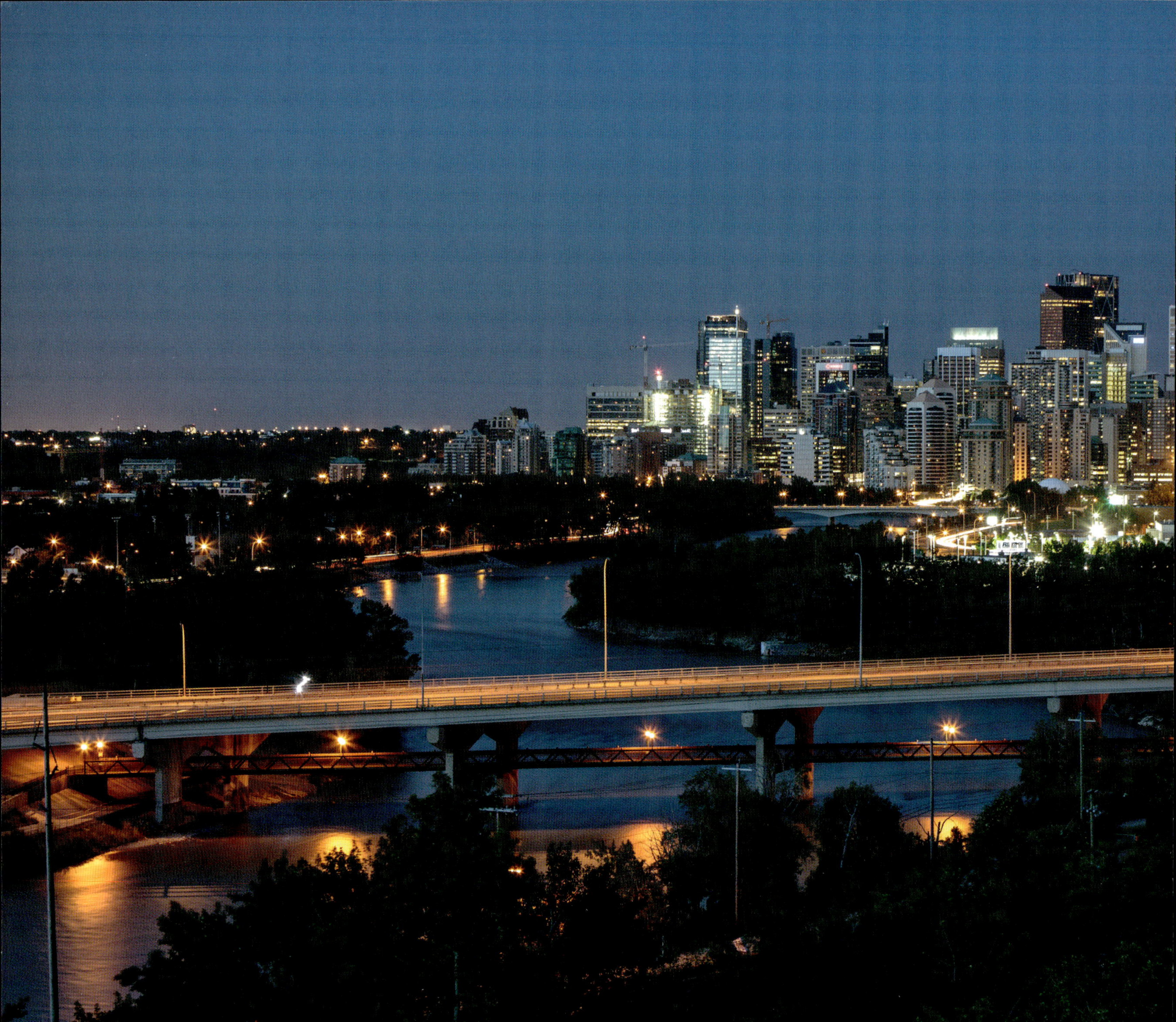

CHAPTER 1

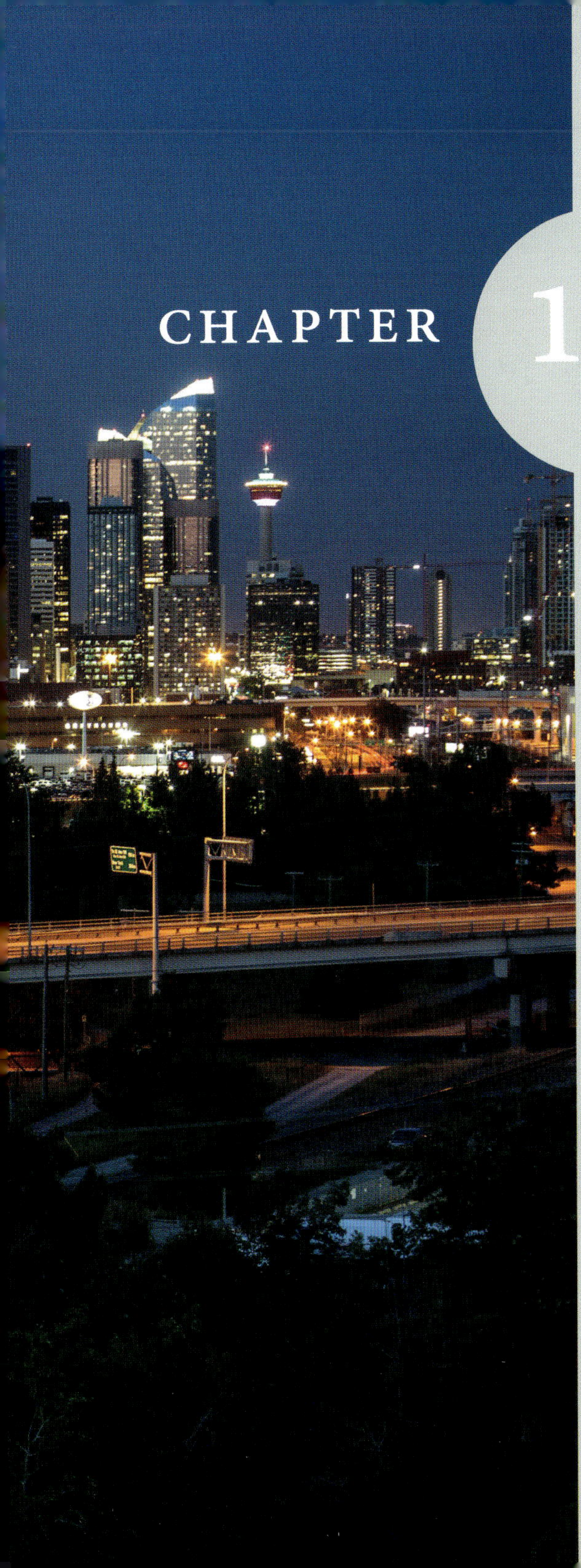

Voices in the Water

SOON AFTER HIS 1876 ARRIVAL at the new fort where the Elbow River merges its waters with the Bow, North West Mounted Police Commissioner Irvine proposed that the place be called Calgary "...which I believe is 'Scotch' for 'Clear Running Water,' a very appropriate name I think."

The Bow River I grew up beside a century later differed from the wild stream that greeted those first NWMP officers. Spring ice jams and flooding meltwaters regularly threatened their fort on the open flats beside the Bow. By my time, upstream dams like Glenmore and Bearspaw buffered the city against all but the most intense of floods. Man-made berms walled off downtown Calgary from the river whose floodplain it had smugly occupied for half a century.

Irvine's river ran blue with glacial silt during the hot days of midsummer, shrinking and clearing as fall drew near and cooling temperatures in the mountains slowed the melting of its headwater glaciers. In winter the stream became so shallow it sometimes froze to the bottom, the resulting ice jams forcing the river to flood overtop of its ice.

My river flowed more evenly through the seasons because of almost a dozen upstream dams that enabled water engineers to reschedule its flows – less water in summer and more water in winter. Silt from the headwater glaciers – shrunken by a warming climate to little more than half the size

Page 10: The Bow River at Calgary.

they had been in Irvine's day – now settled out in the reservoirs behind those dams, so my downstream river ran clearer than in the past.

Commissioner Irvine's NWMP recruits fished for fat cutthroat and bull trout in the river's eddies and beneath its many logjams. Decades later I caught introduced rainbow and brown trout beneath the Crowchild Bridge, the natives long ago having been fished out and the logjams long gone for want of floods and upstream timber.

It was still the Bow River – but in many ways it was a different stream altogether by the time its waters arrived in Calgary.

TOO MANY DECADES have slid by since the late-summer evenings I used to spend with the Bow River. After dinner, I would slip away with my fly rod and a few homemade flies, dodge the traffic on 12th and 11th avenues, pick my way across the creosote-smelling CPR tracks and scramble down rip-rapped banks to where my home river lapped quietly against old slabs of broken sidewalk.

The river was always there for me, hissing through shallow riffles, chattering against bridge pilings, its waters warping into hypnotic lines and swirls, where they parted around partly submerged rocks or slid out of long pools into the sleek, V-shaped runs that broke into standing waves and spilled into eddies where unseen trout awaited. The river was my place of refuge and renewal during those turbulent teenage years. It was an undemanding companion at an intensely self-conscious time of my life. I could lose myself in its quiet chatter and mysteries, unaware of its history and of how changed it was from its original condition. Instead, in my naïveté, for me the Bow was a reassuring constant in a world full of change.

It was the trout that first brought me to the Bow. As cars flashed by on Memorial Drive across the river, and the shadow of the Crowchild Bridge grew longer before merging, at last light, with the long shade of Shaganappi hill, I worked my way along the shadowed shore, watching for rising trout. If there were no rises, I would try to place my handmade flies – messy amalgams of Christmas-tree tinsel, Mom's sewing thread, my brother's model airplane glue, scraps of pheasant tail feathers from last fall's hunting expeditions and snipped-off bits of my long-suffering dog's tail hair – into the current lines where little rainbow trout fed or the eddies behind large boulders where I was sure bigger fish lurked. There was transcendence to that fishing. It immersed me completely in the mysteries of water movement, the challenge of laying out a good cast and a drag-free float, and the suspense of what might happen on the next cast.

One September evening, so late that I had to find narrow aisles of reflected light from streetlights across the river in order to see where my casts landed, my fly swung into a drift of floating leaves at the tail of a long pool and vanished into a massive boil. Half an hour later, heart pounding in my throat, I slid a 46-centimetre brown trout up onto the streamside grass and pounced on it, feeling its cold thickness vibrate in my hand as I subdued it with a stone. Unseen, unnoticed in the shadows beneath the

Sheep River. Each headwater stream has its own character; some carve canyons through shale.

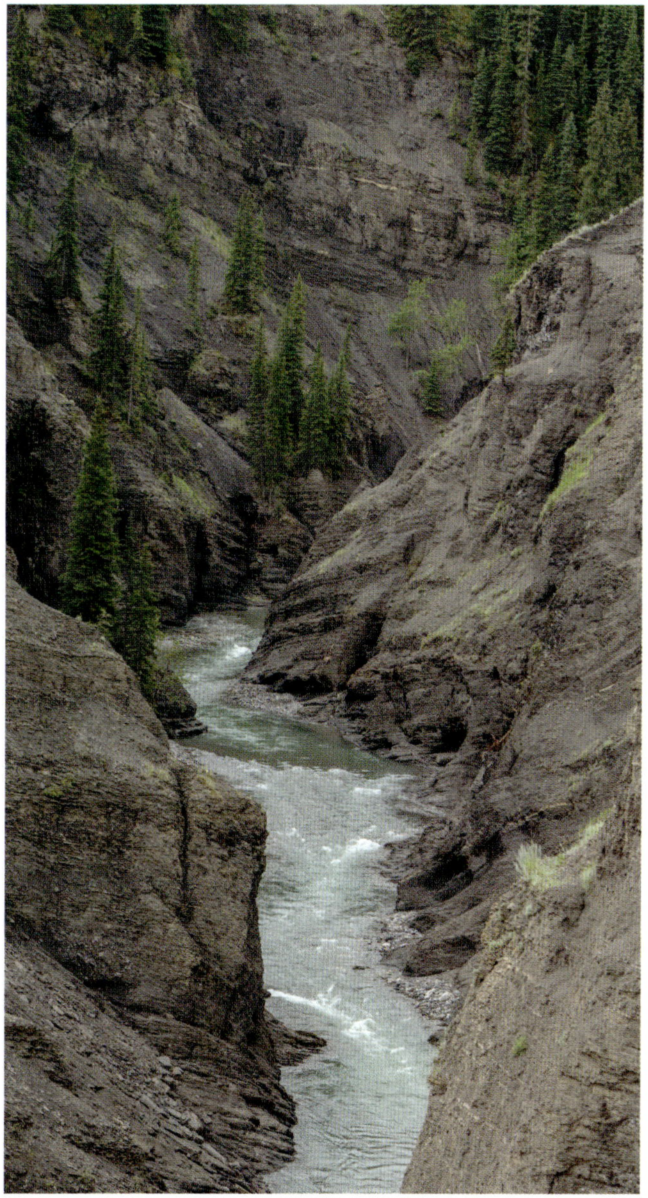

bridge, I sat beside the Bow River and held a creature that, to me, at that time, was the distillation of all the mystery, fecundity and vitality of my home river.

And the water whispered past, dark and secret, unchanging from one moment to the next, yet continually in the process of arriving and departing. Upstream, unseen, its many tributaries coursed constant and true out of shadowed hillscapes and looming mountains to become the river, to become the trout; to become me. I took my trout home through the busy streets like a talisman or a gift of initiation, or perhaps a sort of grail.

Later, we ate it.

The trout brought me to the river because I was part of a trout-fishing family. My father, Jack, took his many offspring fishing as soon as each of us became old enough to keep up with him. Our weekend outings and longer summer camping trips took us to headwater streams surrounded by elk tracks, birdsong, paintbrush flowers and forested hills. In my heart's eye, I see those places with crystal clarity even now, all these many years later.

Childhood may be brief, but childhood summers seem eternal and more intensely real than any other time in one's life. Those were bonding times – bonding to family, to landscape and to the living waters that tumble out of western Alberta's high country. But they were too brief. Dad wasn't available to take me fishing as often as I wanted. So, although it wasn't a small foothills stream like

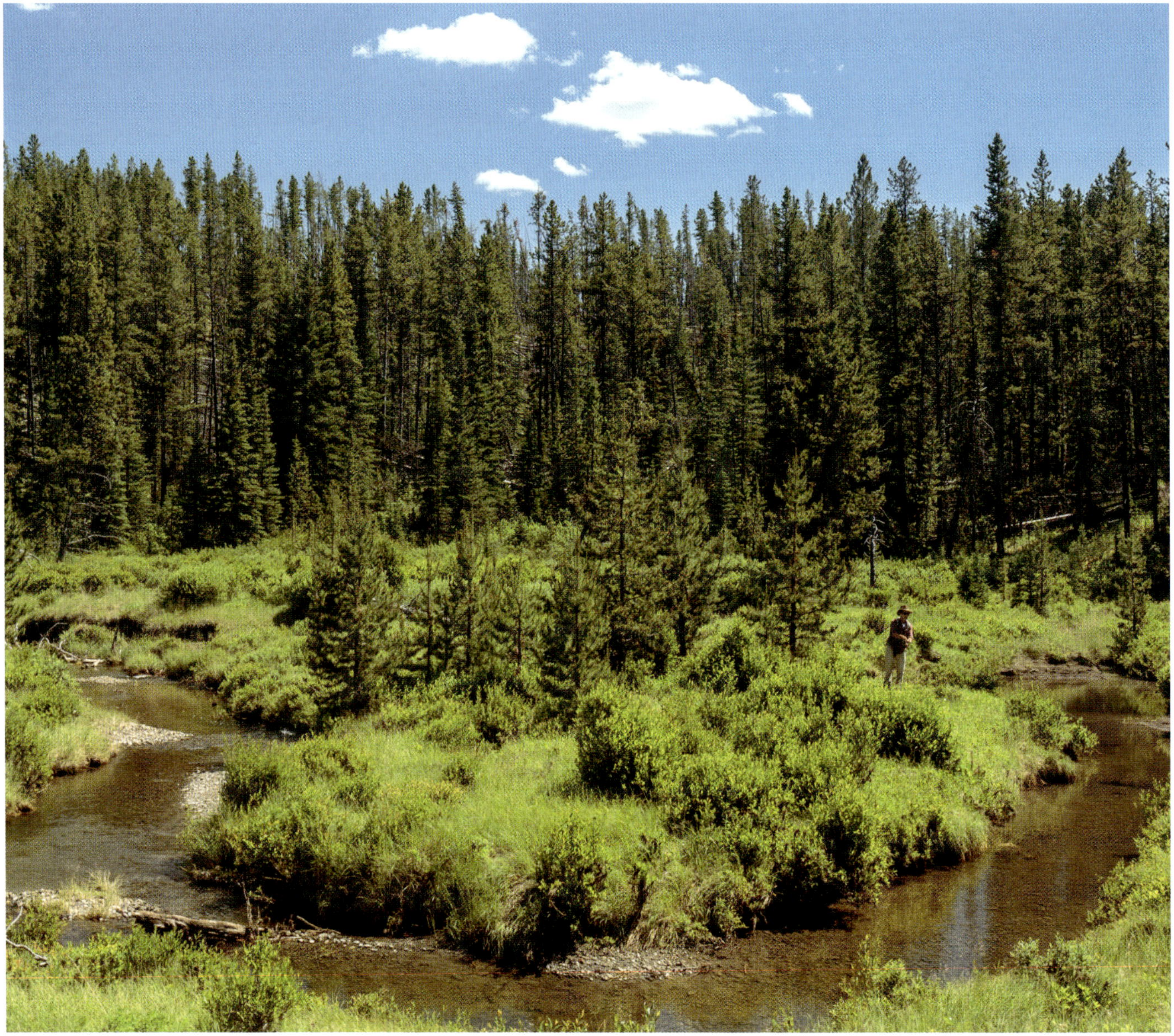

Unnamed tributary of Waiparous Creek. Foothills streams store massive amounts of water in their riparian meadows and groundwater aquifers.

the ones we usually fished, I found my way down to the Bow, a river that held the intermingled waters of so many of those far streams where I would rather have been.

A river has its own music: rhythmic sounds and recurring tonalities. Small waves slap and chatter, current tongues lap against stone, sediment hisses around cobbles, deeper resonances seem to murmur from the depths. There is no one river sound; there are many. They overlap, harmonize, ebb and flow, and the many sounds become one voice: the voice of living water telling of the far places from which it has come.

Behind that water noise, the chatter of other, almost-heard voices rises and fades, just beyond the edge of hearing. Secrets are being whispered, stories being told … but one can't quite make them out before they are subsumed again in the endless, complex rush and rustle of water sound.

Bemused, immersed, I would find myself contemplating the contrast between the voices buried in the rhythms of those dark, insistent waters, and the seemingly mindless rush and scurry of urban life just beyond the river's edge.

Calgary was growing from an almost rural town/city into a modern metropolis, people flocking from across the continent to add to this population at the forks of the Bow and Elbow rivers. Across the river from where I fished, cars streamed endlessly past, each full of Calgarians going about their daily lives in the city of "Clear Running Water." None could hear the whispered river-tales; few probably even noticed the river or wondered where it came from. All depended on it utterly, and their daily decisions, in many ways, controlled its fate. That seemed a dangerous sort of disconnect; it still does.

A RIVER IS AN AGGREGATE of waters. Each molecule of water in a river comes from somewhere in the headwaters. Jostling, joining: all those molecules hurry from their upstream origins to a far rendezvous with the sea. Some of those bits of water emerge from spring seeps in shale slopes pocked with the tracks of bighorn sheep. They merge with other water molecules to form headwater springs that seep into shadowed creeks at the bottoms of dark canyons. Others dissolve calcium from cold stone caves deep behind limestone mountain walls, then spring from fissures into sudden sunlight to tumble down wind-blasted cliffs into other headwater streams, where glacier lilies nod and grizzly bears feed. Depending on the nature of their headwater streams, some pause repeatedly in beaver ponds while others race in turbulent arcs from one noisy rapid to another. Each molecule of water has a different story, has travelled a different route, to become a part of the Bow River.

Perhaps those voices I could almost discern were the stories of the Bow's birthplaces, the chatter of water voices telling where they had been, how they had come at length to be a part of the Bow, and what they had left behind. Perhaps the reason one can never quite make out what the voices are saying is that they tell so many stories – the river has assembled the waters of so many headwater rills and riffles, so many living places.

I don't know when this notion first took hold for me, but often I would find myself listening to the river's muted harmonies for the sounds of streams I had visited with my family – Ware Creek, Lesueur, Johnson or Quirk. Sometimes it seemed I could hear them, too, just for a moment, before they were drowned by the clamour of other water voices telling of places I had yet to find.

THOSE ADOLESCENT EVENINGS BY THE RIVER of my childhood are well behind me now. Calgary's then-population of 300,000 has now grown well beyond a million human souls. It will continue to grow until the oil and gas run out. It will face droughts more severe than the 2001–3 drought that forced urban water rationing, resulted in negative farm income for the first time in over a quarter century and caused a major coal-fired electric generating plant to shut down for lack of cooling water. It will face floods worse than the June 2013 deluge that left Calgary's downtown swamped, High River devastated, five people dead and cost billions of dollars in cleanup costs across southern Alberta. With many more people living along and relying on the Bow River, those events will have massive impacts, especially if the river's floodplain is clogged by development and its headwaters reshaped so that they shed runoff water faster than ever before.

On the leeward side of the Rocky Mountains, where water is relatively scarce, so large a city makes great demands on its river – both for water supply and wastewater removal and also, in countless indirect ways, to sustain its economy and the quality of its citizens' lives.

High-elevation snows account for most of the water in rivers draining east from the Rockies. Sulphur Mountain, Banff National Park.

But a river, ultimately, is its watershed. Every human decision influences some part of that watershed. Consciously or unconsciously, we daily decide the well-being of the Bow River, its tributaries, and all the tangible and intangible benefits that flow to us from them.

THE BOW – FROM BOW GLACIER, on the Continental Divide in Banff National Park, to its confluence with the Oldman River upstream from Medicine Hat – is about 645 kilometres long. Its watershed includes Canada's oldest national park, historic cattle ranching landscapes, world-renowned trout streams, Alberta's first oil discovery site, the home places of the Siksika, Stoney Nakoda, and Tsuu T'ina peoples, and a city containing more head offices than any other in Canada.

Almost three million people live along the river and its tributaries. They drink of its waters, dispose their domestic and industrial effluents back into the same waters, and continue to arrange and rearrange its 25,000-square-kilometre watershed in ways that influence both the quality of its water and the amount and timing of its flows. Everything else in that watershed – from red-backed voles to brook sticklebacks to thorny buffalo berry thickets to yodelling late-night coyotes – depends on the health of that watershed and the reliability of those waters, too. The future of everything that lives here is intertwined with

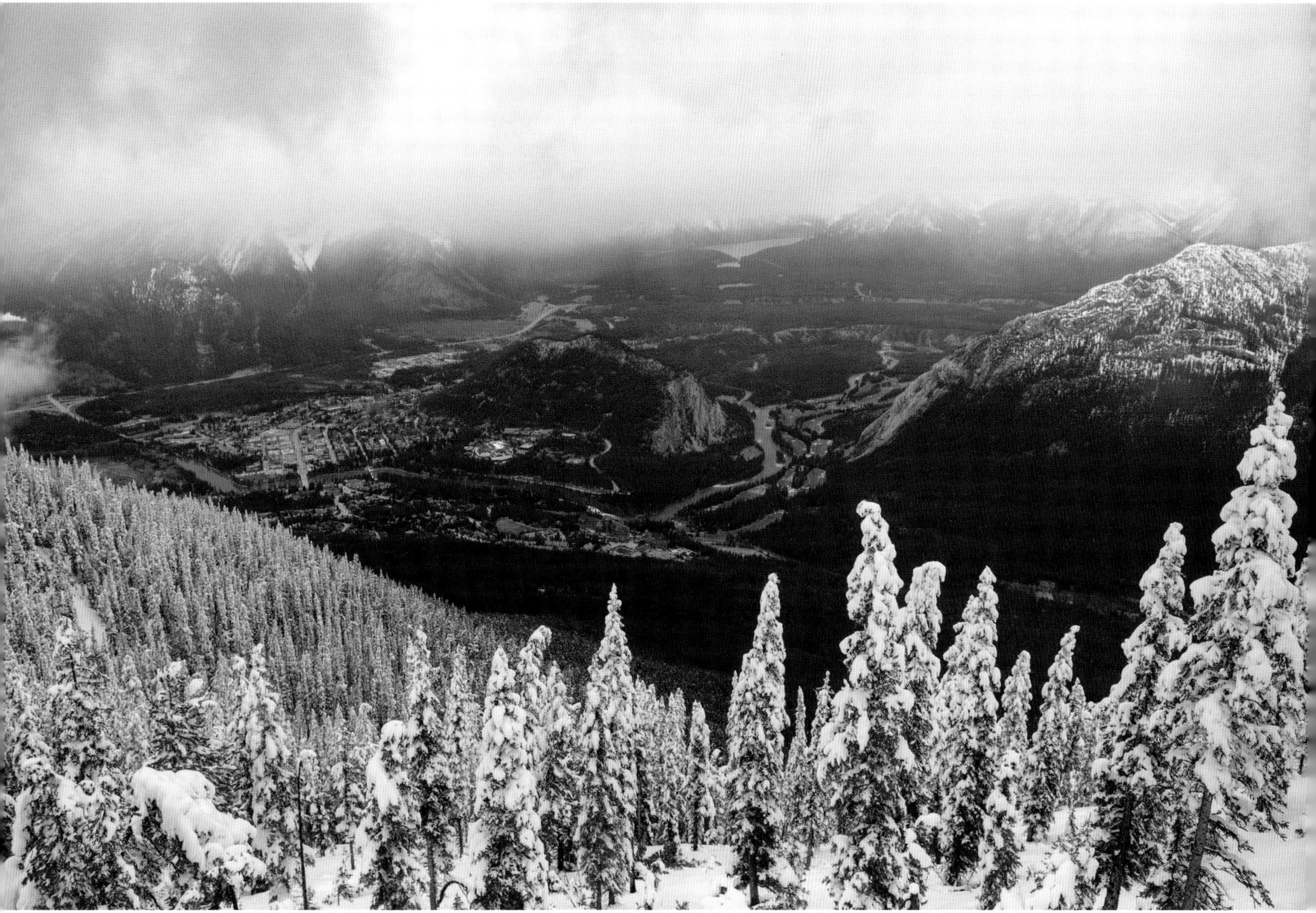

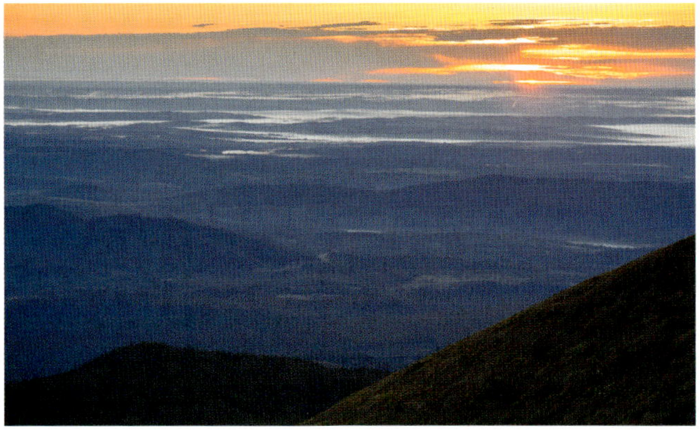

Left: The Bow River headwaters originate from a narrow band of foothills and mountains where clean, cold creeks arise from springs fed by last winter's snows.

Calgary's downtown towers rise behind the morning mists of its headwater valleys.

ours and, given the scale and impact of our activities, that future depends on the quality of our choices.

Recently I went back to the edge of the Bow River just upstream from the Crowchild Bridge, where I had spent those intense, quiet evenings of my adolescence coming to know my home river. It felt reassuringly familiar. What changes I could detect were mostly for the better. Where Calgary used to ignore its river valleys or, worse, simply exploit them as dumping places for demolition waste and unwanted fluids, there are now paved pathways and restored green areas full of people enjoying healthy exercise in urban nature. Birds are everywhere. Storm sewers rarely spill an oily sheen into the river, and the water seems at least as clean as, if not cleaner than, I remember from a few decades ago.

But the rush and scurry of urban life is, if anything, more intense and distracted than in the past. Since the evening I sat beside the river in the darkness, a brown trout resting in my hands, striving to hear what it was that the passing water seemed so urgently to murmur, Calgary's growth has given it three times more people to take its river for granted. Even the cyclists and runners on the river trails, more often than not, sport earplugs that shut out the music of the Bow's living waters and the whisper of its stories in favour of the generic sounds of consumer culture.

Those voices in the river do more than speak to us. They speak *about* us, because the stories of the Bow River's headwaters have become, increasingly, the stories of our choices: our successes and failures. Calgary is, ultimately, defined by the river at its heart in a deeper manner than Commissioner Irvine ever imagined.

The river we too often take for granted is patient, though; it will be there when we are ready to listen. The voices in the water may be subdued and elusive, but we would do well to try and hear what they have to say. They may be telling us things we need to know: who we are, where we've been and how we're doing.

Or maybe they are just telling us about where they have been. That, in itself, is worth knowing.

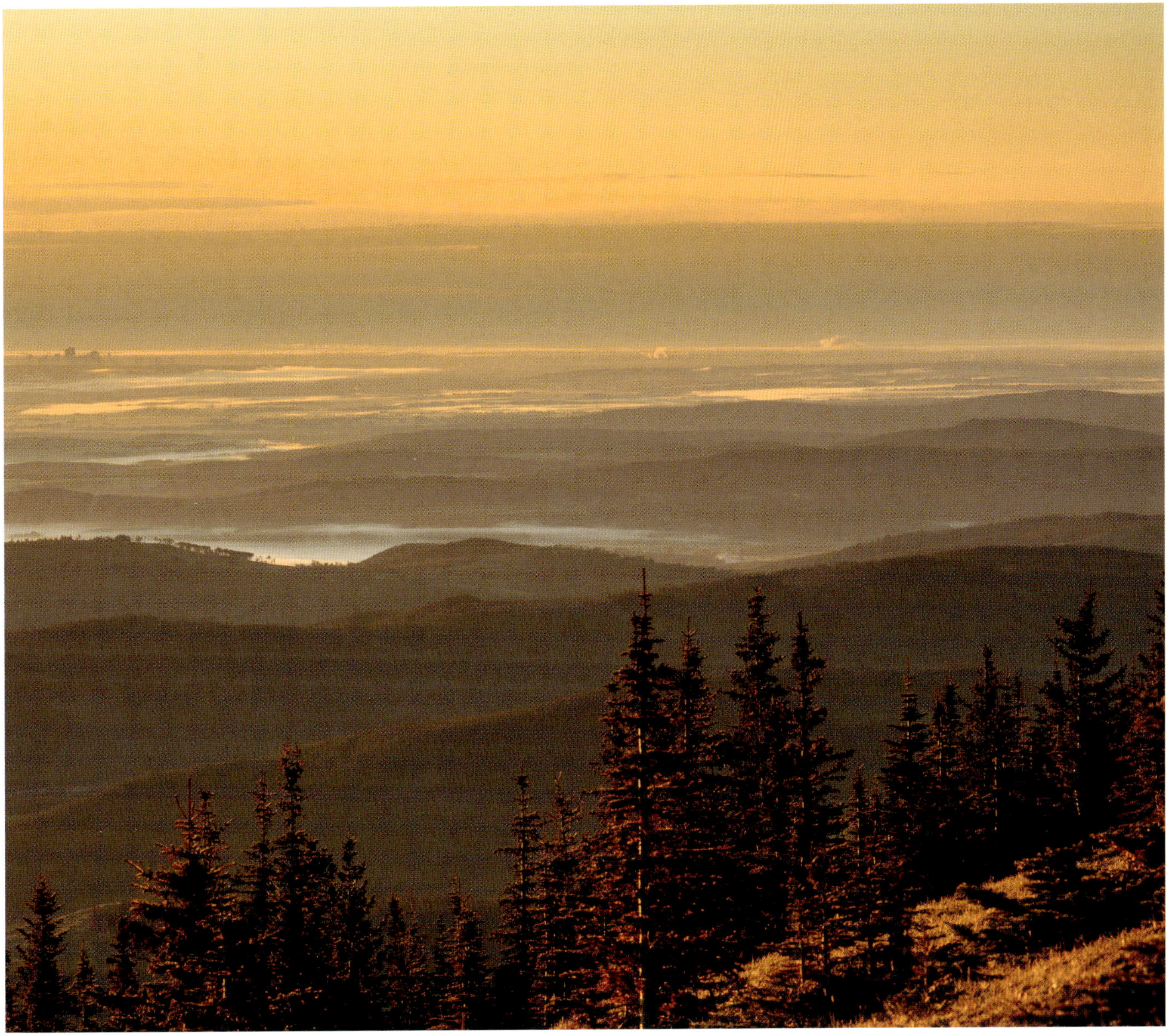

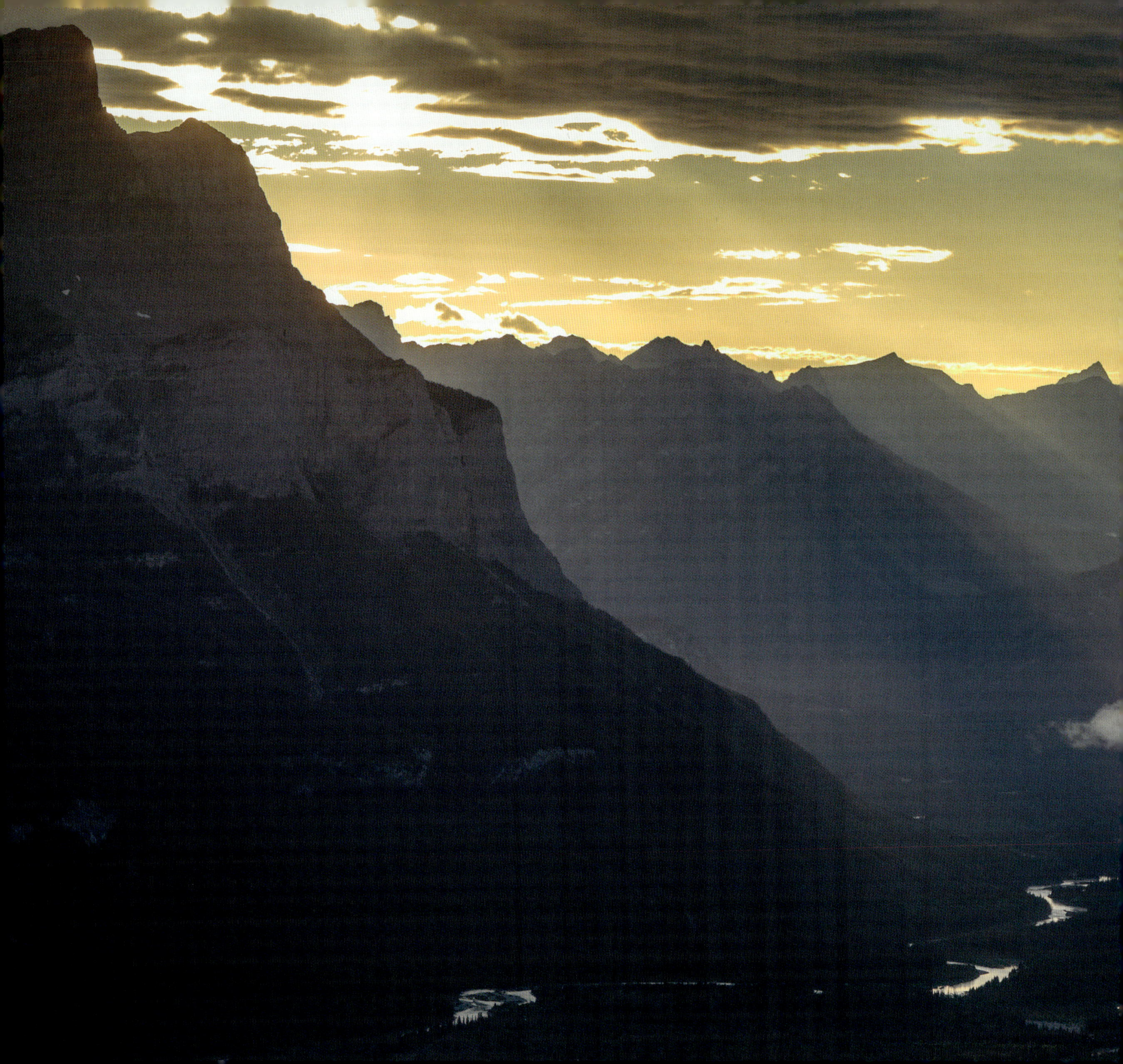

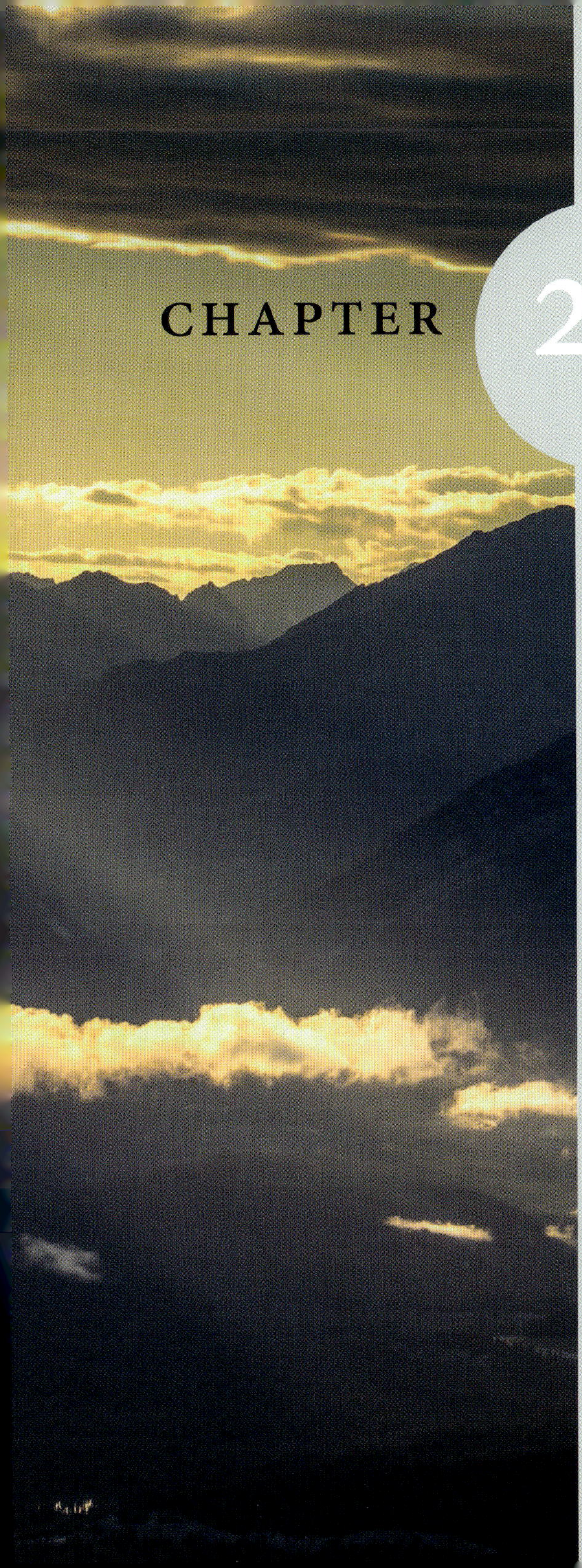

CHAPTER 2

River Origins

Bow River

Oceans in the Sky

David Thompson's journal notes on November 30, 1800, after he had climbed to the summit of Loder Peak, near the current site of Exshaw, provide the first written record of an impression that has registered with many others since:

> Our view from the height to the eastward was vast and unbounded. The eye had not strength to discriminate its termination. To the westward, hills and rocks rose to our view, covered with snow. Never before did I behold so just, so perfect a resemblance to the waves of the ocean in a wintry storm.

The long ridges of limestone that look so much like giant breakers are, in fact, ocean – ocean floor. The stone that scrapes the western edge of the Alberta sky was ocean-bottom sediment long before humans existed to wonder about the forces that could harden them to rock and push them so high into the atmosphere.

Most of this is carbonate rock. Ironic that those solid walls of limestone

Page 20: *Oceans of moist air spill across the Rockies into the glacially carved valleys of the Bow River and its tributaries, bringing snow and rain to the prairie headwaters.*

Right: *Bow Glacier Falls, Banff National Park. Glacier melt accounts for only 2 per cent of the Bow River's flow on an annual basis, but it is disproportionately important during the heat of summer.*

Far right: *Loaded with silt, the newborn Bow River drains across recently exposed glacial moraine to swell the clear flow of a tributary stream from nearby Bow meadows.*

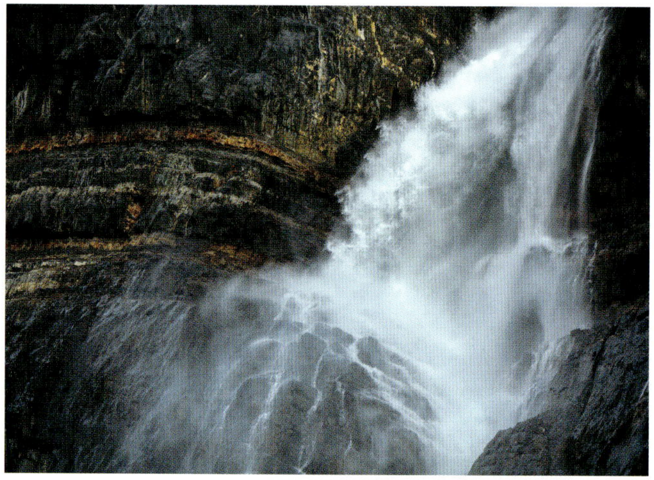

and dolomite were formed, to a large degree, from a gas – carbon dioxide. That's the same gas whose growing concentrations in our modern atmosphere has become a source of consternation for people who prefer stable and predictable climatic conditions to the atmospheric warming, extreme weather events and climate change that increasingly beset us as we near the end of the hydrocarbon-fuelled Industrial Age.

Carbon dioxide from young Earth's atmosphere dissolved into ancient oceans over many hundreds of thousands of years. Primitive ancestors of modern coral algae and phytoplankton, while converting sunlight to energy, transferred carbon molecules from the dissolved gas into calcium carbonate in their shells and other limy structures. As the ancient organisms died, their bodies settled to the ocean floor and began the process of turning into rock.

Sun and wind increased the limy marl on the seabed by evaporation, which reduced the amounts of dissolved material that the remaining water could hold. Calcium carbonate deposits gradually deepened on the shallow ocean floor. Rivers draining long-gone continents washed silt and sand into those same ancient seas. Just as happens in today's oceans, currents and tides sorted the sediments as they settled out on the ocean bottom; these became the shales, siltstones and sandstones that also outcrop along the Front Ranges and foothills of the Rocky Mountains, where the Bow is born.

It is impossible for human beings to comprehend the lengths of time those ancient oceans were in place, quietly conceiving mountains in their depths. Nor is it possible fully to imagine the depths of sediment that accumulated at the bottoms of these oceans. Geology texts illustrate geological time with charts that show our modern era as the thinnest sliver at the end of a long line of events in

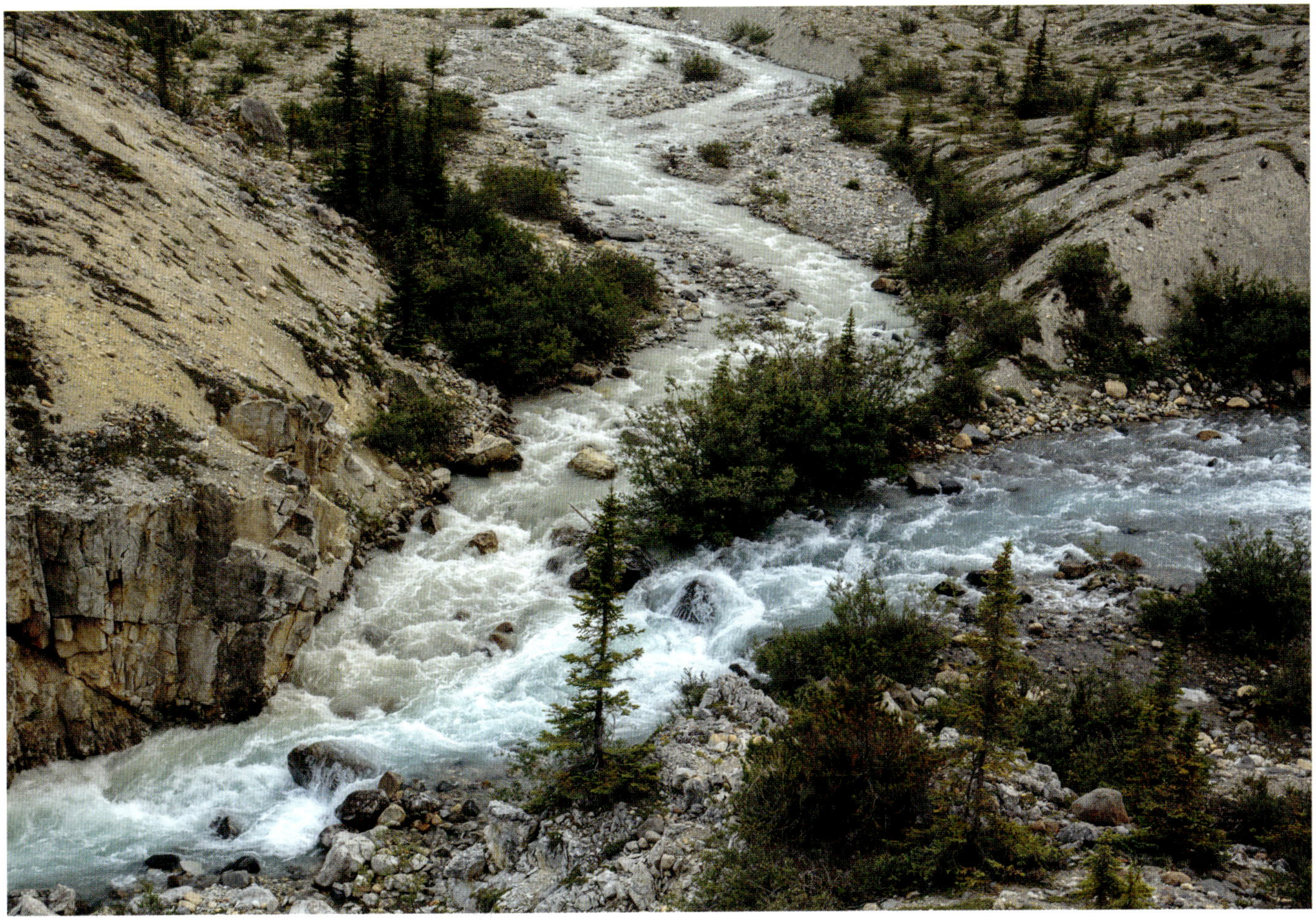

Earth's history, but our imaginations simply can't reach that deep, neither into time nor into the ocean sediments that eventually became the rocks underlying the Bow River headwaters.

The sheer weight of accumulated lime marl, silts and clay gradually pushed down Earth's crust beneath the oceans. As a result, the oceans never filled up with sediment – the sea bed simply sank deeper beneath its weight.

The weight of all that accumulated material did more than depress Earth's surface. It compacted and heated the deepest deposits, squeezing out water and gases until what had originally been soft, slimy ocean floor hardened into stone.

Mount Rundle's massive walls of limestone tower one thousand metres above the floor of today's Bow River valley. There is a lot more rock beneath the ground. It was all ocean bed at one time.

David Thompson was being metaphorical when he saw ocean waves in the shapes of the Rockies, but he was looking at an ocean nonetheless. The headwaters of the Bow River flow from the crumpled remains of a fossilized sea floor that got pushed into the sky between 140 and 40 million years ago. Some of the earthquakes must have been impressive. There must have been a lot of them, and they went on for millions of years. The bottom of an ocean doesn't get shoved two kilometres into the atmosphere overnight.

The forces that lifted all that rock into the sky likely involved both the long, slow collision of two parts of Earth's crust – one underlying the North American continent and the other supporting the weight of the Pacific Ocean – as well as the inevitable bounce-back of so much weight being pressed down into Earth's soft-molten crust. Push a sheet of ice down into a puddle, and you see the same effect; at some point it bends and bounces back to the surface.

The thickest rock deposits in the Front Ranges are carbonates. Those limestones and dolomites are interspersed with beds of shale, siltstone and sandstone. Farther west, in the Main Ranges of the Rockies, the peaks of the Continental Divide are mostly older rock that was originally

A broad U-shaped valley and sparse vegetation betray the recent glacial origins of this headwater valley, where the meltwater from Bow Glacier drains down to Bow Lake.

sedimentary. Pressure and heat deep beneath Earth's surface recrystallized it into metamorphic rock such as quartzite and schist, before promethean forces lifted those peaks to the clouds.

And so ocean bed became rock, and the rock slid up into the sky, and the Rockies were born. The brachiopod fossils exposed along the top of Forgetmenot Ridge and other mountaintops in the headwaters of the Bow were sea creatures once. They are still at home in the bottoms of their ancient oceans – up there in the alpine wind.

TODAY'S OCEANS, LIKE THE PACIFIC, build rock in all the same ways as the ancient seas that birthed the Rockies. And above our modern seas are vast oceans of air that, like the waters below, have tributary streams, turbulent flows, seasonal currents and even the ability to carry sediments – they absorb vast amounts of evaporated moisture from the briny waters and carry it inland to shed it as fog, rain and snow.

In winter, at our latitudes, the Pacific Ocean is warmer than most of the continent. Its waters warm the air and fill it with moisture. Between about 35 and 60 degrees north, winds tend to flow from the west toward the east, bringing a lot of warm, moist air inland from the Pacific toward Alberta.

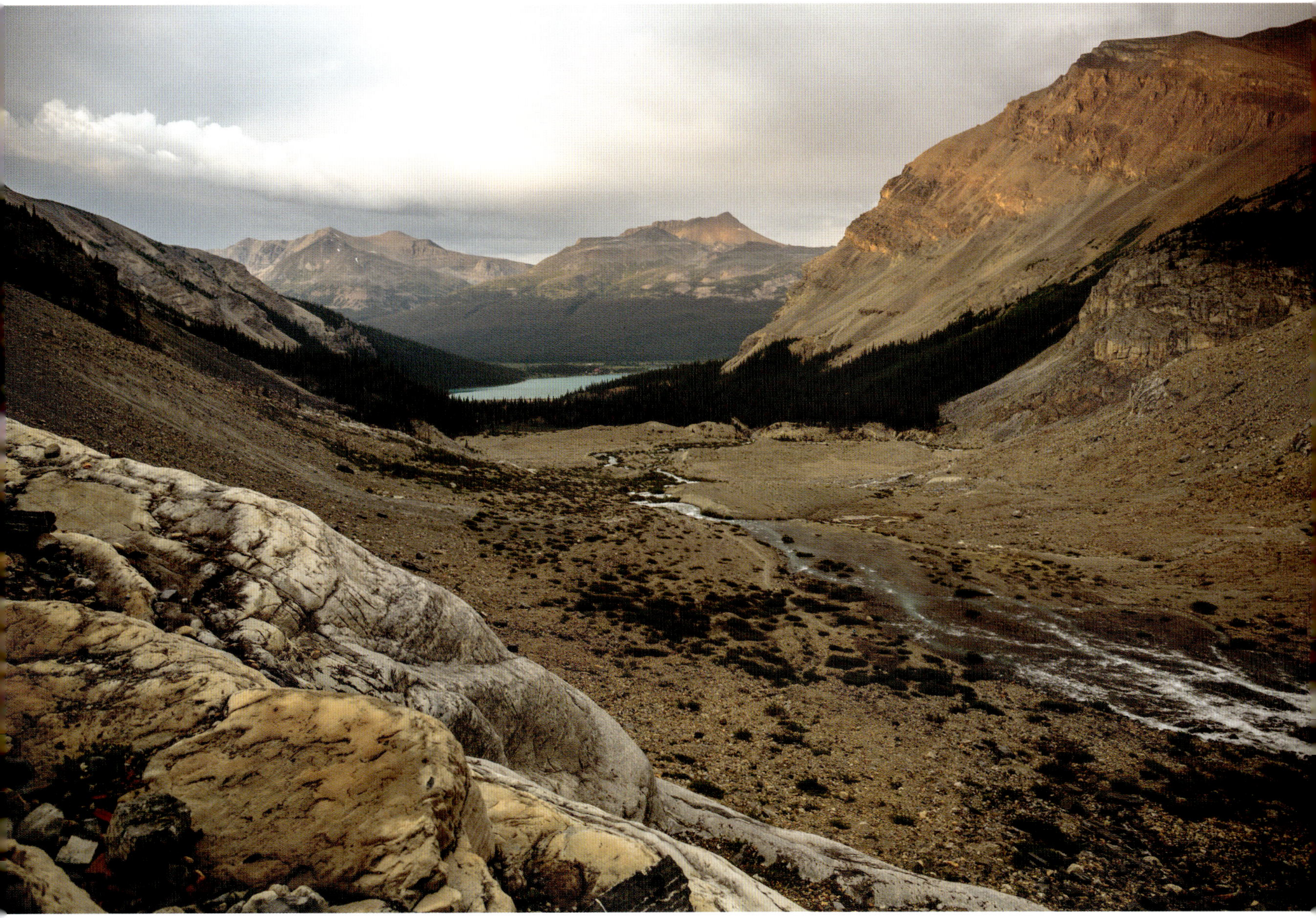

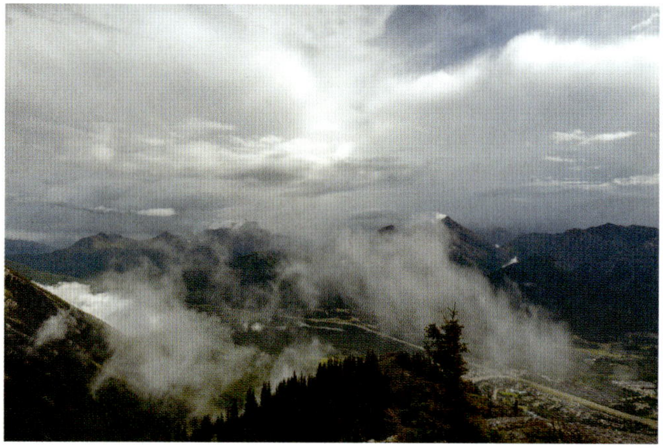

Oceans of moist air spill across the Rockies into the glacially carved valleys of the Bow River and its tributaries, bringing snow and rain to the prairie headwaters.

Forced up by the abrupt rise of coastal mountain ranges in British Columbia and the northwestern United States, the damp air cools as it loses pressure. Cooler air can hold less moisture than warm air, so the relative humidity of the air increases until clouds form, shedding copious precipitation on the rainforests of the Pacific Coast.

Water vapour is full of latent energy. As soon as the vapour condenses into liquid form, it releases that energy as heat into the air around it. Even though the air cools as it rises over the mountains, some heat gets added back into it from the condensation of its moisture. As it begins to descend the other side of the mountain, however, the increased air pressure means that it warms again. A strange but fortuitous result for those of us who live in chinook country is that the air, because it now contains less moisture, warms faster as it descends on the lee side of the mountains than it cooled on the rainy side.

Pacific Ocean weather systems become drier and warmer as they repeatedly cross mountain ranges en route to the headwaters of the Bow River. By the time the ocean of air begins to subside down the east side of the last mountains and out onto the interior of the continent, it has lost much of its moisture and gained considerable warmth. That's why southern Alberta winters are interrupted repeatedly by warm, dry chinook winds even while the same weather system deposits another big dump of snow in the high country. If Calgary were at sea level, in fact, those winds would be hot, not just mild, because of the imbalance between the rate of cooling as moist air rises and the rate of warming as the drier air descends again.

Even when no chinook wind is blowing at ground level, winter systems often bring moisture from the Pacific and deposit it as snow in the high headwaters of the Bow. Other times, especially in early spring, moist air masses work their way northwest across the US plains from the warm Caribbean seas and, encountering cold air that bulges down from the Arctic, cool below the condensation level and deposit snow or rain along the foothills and up into the mountain valleys.

Regardless of what weather system is dominant, the fact remains that all the water in the Bow River is brought by oceans of air from distant oceans of water, to be deposited on the remnants of ancient ocean floors that comprise today's Rocky Mountains and foothills.

Thompson had the right idea. The Bow River does arise from oceans.

Water in the Landscape

Water molecules don't take kindly to getting torn away from their ocean homes. The moment those molecules get pulled up into the air as vapour and carried landward, they're waiting for the chance to start home to the sea again. The law of gravity is on their side; water runs downhill to the sea.

The healthiest watersheds are those that do the best job of frustrating those little molecules at every turn. Generally speaking, the longer that water has to spend working its way down the watershed, the more that watershed benefits from its visit. The slowest water is groundwater, which is why healthy watersheds are good at trapping water in soil and deeper rock deposits. The faster the water makes its escape, the greater the likelihood that it will do some harm along the way and leave a thirsty landscape behind.

Most water molecules don't even make it to Alberta before they begin their journey back to the sea. Tofino, on the west coast of Vancouver Island, gets about three metres of rain every year. That's a lot, considering that rainy Vancouver receives only about 1.2. On the west side of the Selkirk Mountains, Revelstoke gets almost the same amount of precipitation as Vancouver. All that wet weather represents water molecules making an early escape back to the Pacific.

Water molecules that fail to escape those big Pacific weather systems before they reach the Rocky Mountains are most likely to make their getaways near the Continental Divide. Lake Louise, averaging 720 millimetres per year, gets less than half as much precipitation as Vancouver, but that is still well more than the 450 millimetres received by the town of Banff, which, in turn, gets more than Calgary. Calgary gets barely a third as much water from the sky as Vancouver.

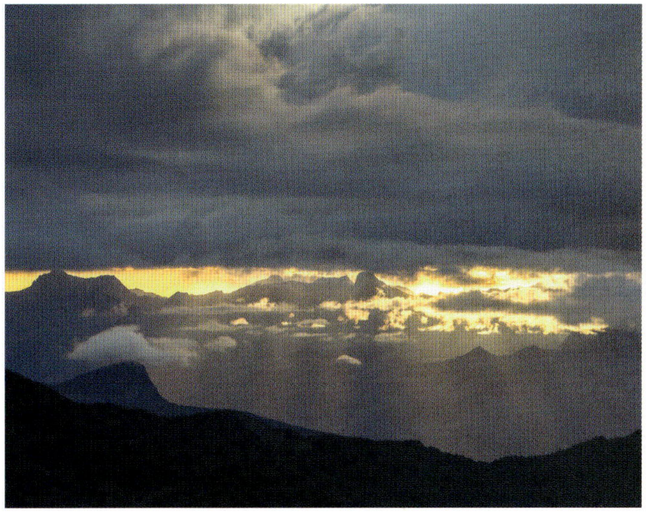

The Bow River is born where the bottoms of ancient oceans have been raised into the oceans of air that bring moisture from modern oceans across the North American continent.

Rain is the means by which most water molecules escape from the skies over the Bow River headwaters. Although winter snows get deep – especially along the Continental Divide, where up to 3.5 metres of snowfall

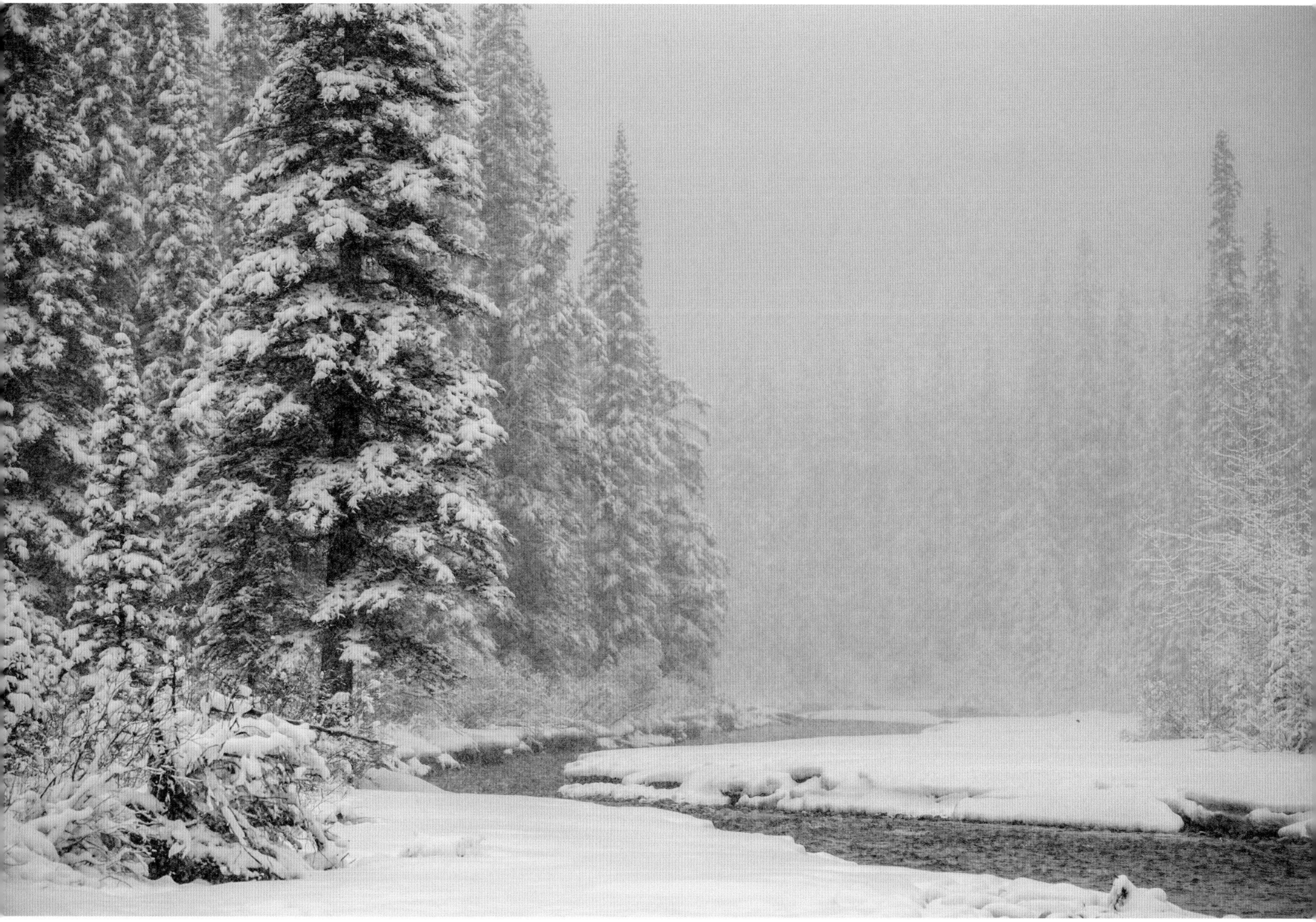

Winter on the Spray River. Mountain and foothills snowpack account for about 80 per cent of the annual flow in the Bow River.

can be expected during an average winter – snow holds less water than the same amount of rain, because snowflakes are full of air. Even so, most of the water in streams is from snow; growing vegetation uses up a lot of the spring and summer rainfall.

In coastal British Columbia, where the ocean has an overwhelming effect on weather patterns, most precipitation falls in winter. Farther toward the centre of the continent, this maritime effect weakens. Lake Louise, which is tucked beneath the Continental Divide and is consequently more influenced by maritime conditions, receives half again as much snow as falls in the town of Banff, which lies farther east. On the other hand, both places get about the same amount of summer rain.

When the Ghost, Bow, Kananaskis, Elbow and Highwood rivers turn brown and surly in late spring, spilling out of their channels to seethe across their floodplains, they are responding to both the annual peak in rainfall and the annual peak in snowmelt. The memorable floods – the ones that fill basements in High River, wash down Okotoks's Main Street and devour buildings and fences on their floodplains – often coincide with a cool, late spring, followed by a warm spell that primes the snowpack, and then an intense, sustained rainstorm in late May or June that not only contributes its own copious water to the landscape but helps melt the previous winter's snows, too.

Although rain usually accounts for the highest stream flows in spring and early summer, it's the mountain snowpack that sustains the streams and rivers through the rest of the summer. Because the snowpack is deepest at the highest elevations, where air is generally much cooler, densely-packed snowdrifts often survive until well into August, especially on the sheltered north aspects of the mountains along the Continental Divide. Because of the thin mountain air and the shadows cast by mountains at a latitude where the sunshine always comes in at a slant, some slopes almost never get warm. Even the earlier-melting snow is important to summer stream flows, because it's the source of the groundwater that, emerging as springs, provides a sustaining base flow.

Glaciers survive in high places, too, their lower-elevation toes melting back each summer only to be replaced by new ice squeezed downslope as new snow accumulates on the upper parts of the glaciers, gradually hardening as it deepens. Most surviving glaciers in the Bow watershed have a northeasterly aspect, an advantage in two ways. For one thing, they are shaded during most of the day. That slows the rate of ice melt. In addition, because prevailing winter winds are out of the southwest, considerably more snow accumulates in their sheltered alpine nooks than on more exposed slopes.

Very little glacier ice remains in the Bow watershed. In fact, the total area covered by glacier ice is 25 per cent less than it was in the late 1900s; some climate-change projections suggest that all the remaining ice will be gone by the end of this century. Even though glacier meltwater contributes barely 2 per cent to the Bow River's total annual flow, that will be a big loss. That 2 per cent enters the river mostly in the hottest part of the summer, when other water sources are scarce. In years with low snowpack, glacier meltwater can be as important as groundwater for keeping the upstream reaches of the Bow River wet. In August 1970 – a drought year – hydrologists estimated that almost 60 per cent of the flow in the Bow River near Banff was meltwater from alpine glaciers. Once those glaciers are gone, the midsummer Bow River will be a smaller, warmer stream, far more vulnerable to droughts.

Even where glaciers have already vanished, however, the cool, shady sides of mountains retain moisture, sometimes locking up those homesick water molecules for many years. Soil scientists, classifying the landscape of Banff National Park in the 1970s, found permafrost under high-elevation spruce forests on some of the northeasterly slopes along the Front Ranges. These sites receive less winter snow than the higher mountains farther west, and the shallower snowpack results in less insulation for the ground below. Winter cold can penetrate deeply. In summer, with little direct sunlight and a good insulating cover of spruce trees and moss, the frozen moisture deep in the soil never gets a chance to thaw.

Most winter snow, however, melts before the end of summer. The runoff seeps through the snowpack to the ground below. There, some of it soaks in. The rest runs off the surface, emerging at the downstream edge of snow patches. At higher elevations, this seepage water produces lush meadows of valerian, mountain marsh marigold, windflower, glacier lilies, rushes and willows that can cope with a short growing season while thriving on the abundant moisture. Farther below the treeline, snowdrifts melt earlier and produce wet meadows of more lushly growing vegetation like cow parsnip, larkspurs and grasses like tufted hairgrass. Bears, elk and other salad-loving animals spend a lot of time in these places.

Groundwater springs emerge from sandstone in Big Hill Springs Provincial Park, many kilometres from the melting snows that feed them. Carbonate tufa mounds have slowly grown up around the spring outlets as bacteria extract dissolved calcium from the water.

BOTH MELTING WINTER SNOWS and the rains that fall through the warm season produce water that has to go somewhere. Growing vegetation uses a lot of the summer rain. The remainder, along with most of the winter snowmelt and spring rains, ends up in creeks or rivers or goes into the ground. Some of the groundwater also ends up in creeks, but it takes a longer time to get there than water that runs off overland. Sometimes it emerges in springs kilometres away from where it went into the ground. Foothills springs and bogs, for example, are often fed as much by melting snow and rain that seep into the ground in the mountains to the west as by more local sources. In 1948, near Turner Valley, a Royalite Oil Company drilling crew hit a pressurized spring of water 35 metres beneath the ground surface. Forty years later, the artesian spring they brought to the surface was still flowing with pressurized water that originated at higher elevations to the west.

High-elevation mountain soils are generally thin,

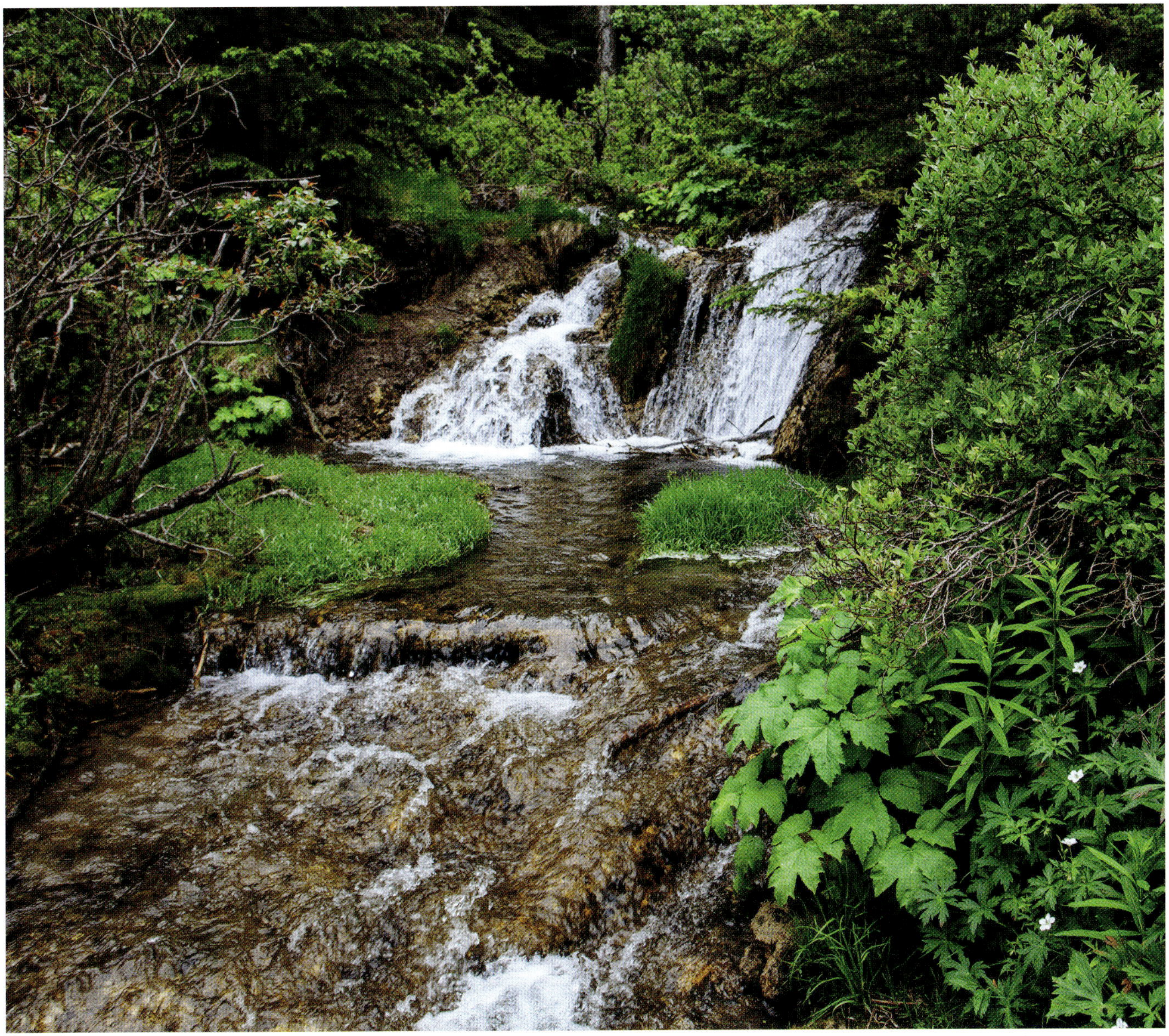

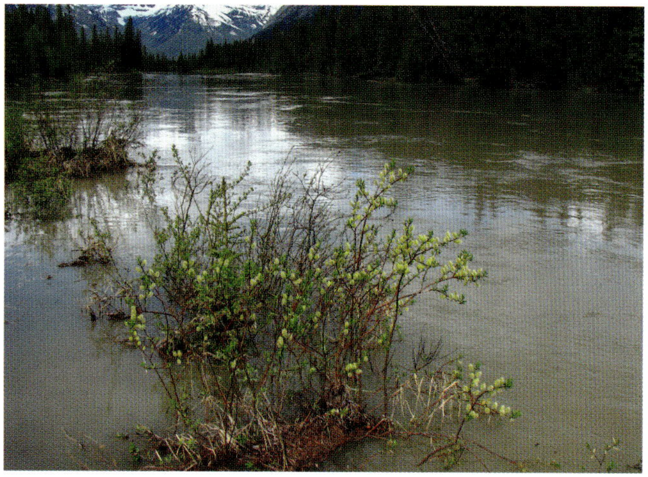

Spring runoff brings high water and silt to rejuvenate the Bow River floodplain near Canmore. Photo: Kevin Van Tighem

but they often lie on top of frost-shattered and pressure-cracked rock. Water that doesn't flow away overland seeps into the ground. Some becomes shallow groundwater; the rest works its way downslope and into the cracks below, penetrating into rock aquifers that can store massive amounts of water for centuries. Limestone, common in the Front Ranges of the Rockies, is soluble in water. Where water has worked its way through limestone over many millennia, deep hidden streams have dissolved and eroded impressive cave systems. Gushing streams burst full-grown from the rock at the downstream ends of some caves; other caves are dry today, the water that created them having found newer channels through the rock.

In many places, especially lower on the mountain slopes, a veneer of glacial till lies between the rock below and the vegetation above. Till is the jumbled mix of boulders, pebbles, sand and silt that remains behind after glacier ice melts back. It soaks up water quite nicely, except where it contains a large amount of clay. The thicker the till, the more water it can absorb.

Where snowdrifts melt slowly and the ground has a continuous cover of vegetation, most of the water goes into the ground. Some goes deep into hidden aquifers and only emerges again, many kilometres away, decades or even centuries later. Some only penetrates a short distance and simply moves to the valley floor underground, arriving a lot later than the overland runoff above. If the groundwater encounters a cut slope or a bed of underlying rock that forces it back to the surface, it emerges again as a spring.

The creeks and rivers continue to flow as the mountain snowpack dwindles. Their flow is sustained now not so much by overland runoff as by baseflow – the springs and seeps that emerge from the bottoms of valley slopes, and from the banks and beds of the creeks themselves, into the living channel. It's still mostly snowmelt water, but it's the part that went underground where it oozed slowly downslope, slowed by friction and hydrostatic tension as it seeped between soil particles and glacial till, through the rotted-out channels of old tree roots and pale, inverted forests of grass, forb and shrub roots that finger their way down into the darkness and away from the sky, sharing the cool stillness of the earth.

Where snowdrifts melt rapidly, where vegetation cover has been damaged or the soil compacted, and during extended rainstorms, the ground often cannot absorb all the available water. Instead, water flows over the surface of the ground. There it forms channels as it follows the path of least resistance downslope. Surface water drains much faster than groundwater. Along the way, it picks up and moves anything loose. When water is able to make a quick getaway from unhealthy watersheds, it takes a lot of soil with it – soil that would have done far more good if it had stayed where it belonged rather than silting up reservoirs and estuaries farther downstream.

Extreme weather events, like extended heavy rains, are becoming increasingly common as a warming climate moves greater amounts of water vapour and energy around the planet; those events are most damaging where unwise or irresponsible land use has exposed raw soil to erosion or weakened the banks and floodplains of streams.

Rivers of Ice

Before the last major ice age, the Bow River turned north near where the town of Banff is today. It flowed out of the mountains through the valley now occupied by Lake Minnewanka. Essentially, the Bow River flowed down the path now followed by the Ghost River until mountain glaciers, thickening and spreading about a million years ago, filled the valleys so deeply that only the highest peaks showed. Although the mountain glaciers grew and shrank several times during the ice age, the mountains spent most of those millennia swamped by ice. Rivers still flowed, but they flowed under, through and over the ice.

Like water, glacier ice flows downslope, but its behaviour is more like butter than like water. It doesn't cut down into the land beneath it so much as spread out and ooze across it, eroding valley edges more than the valley floor. Like butter, it's sticky, picking up anything loose as it spreads down-valley incorporating everything it gathers into the moving mass. Along the edges and bottom of a glacier, water repeatedly freezes and thaws, cracking rock loose. As the glacier undercuts the surrounding mountain slopes, rock also falls onto the ice above. All those rock fragments become frozen into the ice. Like a massive rotary sander, the rock-studded ice grinds against the mountains. Massive amounts of sand and silt, chiseled and ground out of rock in this way year after year, either freeze into the glacier ice or get washed away by meltwaters.

During the countless millennia that ice-age glaciers filled the mountain valleys, they carved many millions of tonnes of rock loose. Narrow mountain valleys became wider, with steeper side walls, as the ice ground and plucked away at the mountainsides. Like a slow-motion conveyor belt, the ice carried all that rock debris until it reached the point where summer's warmth melted the ice back faster than new ice could replace it. There, the loose material melted out, accumulating into hummocky ridges called moraines.

By the time the glaciers began to melt back, several thousand years ago, they were loaded with massive amounts of mountain rubble. The Bow valley glacier

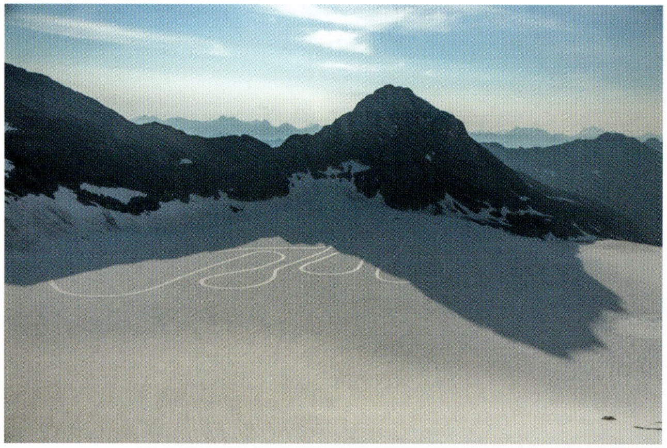

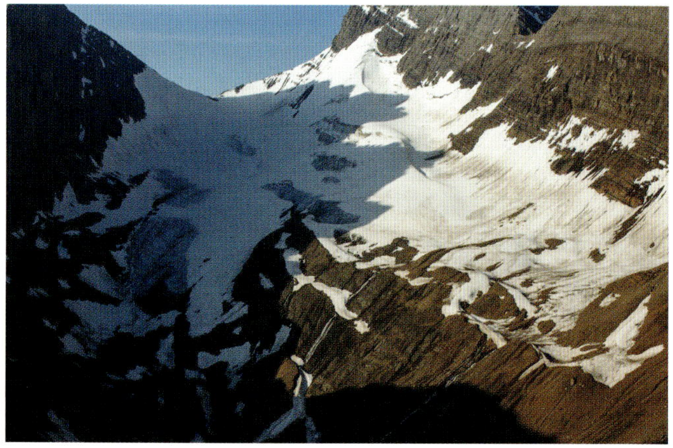

Left: *Haig Glacier is marked by training courses used by Canada's Olympic skiers for summer training after lower-elevation snow is gone.*

Right: *Most surviving mountain glaciers, like French Glacier in the upper Spray valley, are on shady northeast or north-facing mountain slopes at high elevations.*

left so much of this debris between Tunnel and Cascade mountains that the newly emerged Bow River flooded the Bow valley and then spilled through a narrow gap between Tunnel Mountain and Mount Rundle. Bow Falls is the result of that glacial river rerouting.

The volumes of water rushing through the Front Range valleys during the peak decades of glacier recession must have been incredible. Huge rivers of muddy, sediment-laden waters from the mountain glaciers roared out of the mountain valleys, eroding new channels into the exposed moraine that carpeted the foothills, only to encounter the much larger continental ice sheet that still covered the plains. Dammed by the continental glacier, the waters pooled back into the foothills in an immense lake that extended from east of Calgary to well west of Cochrane.

Upstream from glacial Lake Calgary, the Bow, Ghost and Kananaskis rivers continued to rush out of the Rockies. Now, however, they lost momentum upon encountering the new lake. Without the force of gravity to help, their waters could no longer carry all the sediment with which they were loaded. Instead, it settled out onto delta floodplains where the muddy rivers meandered and shifted, changing course each time the accumulating sediments blocked their course.

Morley and Chiniki flats are the remains of broad, gravelly floodplains that the ancestral Kananaskis and Bow rivers built upstream from Lake Calgary. The flats along the Forestry Trunk Road north of Highway 1A are similar, postglacial floodplains formed by the Ghost River as it slowed upstream of the immense lake in the Bow valley. It's still possible today to see the kind of landscape that existed then, simply by driving the Icefields Parkway north from Saskatchewan Crossing. There, the North Saskatchewan River continues to build a similar-looking floodplain below the receding glaciers at its headwaters.

Lake Calgary likely persisted only a few decades. As the continental glaciers melted down, the river draining out of the lake began to erode its ice dam. There were probably several phases of catastrophic dam failure as the river broke free from rotting ice, each resulting in a massive release of flood waters that scoured out huge coulees eastward along the paths of least resistance. Geomorphologists have mapped several old beach terraces in Cochrane, Bowness and Calgary that correspond with different phases in the shrinking of Lake Calgary.

Finally, about 12,000 years ago, Lake Calgary drained out completely. The Kananaskis, Bow and Ghost rivers and Jumpingpound Creek, no longer held back by lake waters, began to erode the upstream landscape down toward the new base level established by the Bow River at the bottom of the former lake bed. The renewed – but much smaller – river began working and reworking its new floodplain.

TODAY'S LANDSCAPE would have been recognizable at that point, but only in its broad outlines. Until continuous vegetation cover became established, the raw glacial till, old lake bed silts and river deposits were at the mercy of the winds, rains and spring floods. Chinook winds chased huge dust storms down the Bow valley, depositing fine silt all across the prairie landscape to contribute to future soils. Over-steepened hillsides collapsed to more stable angles. Gullies formed along the edges of the former Lake Calgary and began to grow back into the foothills as newly freed creeks and rivers took up their work of bringing their stream beds down closer to the level of the new Bow River floodplain.

A green wash of vegetation, starting with species like spruce and willow, whose seeds are easily spread by wind, began to spread across the new landscape. At first, sedges, grasses, sage, willows and poplars became established in a kind of open, tundra-like vegetation that persisted for a few centuries. Animals that thrived in these new postglacial plant communities followed: mammoths, horses, antelope, moose, long-horned bison and deer. Packs of dire wolves and timber wolves hunted them, as well as short-faced long-legged bears, sabre-toothed cats and, of course, Aboriginal humans.

The first few centuries after the ice melted saw an explosion of life. More and more kinds of plants arrived to replace the original open shrub-steppe vegetation with a greater variety of vegetation similar to what we see today – grass-dominated prairie on the drier, windier sites; spruce forest in the moistest, most sheltered places; and willow thickets, aspen groves, sedge wetlands and various other habitats in between. Many of the Pleistocene animals died out either because of those habitat changes or because growing numbers of Aboriginal hunters killed them off – most likely for both reasons. A massive volcanic explosion in what is now Washington State, about 7,700 years ago, may have contributed to the great extinction, too, by plunging the world suddenly into a series of dark, cold years until the dust from the explosion of Mount Mazama finally settled out of the atmosphere.

Whatever the case, other animal species better adapted to the new habitat mix and better able to avoid human hunters soon took over.

And, perhaps eight thousand years ago, the place that would someday be called Alberta began to look very much like it did when the first European explorers stopped at the edge of the Bow valley and looked west across bunchgrass hills to the shining mountains.

Today's streams and landscapes betray their glacial origins only to those who can see through scenery to the stories its patterns reveal. Bighill and Nose creeks, like the lower end of Fish Creek and the Bow River itself downstream from Calgary, flow in the bottoms of broad coulees. Their valleys were scoured into the plains by flood waters released by the collapse of ice dams that held back meltwater lakes along the edges of retreating ice sheets.

The Kananaskis River at Morley Flats and the Ghost River at Benchlands and Waiparous have worn their way down into the broad, sloping deltas they formed back when they were larger streams pouring meltwater into those same periglacial lakes. The middle reaches of Fish Creek, Jumpingpound Creek and other foothills streams occupy sunken valleys, too, carved not into old deltas but into glacial till deposits. They've been reworking those deposits for the 10,000 to 15,000 years since the big glaciers retreated. The work continues today, albeit more slowly, because erosion takes longer when the landscape is covered with vegetation. Today's waterfalls and canyons mark the places where down-cutting streams once reached bedrock ridges that ice had failed to flatten.

Bow Lake, in Banff National Park, is one of many lakes and wetlands that store snow meltwater and serve as settling ponds for silt and sediment.

The more mountainous headwaters – the upper Highwood, Sheep, Elbow, Bow and Ghost rivers and their Front Range tributaries – follow ancient glacier tracks, too, having built up broad and deep floodplains from the gravels, cobbles, sand and silt originally deposited on the side slopes by melting ice and subsequently rearranged by centuries of spring floods. Each big flood brings more material across their floodplains, pushing the active river channels from side to side as the valley bottoms, filling with sediments, slowly rise.

Farther west yet, at the very farthest reaches of the watershed, silty-grey meltwater still drains today across newly exposed glacier debris from the final remains of the once-great mountain glaciers – Robertson and French glaciers in the Spray River valley, Haig Glacier, the shrunken Rae Glacier at the head of the Elbow, hanging glaciers behind Lake Louise and Moraine Lake, and the Wapta Icefield and Bow Glacier.

These are still rivers of ice, long after the ice age.

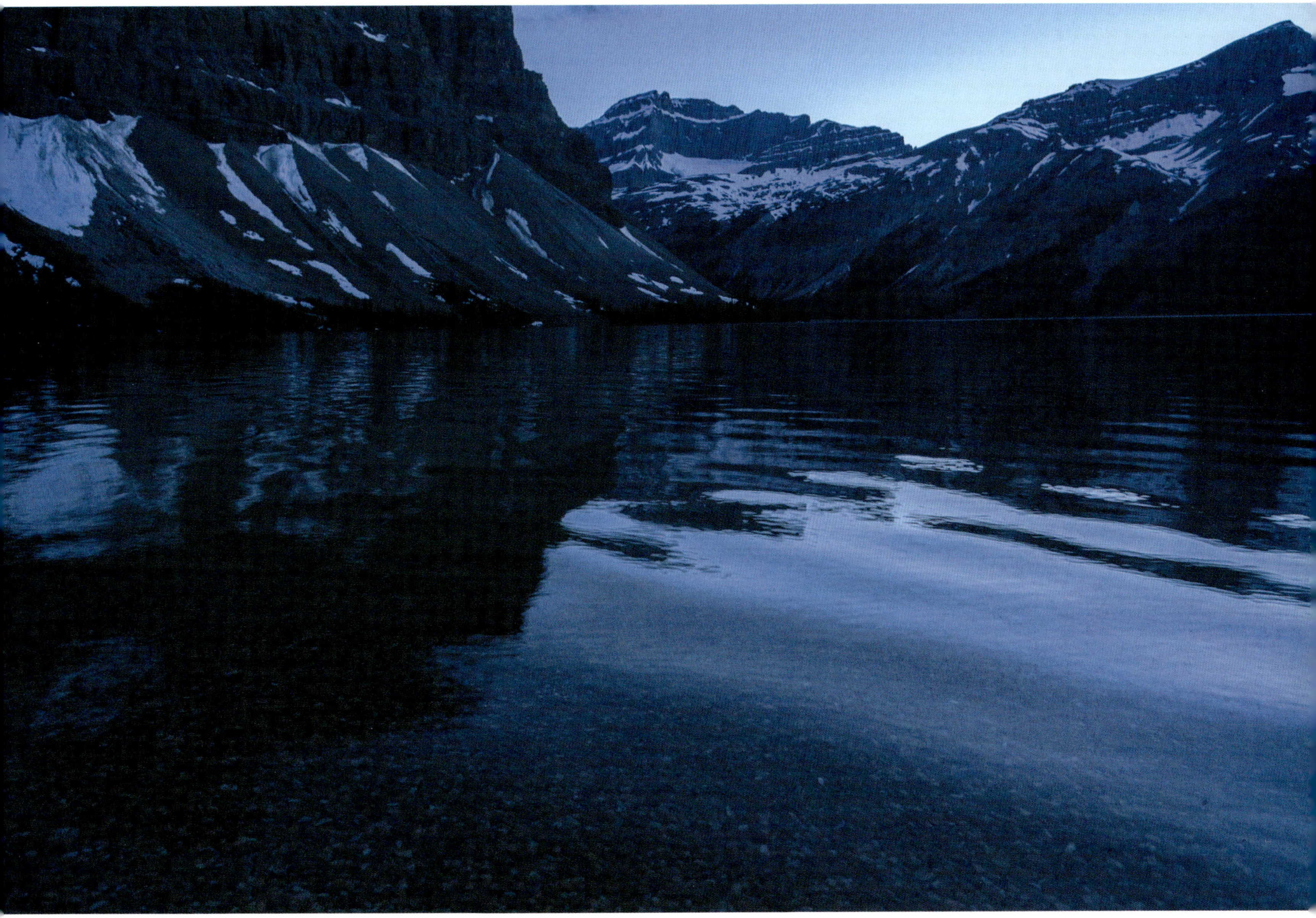

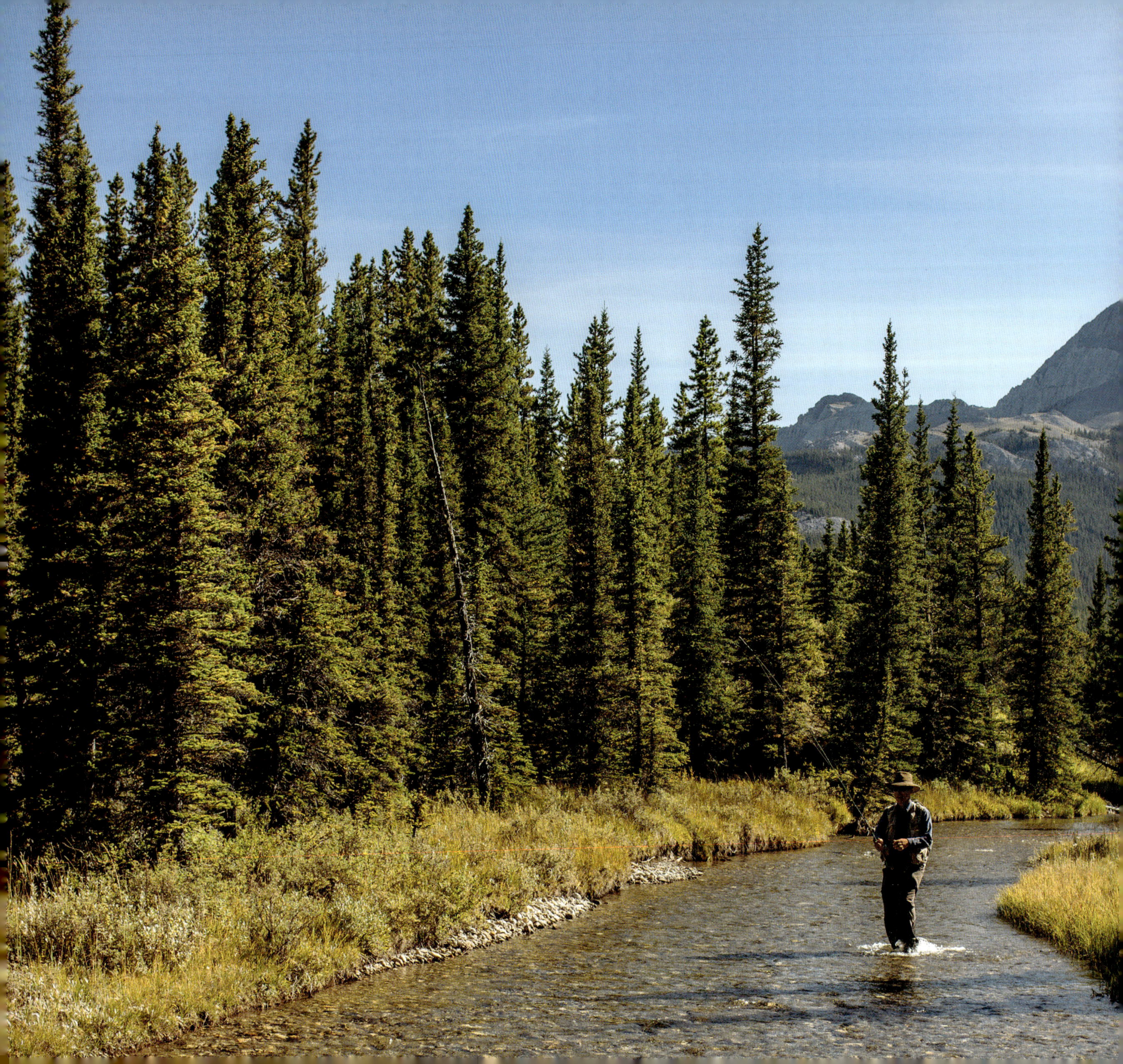

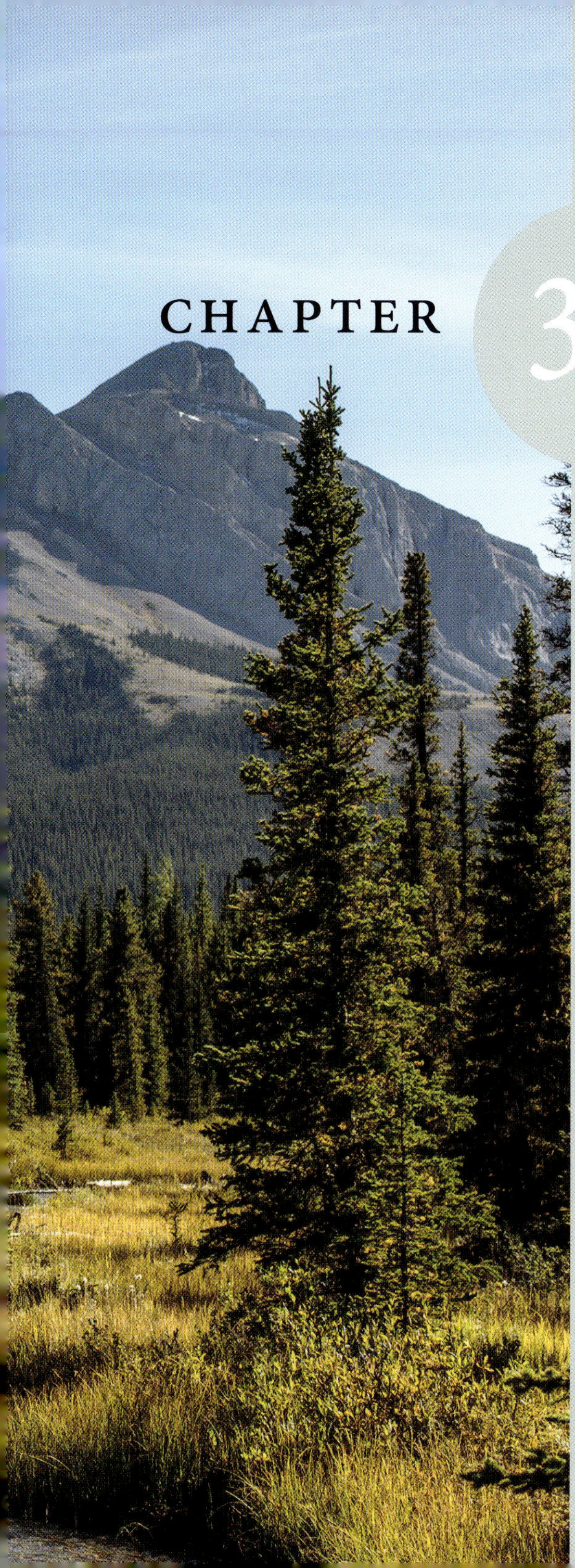

CHAPTER 3

A Prodigal's Return

Johnson Creek

I WAS PROBABLY SEVEN before I could keep up with Dad on his long walks into unnamed (at least for us kids) fishing streams. Less than a decade later, adolescence stole me away from the woods to deal with what seemed like more pressing matters. It's strange, then, the degree to which those few short summers came to define for me the idea of Alberta, and of what it means to belong to this place. Camping, long dusty drives into the pine-clad foothills and the perpetual search for good creeks played a surprisingly powerful role in shaping my sense of who I am and what life is all about. What a country in which to be young.

The good creeks were the ones that required a long hike and, preferably, a river crossing or two to add to the sense of remoteness – which, to my older brother Gordon and me, always translated into the possibility of big, wild trout. An exotic-sounding name helped, too, especially if it was one we had first heard from the lips of Pop-Pop – our maternal grandfather, Alban McParland. In my mind, at least, he'd been there when it was most real. It was

Page 38: *Clean water, clean gravels and lush riparian vegetation: a healthy headwaters creek.*

his country we were searching for, his stories we wanted to live.

Johnson Creek was a good creek, in spite of its mundane-sounding name and the fact that Pop-Pop had never fished it. Dad found it as a potential-laden blue wiggle on one of his first-generation foothills land survey maps. After an exploratory trip with Gordon, he soon adopted it as a favourite cutthroat trout stream. The creek might not have had much of a name, but the creeping, tortuous ride along a rutted two-track jeep trail offered occasional glimpses of gravel flats, flickering water and far mountains that definitely set the mood. Past the point where the road was no longer passable for Dad's station wagon, a hike through lodgepole pine forest brought us to an old seismic cutline crossing of Waiparous Creek. "Waiparous" more than met the requirements for an exotic name, and by the time Dad had set down his cargo of one, two, three or more young fishermen among the feather mosses and bunchberries on the far side of the creek's tumbling waters, we felt like we were well into the kind of wilderness where legendary trout might be found.

I was about nine when the Waiparous itself produced a legendary trout. Dad had decided to see how far up that perilous little jeep track he could coax our old station wagon to go. It was going to be an adventure, complete with camping rough rather than in our usual roadside campground. In Dad's view, such an adventure was acceptable for my older brother but not for me. In my view, it was unimaginable that they could leave me behind. Dad's view prevailed. I was heartbroken.

When they got back, Dad pulled out a large object wrapped in damp newspaper from the bottom of the cooler. Unwrapping it, he laid it on the sideboard in the kitchen, where we always cleaned our catches. It was a fish like I had never seen before – 45 centimetres long, densely covered with white spots and sporting a more deeply forked tail than the cutthroat, bull and brook trout we normally caught in those headwater streams. I had used the earnings from my first newspaper route earlier that year to buy A.J. McClane's *Standard Fishing Encyclopedia*, so we promptly began flipping pages to see if we could identify the fish he had caught in a deep pool far up the Waiparous.

It was a lake trout. What had compelled it to make the long journey upstream from Ghost Reservoir – the nearest water body with lake trout – is anyone's guess. But it confirmed for me that my father and older brother had deprived me of the kind of wilderness adventure and legendary fishing I'd always dreamed of. I was bitter and made sure they knew it as long as I could, which was probably only until the next weekend's fishing trip.

Johnson Creek was a very different stream from the Waiparous. The Waiparous is a braided mountain river. Its crystalline waters tumble and dance in sinuous channels through a spreading floodplain of rounded cobbles woven together by mats of yellow dryas and occasional carpets of river beauty. It didn't seem all that fishy to me then and still doesn't today, although I'm told by reliable sources that it has good populations of cutthroat trout, too many non-native brook trout, and still a few bull trout. The water seemed to spend too much time scurrying across long, gravelly riffles and too little time forming pools. Each spring, after the annual spring runoff floods abated, the stream would have abandoned many of its former channels and opened new ones, as if it just couldn't make up its mind. So indecisive a little river seemed too flighty ever to be a proper trout stream.

Johnson Creek, on the other hand, meanders from pool to pool in a well-entrenched channel through lush, grassy meadows full of shooting stars, larkspur, willows and swamp birch. It is a small stream by comparison with the Waiparous, but it clearly knows its job, which is to create as many curves and corners as possible to bemuse and tempt the visiting angler. Each corner holds a pool whose shadows whispered to me that this was it: this was where I would catch my own legendary trout.

One pool even kept that promise. It was a long run that had incised a good undercut beneath the far bank. Unfortunately, the spring floods had worked that far bank so hard that they had also undermined a good-sized spruce that, having finally fallen, now lay awash with its tip downstream, almost touching my bank. I recognized that tree for what it was: a fly thief. I couldn't afford to lose too many flies because I only owned a half-dozen, and Dad, who could usually be prevailed upon to lend me one of his lures if I let him grumble enough about my plaintive request, was far upstream.

I dropped my little Grizzly King fly into the current at the head of the pool and watched the curve of the line as it hurried down toward the sweeper. At the last moment, just as I was about to whip my fly to safety, there was a silver-green flash in the depths and the rod jerked in my hand. I tightened the line, excited, only to feel a bit of a letdown as the vibrations shivering up the line and into my hand revealed that I'd hooked only a small fish. Then, as if to add insult to injury, before I could lift it out the little fish dove for cover beneath the tree.

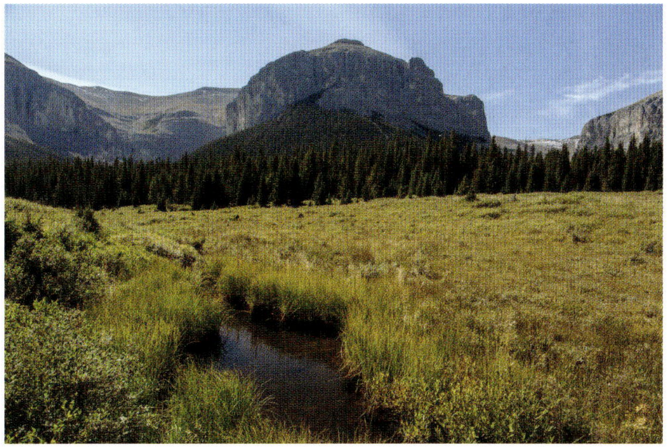

Fen meadows along headwater streams like Johnson Creek store far more water than downstream dams. Kept healthy, they also release that water cold and clean when it's most needed.

Muttering some words that Dad likely wasn't aware I knew, I hauled back on the rod. It was too late. The line was stuck. I tried to jerk it free, but it felt solidly anchored. Still hoping I might save my fly if the branch broke, I began to back up the bank, keeping the line tight. Sure

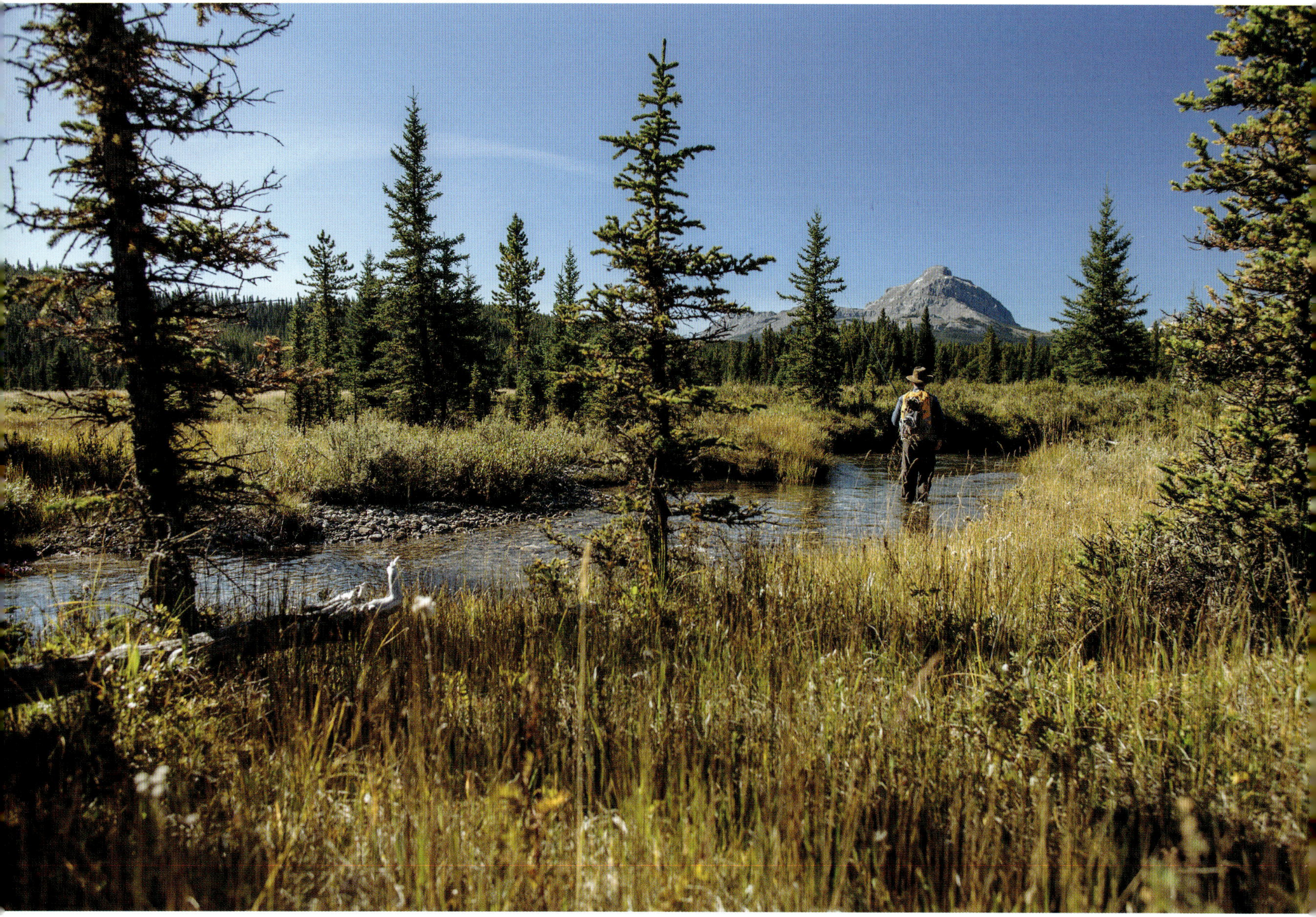

Johnson Creek's lush floodplain is a living reservoir of groundwater that sustains summer flows long after the spring runoff is past.

enough, I felt it give a little and then begin sluggishly to emerge from the depths. Then my heart stopped: the biggest fish I had ever hooked was struggling sullenly at the end of my line.

I backed up faster. The leviathan began to flap and twist as it found itself in shallow water. With one massive tug I slid the fish up onto the gravel bank and pounced on it. Only as I closed my hand around its slippery grey sides did the big bull trout open its mouth and release the little six-inch cutthroat I had actually caught. Holding it down with one hand, I found a rock with which to club the big fish. Only when it lay still and secure, well up among the willows, did I go back to release the cutthroat. The poor little thing had succumbed to the trauma of the experience, however; it went onto my willow branch, too.

That bull trout was 43 centimetres long, and I was vastly proud of it. It was almost as big as Dad's mystery lake trout, and when I finally caught up to him a few meanders upstream, he was gratifyingly impressed. We never did catch another fish that large in Johnson. Mostly we took home creels full of little native cutthroat trout, ranging from 20 to 25 centimetres in length. They might have been small, but they seemed the right size for a headwaters creek so small that Dad could often simply step across it.

Johnson Creek seemed pristine to my naive eyes, back in the late 1960s. Cattle wandered the valley in the summer, but not in numbers sufficient to put much of a dent in the lush greenery of creek meadows that extended far to the west. Those shrubby meadows, framed by sweet-scented pine forests, stretched peacefully to infinity – or at least to the backdrop of Black Rock, the Devil's Head and the other peaks along the western horizon.

I came to know those mountains as the birthplace of storms. Often, in mid-afternoon, we kids would find ourselves huddled under Dad's rubberized army-surplus rain cape like a covey of young grouse. There we would listen to thunder rolling across the meadows and the slap of fat raindrops on the forest floor. When the storms rolled on eastward, the sun would turn rain-wet creek meadows into a glowing green paradise. The next hour or two often yielded the best fishing of the whole day.

The peaks that frame the Waiparous and tributaries like Johnson Creek still give birth to storms. Something in the geography of the Ghost drainage makes it a summer thunderstorm engine. To the west, where much of the weather originates, high mountains are crowned with ice caps – the Wapta Icefield, and other big alpine glaciers farther north. The air that spills across the Rockies here arrives chilled and thin. The foothills in the Ghost–Waiparous watershed are high and forested, extending farther east than the hills south of the Bow. The broad basins between those hills have shallow gradients and drain slowly, so they are full of sphagnum fens, beaver meadows and wetness.

Water vapour is released from the leaves of plants as a byproduct of photosynthesis. The source of this water is soil moisture, which is brought up by the roots and trunks to where the leaves can release it through their open stomata as they make sugar from sunlight. The dense pine forests that clothe the hills breathe this moisture into the air, where it joins the water absorbed by evaporation from the wet valleys. The volatile hydrocarbons that give pine trees their distinctive scent combine with dust particles to form condensation nuclei for all the moisture accumulating in the air. As the summer sun heats the air close to the ground, thermals loft all that moisture into the cold air above. There, the moisture condenses into fluffy white clouds. The air becomes more unstable as thermals continue to pump more moisture into the heights; small clouds grow and coalesce into towering thunderheads. Coursing eastward, those thunderheads drag summer rain along a storm track that runs from near Cochrane through the northern edge of Calgary. Often they deliver hail or even short-lived tornadoes to the plains well after the sun has emerged again along Johnson Creek's fresh-washed meadows.

DURING THOSE EARLY FISHING TRIPS, those meadows were spongy with sphagnum moss into which I sometimes sank up to my thighs. In fact, I learned later while pursuing an ecology degree at the University of Calgary, they are a kind of wetland called fens: gently sloping bogs. Unlike true bogs, whose soils are saturated for much of the year by water that barely moves and, consequently, becomes increasingly acidic, the groundwater in fens is always seeping – slowly, of course – downslope. Fens have their own unique chemistry and a suite of plants and animals that thrive in their well-watered, moss-carpeted soils. Deprived of oxygen by constant saturation, the fens accumulate undecomposed organic matter, or peat. As often as not, where downslope ends, sweet springs emerge from beneath the mosses and peat, draining into little trout streams and keeping them cool and fertile during the heat and drought of late summer.

Strange little plants with purple foliage and exquisite pink flowers shaped almost perfectly like elephant heads grew in the mossy hollows along Johnson Creek – members of the snapdragon family. I learned later that their common name, appropriately, was elephant head. They were often associated with Indian paintbrush, grass of Parnassus, tiny saxifrages and insectivorous butterworts, looking like slightly thuggish cousins of the more abundant blue violets also huddled down in the sedges and sphagnum. It was a get-down-on-your-knees garden of unique and beautiful plants woven into a rare mosaic of humming life; an ecological medley scaled ideally to a preteen's height.

The fen meadows might host insect-eating plants, but clearly not enough – the smell of mosquito repellent still triggers vivid memories of Johnson and the other meadow creeks we fished in those days. Fen ponds, orange with iron oxide and sometimes darkened with hordes of toad tadpoles, yielded endless thousands of the little bloodsuckers. Dad usually had a yellow tube of roll-on 6-12 mosquito repellent in one of the many pockets of the old wool Air Force jacket he wore fishing. On the worst days, my fishing would be interrupted every hour or two by the need to look for his fishing rod over the dwarf birch and fight my way through the shrubbery for another touch-up before the whining hordes could suck me dry.

It never occurred to me then to question where all the water that saturated the peaty soils of those stream meadows came from; it was just there. These were the high foothills, lying just to the east of the first ranges of the Rockies. The surrounding slopes were covered with tall lodgepole pines whose understory seemed sparse and dry. They couldn't be the source of the water. The mountains along the western horizon, by mid-July, were no less sere-looking in their grey limestone remoteness. The odd snow patch glimmered through the afternoon haze, but too far away to have anything to do with the spongy grassland, winnowing snipes, willows and birdsong along our little trout stream. In my mind, the stream likely started in the mountains. The springs simply emerged as a matter of course. I accepted the natural world as given – just the way it was. I never once recognized that those meadow springs were, in fact, the source of the stream: that it was continually in the process of becoming itself, from the first spring wetting a rocky mountain slope, to the last mossy seepage near its confluence with the Waiparous, a kilometre or two below where we fished.

Johnson Creek is, in reality, an aggregate of springs, the surface expression of a landscape full of water that originated in last winter's snow and this year's spring rains and, having soaked into the sodden welcome of sphagnum, peat and marl, emerges weeks later to work its way toward a long-distant rendezvous with the salty waters of Hudson Bay. This stage of its journey – the cheery, chattering little wanderer with its countless cutthroats and the occasional

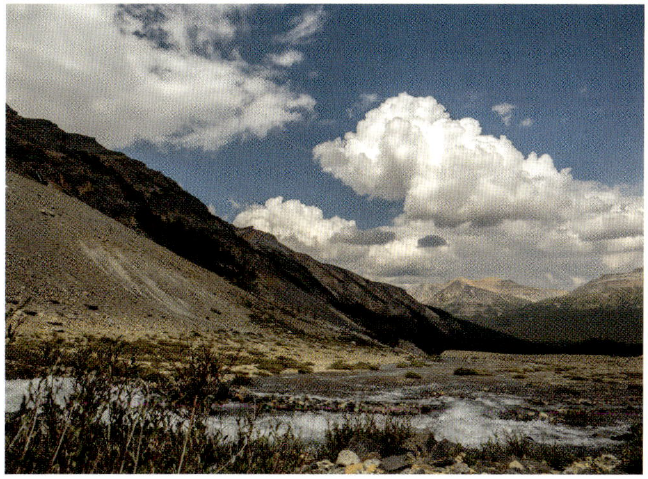

Clouds beginning to form near Bow Lake will grow to towering thunderheads by the time they reach the green foothills valleys of the Waiparous drainage farther east.

legendary trout – was the entirety of the stream to me in those days. There was no hydrological cycle or landscape health involved, just fishing in a good creek at the western edge of a young Albertan's home range.

IT'S TOO EASY TO LET THE YEARS SNEAK BY, to continually put off visits with old friends and loved ones. Then, when at last we reconnect, it can be cause for regret to see how much the years have changed them; how much we missed, how much we could, perhaps, have spared them. So it was with a strange combination of trepidation and guilt that I found myself returning to visit Johnson Creek in 2012, after an absence of more than three decades.

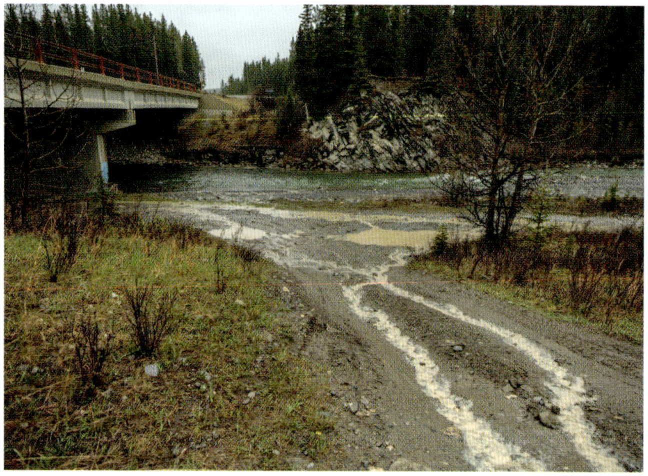

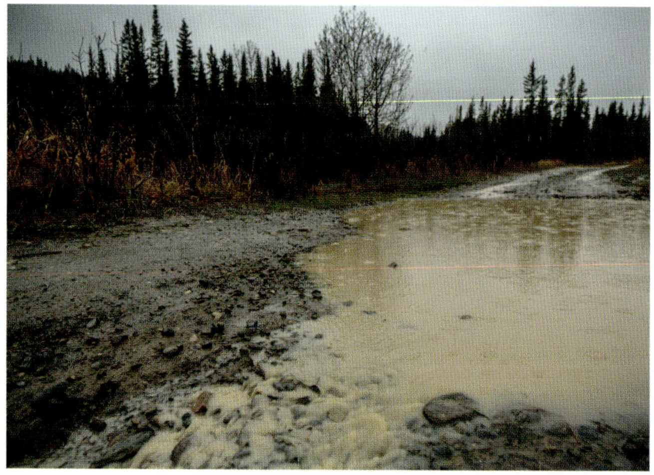

Dad and his kids stopped fishing Johnson Creek in the late 1970s, when the Alberta government decided to turn the Waiparous and Ghost River drainages into a sacrifice zone for a growing minority of well-heeled recreationists who prefer motorized play on off-highway vehicles (OHVs) to healthy exercise. We had no real objection to those who used OHVs responsibly simply to get a little farther into the backcountry, even though that meant by definition that there was less backcountry, but the idea of sharing that once-peaceful valley with a growing number of vandals who felt entitled to tear it apart with noisy dirt bikes, motorized quads and four-wheel drives held no appeal to us at all. We moved on to other, still-pristine streams.

In retrospect, it was a sort of disloyalty to abandon a place that had been so good to us, leaving it to face a future of abuse alone. It's not the way any of us would have treated the people we love, but somehow it seemed acceptable to turn away from places we should have cared for no less deeply. The more I reflected on our faithlessness, the more shame seemed to attach to it. Eventually it became clear: I owed it to Johnson Creek to return.

The old two-track road was a potholed, rocky mess. Beer cans, broken lawn chairs, scorched piles of campfire stones and other debris littered recesses in the spruce forest along an eroded network of vehicle trails with deeply incised ruts. As I eased carefully through muddy holes and over protruding boulders, men on grime-splattered quads and dirt bikes roared past. Some threw me a friendly wave; others glared at me with that too-cool-for-you male aggression that seems endemic to those whose recreation is founded on power and destruction. I was in a Subaru, after all; what kind of man would bring something like that to tough-guy country?

Page 46, left: *Rain that formerly would have soaked into vegetated ground drains down an off-road vehicle track, carrying eroded silt into Waiparous Creek.*

Page 46, right: *An off-road vehicle trail on the Waiparous Creek floodplain becomes a conduit for runoff and eroded soil during a light summer rain.*

Left: *Silted runoff water seeps into the clean waters of Waiparous Creek from an OHV vehicle trail.*

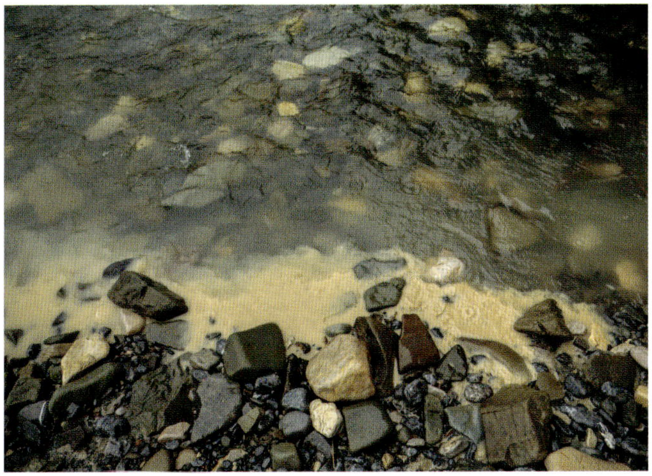

The cutline intersection where we used to park was barely recognizable: dust-coated spruce trees stood in a wasteland of bare soil and tire tracks. The floodplain beyond was trenched with vehicle trails, and the banks were worn down by the passage of countless vehicles. Deep ruts ran up the cutline to an immense mudhole that I remembered as a green meadow of tufted hair-grass. Everywhere were the marks of erosion and hasty runoff – the watershed had adapted to all the motorized abuse by becoming a place of rapid drainage where every rainstorm, rather than soaking into forest soil, now sends miniature torrents of muddy water down countless vehicle trails to the wounded river below.

A 2006 water quality study commissioned by Alberta Environment found the suspended sediment load in the Waiparous to be at least seven times higher after rains than in the similar Elbow River drainage, largely because of erosion from off-highway vehicle trails. I had learned this from the final report on a cumulative effects study by the Ghost Watershed Alliance and had a bit of difficulty really accepting it. That wasn't the Waiparous I remembered. Today, after a week of no rain, the river looked as sweet and clean as ever, but the damage along its floodplain soon made a believer of me. No river can stay healthy with a watershed and floodplain so badly degraded.

Once I waded across the Waiparous, to my relief, there was less evidence of abuse. The cutline was worn to bare soil, but at least it didn't have a network of parallel tracks like the main trail across the river. I turned onto a narrow forest trail worn by range cattle, wild horses and elk. Flattened vegetation showed that renegade off-roaders had used it, too, but only a few. Where it broke out into the shrubby meadows of Johnson Creek, it intersected an illegal OHV trail that followed the edge of the meadows west toward the mountains.

My emotions were conflicted. The valley was as lush and green as I remembered, water flickering behind the same willows and scrub birch, the long line of mountains forming the familiar backdrop of childhood memories. The relief and joy to find it so little changed was like coming home or seeing a long-lost friend. But the muddy vehicle tracks receding up-valley into the trees told me that others who cared less for the place had laid claim to it in my absence – it was like finding that a high-school sweetheart had been trapped in an abusive relationship for the same decades that one had spent remembering her fondly for who she once was.

Down by the stream, however, both past and present vanished into the timeless chatter of living water where Johnson Creek swept, clear and cold, over its bed of clean gravel. It had not forgotten its job during all those long years of my abandonment: the corner pools were as deep and the undercuts as promising as ever. If anything, the little creek seemed to bulge at the seams – too full of water for its own narrow channel. The wet years of the 21st century's second decade had evidently supercharged its fen meadows with groundwater; the creek was straining to carry all its liquid wealth.

With so much water flowing so rapidly, the fishing was challenging. Eventually I landed my first trout. Unlike the sleek little cutthroat I remembered, this one was a stranger. Not only had off-highway vandals invaded the foothills greenery surrounding the stream, but other invaders – introduced brook trout – had worked their way upstream and were in the process, as in too many other headwater streams, of displacing the native cutthroat and bull trout we had found here 40 years previously. I caught only a few more fish that day – all brookies.

Johnson Creek.

The years have not been kind to Waiparous Creek and its tributaries, like Johnson Creek. Its solitude and once-unbroken mosaic of natural vegetation have been marred by motorized vandals, and its aquatic community impaired by misguided mid-20th-century fish-stocking experiments. But as I hiked downstream at day's end on the rutted tracks of an illegal quad trail, the crystalline evening light still slanted, as it always had before, onto shrubby meadows and flickering water. In the few decades since Dad first ushered us into this then-secret place, the creek had changed little. It had suffered, but the injuries were far from terminal. It could be healed – but not if fair-weather friends abandoned it to abuse at the hands of others.

I paused a while to sort out my emotions. At first I was lost in nostalgia and memories of lost childhood, long-departed father and grown siblings – of what used to be and will never be again. But eventually I found the grace to give myself over to gratitude for the moment itself, for the opportunity once again to be alone with the sweet stillness of a foothills valley and the whispered confidences of a headwater creek, its future still full of potential. I promised myself I would never turn my back on this place again, whatever the future might bring to it. Then I went home to write a book.

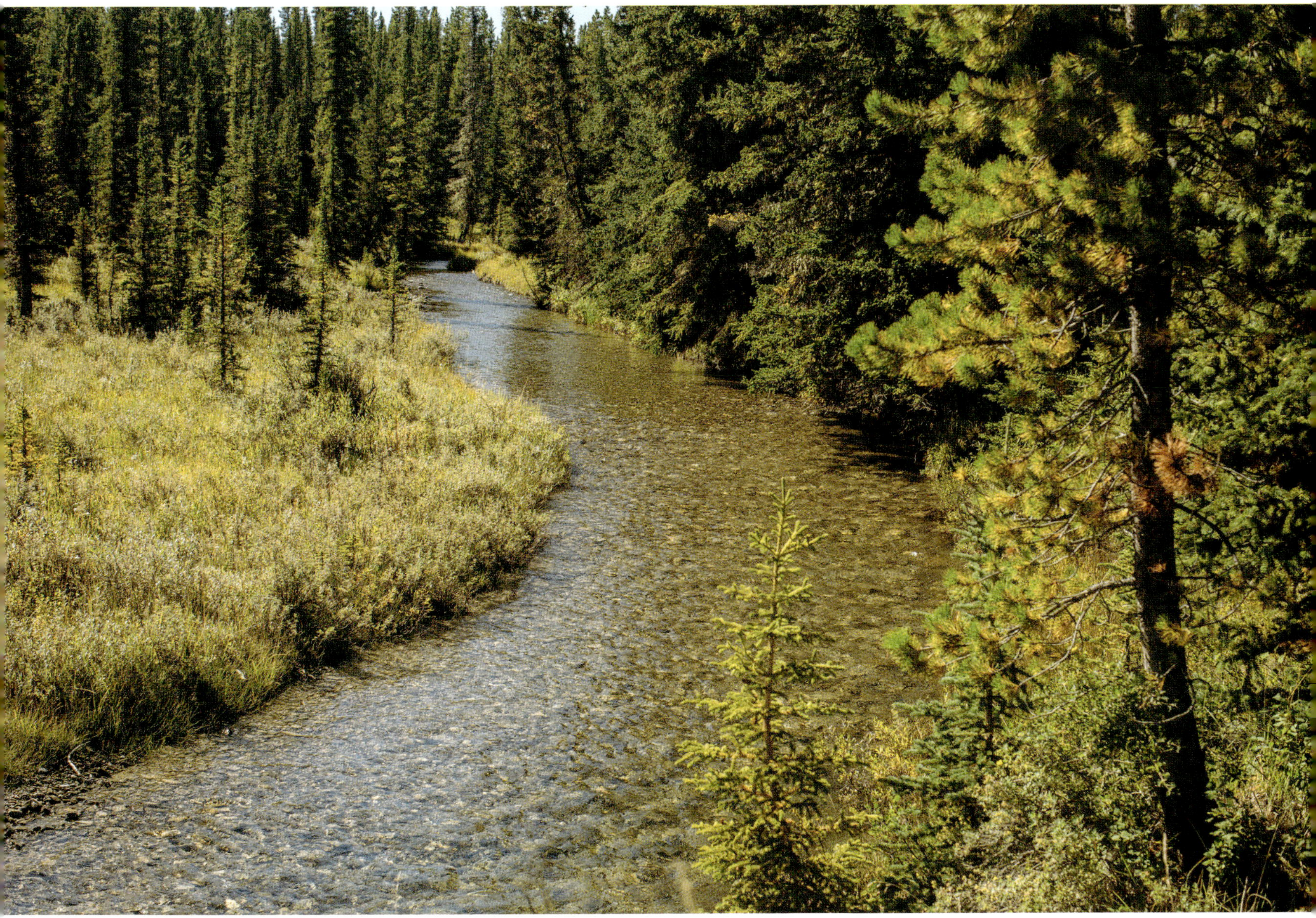

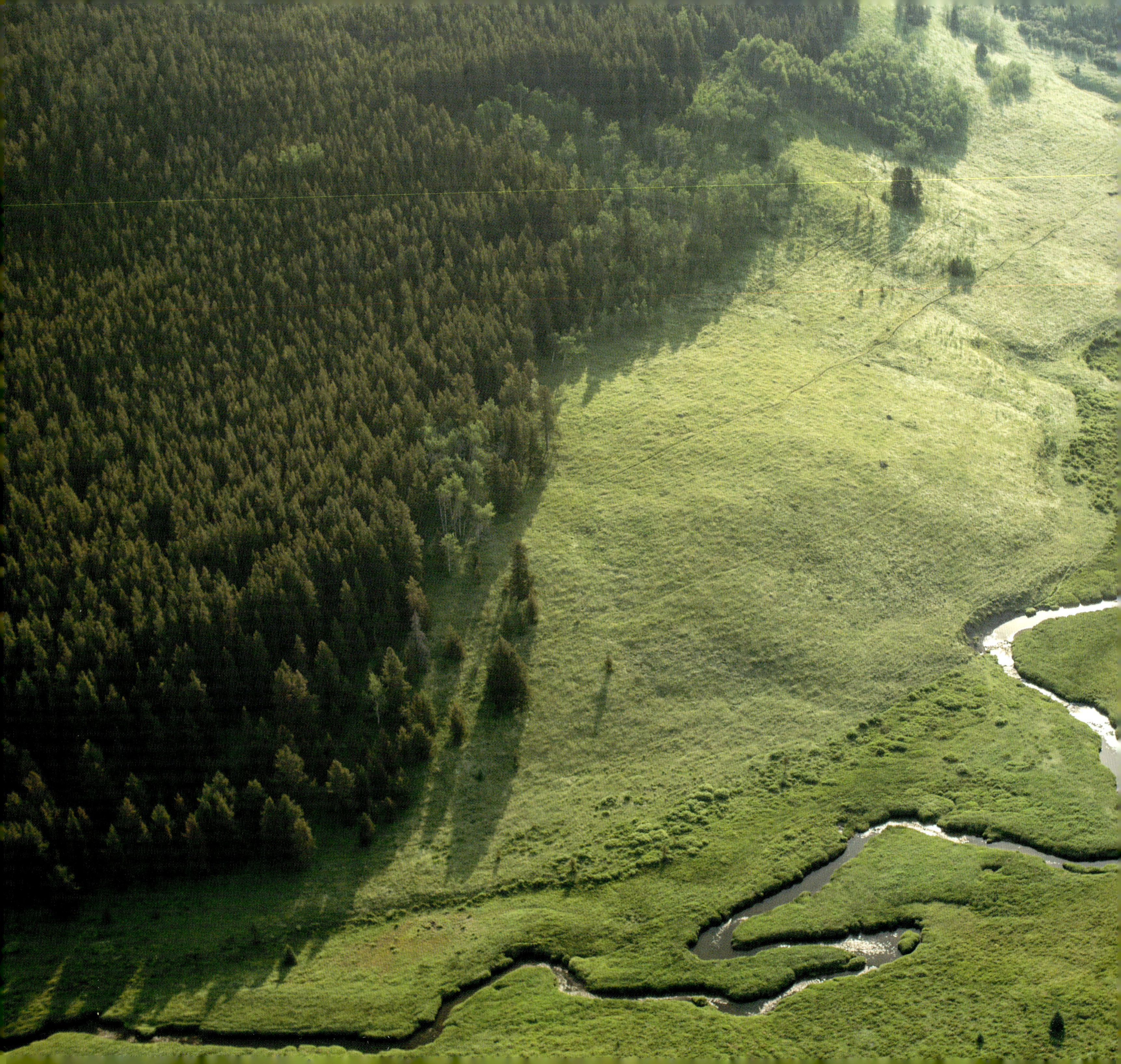

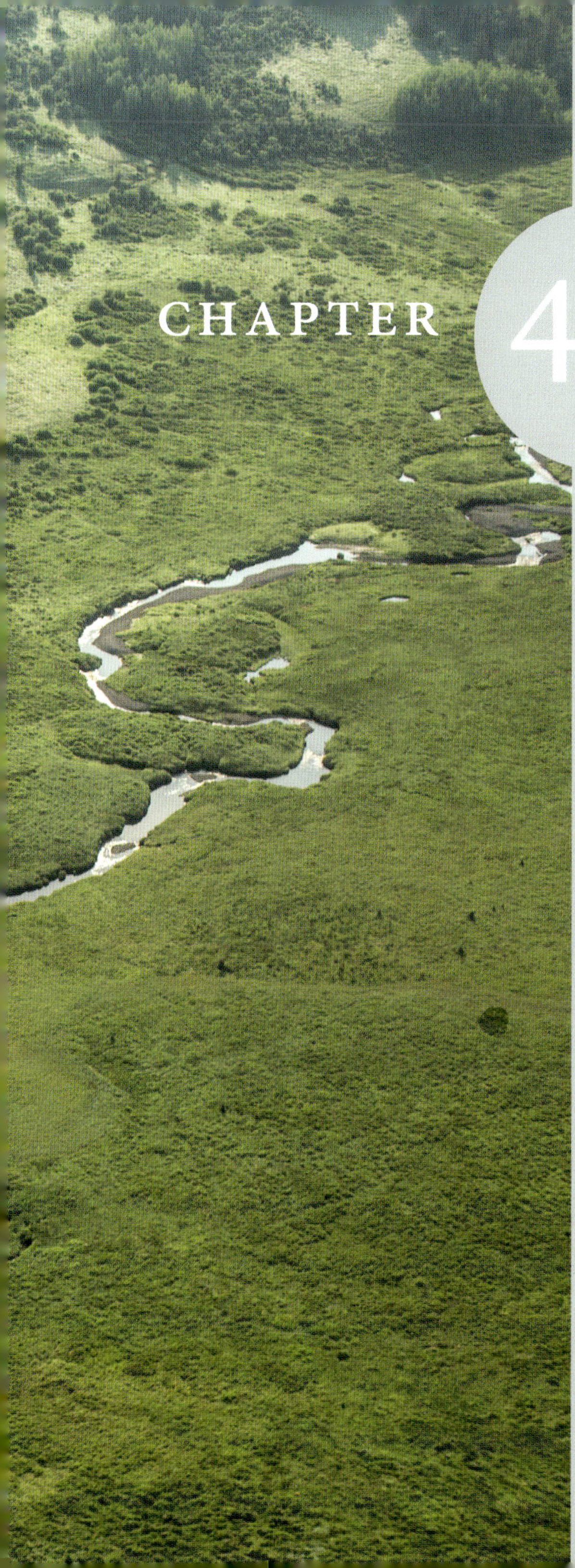

CHAPTER 4

Caterpillars and Cutthroats

Quirk Creek

MY BROTHERS AND I DIDN'T KNOW QUIRK CREEK by its real name until we were most of the way through our teens. Even before he found Johnson Creek, Quirk had become one of Dad's treasured secrets. He wasn't going to risk its true identity to kids who were eager to talk to anyone anywhere, anytime, about fishing. So we called our little Elbow River tributary Muskeg Creek. That was, however, not a bad clue to its whereabouts, as it shares the same high foothills basins with the headwaters of a creek by that name that drains to the Sheep River drainage.

Quirk begins in a series of spring seeps, birch bogs and seasonal drainages arrayed along the east flank of Forgetmenot Mountain. Two tributaries – Mac and Howard creeks – emerge from mossy hollows under ribbons of white spruce and join their newborn waters to upper Quirk Creek after tumbling through cow parsnip meadows where deer, elk and domestic cattle graze.

Page 50: *Quirk Creek's lush green floodplain and intact stream banks reveal it as one of the healthiest streams surviving today in the headwaters of the Bow River.*

Right: *Exposed cobbles, a scour pool and torn-out stream banks reveal the damage downstream from an off-road vehicle crossing on Quirk Creek.*

After winding quietly through several kilometres of grassland, shrubby sphagnum fen meadows and beaver ponds, Quirk awakens, begins to tumble and dance, and slips into the shade of the pines to spend its last couple kilometres of independence as a chattery little forest stream. Then it abruptly spills out onto a sunny floodplain to merge its waters with those of the upper Elbow River.

If you live in south Calgary, chances are you've tasted Quirk Creek, along with Canyon, Prairie, Ford, Cougar and the other sparkling little tributaries of the river that, pooled behind the concrete walls of Glenmore Dam, served as Calgary's original drinking water reservoir until the city grew too large and was forced to tap into the Bow River's Bearspaw Reservoir, too. It's already accomplished a great deal before reaching your glass.

QUIRK CREEK FOUND ITS WAY into my family's lore sometime in the early 1960s, when Dad went to get a haircut. While Dad sat in one of the waiting chairs, surrounded by the smell of pomade and grooming oils, Mr. Osterwercha snipped and trimmed away at the customer ahead of my father. The customer was sharing the tale of a remarkable fishing stream he'd recently found. Dad idly flipped the pages of a *Reader's Digest* magazine, pretending not to be listening as avidly as he was. The only clue the other customer gave was that he had parked at a locked gate on a forest reserve road and walked two hours up a river to get to the tributary creek.

Dad went home with a new haircut and a new project. He dug out his dog-eared set of land survey maps and set to work figuring out which of the many creeks west of Calgary might be the one he'd just heard about. A two-hour walk, he assumed, would be about eight or nine kilometres. So he looked for roads that ended at gates, and then looked for the mouths of tributary streams eight kilometres up-valley.

The gravel forestry road west from Bragg Creek, in those days, was gated near Elbow Falls. Prairie Creek was too close to the end of the road and Ford Creek too far for either to be the mystery stream. There was a south-bank tributary that seemed a likely prospect, however, so Dad decided to give it a shot. On his first hike into Quirk Creek, he later told us, he fished upstream from the mouth and had barely reached the meadows when he ran out of the preserved salmon eggs he used for bait. The fishing was just too good. He ended up completing his daily catch limit of 15 trout with bits of tomato out of his lunch sandwich, and hiked back out along the Elbow that evening with a creel so heavy it hurt his shoulder.

By the time my older brother Gordon and I were old enough to accompany Dad into Quirk Creek, the road had been extended. It was now possible, except in wet weather, to get over the shoulder of Powderface Ridge and

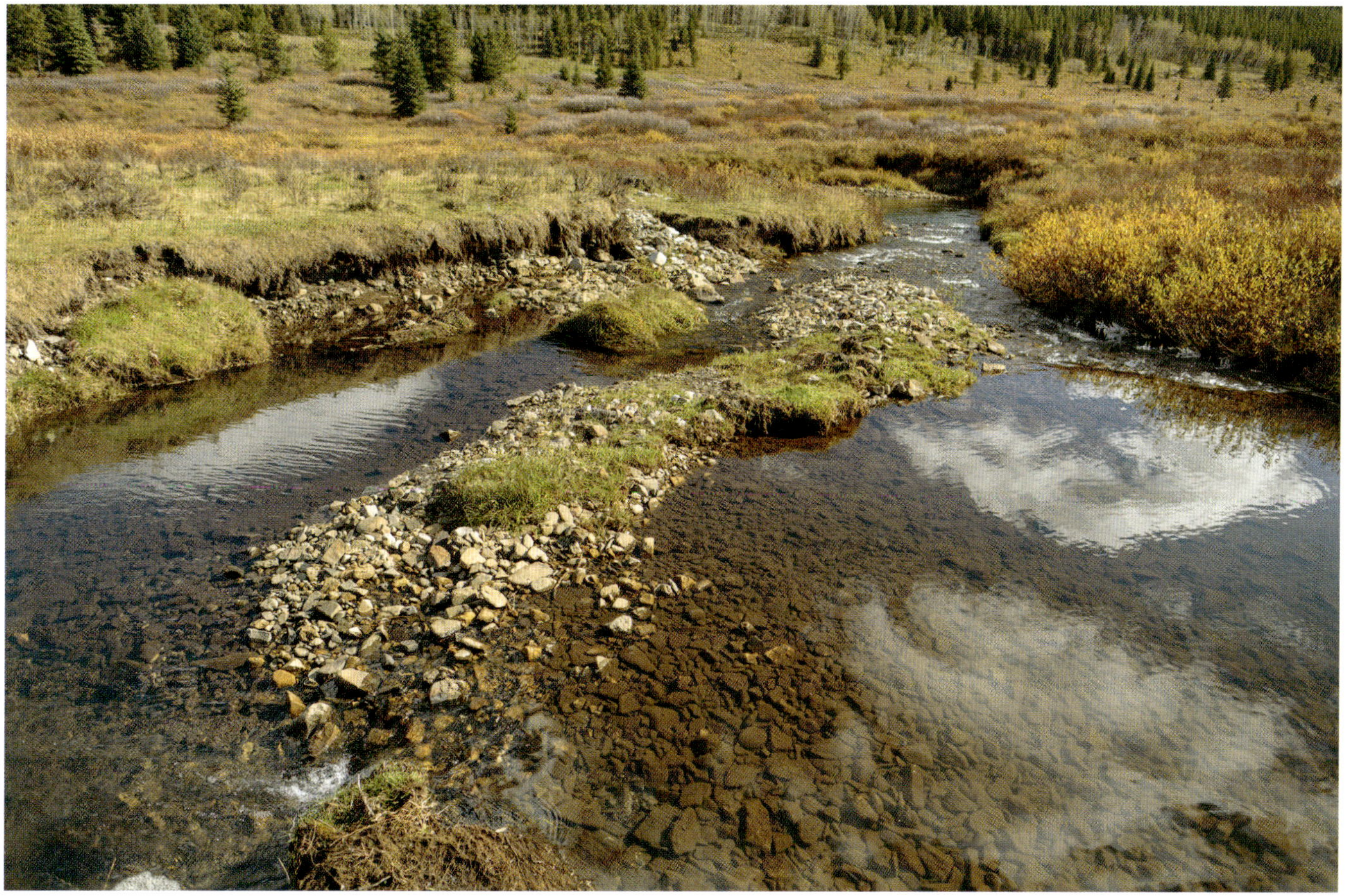

thence down to the open gravel floodplain of the Elbow River, only a couple kilometres upstream from the Quirk Creek confluence. Dad would ferry us one by one across the powerful current of the Elbow and deposit us on the far bank. From there we followed a cattle trail across sparse floodplain meadows to the base of the low hill that separates the Elbow and Quirk valleys. A seismic cutline took us up and over the hill through resin-scented forest of lodgepole pine and, on the other side, spilled us out onto the edge of sloping meadows of shrubby cinquefoil, dwarf birch, stunted willow and timber oatgrass.

Down in the meadows, blinking in and out of sight as

it traced its circuitous way from one long pool to another, the creek beckoned. Usually there would be white-crowned sparrows and ruby-crowned kinglets singing and, in the open timber at the edge of the meadows, the "Quick! Three beers!" call of an olive-sided flycatcher. They may have been declaiming to one another that each had exclusive rights to their portion of this verdant foothills paradise, but from an early age I came to hear those songs as an announcement that a long hike was nearly over and trout were very near.

On one of our earliest visits to Quirk Creek we arrived to find the meadows crawling with billions of tent caterpillars. Dad was six feet tall and he wore hip waders. He could afford to be blasé about those squirming hordes down around his ankles. I was half his height and wearing gumboots. Things looked considerably grimmer to me. Thanks to my short legs and tendency to be distracted by birds and animal tracks, I was well behind Dad and Gordon when I suddenly realized I was alone amid a sea of hairy, wriggling creatures.

As usual, my plaintive cries for help went unheeded. Even when they turned to screams of panic, they were ignored. Dad and Gordon were getting steadily farther away, and I was about to be abandoned to a universe of caterpillars. Finally, as Dad dipped out of sight down by the creek, my nerve broke and I ran, shrieking, into the meadow, like a shell-shocked soldier abandoning his trench and throwing himself into enemy fire.

When I found the others and frantically yanked my gumboots off to shake out the thousands of caterpillars that I was sure must be in them, while sobbing recriminations at an exasperated father and smirking older brother, I was empty-handed. At the start of my panicked dash, Dad pointed out, I had been carrying a rain cape and a fishing rod. They never turned up again. Gordon still reminds me from time to time; it had been his spare fishing rod, after all.

Those long, spongy meadows were the site of many fine days afield, caterpillars notwithstanding. The stream still held plenty of cutthroat trout, albeit not as many as back before Dad and a few other anglers found it and started taking home their limits. It was hard to fish, though, at least for me. The pools were deep and long, some dammed by beavers and others simply held back by caved-in cutbanks or short outcroppings of rock. The banks overhung the creek and the undercuts extended in some cases a metre or more back under the meadow edges. The trout could remain hidden far back under those banks, inaccessible until the right combination of day length, water temperature and sun angle triggered a hatch of mayflies or caddis that would bring them out into the open to feed. The rings of rising trout would form then just off the current line and my heart would begin to pound and my hands to shake. The rise forms inevitably vanished at my clumsy approach as the fish darted back under the banks.

Dad always fared better than me, because he had the sense to step softly across the spongy meadows so as not to send vibrations ahead of him to warn the creek and its denizens of his approach. Gordon sneaked up on each pool from downstream. He had an uncanny ability to put the little red and white spoons he used exactly where he wanted them, and could bring his lure right down the edge of a cutbank the whole length of a pool without disturbing it, so he did well, too.

The fish we caught were pure westslope cutthroat trout – the original native trout of the Bow River headwaters. They were green-backed and golden-sided, sometimes with intense orange stains down each side of their belly, their backs covered with small black spots that became more abundant toward the tail. On our first trip to the creek, Dad took one out of his creel to show me the orangish-red slash marks under their throats that gave them their name.

I doubt that there is a more beautiful fish in the world.

Like the white-crowned sparrows and olive-sided flycatchers and the endless breathing of foothills breezes through the thousands of lodgepole pines that lined the valley, those fish resonated deeply with me. They belonged here; they made the place complete. And the place made me complete, though it never occurred to me at the time; I was just fishing with Dad and my siblings.

Once in a while we caught a different kind of fish, more slender and slippery, with a sort of flattened head and white leading edges on each of its pectoral fins. Gordon, in particular, caught a lot of them, as they were aggressive about chasing hardware. Instead of the black spots that covered the cutthroats, these grey fish had whitish spots with a sprinkling of pale orange ones down each side. Dad told me they were called bull trout and that they sometimes got much bigger than cutthroats, but that most of the big ones were fished out. We added them to our daily limit and took them home and ate them, but they never seemed to fight as hard or taste as good as the cutthroats.

It would have been around 1969 when I caught my first brook trout in Quirk Creek. Well into my teens by then, I had abandoned the meadows to Dad and my siblings in favour of the livelier, gravel-bottomed reach on the stream's final descent to the Elbow. The fish were smaller but more readily caught here, and I liked fishing runs and riffles more than the quiet water of the long pools farther upstream.

One afternoon, where a small rapid eddied into a dark pool, I hooked a beautiful little fish. It had a darker back than the bull trout it somewhat resembled, and its pale spots gave way along the very back to a sort of worm-like patterning. On the sides, instead of pale orange spots it had large yellow spots and a scattering of bright red ones, each with a ring of blue around it. Its belly was orange. At the time, I thought the pretty little trout was a sign of good things to come, as our favourite creek could only be improved by having yet another species of trout in it. In truth, however, it marked the beginning of decline for Quirk Creek's near-pristine aquatic ecosystem.

BROOK TROUT ARE NATIVE TO STREAMS and lakes of eastern Canada and the northeastern US. Although they never occupied Alberta waters naturally, well-intentioned but, in retrospect, sadly misguided early fisheries managers began releasing them into streams and lakes in the early 1900s to replace fished-out native stocks.

Brook trout are pretty, they taste good, and they wreak havoc on native trout populations. But in 1940, long before fisheries managers had realized the magnitude of the mistake they were making, a hatchery truck finally

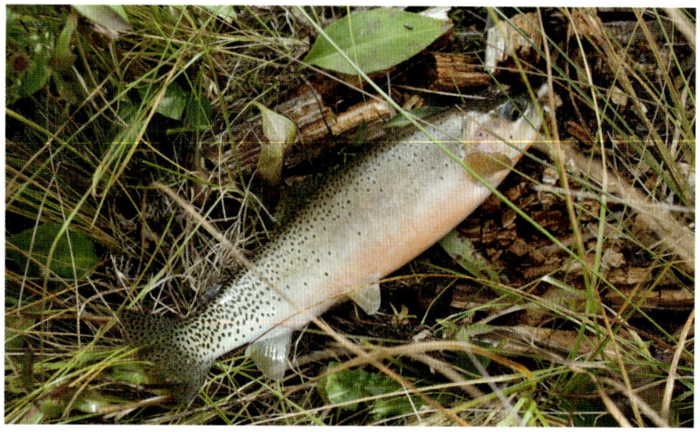

Westslope cutthroat trout, the original native trout of the Bow River headwaters, are now classed as a threatened species because of competition and hybridization with non-natives. Photo: Kevin Van Tighem

arrived to pour a load of the little invaders into the upper Elbow River which, until then, had contained only its original native fishes.

Because they are closely related to the native Alberta bull trout (both are char species in the genus *Salvelinus*) and, like bull trout, spawn in the fall, brook trout hybridize with their larger relatives. Brook trout, however, become sexually mature at an earlier age and continue to spawn later into the fall. As a result, they can overwhelm a bull trout population by filling the stream with early-maturing and aggressive brook trout and at the same time making the surviving bull trout produce maladapted hybrids instead of more bull trout.

Cutthroats spawn in the spring and don't need to worry about male brook trout fertilizing their eggs. Even so, where brook trout invade a cutthroat stream, it isn't long before the cutthroats either disappear or become restricted to the coldest, smallest upstream reaches. Brook trout are aggressive competitors for food supplies and also have an unfortunate habit of devouring young cutthroats.

Jim Stelfox, for many years a senior fisheries biologist with Alberta's Fish & Wildlife Division, found that anglers catch fewer brook trout than cutthroats and bull trout even when the exotics are more abundant. Combine the aggressive feeding and prolific breeding of the brook trout with anglers who are more likely to catch and kill the native fishes, and the result is what happened to Quirk Creek in the last two decades of the 20th century.

A 1978 stream survey showed that brook trout had pretty much taken over the lower three kilometres of Quirk Creek but were still absent farther upstream. A decade and a half later, fishery survey crews found that brook trout had spread throughout the whole creek and now accounted for more than 90 per cent of the fish population.

What had once been a stream full of good-sized cutthroat trout and a few large bull trout – native fish that had evolved through countless centuries in the Bow River's headwater ecosystems – was now crowded with stunted brook trout. It was a familiar, and discouraging, story to the biologists who had only recently seen bull trout designated a threatened species and were trying to come to terms with data that suggested that even the once-abundant cutthroats might soon be a species at risk.

Fish Hatcheries: Nurture vs. Nature

The Canadian Pacific Railway released the first non-native fish into Alberta waters in 1903. Having spent considerable effort attracting well-heeled tourists from the northeastern United States and eastern Canada to Banff National Park, the company was faced with overfishing of the easily captured native bull and cutthroat trout. Tourists still wanted to catch fish, so Canadian Pacific shipped a load of brook trout by rail from Lake Nipigon, Ontario, and followed that with more transplants of the exotic new trout between 1904 and 1908.

The Dominion Parks Service next took over the task of importing exotic fish like brook, rainbow and brown trout. The popularity of stocking programs led park officials to establish a fish hatchery in Banff in 1913 so as to ensure a steady supply of trout for release into streams and lakes. Within two decades Jasper and Waterton Lakes National Parks had fish hatcheries, too. My great-uncle Bill Cable ran the Waterton hatchery for many years.

J.B. Cross, a member of the famous A.E. Cross ranching family, owned the Calgary Brewing and Malting Company in Calgary. In 1936 he opened the first fish hatchery outside the national parks in what is now the Inglewood district of Calgary. The close relationship between beer and trout continued for the next four decades (some might argue it has never ended), until the Province of Alberta, which had been jointly operating the Calgary hatchery with Calgary Brewing and Malting, opened the new Sam Livingston Fish Hatchery on the William Pearce estate in Calgary in 1973 and took over full responsibility for pouring bushels of brook trout into waters they were never meant to occupy.

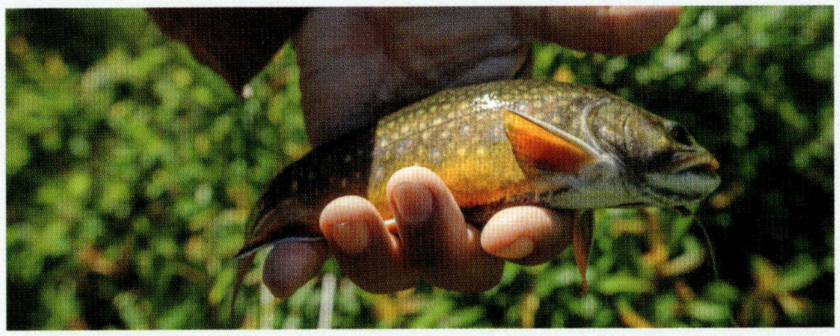

Brook trout are as attractive as they are alien to Alberta waters. These exotics displace native bull and cutthroat trout.

Most Alberta fish hatcheries finally closed down after repeated outbreaks of diseases like infectious pancreatic necrosis (IPN) in the crowded, feedlot-like environments of the rearing facilities. Non-native fish like brook, brown and rainbow trout are no longer released into Alberta streams where they might compete with native species. Most trout stocking is now limited to lakes that are subject to winterkill or ponds that receive heavy fishing pressure. Stocking of streams – in the 20th century, a recurring demand by local fish and game groups as headwater streams became depleted of their native stocks – ended after Dr. R.B. Miller's research on Gorge Creek, a tributary of the Sheep River, showed the practice to be a waste of time, money and fish.

The 20th-century experiment in raising alien fish in hatcheries and releasing them into natural waters to restore depleted fisheries proved to be an unproductive exercise based more on untested assumptions than on science. History has shown that nothing works as well as simply conserving the native fish, whose evolutionary history makes them the best fit for waters they have occupied for millennia.

THE CHANGES TO QUIRK CREEK, however, took place unwitnessed by Dad and his kids. Just as with Johnson Creek, we no longer fished there.

The first unwelcome change to our special place had come in the early 1970s, when an oil company cut a road into the lower part of the drainage and installed two gas wells. The road had a locked gate, however, so the stillness of the valley remained for the most part undisturbed. Even with the scar of a road, the quiet green valley still pulled us back season after season.

We finally abandoned Quirk Creek in 1979. That was when the Alberta government designated the McLean Creek off-highway vehicle use area in the southern part of the Elbow River watershed. The new land-use zone was part of an effort to concentrate off-roading in only a few areas and thereby prevent widespread damage to the Eastern Slopes. The intentions of the government authorities were, arguably, good, but the approach was founded on flawed premises.

One was that off-roading is a legitimate use of public land, in spite of the damage it does to landscapes, wetlands and streams, and in spite of the unnecessary burning of depleting fossil fuels. The other flaw in their reasoning was that the McLean Creek area was suitable or appropriate as a sacrifice zone. My family never accepted either premise, especially since the government planners included most of the Quirk Creek valley in the OHV sacrifice area. Land abuse is always ugly but never more so than when inflicted by uncaring newcomers on a peaceful, near-pristine valley that long-time users have grown to know and love.

Rather than see the damage and cope with the noise and exhaust fumes, we simply stopped going to Quirk Creek. It had, in effect, been taken away from us and given to a new group of people, too many of whom saw it primarily as a place to vandalize with their big, expensive playthings.

Riders were fording one of Quirk Creek's small tributary streams so frequently in the late 1990s that large plumes of silt washed downstream all summer long. The erosion of fine mud into the creek during its lowest flow period fouled spawning areas and clean gravels, adding habitat damage to the challenges facing the creek's native fishes.

Although it was bad land-use policy that opened up the area to off-roading, Spray Lake Sawmills played a key role in triggering the silt pollution problem. Spray Lake extended the original gas well road during the late 1990s to access some cutblocks in the pine forest farther upstream. Off-roaders quickly discovered the logging haul road and appropriated it. When the logging operation ended and the crews pulled out, Spray Lake made no attempt to reclaim the road; they simply pulled out their temporary bridge and left.

The off-roaders kept on coming, but now they drove right through the creek.

Mountain and foothills streams always move a lot of sediment during spring floods, but the high water flows at that season also scour the gravels clean and create turbulent flows that sort the sediments out as they settle. Much of the silt from spring runoff gets deposited up on the floodplain instead of in the active stream channel.

Spring floods have an erosional effect, but they also have a cleansing effect simply because there is so much water at work and so much of the floodplain to work on.

The problem with constant stream crossings during the low-flow periods of late summer and early fall is that all the sediment disturbed at the crossing and washed in from the approaches gets set adrift at a season when the stream, having shrunken to its summer levels, lacks the power to move it far or to flush it out again when it settles into the cracks and crannies among streambed gravels. When mud chronically erodes into a low-volume summer stream, the once-clean gravels of the stream bed can become cemented in place, and the invertebrate life and fish eggs and fry that normally inhabit the spaces in the gravels are thus starved of both oxygen and food. This kind of creek deterioration was already well advanced in heavily disturbed foothills watersheds like the valleys of Nose, Grand Valley, Fish, Fisher and McLean creeks, but it was a new phenomenon on the formerly pristine Quirk Creek.

Kerry Brewin and Dean Baayens, biological staff from Trout Unlimited Canada's Calgary office, became aware of the pollution because of the brook trout. They had begun working with the Alberta Fish & Wildlife Division in 1998 to try and protect the native cutthroat and bull trout in Quirk Creek from the invading aliens, but repeated muddy flows soon told them there was a new problem to deal with.

Brewin and Baayens installed a turbidity monitoring data logger in 2001 to substantiate their concerns about sediment pollution. The Alberta government's reluctant

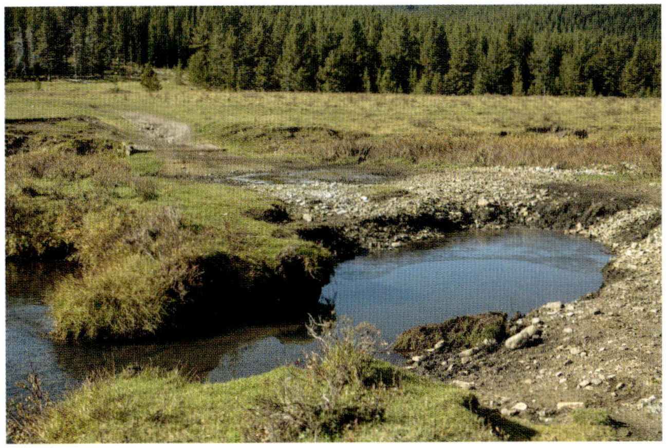

Floodwaters funnelling down an OHV trail and squeezing through a small bridge blew out this once-healthy floodplain meadow along Quirk Creek in 2013. This kind of damage can lead to stream degradation for many kilometres downstream if vegetation doesn't recover before the next big flood.

response, almost two years later, was the too-common half-measure of educating users and seeking voluntary compliance. Education works only with those who are inclined to learn and willing to adjust their behaviour. For the rest, it simply focuses their aggression.

That was the case at Howard Creek, where Alberta Community Development (the responsible agency at the time) put a sign beside the trail asking OHV users voluntarily not to use the ford and advising them that a bridge would be in place the following year. Brewin and Baayens's final report demonstrated the predictable outcome of this voluntary approach:

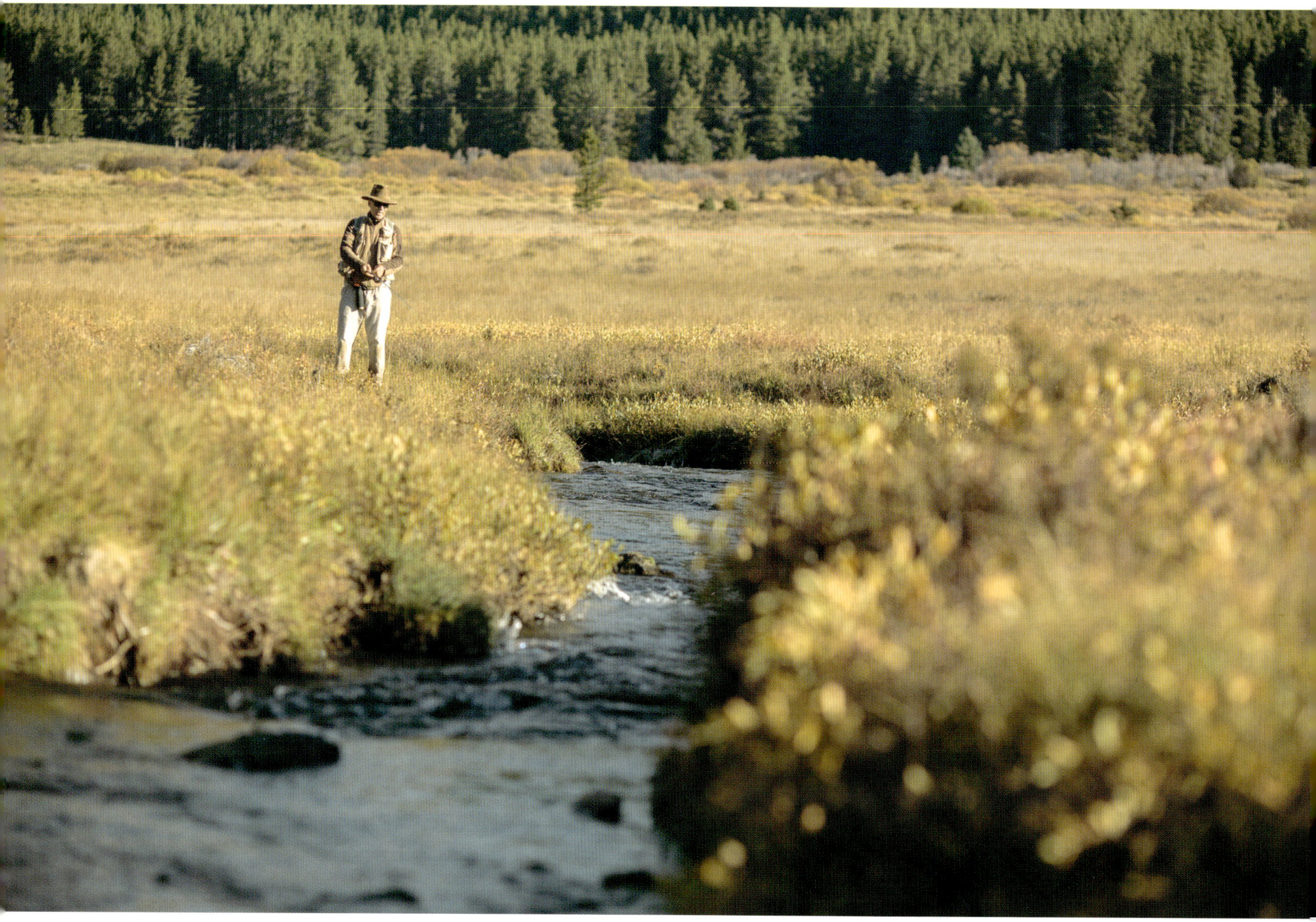

The stable flows and clean gravels of healthy headwater streams like Quirk Creek yield not only a reliable water supply for downstream users but also rewarding angling for trout.

> Among three fording events [witnessed by the authors] by OHV users when the sign was in place, one event involved three OHV users who stopped to read the sign and then drove through the stream. A second observation involved two mountain bikers who carried their bikes across the stream, while the third event involved three quads whose drivers read the sign and then drove approximately 50 m upstream and forded the stream in a new location. In addition .... during the second site visit to Howard Creek after the sign was posted, the sign was found overturned and partially hidden in the brush approximately 20 m from where it had been located during the previous site visit.

Many, if not most, off-roaders in the McLean Creek designated OHV area saw boggy meadows, steep hillsides and quiet little creeks merely as challenges to their ability to take lug-tired motorized vehicles anywhere. Appeals for restraint and stewardship, especially from government agencies for whom the more aggressive off-roaders had no respect, were no more relevant to them than distinctions between the kinds of trout whose habitats they were destroying. Returning home with mud-splattered vehicles – mud that used to be wetland soil – had become a badge of honour to the vandals who had taken possession of the high country.

Quirk Creek's problems were, in fact, mild in comparison to the mud-bogging and landscape vandalism happening in McLean Creek valley itself and elsewhere in the area. McLean and Fisher creeks flow muddy most of the summer today, their watersheds riddled with gaping wounds from motorized abuse. When Kevin Fitzsimmons and Marco Fontana inventoried OHV use in the McLean Creek and Ghost-Waiparous areas for the Alberta Conservation Association in 2002, they found 178 un-bridged OHV stream-crossing points, more than two-thirds of which they classified as heavily or moderately impacted. Most of the remaining third were considered to be deteriorating.

Some users have now organized to promote responsible trail use and to secure grant money to install bridges on designated OHV trails. Members of the off-road clubs, for the most part, aren't the problem. But their values and efforts have no influence on most off-roaders – fewer than 10 per cent belong to responsible clubs. The OHV organizations do just enough good work to ensure the continued goodwill of the land management agencies and to retain a social licence of sorts for off-roading, but in doing so they also provide cover for the many motorized abusers who continue to destroy some of the best and most beautiful of the Bow River headwaters.

In the case of Howard and Quirk creeks, thanks to the persistence of Trout Unlimited biologists, the government followed through in 2003 on its commitment to install a bridge and the damage – at least at that stream crossing – ended. The seasonal cycle of muddy spring floods and clear summer flows returned, and the creek began to heal.

IN 2010 I FINALLY RETURNED to Quirk Creek, this time with my younger brother Michael. It was a pilgrimage of sorts, returning to places we most strongly associate with our dad, who died in 1989.

Stepping into the Elbow River and feeling its cold water surging against my legs, I recalled the water spilling around my father's rubber hip waders and the way his old woollen aviator's jacket smelled to an excited eight-year-old, all those years ago. The old elk trail we used to follow across the river floodplain was still there, but we chose to walk on the vehicle track, since there was really no avoiding it.

The old cutline over the hill was grown in with alder and littered with deadfall: the landscape reclaiming itself. It was a reassuring sight, but not nearly as reassuring as when we broke out of the trees and looked across a valley as familiar to us as a loved one's face, and realized that it was still intact, wild and rich. The worst we had imagined had not happened.

Walking across the meadow to the creek, surrounded with familiar birdsong and bright sun on wildflowers, I fell into a hidden beaver hole well back from the actual creek. Face-first in the dwarf birch, I looked for tent caterpillars, but there were none to be seen this time. I had forgotten those beaver holes, and how hummocky the hairgrass meadows adjacent the creek were. The stream itself was clear with a faint milky hue, barely moving through long sunlit pools whose cutbanks hid shadows that extended well beneath the meadows, then breaking into sparkling little rills before eddying into the next long pool.

My first fish was a 35-centimetre cutthroat, full-bodied and colourful. It seemed almost too big for the creek, and certainly larger than the fish we had caught decades earlier. Working my way toward a lunchtime rendezvous with my brother, whom I could see from time to time along the meanders farther downstream, I caught and released about a dozen cutthroats. The biggest was 40 centimetres in length – a veritable monster. Only once did I find a brook trout on the end of my line.

Something good had happened. On that sun-drenched July afternoon, Michael and I enjoyed even better fishing, for larger cutthroat trout, than in the old days for which

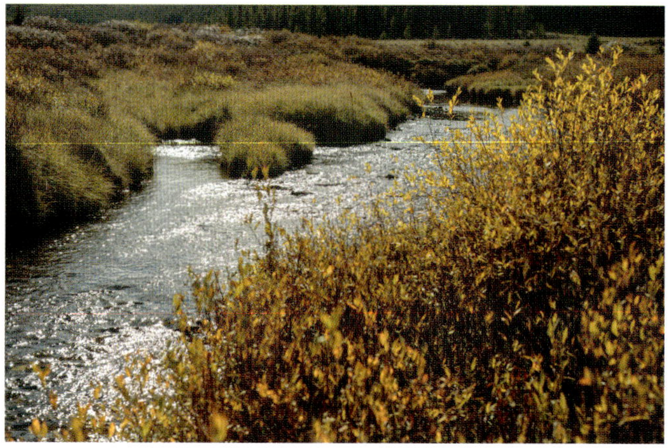

Above: *Robust and healthy floodplain vegetation protects the banks of streams like Quirk Creek from erosion and helps keep the water clean and cool.*

Right: *High water covers grasses along upper Quirk Creek, but the stream's healthy floodplain has kept the water clear of eroded sediment.*

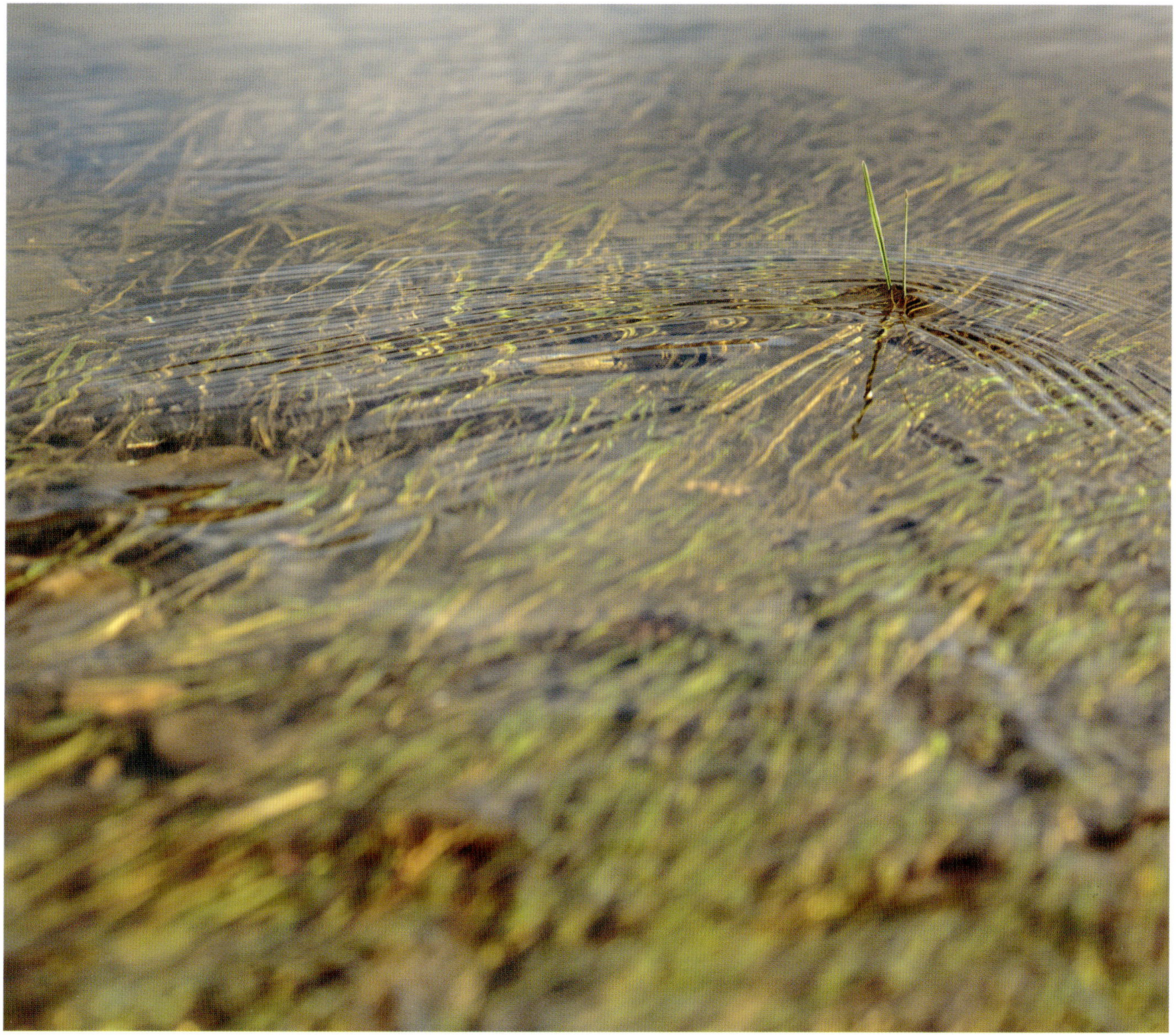

we had been so nostalgic. Could it be that, contrary to Kurt Vonnegut's dour assertion that "things are going to get worse and worse and never get better again," things had actually improved?

I ASKED STELFOX ABOUT the changes in Quirk Creek's fishery. After surveys in the late 1990s showed how critical the situation had become, he explained, fisheries biologists began evaluating options for getting rid of enough brook trout to enable the cutthroats and bull trout to rebuild their numbers. They decided against using selective poisons like rotenone because, in a broad, spongy valley full of small springs and isolated oxbows, many of which now contained brook trout, it would be nearly impossible to kill all the fish. It would be equally impossible, without some kind of intrusive fish-barrier structure, to keep brook trout from recolonizing the stream.

Electroshocking the stream was also a non-starter because it would be prohibitively expensive and labour-intensive, but also because so many fish shelter deep beneath the undercuts, where they are unreachable and undetectable.

It was time for some out-of-the-box thinking. Why not, Stelfox wondered, keep brook trout numbers down by doing away with catch limits for anglers?

In 1998 Stelfox initiated the Quirk Creek Brook Trout Suppression Project. Quirk Creek and its tributaries were closed to fish harvest, except under the authority of a special research licence. Anglers had to complete a fish identification test to qualify for a fish research licence that allowed them to keep all the brook trout they caught.

Quirk Creek's seemingly endless meadows are actually sloping wetlands known as fens — fragile natural water reservoirs rich with life.

Trout Unlimited Canada biologists volunteered to test anglers on fish identification, take them on supervised outings, and to keep track of the program's results.

In later years, qualified anglers were licensed to take brook trout from Quirk Creek on unsupervised outings too. As with the supervised outings, anglers had to release all cutthroat trout and bull trout, kill every brook trout they caught, and document the numbers and sizes of fish they handled of each species as well as how much time they spent fishing on the stream

A decade later the project partners – Alberta's Fish & Wildlife Division and Trout Unlimited Canada – released an interim report. Following the removal of over 9500 brook trout by anglers, the restoration experiment appeared to be working, according to the report:

> Angling, in particular unsupervised outings, appears to be sufficient on the lower reach to keep the number of large brook trout at a relatively low level. Based on the fishing pressure and harvest in 2006, it appears that about 100 angler hours per hectare may be sufficient to keep the brook trout population from rebounding to previous high levels, whereas it took about 200 to 300 angler hours per hectare at the start of the study to reduce the population, when the number of large (>150 mm) brook trout was about four to six times higher. The

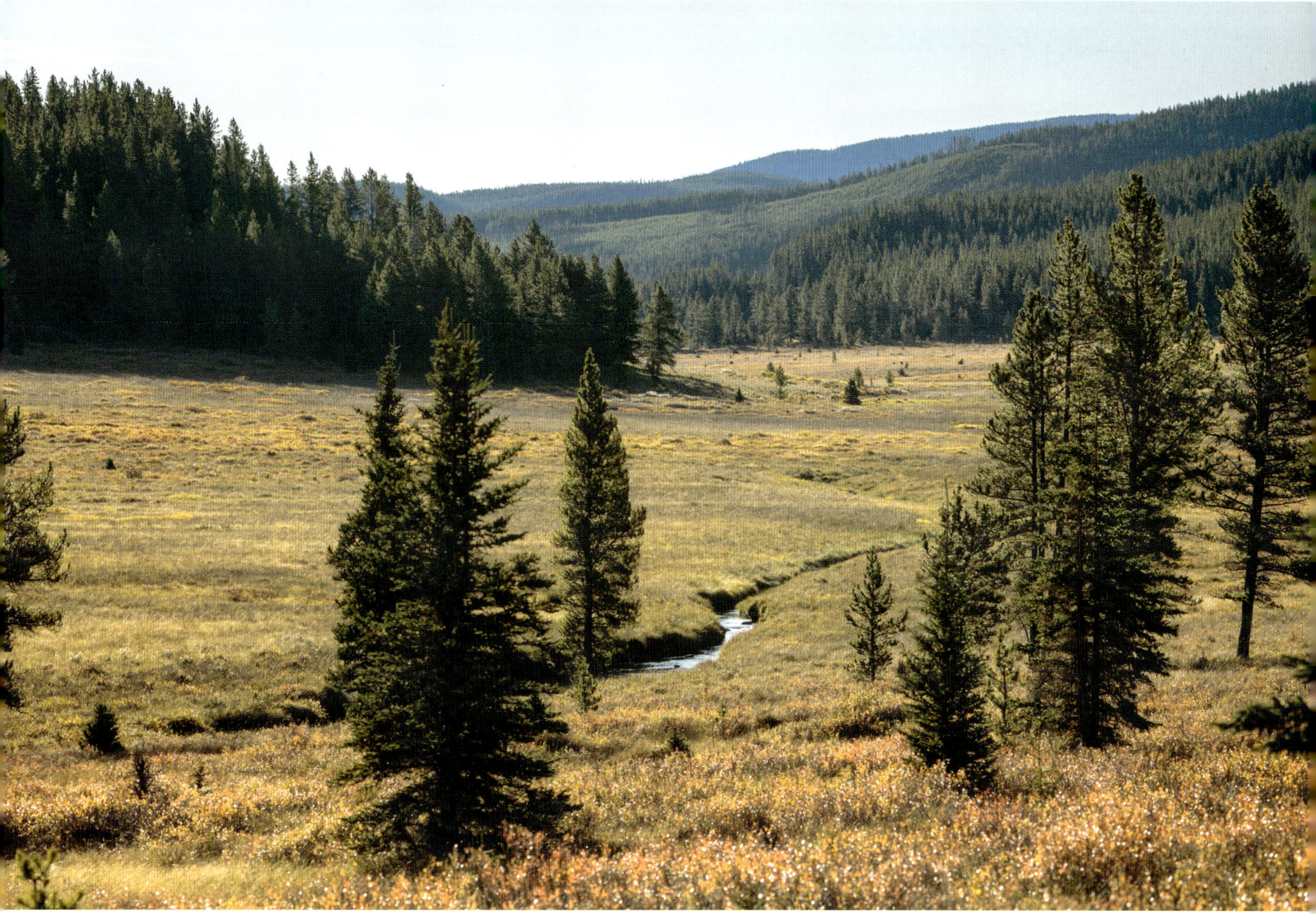

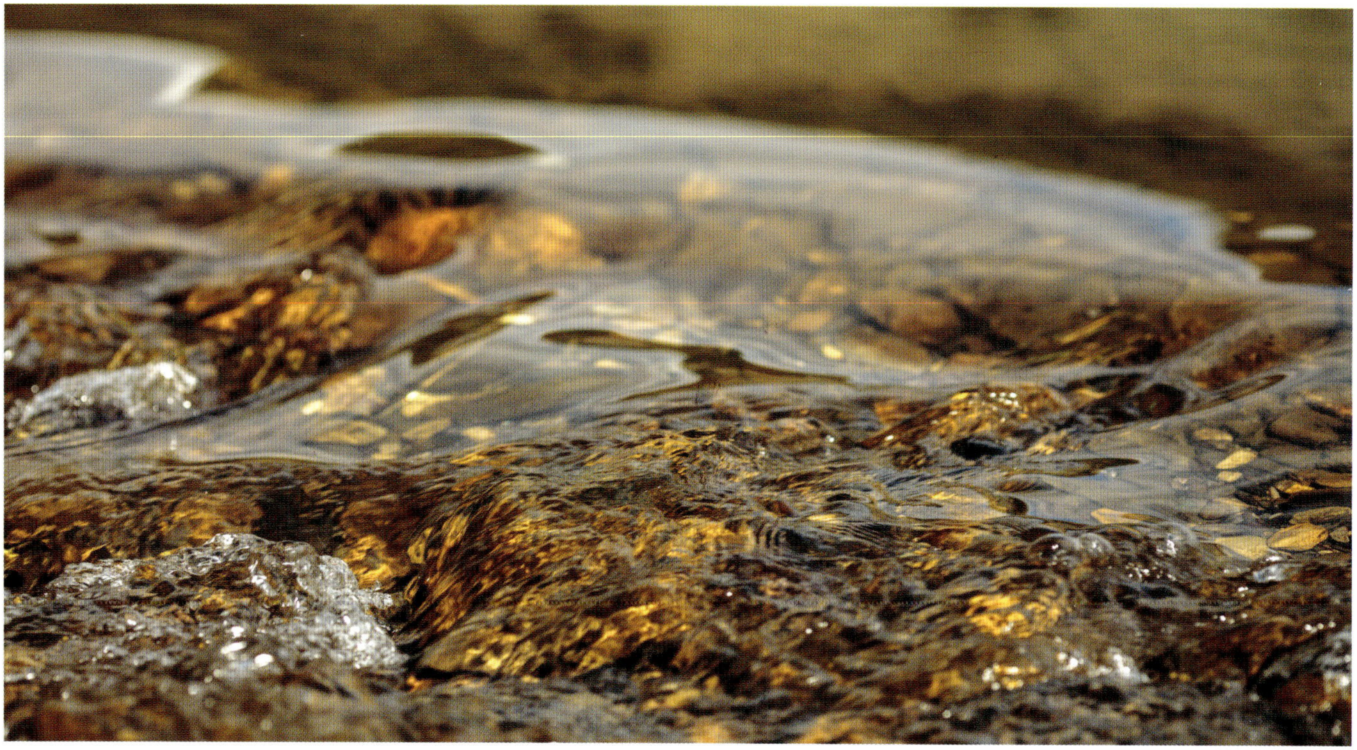

data from this project also suggest that it is necessary to harvest at least 50% of the large (>150 mm) brook trout population to have an effect on the population.

The cutthroat population rebounded as brook trout numbers dwindled. The native fish average larger now, too. It appears that the remaining brook trout, by preying on young cutthroats, may enable the survivors to grow larger than in the past, when there were more fish vying for the same amount of food. It probably didn't hurt, either, that the Alberta government had amended fishing regulations so that anglers could no longer kill cutthroats or bull trout. In the past, as soon as one of those fish grew big enough to fit into a frying pan, it wasn't long before it ended up there.

THE ABANDONED ROAD and ongoing logging still mar the once-pristine landscape, and the sounds and smells of passing OHVs still annoy those seeking peace and clean air. Domestic cows still crop the creek meadows

Quirk Creek. A healthy watershed's gift to downstream communities: clean, cool summer water.

and sometimes trample the creek banks. But the creek is healthy, and that means its watershed is mostly healthy, too. Conservation groups like Trout Unlimited, innovative biologists like Jim Stelfox and a growing number of informed and engaged anglers have made brook trout a minor player in the fish community and given the stream back to the native fishes that belong here. It appears that Quirk's story, if it were to tell one, would be a tale of well-meaning mistakes overcome by determined stewardship, in a place that's more than worth the effort of trying to get things right.

Fisheries managers paid attention to that story and put its lessons into practice more broadly. In 2009 Alberta Fish & Wildlife expanded Stelfox's program to include several other streams where brook trout were crowding out the native cutthroats and bull trout. Anglers who annually pass a fish identification test and participate in a supervised outing receive a special stewardship licence that lets them keep and kill all the brook trout they can catch in Waiparous Creek and its tributaries, Jumpingpound Creek and a few other headwater streams. Sport fishing may have damaged native fisheries in the 20th century, but it has been given a new role in the 21st: helping to restore them.

QUIRK CREEK TELLS its tale in a quiet, understated way. It is a soft-voiced creek, eddying through still meadows, gathering waters from mossy seeps and sparkling rills that emerge from meadows of dwarf birch, larkspur and paintbrush. On summer evenings, with the last anglers having headed back down to the Elbow River and the last chugging engine gone back to the trailheads at McLean Creek, thunderheads sometimes build above the mountain ridges to the west and drag the rumbling darkness of rain clouds east, toward Bragg Creek and Millarville. It's the kind of breathless moment that the valley knows well: a cool stillness when mule deer ghost down from the pines to drink from riffles, and moose materialize in willow swales.

The water dimples with the rings of rising cutthroat trout, rippling and reflecting the last glow from between the clouds and the dark blue silhouette of Forgetmenot Ridge. Nighthawks patrol the meadow edges. Swainson's thrushes query the shadows beneath the pines.

Stream-chatter rises and fades. Green-scented air grows humid and cool. Another foothills evening fades, but the sweetest of Alberta waters whisper on through the night, just as they have done for millennia.

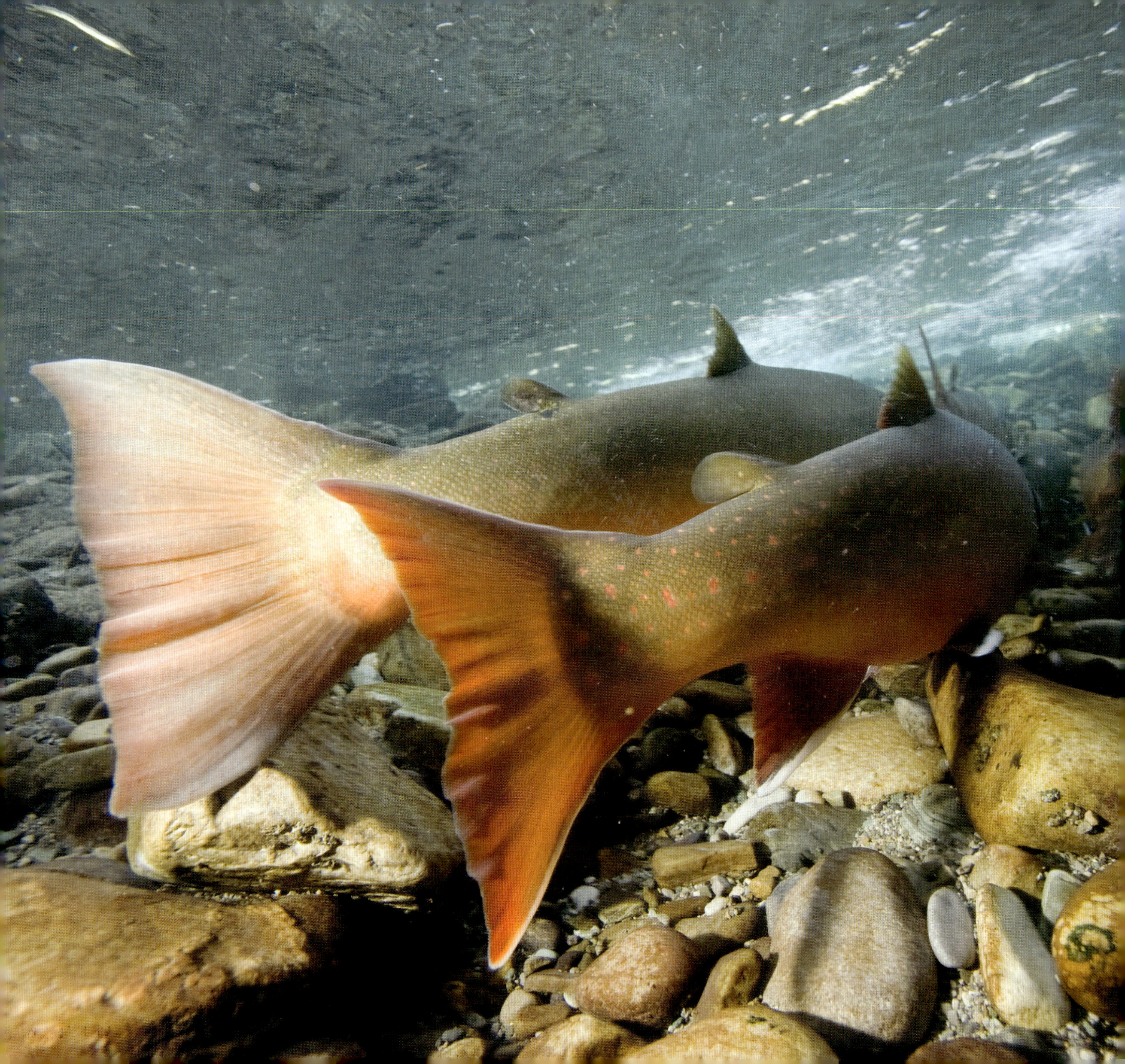

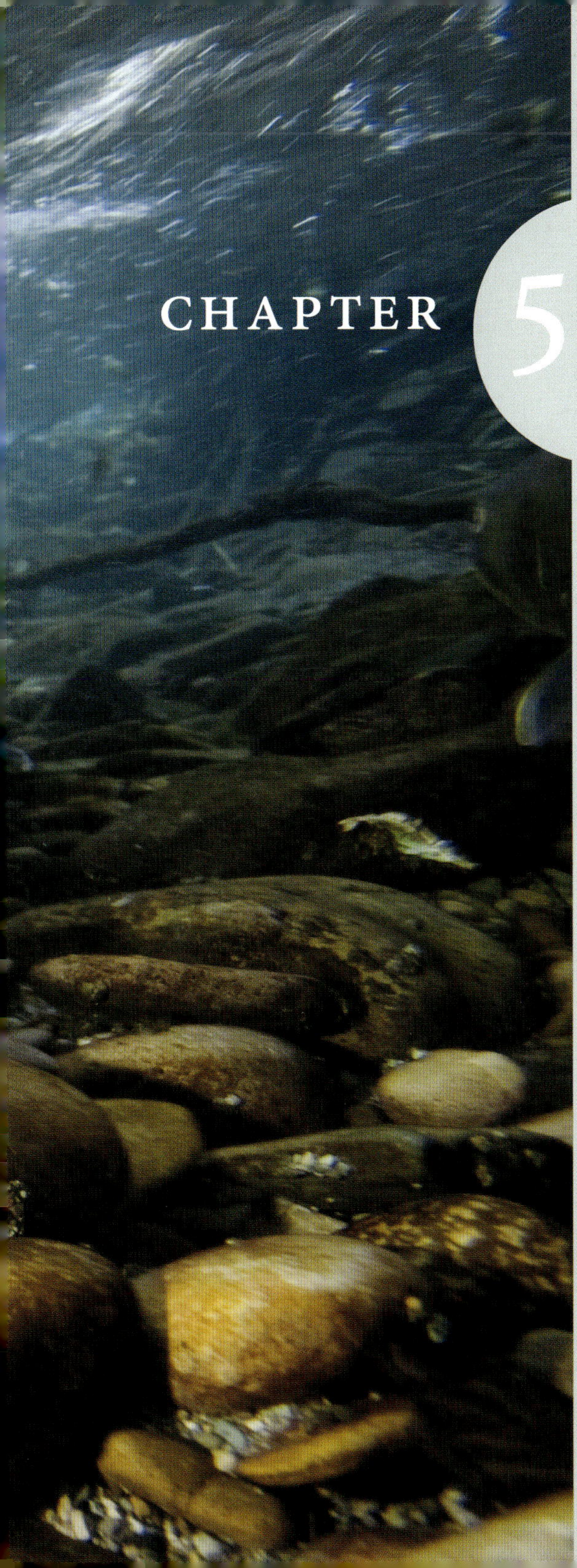

CHAPTER 5

The Past and Future Trout

Meadow Creek

MEADOW CREEK IS A TINY CREEK that winds through a broad valley near the foot of the Rocky Mountains before merging its waters with those of Waiparous Creek. One day Dad saw a submarine there.

Dad wasn't one of those fishermen whose fish continue to grow each time the story's told, so each time he retold his tale I would stare awestruck at that tiny stream, so narrow that we could jump across it in some places.

The submarine, he explained, had revealed itself to him as he peered into a deep hole where a beaver den had long ago caved in, leaving a narrow nick in the deeply undercut bank. First its head appeared: grey and predatory-looking. The head vanished on the upstream side of the nick, and white-edged fins followed it. Then its back went past forever, followed by two more white-edged fins, and finally by a broad tail that waved a lazy good bye as it vanished into the shadowed recess beneath the undercut bank.

Dad always described it as a submarine. "But how big was it really?" I asked in exasperation. I wanted numbers.

Page 68: *Bull trout migrating to their headwaters spawning stream.* Photo: Joel Sartore, *National Geographic*, with Wade Fredenberg

Right: *Bull trout migrate from large rivers and lakes to spawn in small headwater streams where groundwater wells up into clean gravel riffles.*

He spread his arms, and then shrugged. "I don't know," he said. "It looked as big as a submarine. Close to three feet, I guess."

Dad's hands were shaking as he inched along the bank and eased his lure beneath it, where the monster had vanished. It was to no avail; the great fish may have found its way into family legend, but it never found its way onto the end of Dad's line.

The story was enough to motivate me with the hope of a monster fish, but no matter how far I hiked along that creek or how carefully I sneaked up on its most promising pools, the best I could ever find were 25-centimetre cutthroats and fat little brook trout. The submarine was gone.

My grandfather had stories about monster bull trout, too. By the time I was old enough to listen in awed fascination, he was well past the age when he could hike into headwater streams, so his tales held a special poignancy to me. They seemed to represent a frontier time when wild places were as yet undiscovered and unspoiled. He talked about catching huge bull trout with a spoon he called the ruby-eyed wobbler, and floating a dead mouse on a piece of wood into a deep eddy in order to entice one particular giant to bite. His bull trout had been caught in places I was still too young to have fished – Cat Creek, the upper Kananaskis, Little Elbow River – and their names became magical to me. I begged Dad to take us there. As with Meadow Creek, though, when he finally did, the big fish were nowhere to be found.

It's not that we didn't catch bull trout regularly. It was hard not to; they were voracious feeders who would return and bite the hook a second or third time if we didn't get them on the first cast. But they were mostly small fish, rarely the length of Dad's wicker creel – slender grey things that didn't seem to fight as vigorously or taste as good as the other trout we found on our forays into the foothills.

Bull trout were always a kind of paradox to those of us who grew up fishing the creeks and rivers of western Alberta. The really big monsters that our parents and grandparents told us about were always bull trout, so in some ways the bull trout was a symbol of the wildest and finest of places, and of the hidden possibilities of those headwater streams. But at the same time, bull trout were considered nuisance fish by many anglers, greedy cannibals who preyed on the more desirable rainbow, brook and brown trout. The commonly accepted wisdom was that they were unsophisticated fish – too easy to catch, sluggish fighters once hooked and their flesh inferior to that of other species. Some anglers even threw them into the bushes to rot, rather than return them to the stream or take them home for supper.

Ignorance and prejudice, consequently, had a lot to do with the growing rarity of a great native trout in streams

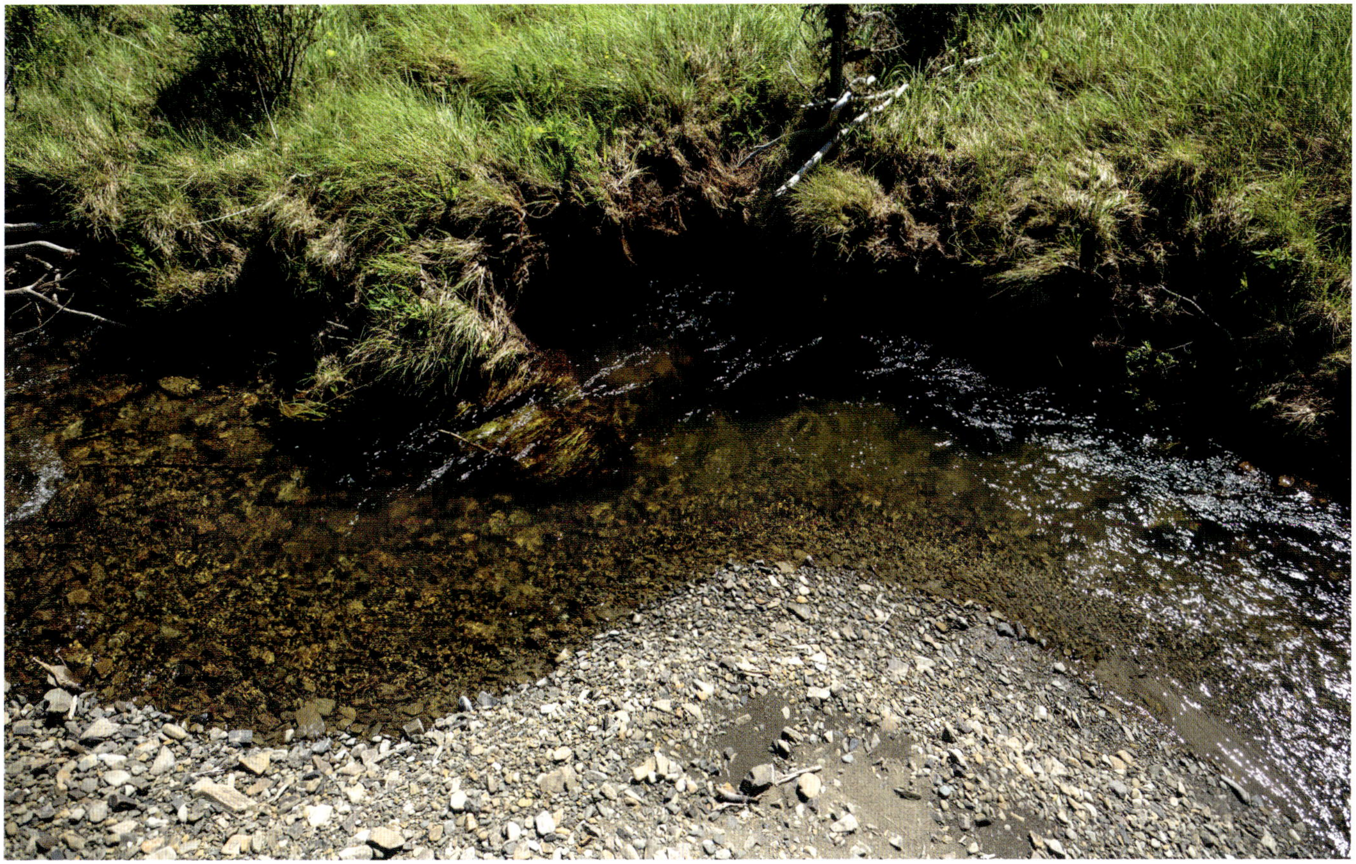

like Meadow Creek. For much of the 20th century, most anglers assumed that one species of trout or char could pretty much replace another. If bull trout vanished, then, it would be no great loss, because a more desirable species would fill in the gaps. We killed our limits of bull trout and hoped for better trout on our next visit.

Bull trout, however, are not interchangeable with the exotic non-native trout that fisheries managers spent decades pouring into headwater streams. They are ecologically as different from brook or rainbow trout as they are from suckers. Their unique adaptations make them the only species that can grow to trophy dimensions in streams that otherwise produce only mediocre specimens of other trout and char species.

Adapted by thousands of years of natural selection to the nutrient-poor, icy-cold and volatile streams that drain from the Front Ranges of the Rocky Mountains, bull trout have life cycles intimately connected to the seasonal cycles of those streams. Biologists studying bull trout in Alberta, Montana and British Columbia have found that their specialized life needs make them susceptible to changes in their headwater habitats, too. For example, bull trout will migrate dozens of kilometres each year to spawn in those few places along gravel-bottomed mountain streams where cold springs well up from below into the stream bottom. They depend on those groundwater springs for their survival across the generations.

Mountain streams often freeze from the bottom up in winter. Since bull trout spawn in late September and early October, their eggs are vulnerable to winterkill from ice that forms in the spawning gravels. By spawning where groundwater keeps the stream bed from freezing, however, bull trout avoid that risk. Reliable underwater springs are only patchily distributed in the headwaters. If road building, clear-cut logging or the gullying that commonly results from irresponsible off-highway vehicle recreation reduces the amount of groundwater recharge on the valley slopes upstream from these springs, the springs can dry up or become choked with eroded sediment. When that happens, entire populations of bull trout lose their spawning beds. Silted gravels and ruined springs help account for the absence of bull trout from abused streams like Fisher and McLean creeks.

After hatching, bull trout remain in headwater streams for at least three years. The young fish feed on insects and live like the cutthroat trout with whom they share those creeks. Unlike cutthroats, however, as they approach maturity, they slip downstream into the bigger rivers and switch to a diet of whitefish, suckers and other small fish. At that point, their growth rate increases dramatically; some mature bull trout can be a metre long and more than five kilograms in weight.

Fisheries researchers were slow to develop an interest in the ecology of native bull trout. Once they did, they were startled to find that some female bull trout don't reach sexual maturity until they are over 50 centimetres long. Other trout species spawn at less than half that size. The bull trout's unique combination of deferred maturity and rapid growth after shifting to a more predatory life phase may both be related to the rigours of life in volatile mountain streams.

Each year, melting snow and spring rains bring brown, roiling floods to the streams that drain out of the Rockies and their foothills. Floods vary in intensity from year to year; the bigger floods move a lot of the gravel in the stream bed. Any fish eggs or newly hatched fry buried in those gravels risk being crushed. Large bull trout, however, are able to dig deep spawning redds into larger gravel than smaller fish can move. Burying their eggs deep in gravel big enough to withstand the next spring's flood waters improves the chances of the next generation's survival. Over the millennia, bull trout that found a way to grow large before spawning produced more offspring than those that didn't; the upshot is that the migratory, river-dwelling life strategy of native bull trout has come out a winner.

Spawning Strategies

For fish to reproduce successfully, their spawning habits need to be aligned to the behaviour of the streams they occupy. Many centuries of natural selection have done just that.

Brook trout evolved in boreal forest streams in eastern North America. Their home waters flow all winter, insulated by heavy snow blankets. There is little risk in the brook trout's habit of spawning in October because those creeks rarely freeze down to the gravel. Brook trout bury their eggs in fine gravel at the bottom ends of riffles, where hydraulic pressure tends to pull water out of the stream bed.

Brown trout originated in Germany and England, regions whose mild winters also make fall spawning a winning strategy. They deposit their eggs in early November at the bottom ends of pools, where hydraulic forces drive water down into the stream bed. The effect is the same as for brook trout: their eggs are constantly rinsed and washed with clean, oxygen-rich water. The eggs of both species hatch in early spring, giving the young fry a whole season to fatten and grow.

Neither brook nor brown trout are native to the Bow River watershed. Its native trout is the cutthroat, which usually spawns in May, and the bull trout, which spawns in late September or October.

Foothills and mountain rivers shrink to very low flows in winter and often freeze solid, from the bottom up. Those can be killing conditions for fish eggs and fry. Bull trout get around this problem by migrating to specific stream reaches where groundwater wells up into the creek bed gravel from below. The springs stop the stream from freezing and flush fine sediment out of the gravel, keeping the eggs well supplied with oxygen. The scarcity of suitable groundwater sites are the reason why, according to fisheries biologist Lorne Fitch, "logging of watersheds with bull trout can be devastating to bull trout, because of the impacts on groundwater flow and over-winter stream flows."

Our streams, unlike those that gave rise to brook and bull trout, are also subject to intense flooding because of their steep gradients and snowy headwaters. Bull trout mitigate that risk by growing large enough to dig spawning redds deep into large gravel. Most years, that puts their eggs and young fry below the scouring reach of a flooding stream.

Cutthroats, Fitch says,

> ... have rolled the evolutionary dice and decided spring spawning, coincident with sediment-clearing floods, is the better strategy. Those eggs incubate under better stream flow conditions (more water) and incubate rapidly so that young can take advantage of higher benthic insect production.

Both strategies are right and both are wrong, depending on the year. But over time the range of natural variation ensures there will be excellent opportunities to balance the years when no eggs survive. Strong year classes from good spawning years sustain the population over the bad years until good times roll again. Cutthroat live about five years and bull trout about ten, meaning there will always be a few good years during a trout's lifespan... unless we humans screw up the watershed.

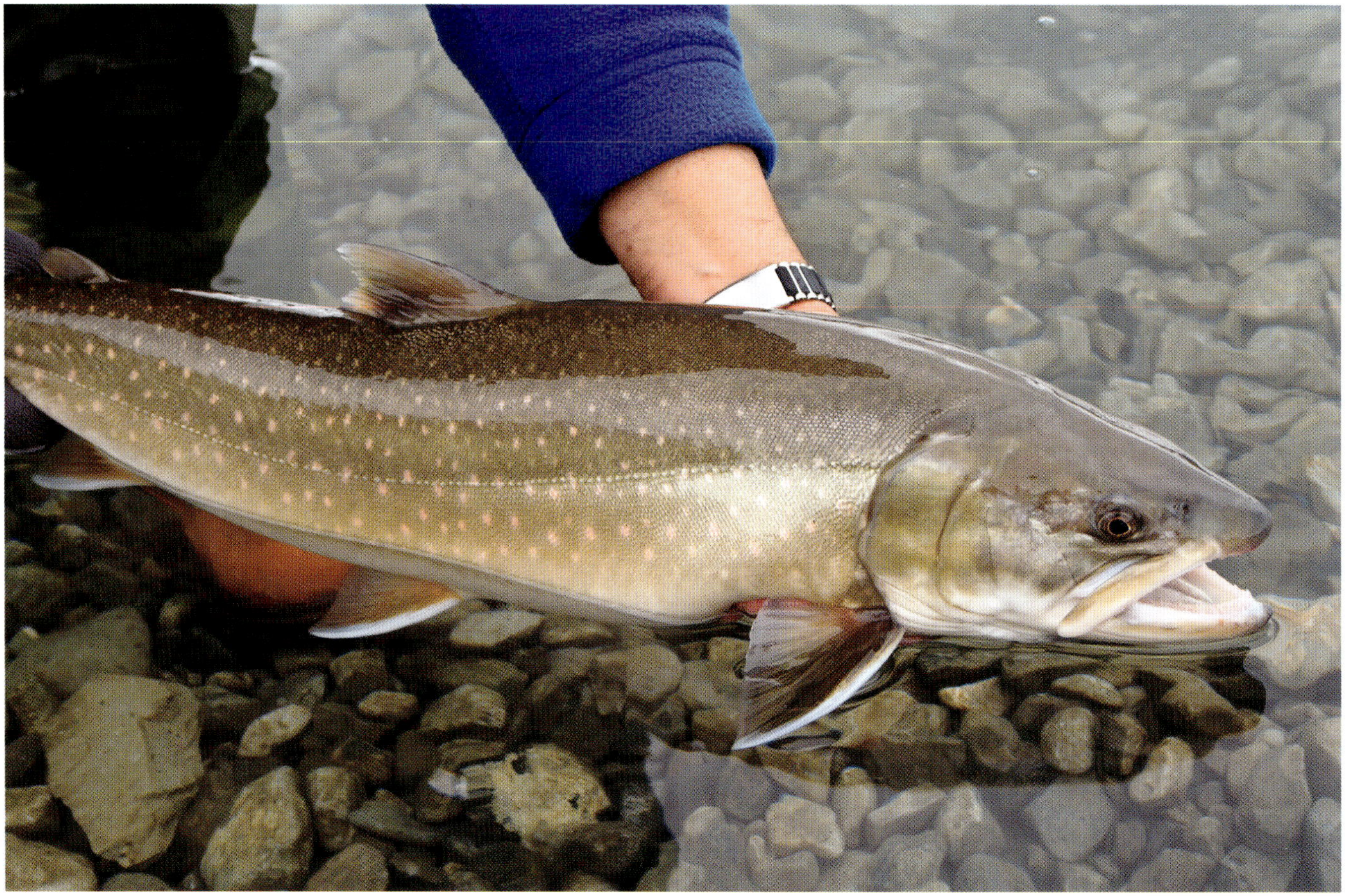

IT WAS A WINNING STRATEGY, that is until the first angler turned up beside a headwater stream looking for a fish to fry. Under the fishing regulations that prevailed until the last decade of the 20th century, most bull trout were killed and eaten before they could spawn for the first time. Managing bull trout as if they were no different from other species resulted in the big natives vanishing, incrementally, from much of their original range.

In 1987 Alberta made the first of a series of changes to fishing regulations to improve bull trout reproduction rates, based on the new insights into its spawning ecology. Anglers were required to release any bull trout under

Bull trout, Lower Kananaskis Lake. Large bull trout spawn more successfully because of their ability to move larger gravel and bury their eggs deeper, safe from floods.
Photo: Frank Wood

40 centimetres to allow more females to reach maturity. It was a step in the right direction.

Many older Alberta anglers found the change puzzling at best and ridiculous at worst. They had always considered bull trout inferior sport fish and harmful predators. They weren't prepared to change their thinking and, in fact, a declining number of old-time anglers still continue to kill and dispose of every bull trout they catch, choosing to become poachers rather than change their thinking. When researchers from the University of Alberta inserted radio transmitters into a sample of 30 Elbow River bull trout during the fall of 2003, they found evidence that five of those fish were subsequently killed by poachers and estimated that 17 per cent of the large breeders in the population had been poached off the spawning beds in the fall of 2003. All the poached fish came from areas readily accessed by off-road vehicles or on foot.

But a growing majority of anglers have come to value the unique attributes of native fish species and to become concerned about the loss of bull trout, cutthroats and, farther north, the Athabasca rainbow trout. The changing culture of recreational angling has also led to greater support for catch-and-release fishing, especially for high-quality fish in high-quality environments.

In January 1993 a group of concerned anglers, biologists, fisheries managers and conservationists formed the Alberta Bull Trout Task Force to develop a recovery and management plan for the province. First they needed information, however, so they organized an international conference where experts in fish ecology could share recent research results and management experience.

The task force couldn't have timed things better. Its May 1994 conference coincided with the completion of numerous studies in the western US, most triggered by an earlier proposal to list the bull trout as an endangered species under US law. Almost two hundred delegates turned up.

Conference speakers revealed many reasons why bull trout are in trouble today. Road building associated with logging and energy development damages headwater streams, clogging once-clean gravels with silt, starving groundwater springs and changing the timing and severity of floods. In some areas, including many parts of Alberta's forest reserves, poorly managed cattle grazing was causing similar harm. Some bull trout stocks were reduced or eliminated by competition and hybridization with introduced brook trout and competition with lake and brown trout.

Dams – including several in Alberta – have devastated migratory stocks, isolating unproductive headwaters populations from the productive lower-river reaches that are often vital to this late-maturing species. TransAlta's power dams extirpated the Bow and Kananaskis rivers' once-productive bull trout populations by cutting off their migrations. The company's 1951 damming of Spray Lakes inundated key spawning areas and gave lake trout a competitive edge. According to fisheries biologist

Jim Stelfox, when the new reservoir was gillnetted in 1953, two-thirds of the 4344 fish captured were bull trout; the rest were native cutthroats. Ten years later, 98 per cent of the catch was lake trout. Bull trout are gone from the Spray today.

TransAlta's river-blocking dams have eliminated large fluvial (river-dwelling) bull trout from most of the Bow River's headwaters. But even in the absence of dams, conference participants found one common thread that has brought bull trout populations low throughout their range. Anglers had been killing bull trout before they were even old enough to reproduce. Overfishing was a problem everywhere.

Where bull trout populations had been protected by restrictive fishing regulations, on the other hand, some spectacular angling had resulted. Lake Billy Chinook, a large reservoir in Oregon's Deschutes River system, was one such success story the bull trout conference heard about. In the 1980s Oregon instituted a one-fish limit and began encouraging anglers to treat bull trout as a trophy fish. Numbers rebounded, and anglers were soon releasing fish in the nine-kilogram class. Early results from Lower Kananaskis Lake reservoir, where the mean length of bull trout doubled annually in the first few years after a zero-kill rule came into effect, offered a similar prospect closer to home.

Brian Evans, then Alberta's minister of Environment, took advantage of the conference to announce a new Bull Trout Management Plan for Alberta that imposed a province-wide zero-kill regulation for bull trout. In 1995 the elevation of bull trout from unloved predator to valued native fish went a step further with its official designation as Alberta's provincial game fish.

Short decades ago, most anglers considered the bull trout a frontier fish whose time was past. New biological knowledge, new regulations and an emerging commitment among anglers to celebrate and treasure native fishes offer belated hope that the bull trout may yet be part of our future, too.

I HAD A GLIMPSE OF THAT FUTURE one September day on a small creek in southwestern Alberta. The fishery had fallen into dark days because of a tradition by local poachers of travelling to the stream's headwaters each fall to kill the big spawners.

Just as conservationists began to talk gloomily of another bull trout disaster, a population explosion of mountain pine beetles swept through the valley, killing many of its older lodgepole pines. The trail to the headwaters soon became impassable for horses, a jackstraw tangle of fallen timber.

One day I set off on foot with a friend, Elliot Fox, to see whether bull trout numbers might be recovering now that the trail was blocked. It was a tough hike. Two hours in, we saw our first submarine: an immense orange-sided bull trout that hung, heavy with spawn, above the crystal-clean gravels of the stream bed. A slightly smaller male tended her.

A little farther upstream, we found a pool full of elongated shadows. Ten huge bull trout lay on the bottom like sunken cordwood, occasionally swirling to chase one another before returning to their positions, heads into the current. For the next two kilometres of stream we found one spawning redd after another, including an immense one that appeared unoccupied until an 80-centimetre female suddenly churned her way upstream out of a riffle and slid quietly into the backwater at my feet.

She held her position against the pulsing surge of newborn waters, gills opening and closing, oblivious to me, obeying an ancient imperative that had guided her kind to these same headwaters for millennia. Standing barely a half-metre away, I looked about at the wild valley and its quiet little stream.

Something began to swell inside of me as I listened to the quiet babble of living water, watched the clouds seething past silent peaks and looked down at that great fish swaying in the current. This stream could have been Meadow or Johnson creek or any of the streams of my youth – streams I once thought I knew well. But I hadn't known them, because only now was I seeing how they really could have been, how they used to be; how they were meant to be. I ached with realization; I wanted to rage aloud.

We treated bull trout like vermin, and in our ignorance robbed ourselves of the opportunity to know the full reality of western Alberta's cold-water ecosystems. All those creeks, all those crystal-clear pools, were only pale shadows of what they could have been, because in our ignorance and our lack of humility we took away the great golden bull trout that belonged there. How could we have been so wrong?

But that was then, and this is now, and although some bull trout fisheries have been lost forever, others wait only for human restraint and habitat renewal to restore them to what they were and again can be. The dark days of the 20th century are now behind a fish that always deserved better.

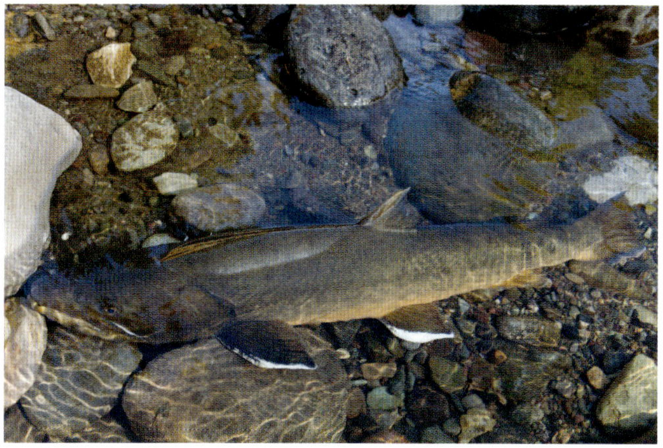

Bull trout are the only native fish that consistently reach trophy size in headwaters streams. Photo: Frank Wood

The bull trout is the living distillation of our headwater ecosystems, part of our shared heritage, and now – if we can sustain a shared commitment to what is uniquely native to the streams draining from the mountains arrayed along the western horizon – part of our common future. In that future, anglers will again see submarines in tiny headwater streams. In that future, bull trout will no longer be the stuff of myth and misunderstanding. In that future, a great native fish will again be a part of how we know our streams, our home landscapes and our selves.

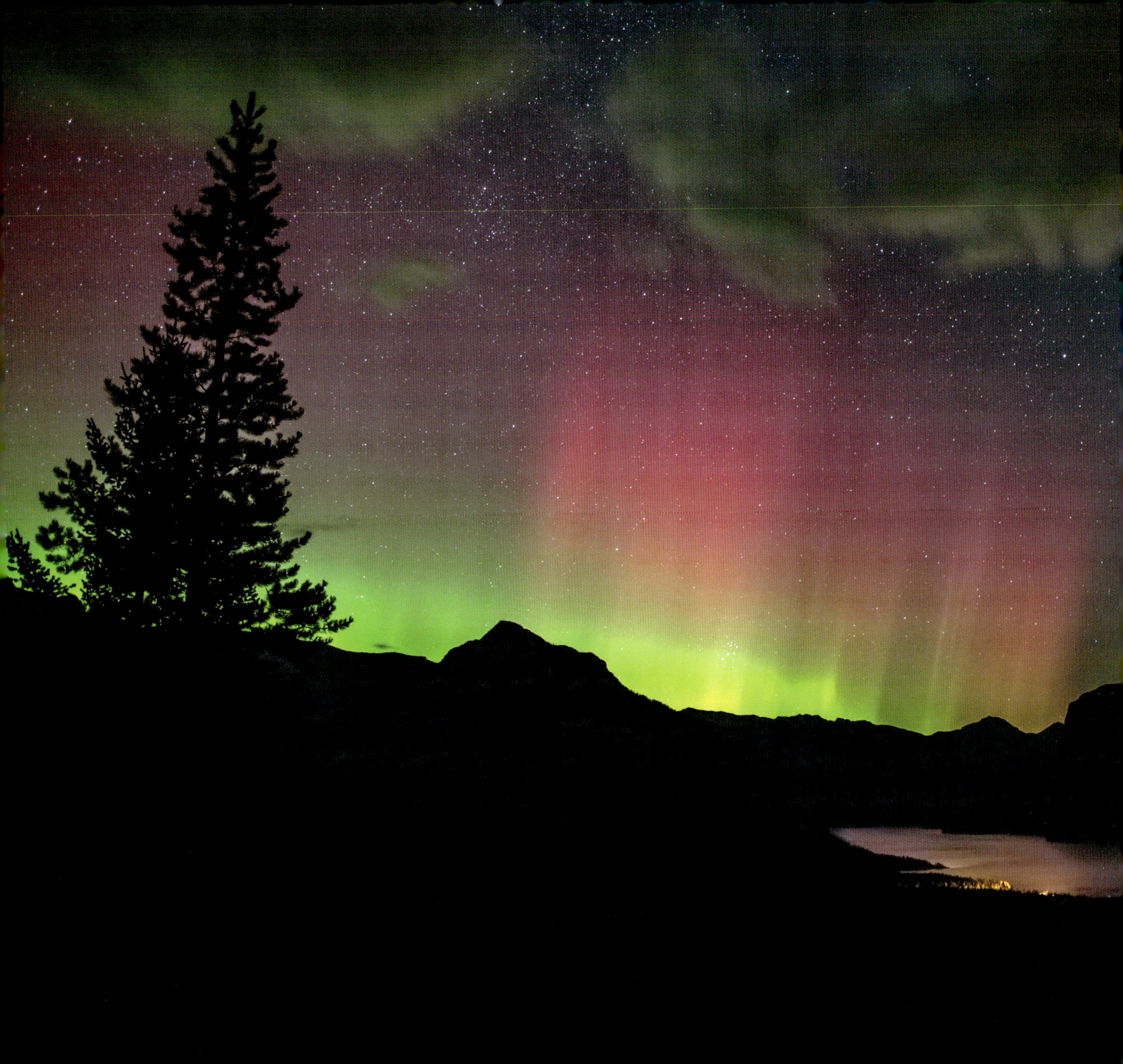

HAPTER 6

Lake of the Spirits

Cascade River and Ghost River

A SMALL BAND OF BIGHORN SHEEP has chosen the middle of a summer morning to hike along the road from the mountain slopes above Stewart Canyon to the grassy meadows overlooking Two Jack Lake. Car doors are open, and cameras and cellphones click as the ewes and lambs dodge the paparazzi while trotting toward this afternoon's grazing spot.

On this August weekend, the local tourism boosters have chosen to stage a dragon boat festival on Lake Minnewanka, swelling the usual crowds of holidayers. In spite of their best efforts to organize off-site parking for race participants and spectators, a goodly number of the dragon boat aficionados have chosen to eschew the free buses and drive their own vehicles to the venue. They're caught in the sheep jam, too.

Banff, Canada's oldest and best-known national park, hosts close to four million visitors every year. According to the local tourism bureau, however,

Page 78: *Aurora borealis — the spirit dancers of myth — play across the sky above the flooded valley of Ghost Lakes and Minnewanka.*

that's just not enough. The idea of hosting special events like this one is to pull even more credit cards into the park. Parks Canada – both because its legislation makes it dependent on user-fee revenues and, more idealistically, because its social purpose is to turn people on to nature, something best achieved by getting them into it, one way or the other – is fully complicit, in spite of the inevitable crowding and commercialism.

Today a couple of uniformed park staff are trying to encourage photographers to get back in their vehicles and move on. The sheep that created the traffic jam, angular and lean-looking in their thin summer pelage, amble between the vehicles with bulging, slit-pupilled eyes, alert for the possibility of a potato chip or Cheezie. The causeway may be asphalt, but it often yields richer forage than the nearby grasslands.

Out on the water, paddles flash in the sun as crews jockey long watercraft into position between lines of buoys set up for the occasion. The race lanes are dwarfed by the expanse of gunmetal-grey water that recedes off into the north, and by the sheer limestone cliffs of Mount Inglismaldie and the Fairholme Range looming above.

If any of the paddlers were to pause and look up into those cliffs, they might see a golden eagle and its shadow tracing the lines of rock outcroppings, as eagles have always done here. Threadlike waterfalls tumble and wisp into cupped-out defiles from unseen alpine basins. Flocks of crossbills tumble drunkenly across the pine-clad slopes below. Even nearer, spotted sandpipers skim along the shoreline or teeter, peeping, on exposed rocks.

But all go unnoticed. For most of the participants, this is just a scenic place for a boat race. The air is fresh, the water is cold, and when the boats come out of the water, there will be parties. This week it's Lake Minnewanka; next week the boats will line up for another race somewhere else.

Minnewanka is a Nakoda term that translates in English, roughly, to Spirit Lake or Lake of Spirits. The broad, steep-walled valley that holds Lake Minnewanka has been a sacred place to the Nakoda people for many centuries. Spirits may still occupy this place in spite of all the hubbub on summer weekends. But a century of development has rendered them as nearly invisible as the eagles, crossbills and sandpipers are to today's dragon boat racers.

THE FIRST ATTEMPT TO EXTINGUISH the spirits in this valley was by Methodist missionaries who came to the upper Bow River drainage in the mid-1800s. Reverend John Rundle, whose name remained attached to a nearby mountain long after he had left, spent a few weeks among the Nakoda in the 1840s. Shortly afterward, George McDougall and his wife and sons established a mission adjacent the Bow River near Morley, just outside the mountains.

The missionaries would only tolerate belief in one Christian God, so the spirits that lived in the landscapes, stories and sacred traditions of the Nakoda had to be assigned an inferior status. One of the rivers draining from this low-elevation valley of marshy forests and small lakes became the Ghost River, and the lakes became the Devil's Lakes. Today's maps still show the narrow north end of the valley as Devil's Gap.

The missionaries enjoyed partial success. Many of today's Nakoda people are devout Christians. But they have not forgotten the spirits that dwell among their sacred mountains. There is room in their belief system for both.

Dragons, though they occupy a similar place in spiritual traditions associated with some of Asia's mountain people, have only recently been introduced to the Rockies. In the late years of the 20th century, some Canadian Buddhists discovered Rockbound Lake, tucked into a cirque basin on the north side of Castle Mountain, and recognized it as a sacred place. One pilgrim told a friend of mine, "Your mountains are younger than the mountains where I used to live. Yours still have dragons." Growing numbers of Buddhists now return every summer to hike to a place that they have come to know as sacred, and as a place of dragons.

The dragons at Lake Minnewanka are a bit more of a problem. A money-making idea dreamed up by the very secular Banff Lake Louise Tourism Bureau, the dragon boat race lacks sufficient spiritual depth to be anything more than a sideshow. And as soon as the tourism boosters began to talk publicly about bringing dragon boats to Lake Minnewanka, local environmental groups took on the role of the early Methodist missionaries and tried to recast the tourism dragons as devils. Keeping dragon boats off Lake Minnewanka and out of Banff National Park became akin to chasing the money-changers from the temple. To local environmentalists, the annual dragon boat races were simply another example of Banff National Park's long and incestuous relationship with the tourism industry, a relationship that compromised the park's core values and confused visitors as to the meaning of a national park.

Letters to the local newspapers and to the responsible authorities pointed out that Parks Canada, by law, has to give first priority in all management decisions to the maintenance or restoration of ecological integrity. How could this fundamental responsibility align with staging a spectacle that had no basis in Rocky Mountain culture and could be held anywhere?

The most compelling argument of boat race opponents was, unfortunately, the weakest from a regulatory standpoint. There can be no doubt that dragon boats and other such commercial spectator events do little to respect the spirit of the place, celebrate the cultural history of the Rocky Mountain national parks or connect visitors in authentic, personal ways to natural ecosystems. But nothing in Canada National Parks Act compels Parks Canada to make decisions based on spiritual, cultural or experiential considerations. They should, but they aren't obliged to.

And the ecological integrity argument – which does carry legal weight – was lost decades earlier.

Lake Minnewanka is not a lake. It is a massive hydropower reservoir that, in 1941, flooded an entire montane valley. Some 15 metres beneath the wind-whipped surface of the unnatural impoundment, lake trout and suckers forage around the edges of drowned cabins, spruce stumps and willow thickets. If spirits still travel the well-worn Aboriginal trade and hunting trails through this once-fertile valley, they are likely very wet and very annoyed. A sterile bathtub ring of wind-washed cobbles and rock surfaces marks the constantly changing boundary between water and land. Engineers in a faraway control centre raise and lower the water levels to feed water down to distant hydropower generation facilities – the Cascade powerhouse, beside the Trans-Canada Highway; and the Kananaskis (Seebe), Horseshoe, Ghost and Bearspaw dams, farther down the Bow.

Very little ecological integrity remains at Lake Minnewanka, even if it could credibly be argued that a weekend boat race beside the dam would impair it. Restoring ecological integrity to the place of spirits would mean removing the dams that hold the waters back and then letting the valley heal. That would be a good idea, but it's not very likely.

THE IMMENSE RESERVOIR – 221,900 dam[3] (cubic decametres, equivalent to about 220,000 Olympic-sized swimming pools) at full capacity – filling the broad, natural basin between the Palliser and Fairholme ranges has its origins in two rivers, the Cascade and the Ghost.

The Cascade River, which accounts for about 6 per cent of the Bow River's flow volume (as measured at the Bassano weir) drains the high country of Banff National Park's Cascade, Palliser and Vermilion ranges. The main

The long-abandoned power plant below the Minnewanka Dam broods over a nearly dry channel where the Cascade River once ran free. Photo: Kevin Van Tighem

river used to receive the outflow from Devil's Lake, the largest of a chain of four lakes strung along the broad Devil's Gap between the Bow and Ghost drainages.

Mountaineer and explorer Walter Wilcox was deeply impressed by the lake and valley when he visited in 1898. In *The Rockies of Canada,* he wrote:

> This lake, which is ten miles long, though very narrow, is like a bit of the Mediterranean set between high mountains. An excellent trail, much favoured by Indians, follows the north shore. On the second day we passed the end of Devil's Lake and made camp finally by the borders of another small lake, in a place almost surrounded by mountains but commanding a view of the plains towards the east. Our camp was located in a meadow where innumerable wildflowers blossomed … These … were slowly drowning under the rising waters of the lake, which was no doubt fed by underground springs from the mountains.
>
> This is the valley of the Ghost River, a strange vale of limestone formation where no streams flow. Torrents descend gullies, and waterfalls dash over the vertical cliffs of this canyon, but each one of them disappears as it enters this Ghost River Valley.

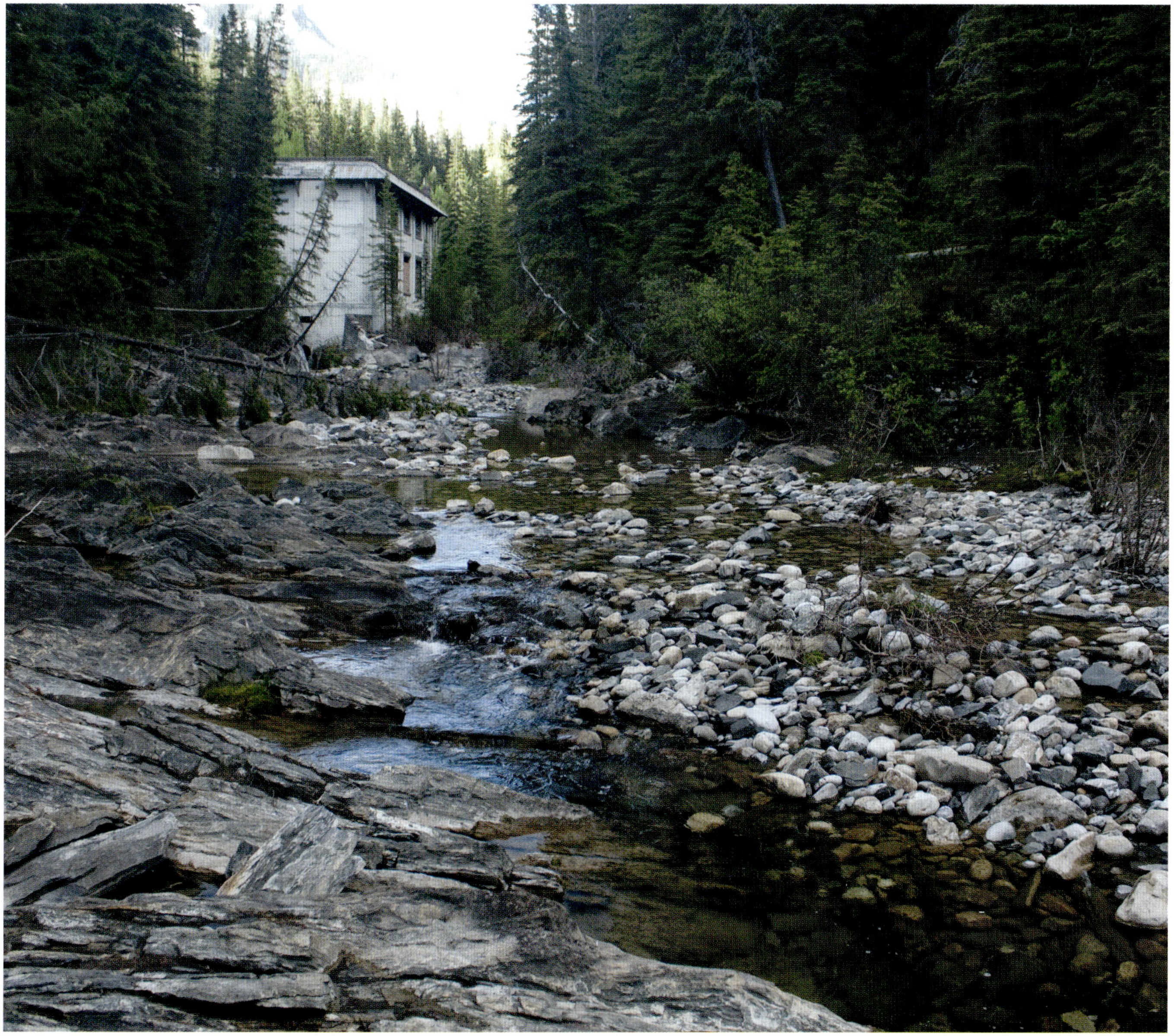

Hudson's Bay Company governor George Simpson had provided the first written reference to the Ghost Lakes in 1841, half a century before Wilcox's visit:

> In the morning we entered a defile between mountain ridges, marching for nine hours through dense woods. This valley, which was from two to three miles in width, contained four beautiful lakes, communicating with each other by small streams; and the fourth of the series, which was about fifteen miles by three, we named after Peechee as being our guide's usual home.

The name didn't stick. Missionaries insisted on calling it Devil's Lake. That unfortunate name also had a short shelf life. When the Dominion Parks Service dammed the outlet in 1908 to improve navigation for small steamboats taking tourists on excursions, the enlarged lake reclaimed its Nakoda name, Lake Minnewanka. In 1912 Calgary Power substantially raised the Cascade River Dam, submerging the original lake under four metres of water to form the Lake Minnewanka reservoir.

The North Ghost River rises from headwaters outside the national park, on the east side of the Palliser Range, in the Ghost River Wilderness. The north fork used to merge with the south fork just east of Devil's Gap, but TransAlta, the successor to Calgary Power, diverted its waters south in 1942 to further augment the Lake Minnewanka reservoir. That project raised the water level another ten metres and inundated the entire valley floor. It also diverted the combined flow of the North Ghost and Cascade rivers into a large penstock that runs to a new hydroelectric plant near where the now nearly dry Cascade once joined the Bow. The 34-megawatt Cascade power plant still stands beside the Trans-Canada Highway.

Downstream from the dam, the channel that once contained the Cascade River now carries a token allowance of water – so little that it has been renamed Cascade Creek. Below the Trans-Canada Highway, what little remains of the once-mighty stream trickles into a bulldozed ditch and simply vanishes into sun-baked gravel.

THE DAMMING OF THE CASCADE RIVER and the diversion of the north fork of the Ghost River were part of a chain of events that actually began well downstream on the Bow River, at the point where it breaks free from the Rocky Mountains.

During a train journey in 1908, Max Aitken, a Montreal-based developer later known as Lord Beaverbrook, spotted the hydropower potential of the Bow River east of Morley. The CP line followed the Bow past two impressive waterfalls between Calgary and Banff. Horseshoe Falls was at the point where the Bow River, cutting down into the glacial and lake-bed sediments that had been exposed with the retreat of the glaciers a few thousand years earlier, encountered the first major bed of erosion-resistant limestone at the edge of the Rockies. It was a spectacularly beautiful cascade and, at more than 20 metres in height, taller than the only waterfall surviving on the Bow River today, Bow Falls in Banff National Park.

Kananaskis Falls, a few kilometres upstream near the confluence of the Bow and the Kananaskis, was a stepped cascade with a total drop of about 50 feet. Although it was Kananaskis Falls that first caught Aitken's attention, the first hydropower dam on the Bow ended up built at Horseshoe Falls.

In 1909 Aitken teamed up with Calgary lawyer – and, later, Canadian Prime Minister – R.B. Bennett to form Calgary Power. The fledgling company acquired development rights to the dam sites on the Bow River and set to work enslaving the river. By 1910, with the dam at Horseshoe Falls already under construction, Bennett negotiated the company's first power contracts with the Canada Cement Company and the growing City of Calgary.

The Horseshoe Falls Dam, however, was plagued from the start by engineering incompetence. The June 1910 flood blew out the cofferdam and scaffolding and undercut the dam footings because the engineers had underestimated the spring runoff. Then, with a completed dam and powerhouse designed for winter flows that the same engineers had blithely guessed would range from a low of 960 to an average of 1,600 cubic feet per second, the company discovered that the winter-flow rate actually averaged less than 725.

Aitken and his colleagues, having failed to do their due diligence, had sunk a great deal of investment capital into an underperforming asset – and taken on binding contracts to sell electricity they couldn't produce. That mistake would lead to dire consequences not only for the Bow, Cascade and Ghost rivers but also for the Spray and Kananaskis. Within four decades, all had been dammed, diverted and re-engineered to make the Bow River dams profitable.

Rather than default on their power contracts, Calgary Power moved quickly to develop the upstream site at Kananaskis Falls. This dam, however, would back up water into Rocky Mountains (Banff) Park. The Department of Interior commissioned a study by C.H. Mitchell, one of Canada's top hydro engineers, to determine whether this dam or a competing proposal would be in the public interest.

In early 1911, Mitchell reported that the upstream dam would produce very little power in winter, because the river flow dropped to about six hundred cubic feet per second. However, he also noted that this shortcoming might be overcome if the company could develop storage reservoirs on upstream tributaries, enabling them to release more water into the river during the winter low-flow period.

Within two years, Calgary Power had completed their second Bow River dam, just upstream from where the Horseshoe Falls Dam's backpool ended. In addition, having persuaded the Department of Interior that hydropower development was sufficiently in the public interest to trump the protection of scenery in the national park, the company began to address the water-storage problem by building a dam on the Cascade River to raise the level of Lake Minnewanka. It didn't help much, however, as most of the water they released in winter simply vanished into the gravel alluvium beneath the Bow River channel. Only an estimated 20 per cent of what they released went through the downstream power plants. It seems likely that some downstream ranchers whose water wells tapped into the alluvial aquifer were pleasantly surprised by increased flow rates in their wells, but authorities also

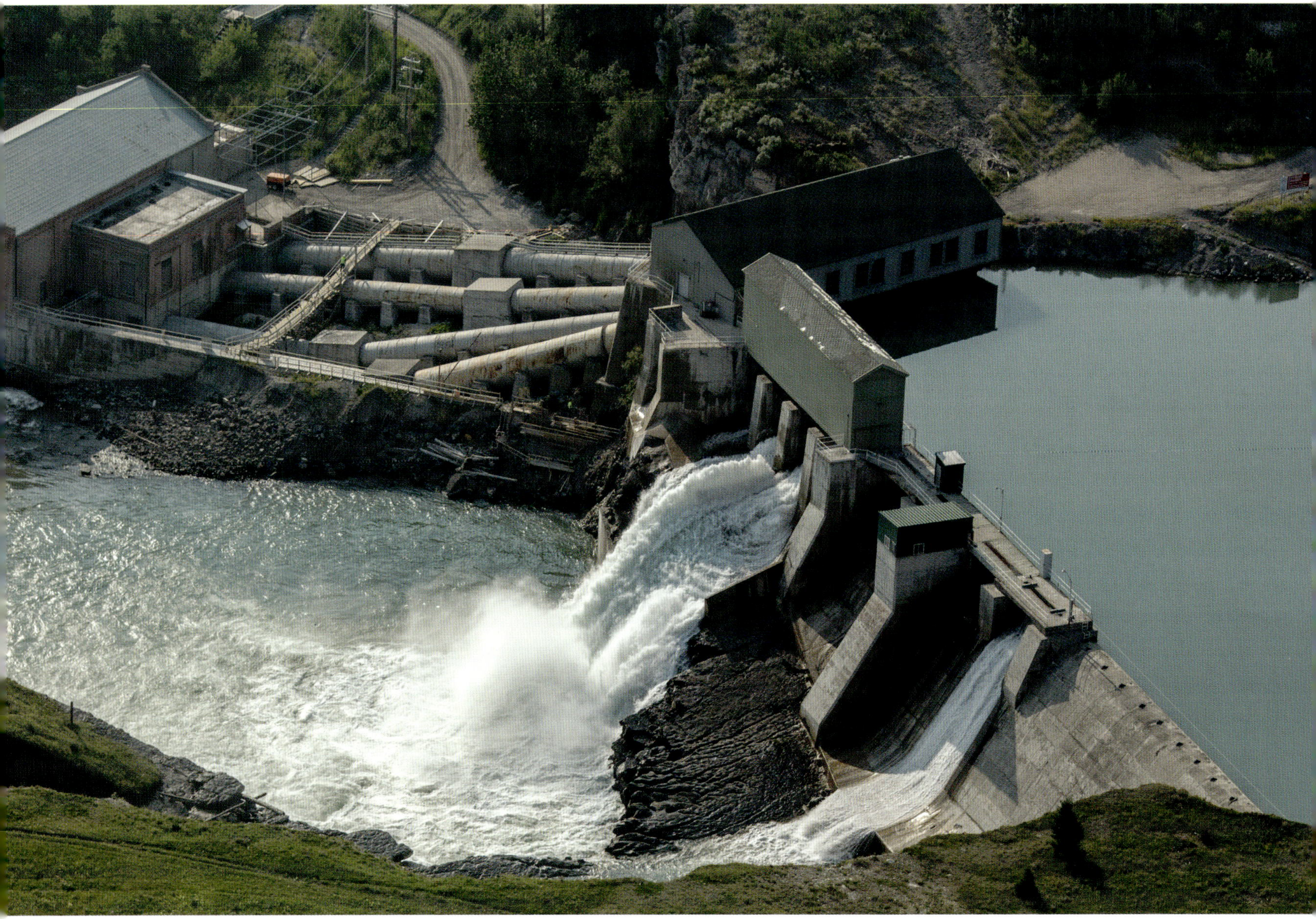

Horseshoe Falls and Kananaskis dams on the Bow River near Seebe set the stage for the flooding of Lake Minnewanka and other headwater valleys.

noted that the Bow River had become more flood prone as a result of the augmented surface and subsurface flows.

Almost as soon as the new dam proved to be yet another underachievement for Alberta's overrated water engineers, Calgary Power began promoting a massive expansion of the reservoir at Lake Minnewanka. Their new concept, developed in the 1920s, involved raising the water level a further eight to ten metres to store more water and redesigning the dam so they could draw it down even farther in winter.

The Dominion Parks Service, which had actually started the process of changing Lake Minnewanka into a giant reservoir, fought long and hard to prevent Calgary Power from flooding the whole valley. The project became unstoppable, however, when TransAlta exploited political connections in Ottawa during the Second World War to get the dam and diversion approved under the War Measures Act. The expansion of the reservoir and the diversion of the North Ghost made this the largest storage reservoir in the Bow River headwaters. With the earlier damming of the Kananaskis Lakes and development of the Spray Lakes a decade later, it finally gave TransAlta enough upstream water storage to operate their facilities on the main Bow River at capacity.

THE EFFECTS OF THE HORSESHOE and Kananaskis falls dams on the Bow River were to eliminate two spectacularly beautiful waterfalls, flood land that had been reserved for the Stoney Nakoda people, and modify the flow patterns of the downstream river in response to hydropower demands. The dams likely had little impact on fish migration, since Horseshoe Falls was already a natural barrier to the upstream movement of fish.

The dam at the outlet of Lake Minnewanka, however, and the diversion of the North Ghost River, dramatically changed the fish populations of both the Cascade and Ghost rivers. The losers were bull and cutthroat trout. The winners were lake trout and mountain whitefish.

Originally, the Cascade was a single, interconnected system. The Ghost Lakes drained by way of a small creek into Lake Minnewanka, whose outlet stream joined the much more substantial flow of the Cascade River near Stewart Canyon.

Large bull trout could fatten on whitefish, sculpins and other small fish in the Bow River and lower Cascade before migrating upstream late each summer, passing through Lake Minnewanka with its resident population of lake trout, to spawn where upwelling springs emerge into the stream gravel in headwater streams like Stoney, Cuthead and Sawback creeks. Young bull trout remain in their birth streams until they are large enough to shift from a diet of insects to one of small fish, at which point they travel downstream to larger waters, where prey is more abundant. When they are large enough to dig redds deep enough in the spawning gravels to protect their eggs from ice scouring and spring floods, they begin to return upstream each year to the small streams where they originally hatched.

The bull trout's life cycle and migratory habit had made it ideally suited for life in the Bow River headwaters. Once a dam goes across a river, however, bull trout populations dwindle and vanish. Sometimes the small fish in the headwaters survive, but the large migratory fish that spawn most successfully are doomed. The diversion of the north fork of the Ghost eliminated any migratory bull trout that might once have spawned in its tributary streams, and the dam at the outlet of Lake Minnewanka doomed any coming upstream from the Bow.

MIGRATORY BULL TROUT might have survived had they been able to use the much-enlarged Lake Minnewanka for the downstream part of their life cycle. The dam, after all, was at the lake's outlet, not its inlet. But the reservoir already held another large predatory fish that consistently outcompetes bull trout wherever the two species occupy the same lake.

In 1858, while staying at Old Bow Fort, explorer James Hector visited with a Stoney man who had

> come through the first range by a pass to the south of Devil's Head in which he says there is a lake the length of a half day's march, where they catch the finest trout and white fish in the country. At the upper end of the lake, which sends a stream into Bow river just below where we camped [Cascade River], he says there is a "height of land" to be crossed, and from the other side of which rises Deadman's River.

Several years later, in 1895, C.H. Eigenmann confirmed that these were lake trout. He reported catching several in Devil's Lake that were up to 43 centimetres in length – the first documented report of the species in what later became Alberta.

Ironically, this artificial reservoir is actually the only lake in the entire Bow River watershed where lake trout occur naturally. Although early fisheries managers successfully stocked lake trout into Bow, Spray and other headwaters lakes, native populations of lake trout were originally found only in a few deep lakes like Waterton, Minnewanka and Glacier, where they had survived the late Wisconsinan glaciation.

Lake trout, like the bull trout, are char. They rarely occupy streams, however, preferring to live year-round in lakes, where they spawn along underwater reefs and rock outcroppings. Biologist David Donald documented 11 lakes in Alberta's mountain national parks that once held bull trout populations but were subsequently stocked with lake trout. In every case, the bull trout numbers dwindled, until only lake trout survived. Given that, it is unlikely that many bull trout lingered for long in Lake Minnewanka.

The flooding of the valley greatly expanded the deepwater habitat available for lake trout and their favoured prey, such as mountain whitefish and suckers. The reservoir today supports a robust population of lake trout weighing up to 20 kilograms.

Although much of the damage was done before the era of intensive fisheries investigations, it seems likely that the Ghost Lakes and Devil's Lakes would have supported good populations of native cutthroat trout, too. Unlike the deepwater lake trout, lake-dwelling cutthroats concentrate in the littoral zone – the shallower edges of lakes, where sun can penetrate to the bottom and insect life is abundant. In their natural condition, the lakes in Devil's Gap would have had extensive shallows ideal for cutthroats, as well as a low-gradient stream connecting them.

Once flooded, however, the littoral zones of the original lakes were swamped. The new reservoir never developed an ecologically productive littoral zone, because hydropower operations result in deep drawdowns in water levels each year. The wider water surface is also more exposed to wind, resulting in waves that wash fine materials away from the rocky shorelines. As a result, even when park officials released non-native fish like brook and rainbow trout to replace the dwindling cutthroats, it was to no avail. The habitat was gone. Lake Minnewanka today belongs to deepwater fishes.

BILL HUNT HAS NO ILLUSIONS about the likelihood that Lake Minnewanka will ever be drained and its valley restored to its original condition. Banff's manager of resource conservation cut his academic teeth on the thorny bio-politics of aquatic ecosystems management. An ecologist as determined as he is pragmatic, he nonetheless sees opportunities to restore some of this much-abused watershed's ecological integrity. His attention is drawn not so much to the big hydropower reservoir as to the small lakes and streams farther upstream and even more to the nearly dry channel below the Minnewanka Dam.

In the headwaters, Bill and his staff have been working since 2011 to eradicate introduced rainbow and brook trout from Rainbow Lake and Sawback Creek. Using nets and electroshocking equipment, the national park crews hope to free the drainage's dwindling cutthroat and bull trout stocks from competition with aggressive non-native fish. There is little unusual in this approach; the project is similar to other native trout restoration efforts being tried throughout the Rockies, from New Mexico to Yukon. When Bill and his staff attend fisheries conferences, they talk to people very like themselves.

Downstream from the Minnewanka Dam, however, the creative challenges facing Hunt and his team are considerably more challenging and complicated. The late Charlie Pacas, long-time aquatics specialist for Banff National Park, was the visionary who first conceived of a project that would bring back not only the river's native fishes, but also the entire ecosystem: a stream, its riparian habitats, its annual cycles and – perhaps – the spirits that once dwelt there.

Pacas envisioned a complex project to solve several ecological challenges at once. Not only was the lower Cascade River dewatered by the Lake Minnewanka Dam, but Parks Canada had mined part of its former riverbed for gravel to supply the Trans-Canada Highway twinning project over two decades starting in the late 1970s. What had once been a sloping, gravelly floodplain covered with spruce forest and grassland was now known as the Cascade Pits – a series of craters and rubble piles covered with weeds. Any effort to bring the lower river back to life would require refilling those pits, digging a new stream channel, and lining it with clay or other fine material to keep water from simply draining into the exposed cobbles and gravel. And it would require water.

Pacas found a clay source a few kilometres west, in a different drainage. The park service had dammed Forty Mile Creek in 1916 to provide water for the nearby town of Banff. Engineers continued to add to the dam until 1949, by which time the concrete wall held back up to 18,000 cubic metres of crystalline mountain water in a narrow reservoir. I recall looking down from the dam in the late 1970s at three half-metre-long bull trout resting lazily on the bottom of their artificial refuge. Before the dam blocked the stream, those trapped fish would have been dwarfed by much larger bull trout that used to ascend the stream from the Bow River each August and September to spawn in the upper reaches.

A generation of baby boomers discovered Vibram soles, aluminum-frame backpacks and their own possibilities in the 1970s. It was no accident that the Town of Banff discovered *Giardia lamblia* – a parasitic protozoan – in its water supply shortly later. Backpackers and other backcountry users had spread the parasite, found in human waste, into headwater drainages. Once there, it was perpetuated in the guts of native animals including the beaver. In an unfair twist of fate, it soon became known as "beaver fever."

The discovery of *Giardia* in the Forty Mile Creek Reservoir was not just a treatment challenge for the town water utility, it pointed out the vulnerability of surface water supplies to contamination. Banff punched new wells into the gravel river aquifers closer

Lake Minnewanka, Banff.

to town and shut down the waterlines from Forty Mile Reservoir.

By then, the reservoir was half-plugged with fine sediment that half a century of spring floods had deposited into the quiet water above the dam. Charlie Pacas looked at the sediment and saw a solution to the Cascade Pits challenge. The abandoned dam should be removed for safety reasons anyway. Why not excavate all that silt and truck it to the Cascade, where it could be spread beneath an artificially restored stream channel? That would reconnect Forty Mile Creek's aquatic ecosystem for the first time in decades while also enabling the lower Cascade River – if TransAlta could be persuaded to release more water from Minnewanka – to build a new floodplain across the scarified gravels of the former gravel pits.

It would be an elegant solution, but a costly one. Time, unfortunately, was not Pacas's friend. By the time he had worked out most of the details, Parks Canada was entering an era of budgetary restraint. Never noted for a lack of persistence where ecological restoration was concerned, Pacas shifted his focus to persuading TransAlta to release an increased flow downstream of the Minnewanka Dam. Meantime, he submitted new project proposals to Parks Canada every year. His case was strengthened when, in 2009, a town-commissioned engineering study raised red flags about the safety of the Forty Mile Dam. If the growing cracks in its cement face were to fail during a spring flood, the town faced an immense liability risk; a

massive amount of water and sediment would be released above the Trans-Canada Highway, the Canadian Pacific Railway line and the town of Banff itself.

Then, on June 19, 2013, a massive rainstorm parked itself over the Rocky Mountain Front Ranges for two days. In less than 16 hours, as much as two hundred millimetres of rain fell on a lingering mountain snowpack, unleashing the biggest spring flood the Bow River basin had seen in well more than a century.

Forty Mile Creek overtopped its dam. To the relief of worried town engineers, the aging structure, though suffering further damage, somehow survived the onslaught.

A few kilometres away, TransAlta's engineers watched with increasing concern as the massive reservoir behind their Lake Minnewanka Dam crept toward its upper limit. If Minnewanka failed, the towns of Canmore, Morley and Cochrane would be hit with an unimaginable tidal wave of water, gravel and woody debris. The weight of so much water and sediment sweeping down the river would almost certainly damage or breach Ghost and Bearspaw dams. Most of downtown Calgary and its inner-city neighborhoods – already swamped by flood waters and mud – would have been destroyed.

TransAlta had never had to use the dam's spillway before. The company's engineers opened the floodgates and let the Cascade back into its long-abandoned channel to reduce the rate at which the reservoir was filling. Unfortunately, the reawakened river was too big for the culvert under the CPR rail line. Water quickly backed up under the adjacent highway and flooded the Cascade power plant, effectively killing its electric systems. With the generating plant badly damaged, operators had to shut down the massive pipe that normally drains the reservoir.

Now the spillway had to handle all the outflow from the reservoir, not just a portion of it ... and still, water was pouring into the reservoir from the upstream watershed. A crew was dispatched to the Ghost River valley with heavy equipment and instructions to breach the earthen berm that diverts the North Ghost into the reservoir. Forecasted rainfall amounts for the next 12 hours had operational staff seriously worried. Although TransAlta insists the integrity of the dam was never threatened, some staff with homes in Canmore, a few kilometres downstream, called their families and told them to get out, now.

The rain, fortuitously, slacked off. The reservoir level stabilized. But by now the full flow of the swollen Cascade River was pouring over the dam spillway and into the river's long-abandoned lower channel. There it scoured out river sediments that encroaching spruce forests had buried decades earlier, redepositing them in long loops and curves as the river undercut new outside bends and built new point bars. Some of the old river pools had been plugged with more than a metre of accumulated silt, but the river made short work of its removal. It may have had a lot of work to do after so long an absence, but there was a lot of water to do the work. The lower Cascade was a river again.

Charlie Pacas, Bill Hunt and others who had dreamed about restoring the lower Cascade were too busy working on emergency response to spend much time marvelling over what was happening along the old stream channel. The flood had breached or overwhelmed the Trans-Canada

Highway in several locations, drowned day-use areas, isolated tourists in wet campgrounds and back roads, and pushed Parks Canada's response capabilities to the maximum. All of southern Alberta was in crisis mode. Still, nobody could miss the fact that the empty gravel channel that, over the past half century, had been vanishing under forest and grass, was now a roaring brown river again.

By the time the flood waters receded, all the pieces were in place for Pacas finally to push his river restoration dream into reality. Only sheer luck had enabled the Town of Banff to dodge the liability bullet their engineers had so recently warned them about. Councillors were now united in agreement that they needed to remove the Forty Mile Creek Dam, and they had access to emergency funding to do so. TransAlta's engineers, after their heart-stopping experience, were more motivated than ever to work with Parks Canada to avoid that kind of stress again. The public had, briefly, seen a reborn Cascade River. Recovery was no longer an esoteric ideal but a tangible possibility.

But in November of that year, in a cruel turn of fate, Charlie Pacas died unexpectedly while enjoying a well-earned bicycling vacation in Europe. He was only 61 years old.

THE SOLUTION TO THE LOWER CASCADE RIVER restoration challenge hangs partly on getting water back into the stream, but mostly on finding a way to seal the porous cobbles exposed by previous quarrying operations. Without a more or less impermeable seal, any increased water flows will simply vanish into the ground. For all Charlie Pacas's creative thinking and bulldog-like perseverance, solutions eluded him to the end.

Unable to persuade Parks Canada or the Town of Banff to move sediment from behind Forty Mile Dam to the Cascade Pits in the first decade of the 20th century, Pacas had come up with a different idea.

Parks Canada's Resource Conservation unit includes not only the biologists and ecosystem-management staff but some of the most advanced fire-management teams in North America. The fire crews use high-powered pumps to lift water to where it's needed. Why not, Pacas wondered, conduct an experiment with those pumps? Pacas theorized that fire pumps could replicate spring flood flows, creating a high-pressure stream of water that would flush silt and clay out of the Cascade River's long-dormant floodplain. With no cleansing flood flows for close to a century, the fine material that washed into the channel after rains and spring mudslides had simply stayed there, cementing the stream gravels in place. A renewed stream would need clean gravel deposits for invertebrate life and fish spawning, so extracting the finer material might serve two purposes: renewing the porosity of the stream bed, and sealing a new channel through the leaky Cascade Pits farther downstream.

Fire crews need to practise their skills. In 2012 the crews loaded up their gear and followed Pacas to the edge of the lower Cascade for a training exercise. They used the firehoses like placer miners, directing a concentrated jet of water into the middle of the channel in three different places along the former river to flush the finest material out to the side of the floodplain. The experiment worked:

the treated river stretches soon had mucky piles of fine-textured goo along their edges and shiny, clean gravel in the middle.

Based on the experiment's success, Pacas arranged for TransAlta to release a flushing flow in 2013. That would subject the whole stream bed to the same kind of pressure-washing. In advance of the experimental flood, the park highway crew cut a channel to divert the mud-charged flow into the Cascade Pits.

But the 2013 flood changed everything. The massive release of water from the Lake Minnewanka reservoir flushed all the fine material out at once – as well as most of the gravel. Instead of pushing it sideways onto the floodplain, the flood waters washed it downstream. The massive flow washed out berms, roads and overflow channels alike, flooding the entire gravel pit before cutting a new channel downstream to the Bow. When the flood waters receded, some silt remained at the bottom of the pit, but most was gone.

The same flood that undid Pacas's plan to use the lower Cascade's own channel as a silt supply shocked the Town of Banff into the need tangibly to address the risks associated with their aging dam on Forty Mile Creek. Pacas's Plan A began to look viable again when, soon after the 2013 flood waters receded, the town hired contractors to breach the dam and remove more than 4000 cubic metres of silt and fine gravel that had accumulated in the reservoir.

But although Pacas had previously lobbied for the sediment to go to the Cascade Pits, the Town of Banff, faced with big flood cleanup bills, couldn't afford the extra trucking costs. Parks Canada, reeling from massive budget cuts imposed by a government more concerned with tar sand exploitation than nature protection, couldn't find the money to make up the difference either. The dam-bottom material got used to reclaim a contaminated site near the old dam instead.

Pacas was gone by then, but Hunt and the project team followed his traditional response to setbacks: they came up with Plan C.

The flood, Hunt points out, had done as much good as harm. It did some of the heavy lifting by scouring away accumulated silt from the stream bed. But, he told me,

> There can be too much of a good thing. The flood also widened the channel well beyond what is needed for future flow levels and removed, from the surface, a lot of the gravels needed for good habitat – so we either need to use a backhoe to redefine a narrower channel and re-expose the deeper gravels, or reintroduce gravels and allow flushing flows to distribute them appropriately downstream.

Every year, meltwaters bring large amounts of eroded material from Cascade Mountain down steep gullies to the valley bottom. Where those gullies intersect the Lake Minnewanka loop road, the debris flows can plug culverts and overflow onto the road. Every year, consequently, Parks Canada's highway crews do preventative maintenance to protect the culverts, excavating tonnes of debris on the uphill side of the road and dumping it over the downhill side.

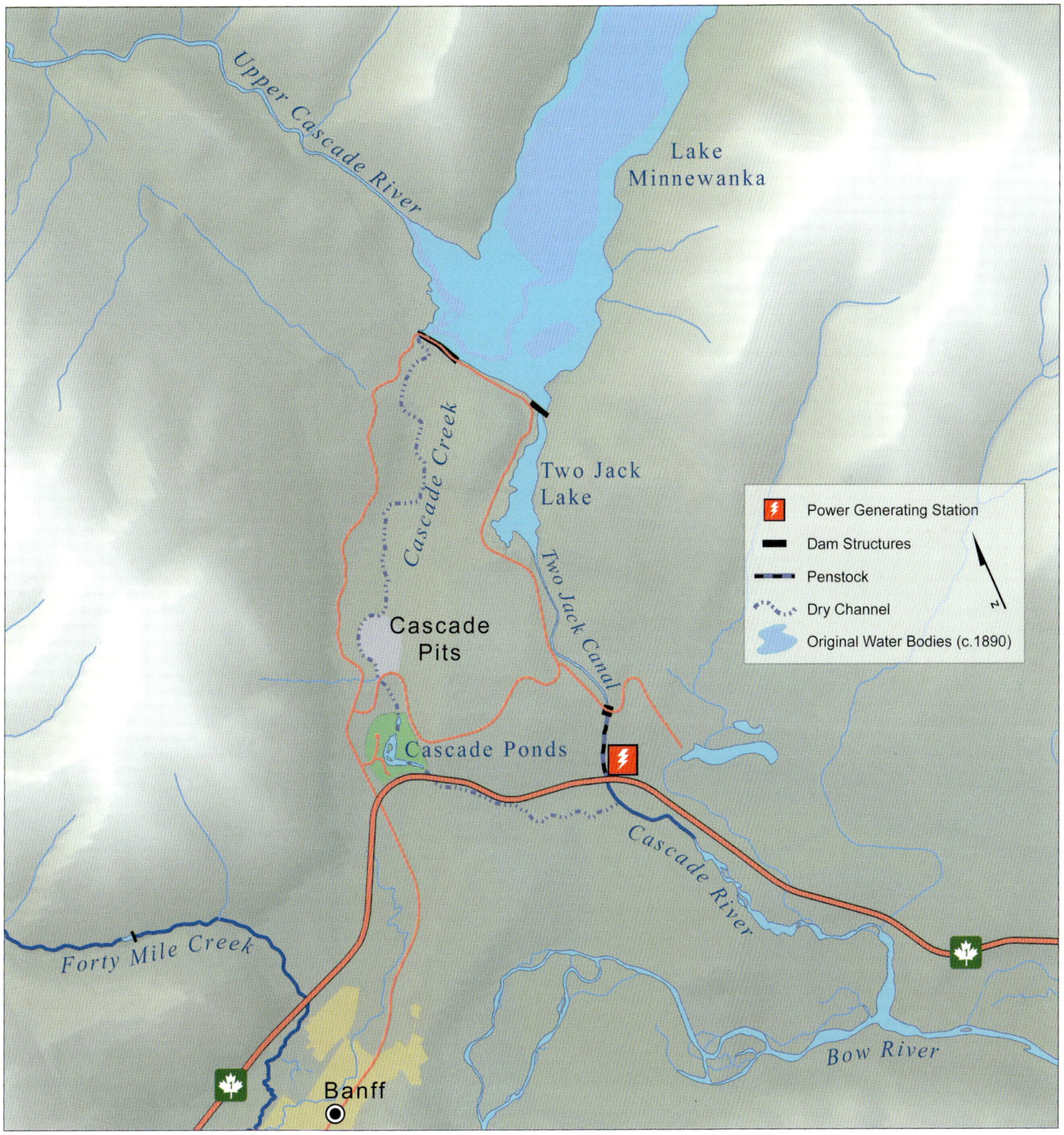

Map courtesy of Jonathan Ball, Banff

Plan C involved creating three or four sites along the upper end of the lower Cascade River channel, where crews would truck and dump that excavated material. If TransAlta could be persuaded to release an artificial spring flood from Lake Minnewanka each spring, carefully calibrated to provide just the right amount of erosion, those freshet flows could be used to flush the finest material out of the debris and wash it downstream to Cascade Pits. It would be an artificial engineering solution, but unlike the engineering that had originally devastated the river, it would be designed to restore the natural ecological processes that keep streams vital.

Water diverted back into the lower river below the Minnewanka Dam would not be available to generate hydropower, but Pacas's work had given TransAlta good reasons to give some water back to the river. While monitoring the effects of their operations elsewhere in the system, Pacas found some awkward problems the company was going to need to come to terms with – or possibly face charges under the Canada National Parks Act and the Fisheries Act. The most onerous involved diced fish.

The Cascade power plant beside the Bow River turns the former Cascade River, diverted through a long penstock, into hydropower. West of the power plant, the former riverbed is a ditch, usually dry, beside the Trans-Canada Highway. East of the power plant, the downstream channel runs brimful when the company is churning out electric power. As partial mitigation for the damage it has done to the river, the company is obliged to maintain enough flow downstream to keep fish from stranding when the plant isn't in use. As a result, however, suckers, whitefish and trout from the Bow River are able to travel upstream to the power station. There, trapped in the churning waters each time the company turns on the generator, hundreds get chewed to bits each year in the unscreened turbines. Pacas suspected that the volume of fish bits he found below the power plant was too great to be only from Bow River fish; he believed that many of the fish had been swept down from Lake Minnewanka because of an unscreened intake at the head of the penstock.

Generating hydropower in a national park might be acceptable, if only as an accident of history. Killing fish isn't. TransAlta doesn't screen the intake because keeping screens clear of driftwood and other debris is a maintenance headache. They might be able to screen the downstream channel to keep Bow River fish out, but that, too would be challenging considering the force of the water coming through the turbines.

But the company knows it needs a solution, because Charlie Pacas's monitoring showed that normal operations wreak continuing havoc on national park fish. The findings even triggered a law enforcement investigation by park wardens. Banff's aquatics visionary may have passed too soon, but he did his work well.

"I CAN'T SEE US EVER PUTTING TOGETHER the kind of money that would be needed to restore the whole lower Cascade," Bill Hunt told me one summer afternoon at his office in the Parks Canada compound in Banff. A framed picture of his long-time friend and colleague Charlie Pacas stood on a bookcase behind him.

> But Charlie put all the pieces together. I think we can bring back the lower Cascade as a restored creek with a population of native westslope cutthroat trout if we work at it bit by bit. There are some good short-term opportunities to deal with the key challenges. And if we do it right, it opens up all kinds of new interpretive opportunities, fish-viewing, lots of ways to enhance the way people experience their national park.

Bill Hunt has continued Pacas's efforts to collaborate with TransAlta on operational changes in the wake of the 2013 flood, and to help the company address its ongoing environmental liabilities. After all, TransAlta has flooded two once-productive valleys, repeatedly scoured most of the Spray River and Goat Creek floodplains with devastating floods, wiped out the middle Bow River's bull trout populations and dried up both the North Ghost and lower Cascade rivers. It owes a massive ecological debt to Canada's first national park – and to Alberta's headwaters.

Hunt sees a potential trade-off that would restore reliable flows to the historic river channel downstream of Minnewanka Dam. If TransAlta were permitted to turn off the water immediately downstream from the Cascade power plant, fish would no longer be able to get into the turbines from the lower end. The company would kill fewer fish. Turning off that flow would leave more than enough water in the reservoir for the company to send a healthy in-stream flow down the 15 kilometres of river below the Minnewanka Dam, as well as to release planned floods each spring. In effect, the company would periodically de-water one hundred metres of artificial tail-race to permanently create 15 kilometres of high-quality stream habitat for native fish, with no loss of electrical production. Given the immense profits TransAlta has earned at the expense of the national park's aquatic ecosystems over the past century, it seems like the least they could do.

An ideal project would also include restoring the Cascade Pits area to riparian wetlands. There is nothing preventing Parks Canada and TransAlta from doing that, too, when the time is right. Bill Hunt also envisions potentially turning an abandoned power generation building near the Minnewanka Dam into an interpretive centre, building a new trail from Two Jack Campground to the restored river and some of its little-known beauties, such as the "travertine wall" – a groundwater spring that has built a dramatic wall of carbonate tufa into the hillside – and offering anglers a chance to catch and release native trout in the more accessible parts of the renewed stream. He sees the restoration of the lower Cascade River not only as an ecological imperative but an opportunity to share inspiration and insight with thousands of park visitors each year.

Listening to Bill Hunt's increasingly animated talk about what could be done to bring life and purpose back to the ghost of a river that once drained the Lake of the Spirits, I glanced over his shoulder again at the photo of Charlie Pacas.

He was grinning.

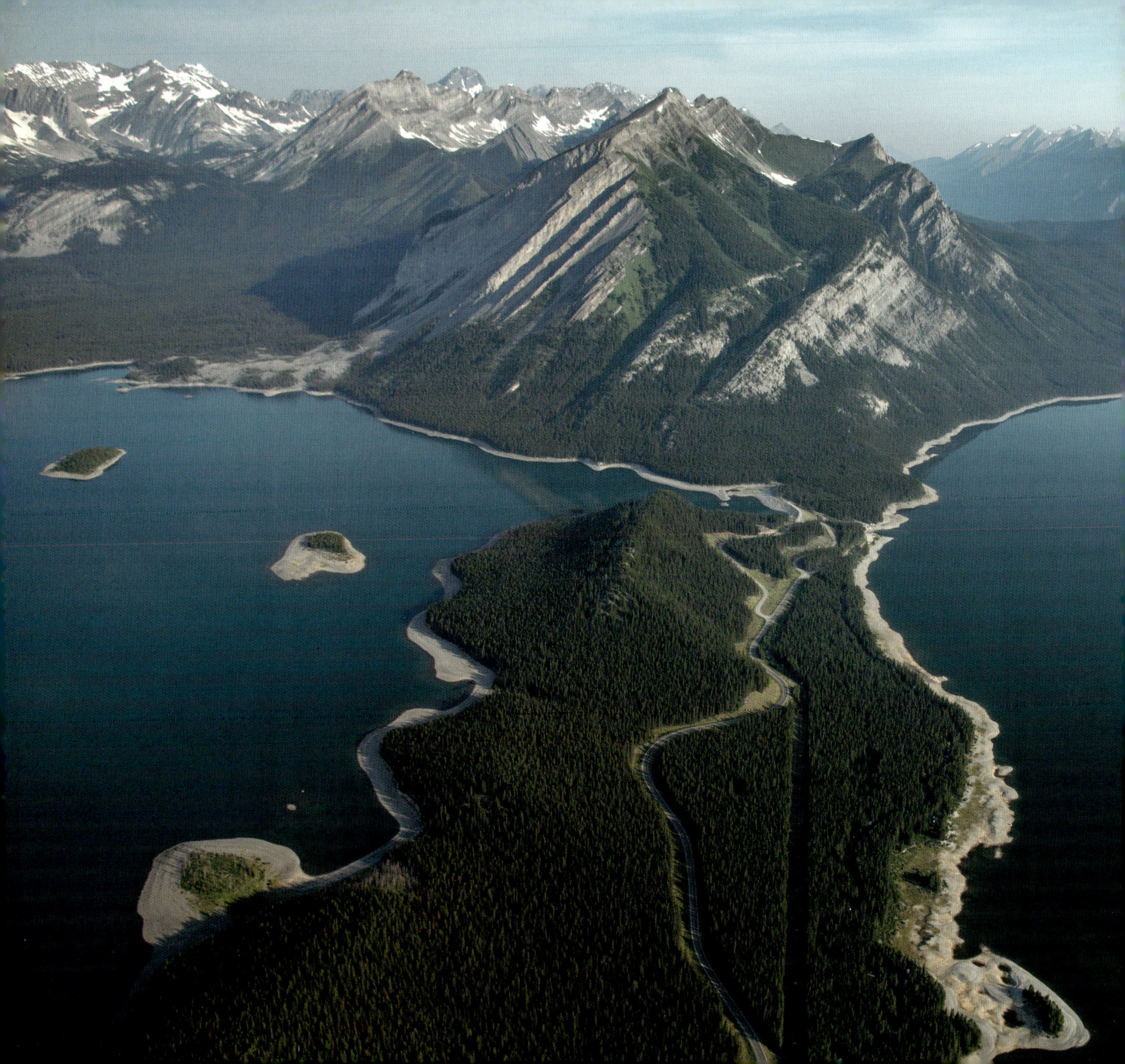

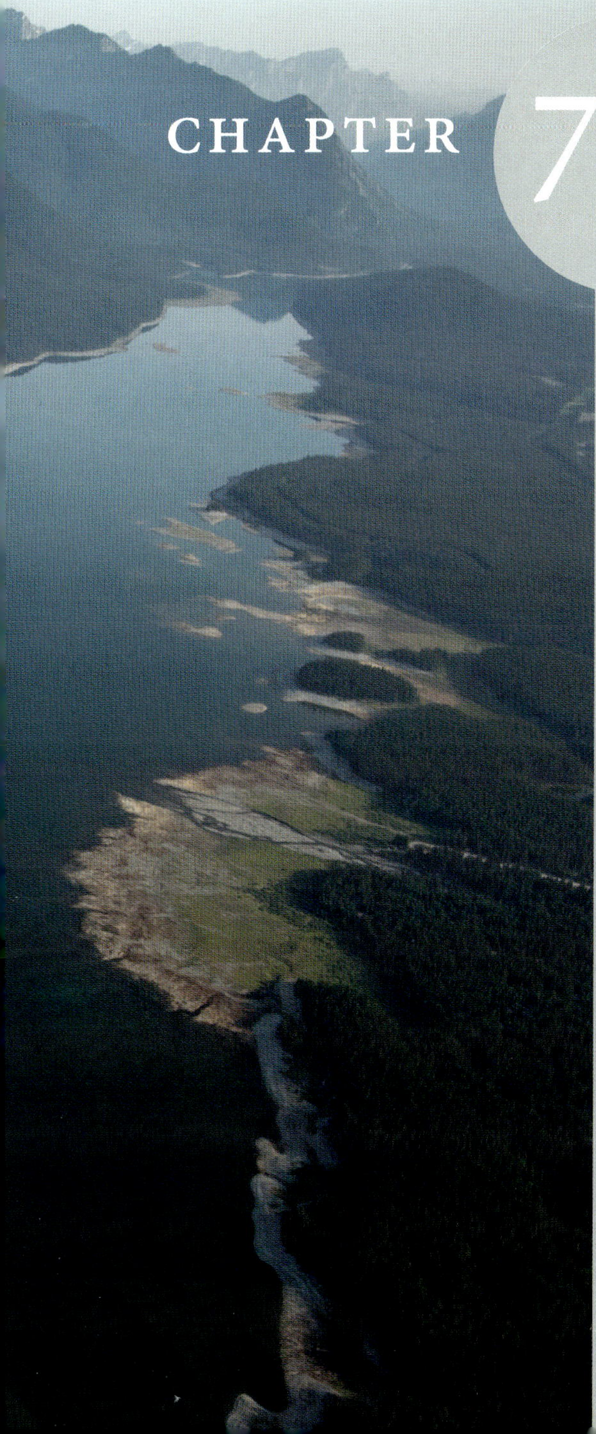

CHAPTER 7

Dammed Splendour

Kananaskis River

THE STONEY NAKODA PEOPLE know the flats where the Bow River emerges from the Rockies as Ozada Imne, or "the place where the waters meet."

The waters that meet within a few kilometres of Morley, one of Alberta's earliest settlements, are from three major rivers: the Ghost, Bow and Kananaskis. For a hunting and trading people, the congress of waters couldn't be a more ideal location. The Stoneys wintered at the Morley Flats for decades before missionaries George and John McDougall first established a Methodist mission there. A few years later, at the signing of Treaty Seven in 1877, their chiefs chose the area for a reserve.

North of the Fairholme Range, the north and south forks of the Ghost River converge beneath the Devil's Head (Phantom Crag) and then arch east and south through high foothills to join the Bow. Before Calgary Power flooded Devil's Gap, the south fork was a major travel route for the original people of the Rockies. The high country at the head of the Ghost has been hunting country for the Nakoda since they arrived in the area in the early 1800s – and for the K'tunaxa even earlier – but its headwater passes lead only

Page 98: *Once considered the most beautiful lakes in the Canadian Rockies, Upper and Lower Kananaskis lakes are now rimmed by sterile drawdown zones of wind-washed boulders.*

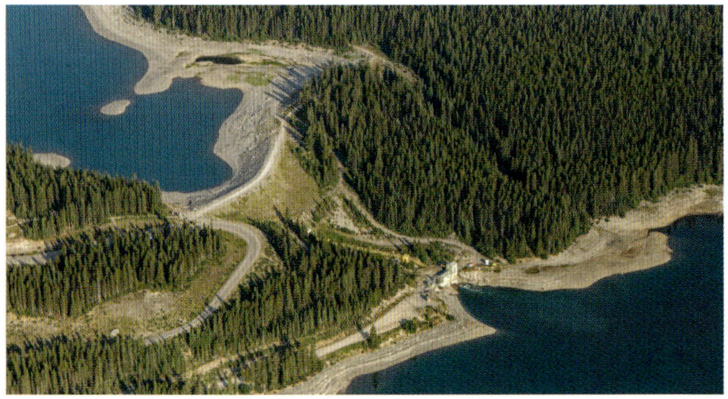

Right: *An earthfill dam, a penstock and a hydro generation plant have replaced the waterfalls and trout spawning riffles that once separated Upper from Lower Kananaskis lakes.*

to more high valleys, so the rest of the Ghost drainage figures hardly at all in the annals of western exploration.

South of the Fairholme Range, the Bow itself spills out of a gap between Heart and Exshaw mountains and, escaping its limestone bounds at Kananaskis and then Horseshoe Falls, becomes a foothills river. For thousands of years the upper Bow valley and its passes – White Man, Simpson, Vermilion and Kicking Horse – have been important travel and trade corridors through the Rockies. The main Bow valley, its horse trails supplanted by highways and a railroad, still is today.

To the south, the Kananaskis River squeezes between Heart and Barrier (now Baldy) mountains into a shallow canyon it carved into the much wider floodplain it occupied 15,000 to 10,000 years ago, when the mountain glaciers were melting back most rapidly. That ancient floodplain, now covered with grass, has come to be known as Morley Flats. They aren't flat; they tilt eastward where the ancestral Kananaskis River used to drain toward glacial Lake Calgary.

Unlike the Ghost, the Kananaskis valley leads to passes into British Columbia that Aboriginal peoples have used as trading routes since time immemorial and that subsequently became important for early European explorers. In that regard it is similar to the Bow, but it differs from that valley, too, because modern transcontinental highways and railroads have not replaced the old Aboriginal trading routes. The Kananaskis is as richly storied a place as the Bow, but in many ways it has retained its wildness and beauty.

The original trails up the Kananaskis were mostly on the west side of the valley, across the river from the route today's Highway 40 follows. The sunny exposure of the southeast-oriented slopes made them relatively warm and dry, with more openings in the forest and abundant wildlife. In trackless country, wildlife trails are often the easiest choice for human travellers. Trails also connected south to the upper Jumpingpound Creek drainage, over Skogan Pass to the Bow, and through Evan-Thomas, Elbow and Highwood passes to hunting areas elsewhere in the Front Ranges.

During what geologists describe as the Hypsithermal

period, about six to eight thousand years ago, western Canada was warmer and drier than today. Trees grew higher up the mountainsides than they do now, and the valley floors were open and grassy because of frequent fires and droughts. Bison, bighorn sheep and elk would have been common in the Front Ranges during that period. The Aboriginal peoples who occupied the Kananaskis valley enjoyed a high standard of living, as well as isolation from potential enemies on the plains to the east. Archaeologists have found evidence that starting soon after the retreat of the glaciers, people occupied the Kananaskis and Bow valleys continuously.

The upper Kananaskis River flows in a trench valley that crosses the Continental Divide. On the Alberta side, the Kananaskis flows north from its headwaters at Kananaskis Lakes. In British Columbia, the Elk River flows south in the same trench valley from its headwaters at Elk Lakes. North and South Kananaskis passes connect this shared headwater valley with the Palliser and White rivers, which drain to the Kootenay. Plains tribes used all these passes to trade pemmican and hides with the K'tunaxa and other mountain tribes, who had access to quarries that provided better tool-making stone than could be found east of the mountain divide.

THE FIRST WRITTEN ACCOUNT of people of European origin penetrating to the head of the Kananaskis River was from James Sinclair, who went over the North Kananaskis Pass in 1854 with a party of Metis colonists en route to Oregon from the Red River country, near what is now Winnipeg. However, it was John Palliser who, four years later, named the valley and left the most detailed account of his travels.

Palliser had been commissioned by the British government to take stock of the western lands that had, for many years, been administered by the Hudson's Bay Company. With the company's original licence about to expire, and mindful of the risk that Americans could invade and lay claim to what Britain considered its territories in the West, the government wanted an objective assessment of the resources and potential of the relatively unknown western lands. Palliser's expedition was also expected to identify the most practical route for a future road to the Pacific Ocean.

Palliser named the valley after a legendary Cree man who survived an axe blow to the head and went on to live until old age in the area. Upon reaching the head of the river, Palliser became only the first of many to comment on the beauty of the two lakes at the river's headwaters.

Originally, a substantial river flowed for a kilometre between the two lakes. The river descended over two waterfalls. One was only 2.5 metres high, but the other, which divided into two around a forested island, was an impressive 12.3 metres. The upper lake was particularly beautiful, with seven islands and numerous peninsulas and bays. Palliser described Upper Kananaskis Lake as

> … a magnificent lake, hemmed in by mountains, and studded with numerous islets, very thickly wooded. This lake, about four miles long and 1½ miles wide, receives the waters from the glaciers above, and is a favourite place of resort to the Kootanie Indians.

George Pocaterra, an Italian-born trapper, rancher and adventurer, saw the Kananaskis Lakes a few years later, in 1905. He described them as the most beautiful mountain scenery he had ever seen.

A young Calgarian, George Edworthy, packed into the valley in 1919 with a friend. They rode by horse from Bragg Creek by way of Elbow Pass. He, too, was moved by the beauty of the upper lake:

> When I first saw that upper lake I thought it was the most beautiful lake I had ever seen. There were a number of wooded islands in it and in the background, there was a tremendous mountain range and a glacier from which there was a very large and high waterfall visible to the naked eye many miles away.

Lower Kananaskis Lake, according to those willing to put in the necessary effort to visit it, was full of large cutthroat trout and even larger bull trout. The cutthroats spawned each spring in clean gravel riffles where the river drained into the lake, as well as in its outlet. The bull trout travelled up tributary streams in late summer.

Upper Kananaskis Lake, which was isolated by two impassable waterfalls from the lower lake, had no fish until George Edworthy and his friend engaged in a little bucket biology. Noting that the upper lake swarmed with pink-coloured freshwater shrimp, the young men made it a project to catch as many as they could of the young trout that swarmed at the head of the lower lake and transplant them into the upper. Within a few years, anglers were catching big trout there, too.

An illusion of wildness: the Kananaskis River, its flow temporarily turned on by TransAlta, offers ideal kayaking water where it drains over and around man-made structures in its bed.

ALBAN MCPARLAND, my grandfather, was one of those anglers. From his home in Strathmore, he and his friends made the long journey into the Upper Kananaskis several times in the early 20th century, following the gravelled highway up the north side of the Bow River from Calgary, then crossing near Morley to pick their way along the rough gravel track that followed the old Aboriginal trails up the Kananaskis valley. I remember him as a wiry Irishman, always with a cigarette smouldering under his trademark cap of Donegal tweed, full of fishing and hunting stories that made me ache to see for myself the wild places he had known. Some of his tales sounded almost too good to be real. Certainly, anglers and Irishmen have a certain reputation for improving their stories, but two photographs on my wall are proof that Pop-Pop didn't need to exaggerate about the Kananaskis.

One shows him standing behind a line strung between two trees at the Lower Kananaskis Lake Campground in 1939. Suspended on the line are 34 trout, the smallest of which appears to be about 35 centimetres and the largest more than 60. Four of the biggest trout are clearly bull trout; the rest appear to be cutthroats. The date inscribed on the original photograph – June 16 – suggests that he and his companions likely caught the cutthroats on their spawning beds either in the inlet or outlet of Lower Kananaskis Lake.

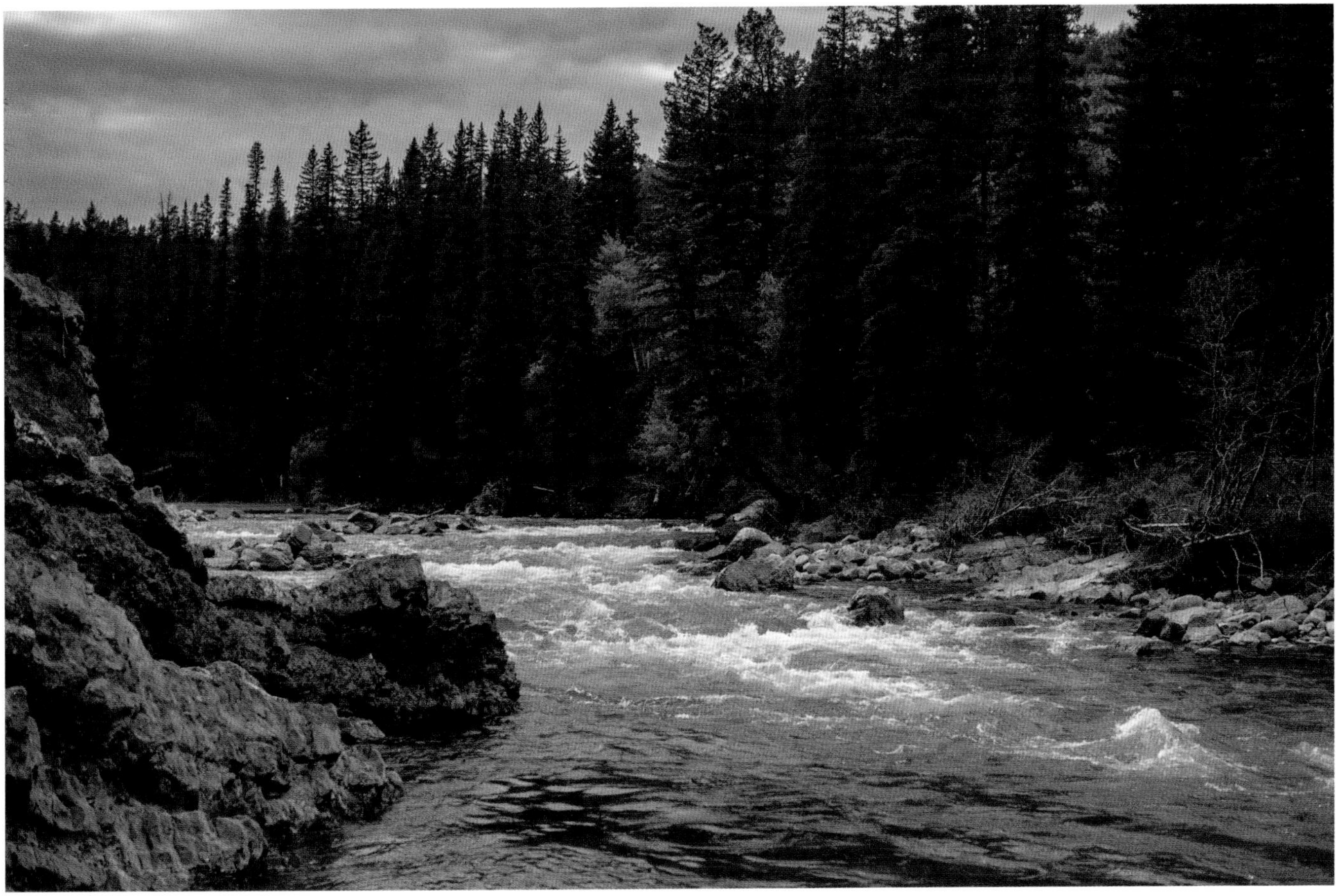

The second photograph shows him kneeling in the Kananaskis River and holding a single trout. On the back of this photograph is the inscription: "6# rainbow caught at Kananaskis June 17.40 on a Ruby Wobbler," and then:

A Fisherman's Prayer
I hope that I may catch a fish
so big that even I,
when telling of it afterwards
may never have to lie.

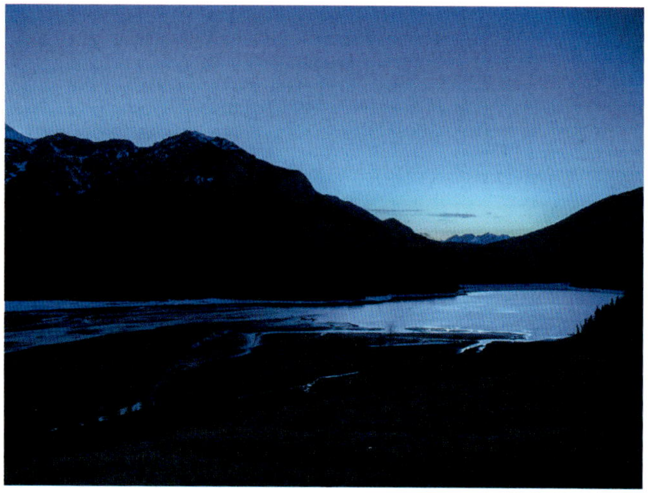

Silt flats mark the Kananaskis River's new delta, where it flows into the biologically impoverished reservoir behind Barrier Dam.

Trout that large are almost unheard of in today's mountain rivers, but the Kananaskis would have supported an extremely productive fishery, possibly better than the famed Elk River that rises from the same headwaters. The large lakes at the head of the Kananaskis not only sustained productive fish populations in their own right, but they would have served as settling ponds for glacial silt, moderated the flow of the downstream river and elevated its water temperature. The gentle gradient of the valley made the Kananaskis a classic pool-and-riffle stream – ideally configured trout habitat. Few Alberta streams can begin to approach the fisheries potential of the original Kananaskis.

Today's Kananaskis River, unfortunately, is a biological wasteland.

AS EARLY AS 1914, the eyes of frontier capitalists were already turning toward the Kananaskis as a possible source of water power to sell into Calgary's fast-growing market for electricity. That was the year that M.C. Hendry published his report after two years of investigating potential hydropower sites in the headwaters of the Bow River on behalf of Calgary Power. He faithfully reported that the Kananaskis Lakes basin had potential for water storage to feed downstream power plants but added that "the beauty of the lake in its natural state and the extreme probability of its becoming a summer resort in the near future should not be lost sight of."

His advice, and the area's remoteness, gave the Kananaskis Lakes a brief reprieve. But in 1932, in response to growing demands for electric power that the 1911 Horseshoe Falls hydro plant on the Bow River could no longer meet, Calgary Power built a ten-metre log dam and spillway at Upper Kananaskis Lake. The engineers channelized the river between the lakes and, in 1942, raised the dam high enough to drown out all but one of the islands on the upper lake. Just to round out the devastation completely, the company then logged off the area around Lower Kananaskis Lake in the early 1950s and built a dam there, naming the power plant after George Pocaterra.

Pocaterra almost certainly would have been deeply offended. After seeing the devastation resulting from the original dams, he had written:

> The most beautiful mountain scenery in the world, as far as I am concerned, was at these lakes but now is completely spoiled by the power dams, the drowning of the marvelously beautiful islands and exquisitely curved beaches, the cutting down of the centuries old trees, and the drying up of the twin falls between the two lakes, and the falls below the lower lake.

With the 1955 installation of a dam and power plant on the lower lake reservoir, the destruction of the once-idyllic Kananaskis Lakes was complete, and the ruination of the downstream river by pulsing rushes of water began. The famed cutthroat trout of the lower lake soon were only memories, as the reservoir covered over the shallow, gravel-bottomed inlet and outlet streams where my grandfather and other early anglers had caught the fish off their spawning beds.

Repeated attempts to stock hatchery-reared rainbow and cutthroat trout into the new reservoirs failed because these species of trout depend on the biologically productive littoral zone along lake shorelines. With huge – up to 16-metre – seasonal water level fluctuations, unlike anything in nature, the reservoirs have no productive littoral zone, just sterile expanses of cobble and gravel. Stocked trout soon died.

The reservoirs, however, produced new deepwater habitats for fishes that don't rely on shoreline areas. It wasn't long before anglers discovered that inundation had yielded at least one group of winners. The native bull trout, a predatory char, thrived on growing numbers of bottom-feeding suckers and other small minnows whose numbers increased as the reservoir grew. Bull trout can grow to more than a metre in length and ten or 15 kilograms in weight, so they are in demand from trophy fishermen. As word got out, increasing numbers of anglers began to converge on the reservoir. Before heading up Smith-Dorrien Creek to spawn, the large fish would concentrate in late summer in the northwest bay, where they were easily visible in the clear, shallow water. Patient anglers could pick them off one by one. Overfishing appeared likely to wipe out the fishery.

By 1992 only 60 adult bull trout survived in the whole reservoir. Trying to avert disaster, the provincial government brought in new regulations requiring anglers to release any bull trout caught in Lower Kananaskis Lake and to stop using bait, which causes fish to swallow the hook more deeply, so as to improve the survival of the released fish. The lake's northwest bay was closed to angling to protect bull trout that become vulnerable when they mass there before going upstream to spawn. Smith-Dorrien Creek was also permanently closed to protect both spawning trout and the young, growing offspring that remain in the stream for several seasons. Within six years, the breeding population had increased to almost 1300, and today the reservoir again sustains a robust population of Alberta's provincial fish.

In 2001, encouraged by results in the lower lake, Jim Stelfox and his colleagues stocked bull trout into Upper Kananaskis Lake. The newcomers thrived on opossum shrimp and suckers. Gillnetting conducted in 2011 revealed that the proportion of sport fish in the catch had increased 20-fold, partly due to an increase in the

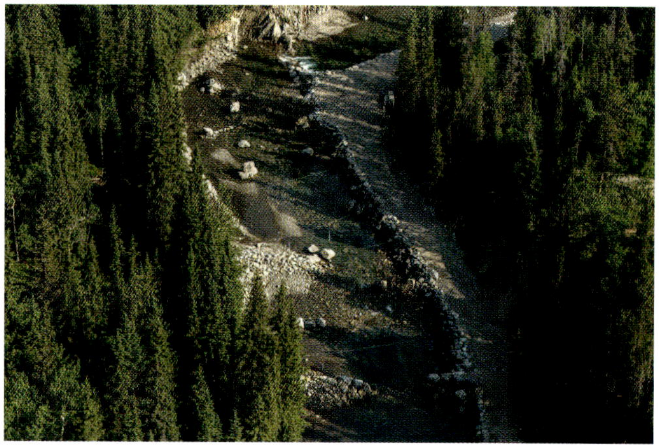

Engineered berms and mid-channel rock placements wait for TransAlta to turn on the Kananaskis River's flow near Canoe Meadows. Daily pulses of water, timed to meet peak power demands, entertain paddlers but devastate the river ecosystem.

density of sport fish (primarily bull trout), but also due to a fourfold decrease in the number of suckers. Anglers today regularly catch, and release, bull trout exceeding 40 centimetres in length.

DOWNSTREAM, where the Kananaskis River used to tumble through the gap between Heart Mountain and Mount Baldy to its final rendezvous with the Bow River, Calgary Power built a third dam in 1947 to create the reservoir now known as Barrier Lake. Together, the three reservoirs are rated as holding a total of 172,000 acre-feet of water, amounting to 30 per cent of the water storage capacity created by dams in the Bow River headwaters. More than half of the stored Kananaskis water is ponded in the Upper Kananaskis Lake reservoir, while Barrier Lake holds only 13 per cent.

Together, the power-generating plants associated with these reservoirs can produce 33 megawatts and account for about 4 per cent of TransAlta's province-wide hydropower capacity. Unfortunately for what remains of the Kananaskis River, however, all three plants are used for "peaking" power. When power consumers need a lot of power in a hurry – for instance, when the city of Calgary wakes up in the morning or, in winter, when consumers get home from work and flick on the house lights, television, microwave and dishwasher all in short order – power companies aren't able to ramp up production quickly enough at the coal-fired plants that produce most of Alberta's electricity. It is considerably easier simply to open up the valve on the hydro plant and pour a lot more water through the turbines to meet sudden peaks in demand.

The river's unnatural behaviour totally discombobulates the river ecosystem. Over the course of most days, the flow level jumps way up during the peak-demand period in the morning, when water is passed through the single turbine at each plant, then plummets when water ceases to be passed through the turbines during midday, then jumps up again during the peak-demand period in the evening, and then plummets again during the night. One moment a group of mayfly nymphs are gripping a midstream boulder, filtering microscopic food particles out of the passing current, and the next moment they are stranded inches above the water line. One moment a trout is leisurely holding behind a stone, and the next moment a turbulent rush of water sends the poor fish rushing for cover. No surprise, then, that few invertebrates or trout actually survive in the main river any more.

Surging flows in the Kananaskis did more than destroy its fishery; they also made the valley unsafe for people who crossed the river to explore its side valleys. Hunters and anglers would wade a shallow river in the morning only to be faced with a rushing torrent when they came back at dusk; the city of Calgary had turned on its lights, and the river's hydropower plants were running at full capacity. Over the years, several elk and sheep hunters were stranded overnight at Galatea Creek or even drowned while attempting the crossing, before a pedestrian bridge was installed. Park status led to a ban on hunting in 2000, when the area became part of Spray Valley Provincial Park; now the bridge saves hikers and climbers.

The unnatural daily oscillations in the Kananaskis River flows devastate the river's ecosystem, but they have become popular with whitewater enthusiasts. Kayakers, rafters and canoeists time their visits to the river based on information TransAlta posts on its website about planned water releases. Elsewhere in North America, as rivers advocate Tim Palmer has pointed out in his writings and during keynote talks he delivered at Alberta's 1987 Flowing to the Future rivers conference, the paddling community has been among the most passionate and determined advocates for dam removals and river restoration. In Alberta, however, paddling groups seem content to see rivers turned into water parks – so much so that in the mid-1980s they lobbied to have large limestone boulders placed into the river bed between Widow Maker and Canoe Meadows. The boulders provide slick water runs and eddies that, when TransAlta turns the river on, guarantee engineered adrenaline rushes for wetsuited paddlers in colourful river craft, unaware or unconcerned that they are paddling a ruined river.

So popular is the artificial whitewater course along the lower Kananaskis River that Alberta Parks and Tourism, which administers Kananaskis Country, arranged in 2008 for Lafarge Canada to donate a further 1500 tonnes of limestone slabs from their quarry on nearby Grotto Mountain to restore the original features that the river had been working hard to reclaim. Five years later, when the massive 2013 spring flood washed out and buried the new boulders, replacing the playground rocks became one of the area's first flood recovery projects. The river's brief attempt to escape control was soon defeated.

It's a beautiful river when the flow is turned on. The headwater lakes – now reservoirs – remove most of the glacial silt that clouds other mountain rivers, leaving the water dark, clear and gleaming with rich greens and blues. Its music is sweet where smooth tongues of swift water split around the grey boulders – certainly as sweet as in more natural rivers. Where waves break and foam into tight, hard eddies, the roar and rush is as wild and rewarding as any kayaker could ask for. It seems so wild and free – but this is an abused and lonely river that has been tortured into domesticity for close to a century. Those who should be its rescuers are barely aware of its suffering and deluded by its continuing beauty into thinking all is well.

IN 1992 THE ALBERTA GOVERNMENT commissioned a Fisheries and Recreation Enhancement Working Group to take a fresh look at TransAlta's hydroelectric facilities in the basin. This was prompted by the near-loss of Lower Kananaskis Lake's bull trout after the river's pulsing flows had already decimated many of the other native fish stocks in the Kananaskis River system, and also by the growing popularity of the valley for nature-based recreation in the wake of the establishment of Kananaskis Country.

In its final report, nearly a decade later, the working group recommended new operating rules for the dam on the lower lake and the Pocaterra power plant, to again give Lower Kananaskis Lake a stable shoreline and restore more stable flows to the downstream river. It predicted that its preferred option would triple the biological productivity of Lower Kananaskis Lake, improve access to and aesthetics of the shoreline area, restore the river's ecological health and reduce winter ice jamming. One variant of this plan additionally restores river flows below the Bassano Dam, where the Bow currently runs nearly dry many years due to irrigation water withdrawals.

The cost of the recommended changes, however, was estimated at around $2 million in lost power revenues annually. Under the revised operating plan, TransAlta would still generate the same amount of electricity, but less would be produced in winter, when high demand yields higher prices. Instead, more power would be generated in the less-lucrative summer season.

The Kananaskis valley, once one of the most beautiful and productive of headwater ecosystems in Alberta, is today a sort of false-front paradise. The expanses of water –

Upper and Lower Kananaskis lakes. Photo: Gail Van Tighem

TRANSALTA'S DAMS AND HYDROPOWER GENERATION FACILITIES IN THE BOW RIVER HEADWATERS

Plant	**Reservoir**	**Primary Supply**	**Installed Capacity** (megawatts)	**Live Reservoir Storage** (cubic decametres)
Cascade	Lake Minnewanka	Cascade River North Ghost River	34	221,900
Spray Group (Three Sisters, Spray & Rundle)	Spray Lake	Spray River Bryant Creek	155	177,600
Interlakes	Upper Kananaskis Lake	Kananaskis River	5	124,500
Pocaterra	Lower Kananaskis Lake	Kananaskis River	15	63,100
Barrier	Barrier Lake	Kananaskis River	13	24,800
Kananaskis	forebay	Bow River	19	n/a
Horseshoe	forebay	Bow River	16	n/a
Ghost	Ghost Lake	Bow River Ghost River	56	92,500
Bearspaw	forebay	Bow River	17	n/a
Bow River upstream from Calgary		**Total**	**330**	**704,400**

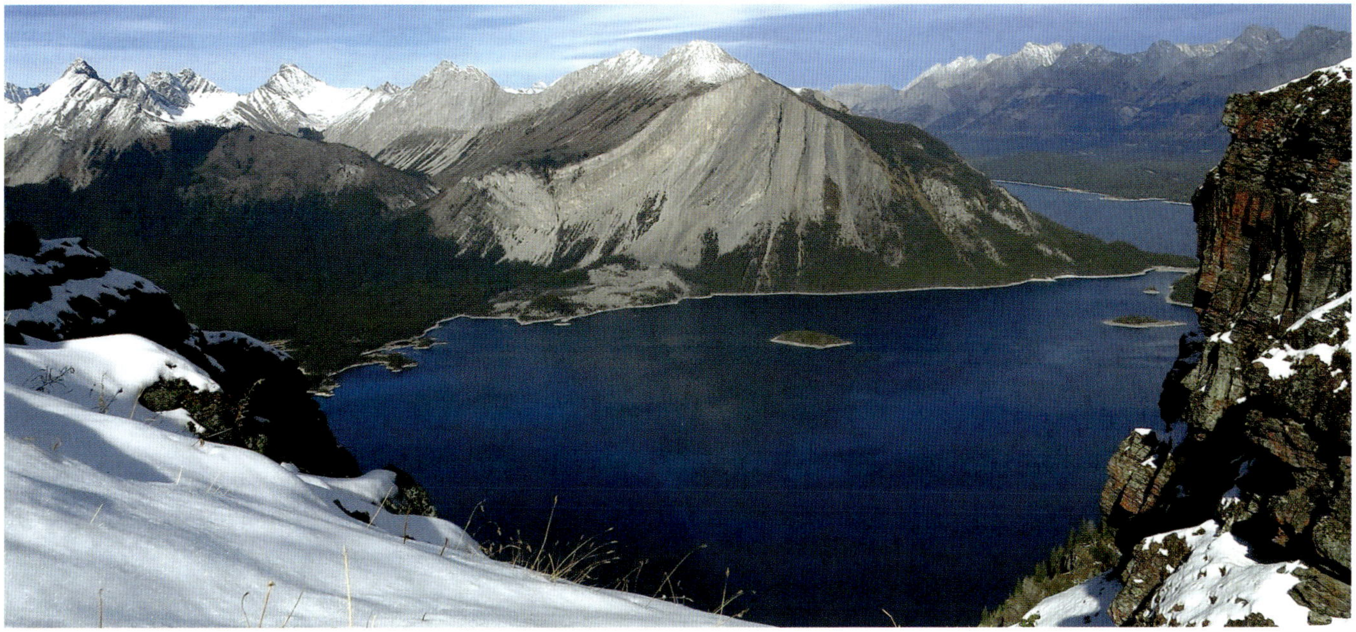

reflecting spectacular mountain arrays, shimmering under morning mists, or glowing in the surreal light of an alpine evening – are reservoirs, not lakes. The lifeless bathtub ring of wave-whipped cobbles that ring those reservoirs most of the year, and the extensive mud flats exposed in spring and early summer, are sad substitutes for the once-healthy shoreline and productive littoral zone bordering the island-pocked lakes that Pocaterra and Edworthy marvelled over. From Highway 40, the Kananaskis Trail, visitors get tantalizing glimpses of a river so lovely that it seems almost idealized – as if nature were imitating art – but it is a sick river whose flows have no logic or pattern that nature can recognize. Its waters are as sweet and cold as the very best of rivers anywhere in the world when they splash over the faces of excited paddlers carving perfect turns into man-made eddies – but that near-lifeless water is controlled by faraway computers, not by nature.

It may be an empty sort of beauty, but that it has persisted in spite of so much engineered abuse offers hope. If Alberta should ever insist that the engineers who control the Kananaskis dams reprogram their operations to restore more normal flow patterns to the downstream river and to maintain stable water levels in the reservoirs – the way nature had done for thousands of years before the first power planner arrived in the valley – that illusion could become reality.

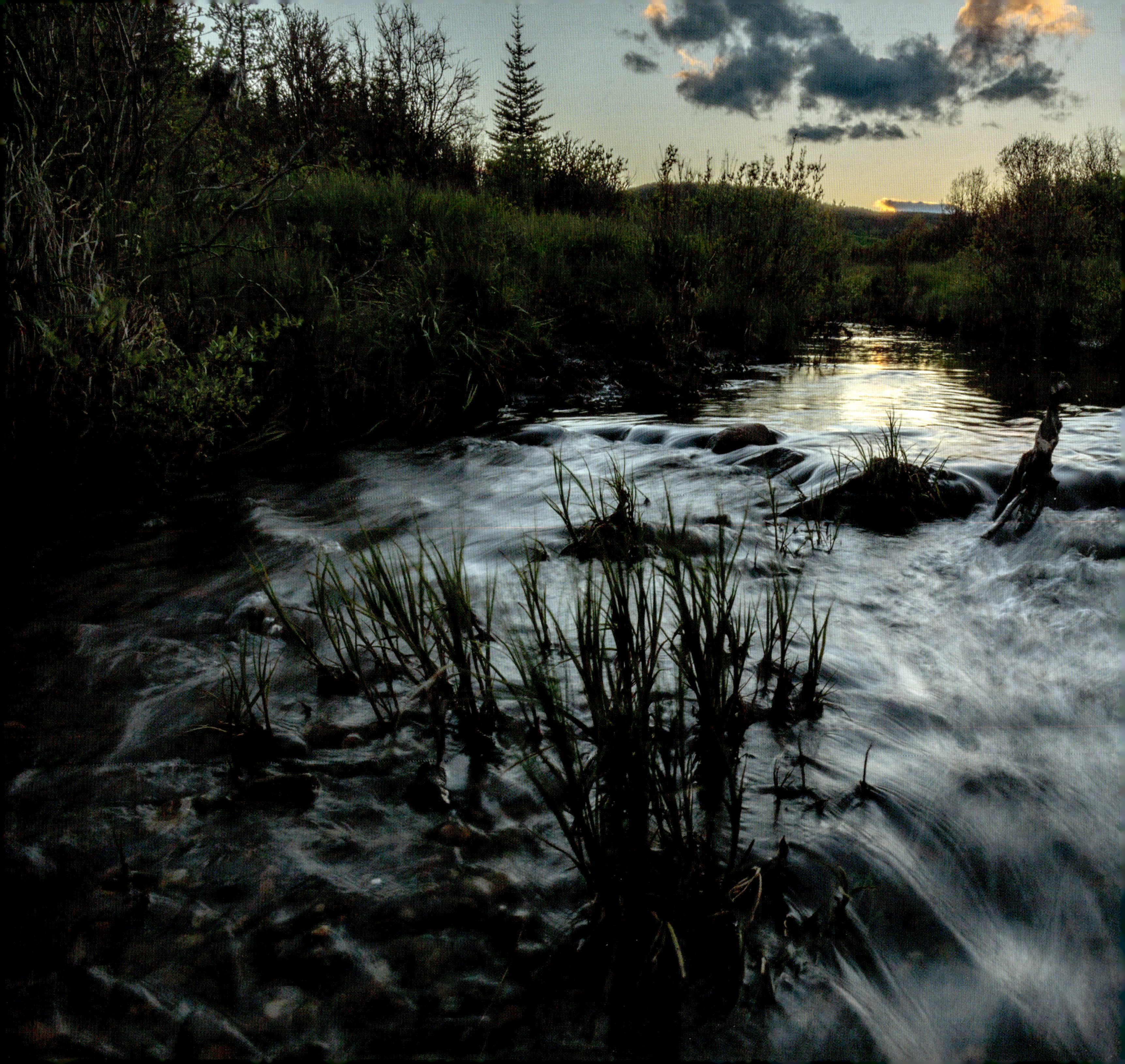

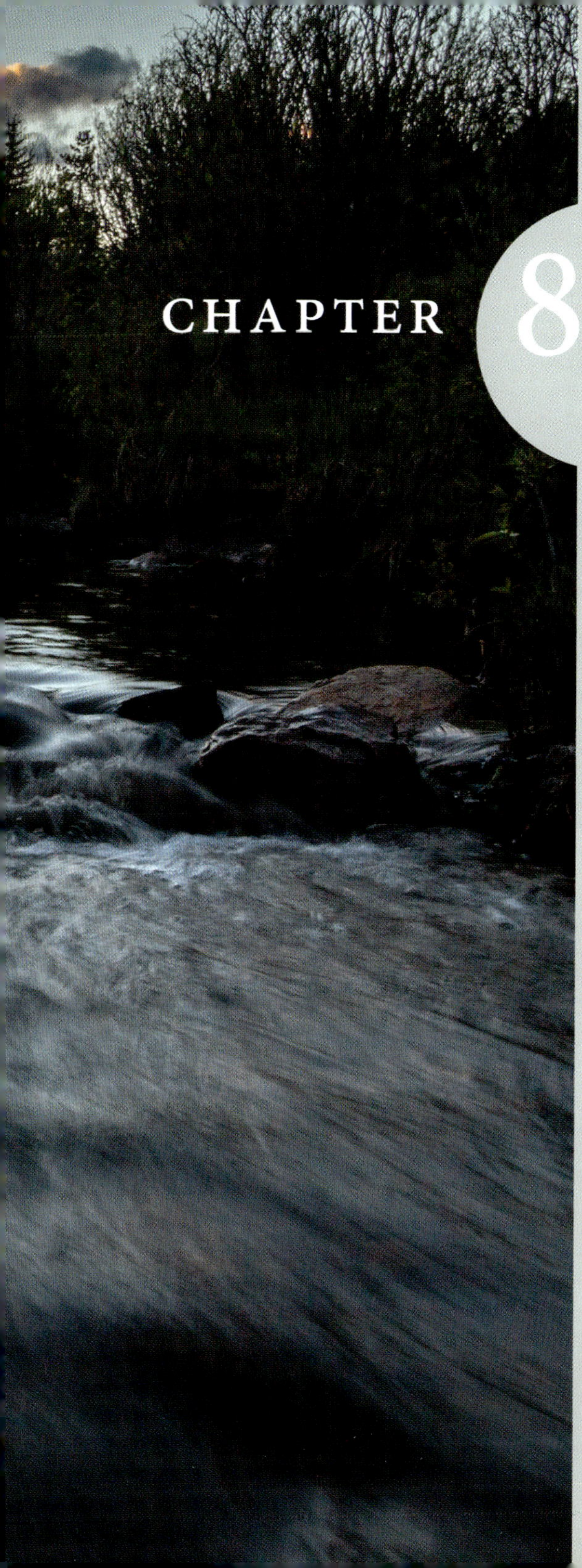

CHAPTER 8

Buck-Toothed Volunteers

Bateman Creek

EARLY-MORNING BEAVER PONDS discourage visitors. The air is cold and damp. Sedges and willows are silvered with dew and whine with mosquitoes. Shadows are dark beneath the trees; it feels like unfriendly creatures may lurk there.

Not until the sun has cleared the easterly ridgetops, and the morning chorus of kinglet, yellowthroat, robin and redwing song has chased the gloom from the woods, do the first human visitors usually appear. If it's a foothills beaver pond, chances are the visitor will be an angler hoping to catch a trout.

The morning shift is over by then. Come a bit earlier, in that chilly dawn half-light, and lines of smooth ripples may betray activity back where the water has flooded the willows. The beavers at work there are undaunted by early-morning discomforts, although they remain constantly vigilant for wolves, bears and other prowlers. Like brown cursors dragging v-shaped waves across the pond's glassy screen, those daybreak beavers quietly add to their underwater stockpiles of willow and aspen branches, build and repair their dams and deepen their swimming channels. Move quietly and stay well

Page 110: *Bateman Creek*

Right: *Beavers work incessantly to keep their dams in good repair, as well as digging swimming channels and storing branches underwater for winter food.* Photo: Mike Kelly

Far right: *The roots of willows are like living rebar, binding beaver dams together and helping them stand against spring floodwaters.*

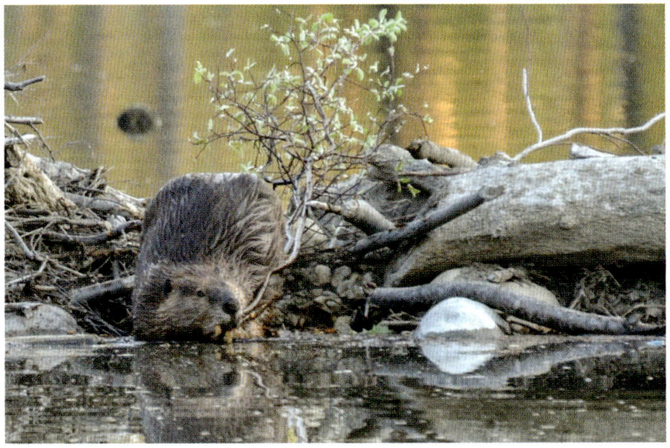

back, and they might tolerate your presence; make yourself too obtrusive, and chances are that a sudden loud crack will shatter the stillness as the nearest beaver alerts the rest of the colony to danger, and the show will be over.

Not that it's a show. Beavers have serious work to do. The fact that we find it fascinating to watch means nothing to them; their labours are about food, safety and winter survival. They spend a great deal of each year ensuring that their ponds are full, their winter food supply sunken deep enough that it won't freeze solid during the coming winter, and their swimming channels deep enough to keep them out of the reach of predators.

In the process of taking care of their own needs, however, beavers serve the interests of countless others, too. That daybreak chorus of wetland-loving songbirds wouldn't exist in the absence of the wetland mosaic of tree thickets, shrubbery and sedgy meadow that develops upstream of each beaver dam. In midsummer, as the surrounding hills become increasingly sere, deer, elk, moose and bears forage along the edges of the ponds, where stored water keeps vegetation green and lush. Fishes, frogs, dragonfly nymphs and countless other aquatic creatures find abundant food in the sun-warmed water behind the dam during summer, and then survive the winter in unfrozen deep spots.

Dr. Glynnis Hood, an ecology professor at the University of Alberta, did her Ph.D. research on beaver ponds in central Alberta. She found that the compulsive dam building and channel digging of Canada's national mammal has benefits that span whole landscapes and extend over many years. Beavers, by building and maintaining their dams, store water not just in the ponds they back up but in the peaty margins and adjoining soils. During drought years, even when other wetlands dry up, beaver complexes retain water, both because their dams hold back so much in the first place and because beavers dig their swimming channels deeper as the water table declines, ensuring that there is always open water. Beavers, in effect, droughtproof the landscape.

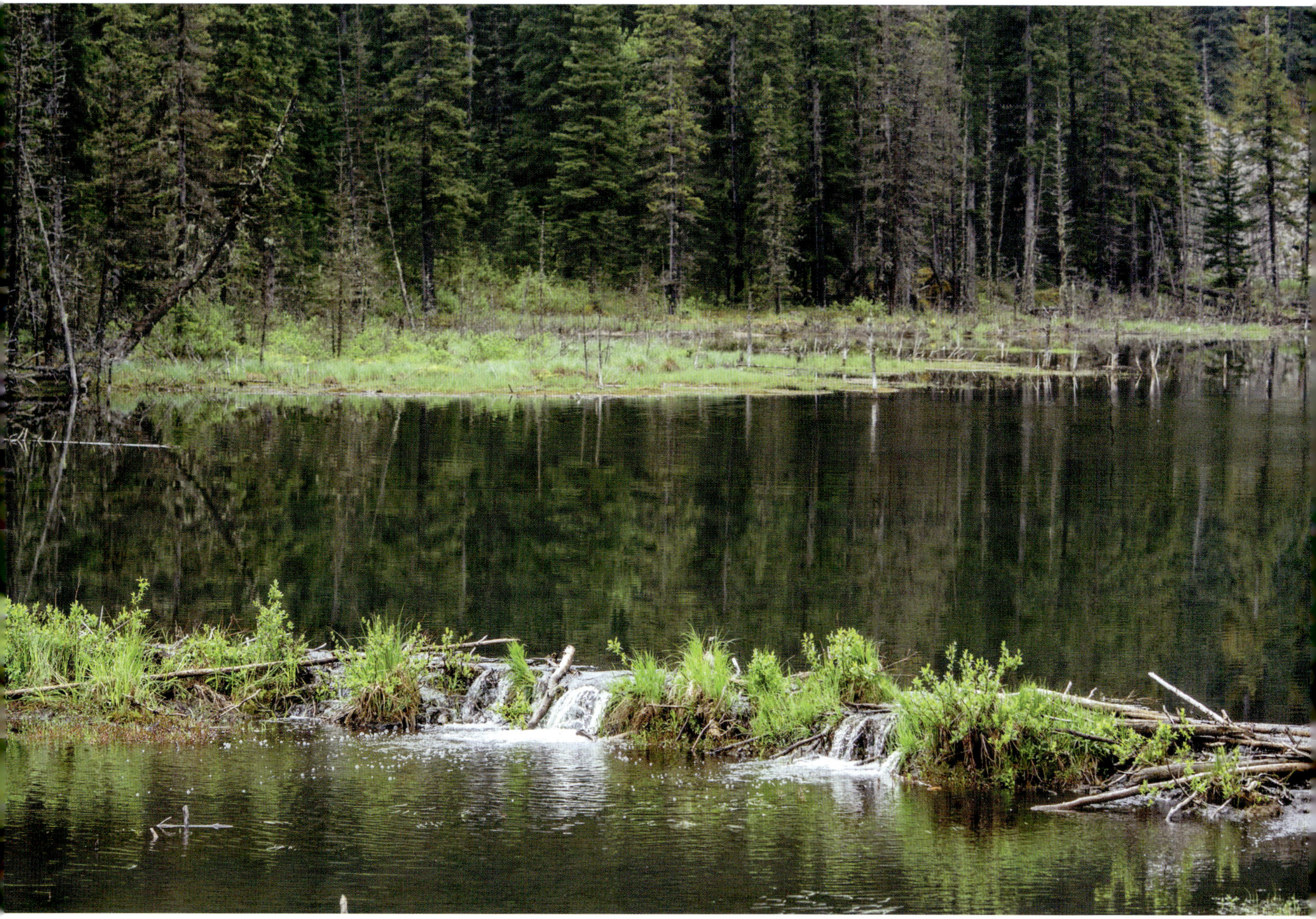

Hood was able to locate a set of 1950 air photos from her Elk Island National Park study area. Beavers had all been trapped out a few years before those pictures were taken. Most of the wetlands were dry. When she looked at air photos from 2002, however, she found 61 per cent more open water, even though that year was by the far the driest on record: barely half as much rain and snow fell in 2002 as in 1950. The difference: beavers that had returned to the area during the intervening years had rebuilt the wetlands and raised the regional water table.

The ability of beavers to keep a landscape wet even when the rains are disappointing is no secret to long-time foothills ranchers. During an interview at his home ranch, Gordon Cartwright told me:

> My parents reintroduced beavers into the upper Pekisko watershed in the early 1950s, with problem beavers they got from the Forest Service. Beavers now store water in all the small tributaries that used to dry up in summers. That helps to maintain the water table. Beavers are why there is water in Dickson Coulée now. In the 1970s and 1980s, a trapper from the Nanton area came in and harvested about 50 beavers each year out of the main creek. That population control helped keep the beavers balanced with their food supply and kept them out of the main creek, where there were fishery and flood concerns.

Other ranchers told me how they always make sure that trappers leave at least a few beavers untrapped on their property as drought insurance. If the following year is dry, cattle can at least find water in the beaver ponds.

Dr. John Pomeroy, director of the University of Saskatchewan Centre for Hydrology, bases his research out of the centre's Coldwater Laboratory in the Kananaskis valley. He says that the cumulative effect of many small beaver dams on water storage is similar to that of one large engineered dam, but with few of the negative side effects. Wetlands, like those formed by beaver ponds, give landscapes "hydrological memory." Elk Island National Park had flowing streams throughout the 1980s drought, even while surrounding areas went dry. The effect of stored water in prairie wetlands can persist for up to six years; this is particularly meaningful since few droughts last more than four or five years.

Biologist Lorne Fitch says that the value of beaver colonies both for flood control and drought mitigation is far greater than most people realize. He points out that not only have beavers been found to increase the amount of open water by almost 10 per cent in some drainages, they store five to ten times as much water underground. When beavers move into a stream, their dams can eventually increase stream flow by 200 to 1000 per cent. But since the dams can also make the effective floodplain up to 12 times as wide as it was before, the increased flows don't translate to bigger floods. It's the size of a stream's floodplain that determines how fast its flood flows drain out; beavers reduce flooding by enlarging the floodplain.

Beaver pond complexes and other wetlands recharge shallow aquifers, which are the source of the springs and seeps that sustain stream flows through late summer and winter, when snowmelt is no longer available. Anywhere from 25 to 45 per cent of total stream flows in Alberta comes from groundwater discharge into the active channel. Jumpingpound Creek, in fact, gets almost two-thirds of its flow from groundwater springs sustained in part by beaver dams on tributaries like Sibbald, Bateman, Bryant and Little Jumpingpound creeks.

The ability of beavers to turn fast-draining valleys into spongy reservoirs is no recent discovery. Biologist Constance Hunt worked for the National Wildlife Federation for many years as an advocate for river restoration. She points out that Aboriginal tribes in the semi-arid desert uplands of Arizona used to weave barriers of seep willow, burrobrush and mesquite and anchor them to streamside trees to slow the streams and encourage sediment deposition. These man-made beaver dams anchored the riparian fields that the Native people used for agriculture – just one example of how Aboriginal cultures studied nature to learn how to sustain their societies. Hunt says we would do well to emulate them:

> Introducing beavers into headwater streams can indirectly increase summer flows, so long as riparian vegetation is present to provide the animals with building materials for dams and food. Installing small water-spreading dams can produce the same effect. Small dams on headwater streams, whether created by man or beaver, increase summer flows, possibly because they increase the zone of saturation within the valley bottom. Beaver dams also reduce the ability of small streams to transport sediment by reducing the gradient and velocity of the streams. Deposition of sediment raises the elevation of the water table and the water table's ability to store water for much of the growing season.

CANADA IS A COUNTRY FOUNDED in absurdity – hats built our nation. It was the European taste for fine felt hats made from the outer covering of an aquatic rodent that drove the colonial exploration, border skirmishes, Aboriginal treaties and settlement patterns that gave rise to our nation. The beaver is the central element of Canada's coat of arms and our national symbol. Revisionists like to suggest that the beaver represents the best attributes of our national character – industrious, co-operative, humble and persistent – but the truth is that the defining characteristic of the beaver that gave rise to Canada was its fine, dense inner fur. That was what the hat makers of Europe would pay top dollar for. Men's fashion made Canada possible.

Glynnis Hood, in her *Beaver Manifesto*, has chronicled some of the consequences of that long-lasting fashion trend to the ecology of the North American continent. The first Europeans to land on North American shores didn't find the rich spices and precious metals that they'd hoped to discover. Instead they found a treasure trove of beavers, an animal already trapped to near extinction back home. They also found people whom they chose to call Indians even though the new continent was not India. Those indigenous people had a strong trading tradition and intimate knowledge of the travel-ways and resources of the new land. It wasn't long before cooking pots, glass beads and other goodies of European manufacture were being exchanged for the stretched skins of an animal that the bemused Indians had never really considered to have any particular commercial value.

As the fur trade extinguished one beaver population

after another, it swept west and north into the continent's interior in the search for more. The British-based Hudson's Bay Company organized and for many years controlled the fur trade throughout much of what would eventually become Canada, until challenged by the more entrepreneurial and adventurous North West Company. The competition led to the establishment of forts in the North Saskatchewan, Athabasca and Peace drainages that would eventually become thriving Alberta cities. One of those cities is Edmonton.

The fur trade was a more furtive venture in the Bow River headwaters because the tribes of the Blackfoot Confederacy – the Siksika, Piikani and Kainai – were primarily a prairie people concerned more with bison than with beavers. Having watched other Aboriginal groups displaced from their homes, suffered from the spread of European diseases and witnessed the double-dealing and murder that accompanied the spread of white people into the American West, they were determined to hold on to their traditional lands and resist change as long as they could. Trappers had to deliver their fur to Rocky Mountain House on the North Saskatchewan because it wasn't safe to establish a trading post along the Bow. Commerce had to wait for the arrival of the North West Mounted Police in Calgary late in the 19th century, by which time the fur trade had crashed as silk eclipsed beaver as the height of fashion for hat making.

Beavers had occupied the headwaters of the Bow for more than 10,000 years by the time the first one stepped into a steel trap. Over the course of those many centuries, their dams built stair-step wetlands up most of the region's low-gradient streams. Some dam complexes had been in place so long that the wetlands had filled with peat and silt, becoming lush, sub-irrigated grass meadows or shrubby forests. Small creeks flowed out of countless small coulees that would have been dry in summer if pioneering beavers, many centuries earlier, hadn't dammed the spring runoff at the mouth of the coulee and their offspring then moved incrementally farther up the coulee to dam the spring runoff even higher, until what had been an ephemeral stream flowing only during spring runoff became a perennial stream spilling from one wetland to the next.

Nobody can say how many beavers occupied the headwaters before the fur trade led to their near-extirpation in the 19th century. Alasdair Morrison, a University of Saskatchewan Centre for Hydrology graduate student, used air photos to map wetlands in Kananaskis Country and then followed up with ground surveys to look for evidence of current or historic beaver activity. He found that at least a third of the wetlands in the headwaters are associated with beaver activity. But that sort of study doesn't take into account the many fens, meadows and spruce hollows that, having lost their beaver populations a century and a half ago, now appear simply to be lush riparian areas along chattering little creeks. Nor does it take into account the many small side drainages that have gone dry for lack of the workaholic little animals that used to trap their spring freshets and hold the water year-round. Glynnis Hood suggests that the loss of beavers came so early in our history, and was so extensive, that we can barely begin to imagine the degree to which their original abundance once shaped the landscape. Natural

Streambank erosion reveals alternating layers of stream gravels, peat and silt from the bottoms of past beaver ponds, evidence of how beavers have raised the valley floor over many centuries.

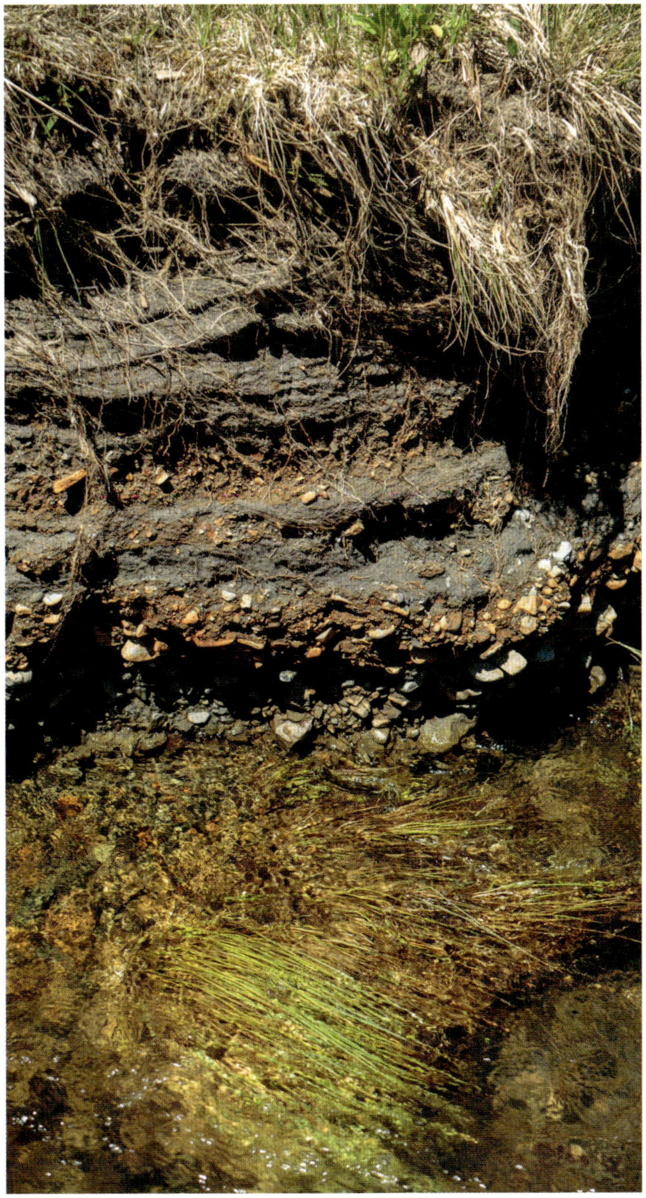

processes of forest succession and stream down-cutting have obscured much of the evidence. Encouraging beavers to return to their former ranges would be one way to find out.

Beaver hats are an anachronism now, but there is still a commercial market for beaver furs. Combined with trapping for other furs – lynx, marten, fisher, mink and coyote – it's lucrative enough to support some full-time trappers in northern and west-central Alberta. Most of the trapping in the East Slopes of the Rockies, however, is now a part-time recreational activity. It appeals to those with a nostalgic affinity for the frontier and a desire to develop woods skills and the intimate connection to nature that comes with the challenge of becoming a successful predator. Arguably an activity that maintains a set of skills and relationships that have long been part of the character of our nation has cultural value. But it's still a hobby. That makes it optional.

It's a hobby that keeps beaver populations suppressed. Province-wide, Alberta's trappers kill from 10,000 to 14,000 beavers each year. In Fur Management Area 6, which includes the Bow River's headwaters, the take is lower: depending on fur prices, it ranges from as low as 40 to as high as 730. Based on trapper records maintained by Alberta's Fish & Wildlife Division, the average kill between 1985 and 2012 was 265. Every one of those

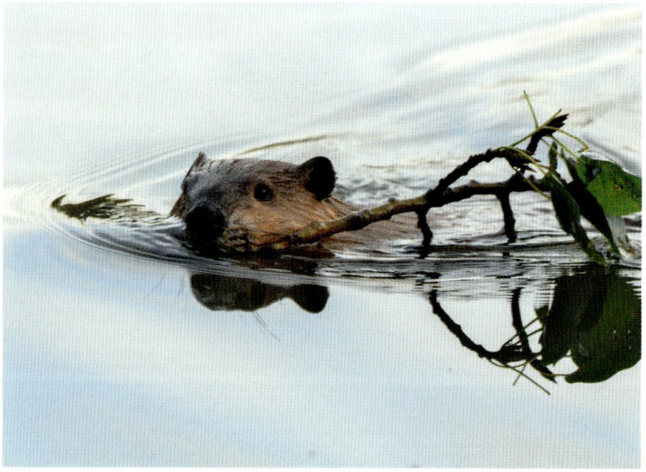

Left: *Beavers work incessantly to keep their dams in good repair, as well as storing branches underwater for winter food.* Photo: Mike Kelly

Right: *Saturated soils around beaver ponds develop lush meadows and willow thickets while storing copious groundwater long after the slopes above have begun to dry.*

beavers, if left alive, would have spent thousands of hours working to keep water in the headwaters. Dead, a beaver buys a day or two of fuel for the trapper's truck. In a region that alternates between extreme floods and extended droughts because of rapid drainage from the headwaters, that seems a questionable exchange.

DR. CHERIE WESTBROOK'S interest in beavers is driven less by curiosity about their ecology than by an interest in how they change headwaters hydrology. Although she is a hydrologist with the University of Saskatchewan Centre for Hydrology, Westbrook and her students study beavers in Bateman Creek, a tributary of Jumpingpound Creek, west of Calgary.

Westbrook's graduate research was near Estes Park, Colorado. She measured water storage both in the open-water channels behind dams in Rocky Mountain National Park and in the adjoining landscape along valleys with active beaver colonies. Not surprisingly, she learned that groundwater levels were elevated not only adjacent the ponds and up the nearby slopes, but also well downstream. The dams stored as much groundwater as a 1-in-200-year flood – but without flood impacts.

Westbrook shifted her attention to Bateman Creek in 2006 – a timely choice, as it turned out. When a massive flood drained out of the Front Ranges of the Alberta Rockies in June 2013, she and her students had amassed a considerable amount of baseline data against which to evaluate the effect of the flood on the creek's beaver dams, as well as the effect of the dams on the flood.

At least one previous study had shown that beavers don't just ameliorate drought conditions but also help to reduce the power of floods. Graham Hillman was studying the effects of logging near Rocky Creek, a tributary of the Simonette River, when a beaver dam broke during a period of extended rains in June 1994, possibly because it had been weakened by muskrats burrowing into it in the weeks preceding the rains.

The dam failure sent an estimated nine thousand cubic metres of water, mud and vegetation down the valley,

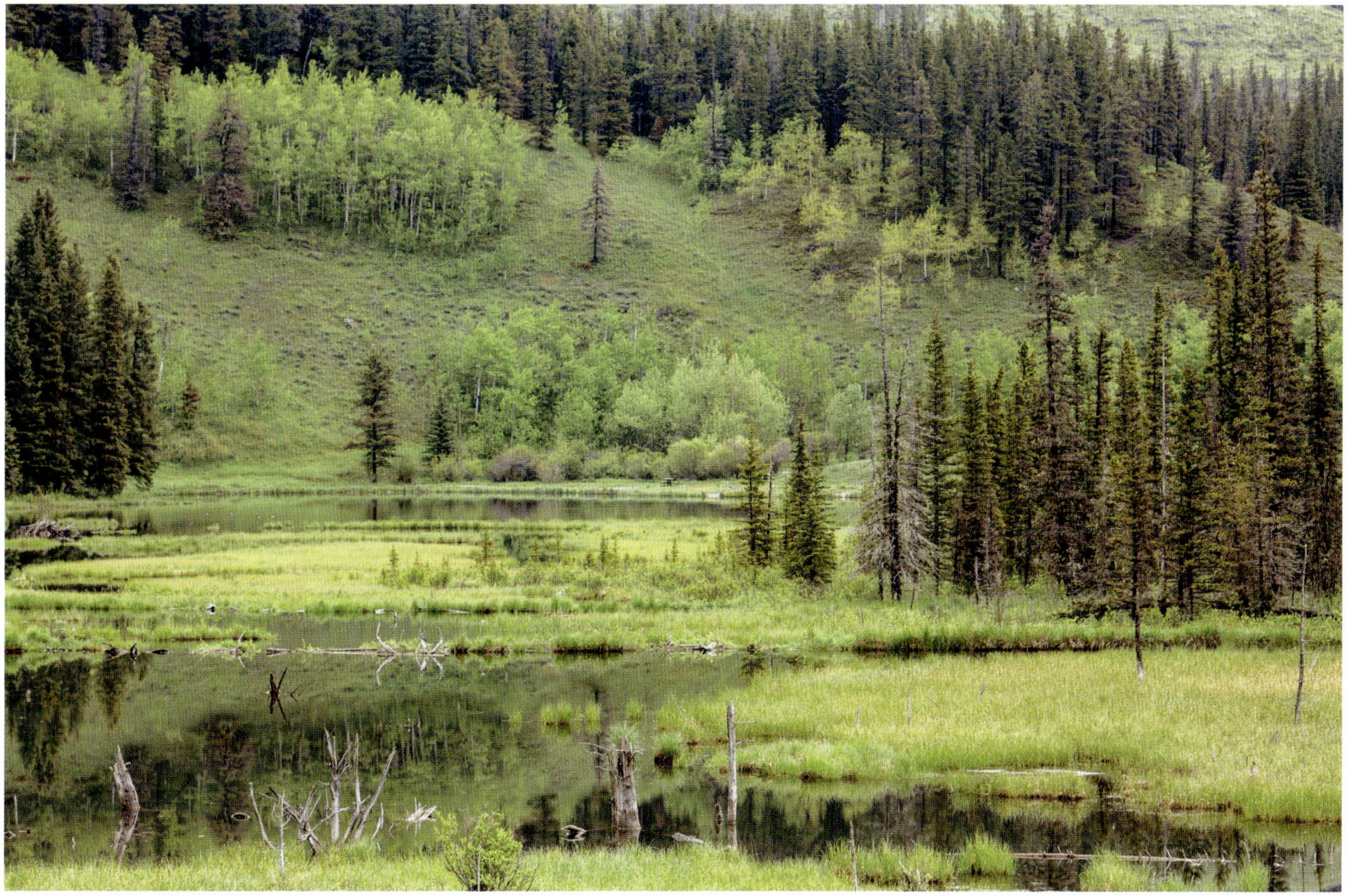

washing out five hydrometric stations along the creek. It was a massive flood that scoured out almost two kilometres of stream channel and spilled far up into the surrounding trees. Even so, it had virtually vanished within five kilometres – because of the effects of a series of downstream beaver ponds in a wetland complex that had developed as the result of thousands of years of beaver activity. When the flood wave hit the wetlands, it spread out and slowed, trapping much of the water and sediment behind beaver dams rather than flushing it downstream.

Hillman's flood was caused by a beaver dam's collapse – but it was a downstream wetland created by beaver activity that quickly absorbed and dissipated it. Nobody camped beside the confluence of Rocky Creek and the Simonette River would even have known that a record-breaking flood had been heading their way a few kilometres upstream; it never got there.

THE TWO RESEARCHERS who preceded me up the marshy edge of the Bateman Creek valley smelled like mosquito repellent and were clad in chest-high waders. Those waders should have warned me what was coming; my hiking boots were soon slimy with mud and my pants slopping against my legs. The trail into the research site was a narrow swath through waist-deep sedges. Black muck showed through trampled green stems, and the track was a ribbon of muddy water. After the first time my foot punched through to the soupy peat beneath, I walked gingerly, trying to levitate my way past the orange-flagged markers and protruding polyvinyl chloride pipes where Dan Karran and his colleagues, graduate students working under Cherie Westbrook's supervision, had pulled long cores of sediment out of the valley floor in an effort to unravel its history.

When I caught up to Karran and his summer assistant, they were about to stop for lunch beside a partially drained beaver pond. Thirteen months earlier, during the June 2013 flood, the dam had been partially breached. Already, however, the muddy pond bottom was a blanket of green wetland plants colonizing the rich mud the dam's failure had opened up to them.

Half a metre of water was still pooled in a trench along the upstream face of the dam. Dan explained that the beavers had excavated pond mire there to build the dam, leaving a deepened moat that now captured part of the creek's desultory flow. Even liberated by the breach in the dam, the creek still ran sluggishly here because the valley floor is nearly flat, tilting gradually toward the valley of Jumpingpound Creek a couple kilometres away. Besides, another dam a few metres downstream still blocked the flow. As Dan put it:

> When a pond fills, it creates hydraulic head. That tends to drive water under the dam, where it can undermine the whole thing. So you'll often see a sort of stair-step profile where the beavers have built one dam below another to reduce the upstream pressure. They are deliberately slowing drainage from the upstream dam, and it slows down the whole movement of groundwater through the valley at the same time as it raises the water table, not just along the valley floor but up the sides.

"I think this entire valley was completely transformed by beavers since the beginning of the Holocene," Dan said, pointing out lines of willows running in graceful curves across the valley at various angles, marking abandoned dams of varying vintages. Pointing to a nearby rise dense with willow shrubbery, he said, "That whole hill is a fen. It's full of peat and groundwater. I can't think how it could have gotten there except that we're looking at an old beaver complex perched above this one."

Dan's vertical cores of the valley floor reveal microcosmic slices of the landscape's history. His challenge is to cross-correlate them enough to weave together a story of how the valley evolved. It isn't easy; when beaver dams originally built at right angles to the stream eventually fail, they become stream banks that divert the flow at a right angle to its previous direction. Sometimes dams fail at both ends and the stream temporarily splits, each channel going in a different direction. Then the beavers dam one or both new channels, creating new ponds that eventually drain out, diverting the creek yet again. Dams, ponds and creek channels are overlaid on one another in an almost impossibly complicated maze.

Dams fail, usually, because they lose their beavers. Trappers, wolves or other predators may kill the beavers, or the animals may simply use up the most easily accessible food supply and move somewhere else. Some of the ponds in Dan's study area were still full of water, but the beavers were gone; the rodents were most active in the east branch of the stream this year. Even without beavers to maintain them, their old dams, reinforced by the living roots of willows and slough grasses, still held water.

> What we're finding is really interesting. Some of the cores go through peat, then silt with snail shells and carbonate marl in it, then sometimes a band of gravel that's clearly from the creek bed, but then below that you find more peat. So there were times when the creek was flowing and could build up a gravelly bed, but that was laid overtop of the peat that came from vegetation invading an older beaver pond.

At one site, Dan's auger suddenly dropped almost a metre and a half. He had punched into a buried lens of water. It was startling, but not completely a surprise.

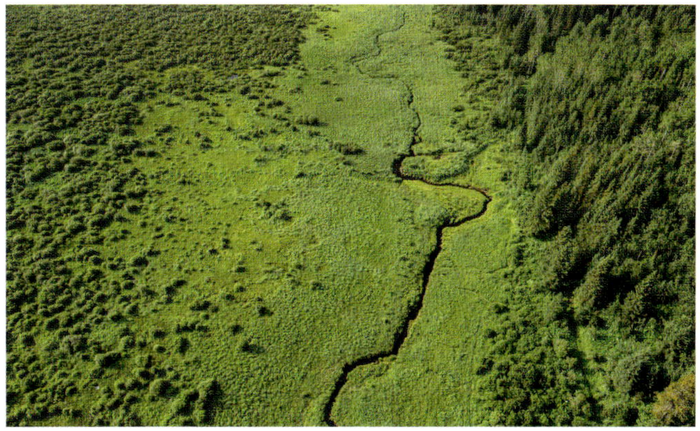

Upper Bateman Creek flows through a landscape formed by past beaver activity. Abundant willows are evidence of the high water table in the fen meadows.

> Wetland ecologists talk about "terrestrialization." When beavers abandon a pond but the dam doesn't breach, then you get a standing pool of water the height of the dam. Without beavers to maintain the pond, peat starts to creep out on the open water as mats of sedge and other plants spread.

Eventually the pond is completely covered with a living mat of vegetation. The peat – which is simply undecomposed vegetable matter – becomes thicker each year as more roots grow and die. Karran's auger had evidently punched into one of those peat-covered ponds that had subsequently been buried below the silt bottom of a more recent beaver pond.

> I think beavers have actually changed the elevation

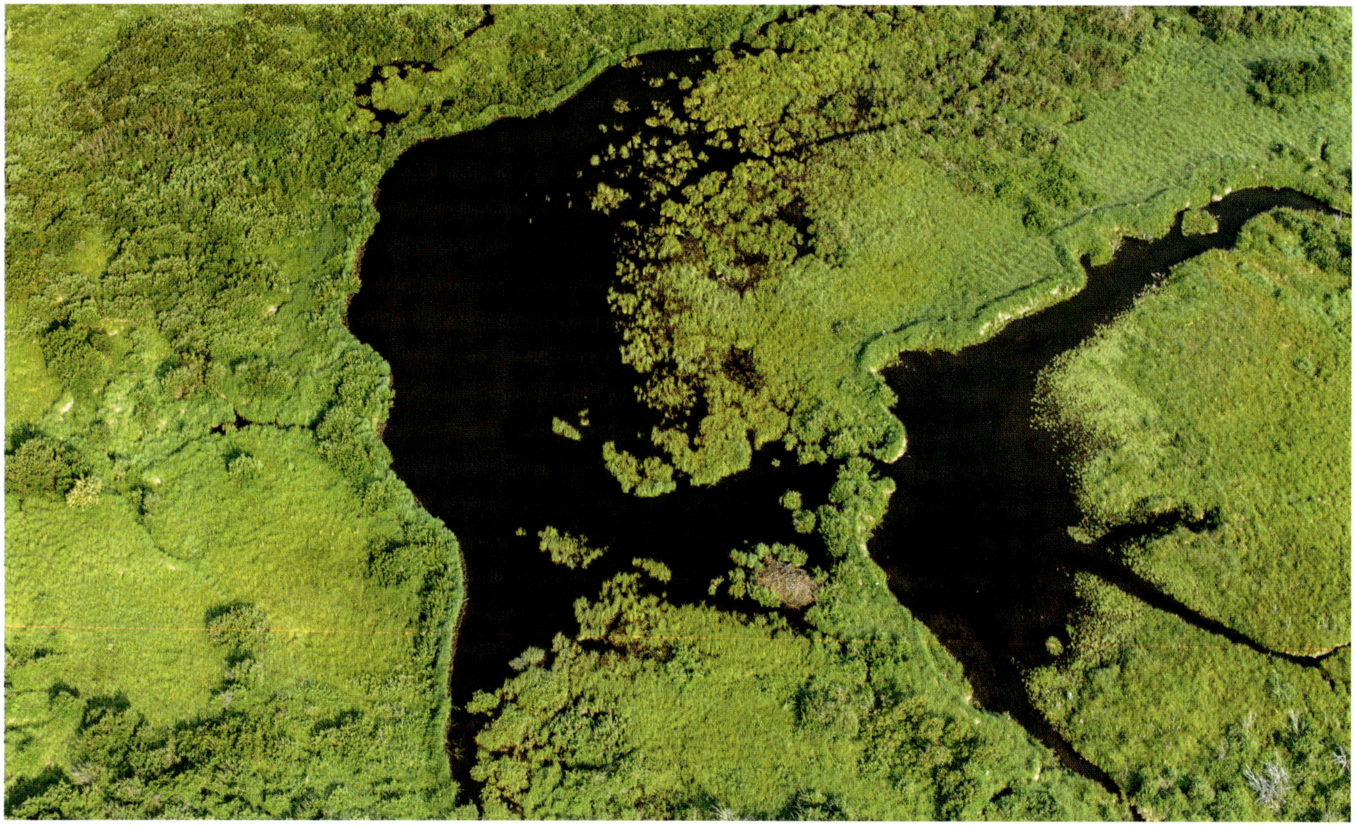

of this valley. It's higher, wider and more gently sloped than it was a few thousands of years ago. If what I'm beginning to suspect is true, then what we've postulated in the past about beaver landscapes and the role that beavers have played in building the floodplains and valley floors all through the foothills barely begins to scratch the surface of how important a role they've actually played.

After the glaciers retreated from the foothills about 12,000 to 15,000 years ago, the valleys went through a period of peat formation as wetland vegetation invaded the shallow lakes and saturated soils along the edges of the receding ice. Eventually willows and other woody plants were able to get a toehold in the peaty soils and valley edges; not long after that, the first beavers appeared on the scene. They have been working to keep water from

Active beaver ponds in the peatland meadows of Bateman Creek, tributary to Jumpingpound Creek.

escaping those valleys ever since. Thousands of years after the first dam appeared along a foothills creek, today's valleys are living reservoirs of groundwater trapped in layers of silt, peat and gravel where the big aquatic rodents redesigned the postglacial landscape into a mosaic of open water, sedge meadows, shrub thickets and forests. And where they can evade trappers and four-legged predators, they are still hard at it.

THE HEAVY, SUSTAINED RAINS that drenched the Bow River headwaters in the spring of 2013 didn't spare Westbrook's and Karran's study watershed. The most intense flooding was along rivers in whose headwaters the rain fell on mountain snowpack. No snow remained in the Bateman Creek drainage, but close to two hundred millimetres of rain over two days was more than enough to send water streaming down every hillside and draw to the grassy peat meadows along the normally placid foothills creek.

Native fescue grassland of the kind that carpets the hillsides along Bateman Creek is dense with tangled greenery. The fescue itself is a bunchgrass that forms large tussocks. Each year, dead grass stems accumulate at the base, forming a thatch of fibrous material. Close to one hundred other native species of plant, from *Tortula ruralis* – a bristly little moss that carpets the soil in places – to shooting stars, wheatgrasses, sticky purple geraniums, wild strawberries, pea vines and vetches, contribute to the tangled web of interconnected life that comprises Alberta's signature type of grassland. Their living green parts and the decaying remains of last year's growth make the grassland spongy and resistant to water flow.

Pine and aspen forest on the surrounding hills temporarily slowed the sheeting rain, but the deluge soon overwhelmed the tree canopy's resistance. On the forest floor, water adhered to understory vegetation and soaked the organic duff, but within an hour or so all was drenched. The rain kept coming. Within a few hours the forest soil was soaked, forcing the water to run off overland.

At the forests' margins the overland flow drained into fescue grassland already heavy with water. Like a living sponge, the tangled, thatchy grassland slowed the runoff even more, giving it more time to seep into the soil, but still the rain continued. Soon, little rivulets of clear water were draining everywhere through the vegetation, down to the valley floor. Converging there, all the overland flow slowed as it hit the flatter areas that had been built up by millennia of beaver activity. The pooling water grew deep among the sedges and willows. Where only hours ago there had been a carpet of green, soon the rain was slashing into standing pools of water. The pools coalesced and overflowed, draining into the centre of the drainage, where Bateman Creek, already swollen with water farther upstream, was turning brown and grim. The creek needed more room to hold so much water, and the water gave it the power to make more room by eroding its banks at the outside of each bend.

But Bateman Creek's beaver-maintained riparian zone is thick with greenery, its peaty floodplain stitched together by living tangles of fibrous roots that protected the soil along most of the creek from the hungry water. Unable to open up a bigger channel, the creek overflowed its banks and spilled across the floodplain, a temporary sea of brown water pouring down the green valley toward the first in the string of beaver dams along its upper reaches.

There the flood slowed. Beavers had put a flood barrier in the way. The water spread out against the dam, growing deeper. Deprived of the energy of gravity's downward pull, the creek became marginally less dirty as the coarsest of the silt and mud it was carrying settled to the bottom of the pond: another year's contribution to the valley floor. But then the flood wave overwhelmed the dam and began to pour over the tangle of sticks, mud and living vegetation into the wetland below.

Another dam not far below the first again forced the water to pause and pool and spread, but again it soon exceeded the capacity of the pond and spilled over the dam in a dozen places. Again it left some of its eroded sediment load behind. The willow branches that the beavers had woven into their dam worked like the living roots in the stream bank, armouring the structure's softer mud and gravel against the erosive force of the flood. The dam stood.

With each downstream beaver dam that delayed the release of Bateman Creek's flood waters, the flow swelled even more. The last beaver pond the stream encountered was the biggest, not far upstream from Sibbald Lake, a popular fishing and picnicking destination in the

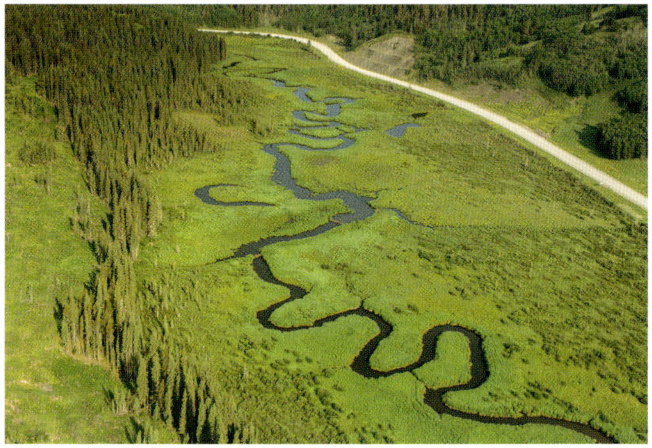

Sibbald Creek. Where beaver dams reduce the gradient of streams, the channels become sinuous and deep, and water migrates laterally into the valley-bottom soils.

Right*: A beaver pond stores water in the open channel but also in the wetland soils from one side of the valley to the other.*

Jumpingpound drainage. Because the pond was bigger, it could absorb more of the flood water. Because it absorbed more of the water, the pressure on the dam was greater and – when the rising water finally overtopped the dam – the erosive force was greater. Unlike the upstream dam, this one failed beneath the onslaught. The sticks and mud of the dam, and a good portion of the accumulated mud from the centre of the pond, went with a roar into the churning flood waters. Bateman Creek would brook no further delay: it was on its way to the Bow.

Although the 2013 flood waters breached the lowest dams in Westbrook's study area, the upstream complex of

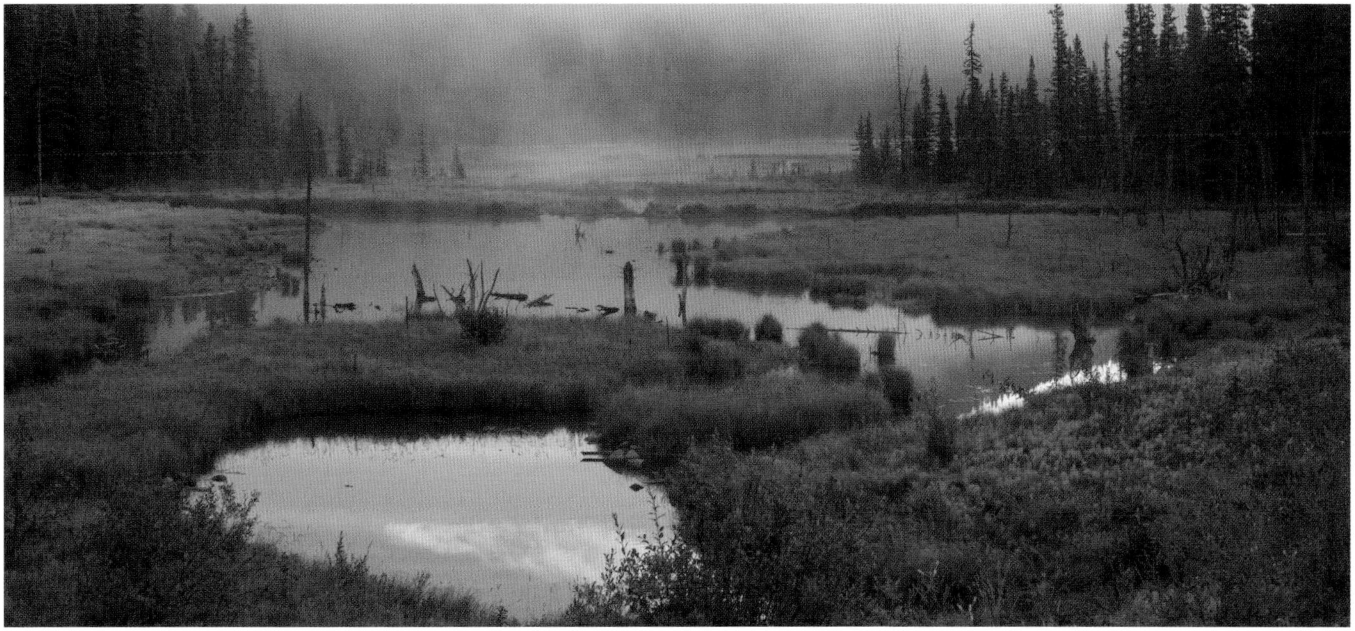

dams retarded the flood flows. Beaver dams on nearby Sibbald Creek, Bryant Creek and the Little Jumpingpound also did their part in holding back the runoff. Had there been no beavers in those valleys, the streams would have drained far more rapidly to Jumpingpound Creek, and its flood crest would have been considerably higher. By holding back the flow as long as they did, those dams also enabled more of the water to soak into the silty floors of the creek valleys, recharging the groundwater aquifer beneath rather than adding to the flooding above. For all the flood damage that Cochrane and Calgary experienced, it would have been worse without upstream beaver dams. More beaver dams would likely have reduced the flood peak even more, but trappers had taken out a lot of the maintenance crew during the previous winter.

The 2013 flooding cost Alberta more than $6 billion. Much of that money went to highly paid engineering consultants to come up with ways to mitigate future flooding by holding water back longer in the headwaters.

Bateman Creek's beavers – and those whose dams slow the flow of Meadow, Margaret, Little Jumpingpound, Bryant, Sibbald, Prairie, Quirk, Silvester, McLean, Stimson, Flat, Pekisko and other headwater creeks – having done their part in keeping the damage costs from rising considerably higher, submitted no invoices. They just went back to repairing their dams.

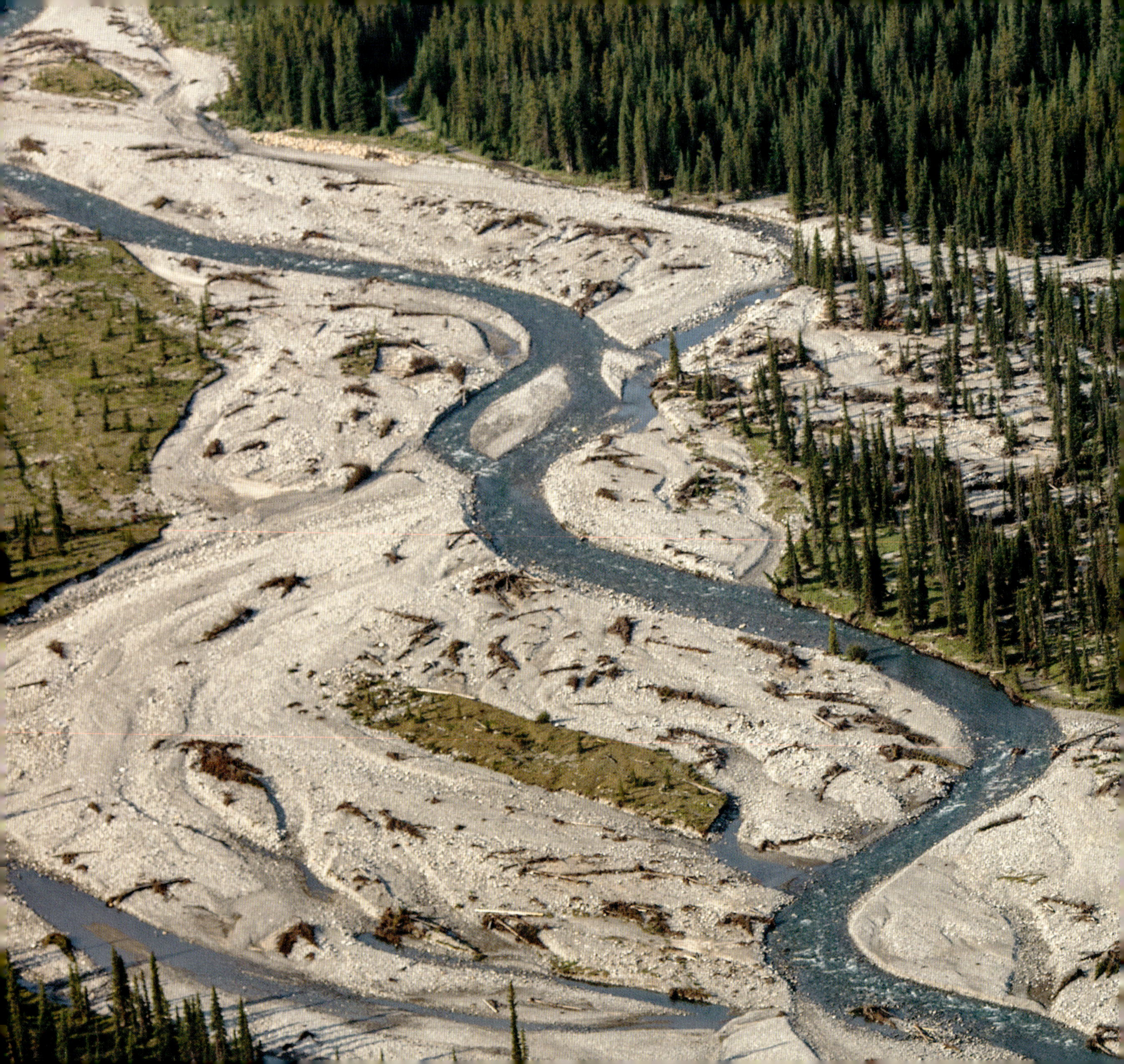

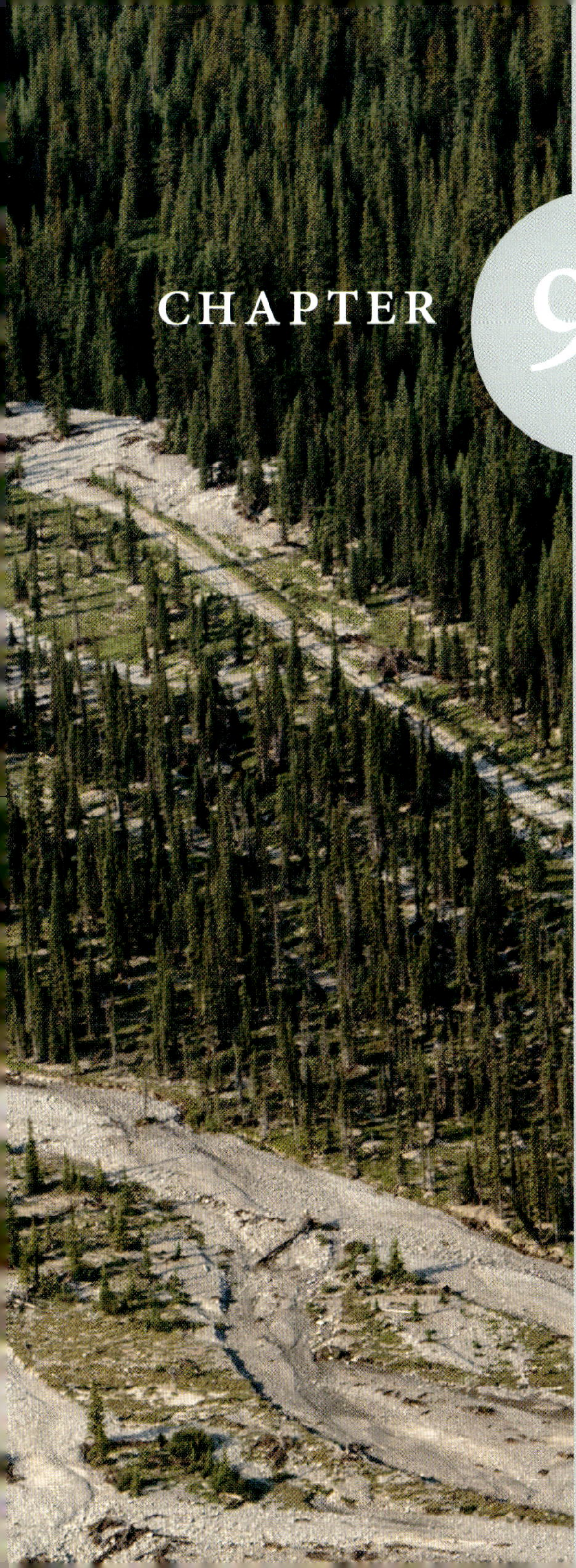

CHAPTER 9

The Under-River

Middle Bow River

POLICEMAN CREEK ARISES like magic, seemingly out of nowhere, in the middle of the town of Canmore. A series of shallow boulder fields in winter, by late May or early June, it becomes a series of long, shallow pools connected by burbling riffles, its several branches snaking among the quiet streets of the mountain resort town. Pathways follow the edges of the creek through white spruce forest and willow thickets, emerging from time to time as sidewalks along quiet residential streets.

By midsummer, Policeman Creek and its tributary, Spring Creek, are bulging at the seams. Water laps back into side bays full of willow, sedges and wetland vegetation. Red-winged blackbirds declaim from the taller shrubs. Yellow warblers, song sparrows and willow flycatchers conceal their nests in the shrubbery and sing from the forest edges. Young mothers push strollers, leashed dogs panting behind, while joggers and bicyclists hustle in and out of forest shadow, accompanying the stream on its meandering way through the former coal-mining town. Long mountain evenings spill golden light onto the quiet riffles. Brown trout rise quietly to hatching mayflies along the grassy banks, while the more numerous brook trout pock the tailwater of each pool with splashier rise forms.

Then, in late September, the stream begins to shrink. As autumn deepens into frosty mornings and shadowed afternoons, the wetlands become meadows, side channels drain, riffles go dry, and Policeman Creek dwindles to almost nothing. By December, only a few short reaches still flow, their open water crowded with overwintering mallards. The deeper ponds become skating rinks. Shallower ones dry up completely, ice riming their exposed boulders.

The rounded boulders and cobbly flats of Policeman Creek are actually the surface of a gravel aquifer – an underground zone of slowly seeping water – that extends deep beneath the valley floor.

During the last ice age, immense mountain glaciers filled the valleys with loose gravel and sand. The ancestral Bow River – a much larger stream than today – washed that material across the valley floor until it was more than one hundred metres deep in some places. As the meltwater flow from shrinking glaciers diminished, so did the Bow River. Vegetation gradually carpeted the valley floor. Soils began to form. Except for the active channel of the modern river, most of the postglacial river's cobbles and gravels vanished beneath greenery.

The unconsolidated gravels that underlie today's Bow River valley may no longer be moved by running water, but they are still full of water seeping and trickling eastward toward the prairies. The whole Bow valley, in fact, is underlain by moving groundwater. What hydrologists describe as an unconfined alluvial aquifer, the buried flow remains unseen except in summer when, swollen by snowmelt and glacier runoff from dozens of tributary drainages, it bulges to the surface as seasonal streams – like Policeman, Spring and numerous other floodplain creeks that appear and vanish annually. Some floodplain streams – like Bill Griffiths Creek, just downvalley from the town – flow year-round from groundwater springs, although their levels fluctuate with the seasons. Those streams aren't really discrete creeks; they are more like places where a giant underground flow surfaces briefly. The swift-moving Bow itself could be seen as the permanent surface expression of that hidden aquifer.

Page 126: *Three deer stand midstream in the braided channel of the upper Elbow — a classic gravel-bed river.*

Right: *Policeman's Creek, one of Canmore's lovely urban streams, is one surface expression of the Bow's under-river — the top part of a groundwater aquifer that fills the valley floor and bulges to the surface where squeezed by bedrock or swelled by high summer water volumes.*

IT WAS A CAMPFIRE CHAT WITH Dr. Ric Hauer one evening beside the Flathead River, a few hundred kilometres south of Canmore, that changed my whole understanding of Rocky Mountain rivers and brought Canmore's vanishing streams into clearer focus.

Our fire was in a grassy clearing surrounded by spruce

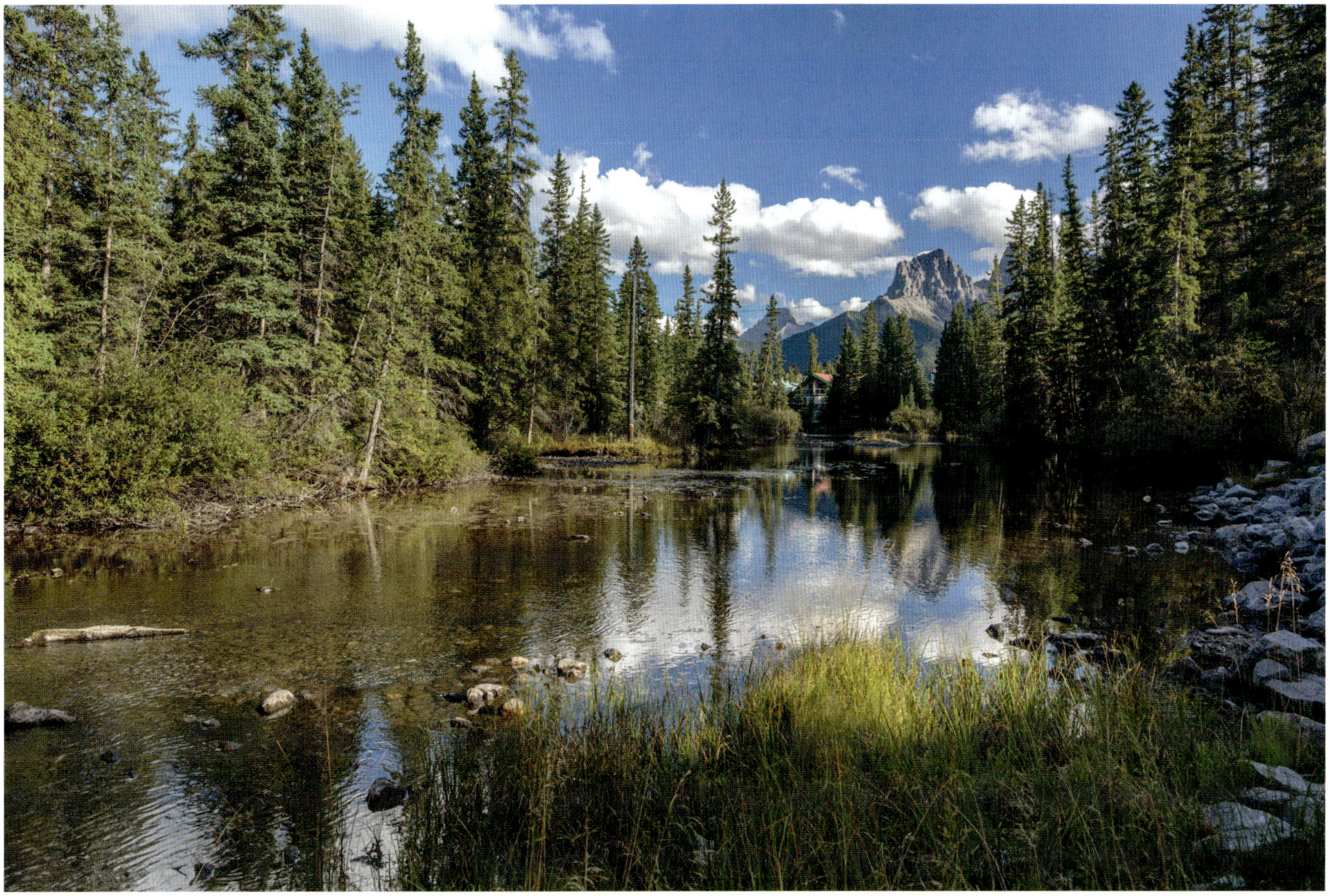

and pine, the river flickering and shimmering a dozen metres away below an eroded gravel cutbank. Cutthroat trout were rising splashily to a hatch of caddis flies along the seam where two lines of current, split around a washed-out poplar, converged again above the shallow tail of a long pool. The evening sun lit the tops of the trees far across the river flats and, perhaps a kilometre or more east, bathed the slopes with a glowing emerald green.

Hauer started studying the Flathead River in the mid-1970s from his home base at the University of Montana in Missoula. He never stopped; the river still enchants him. In the course of a long academic career, he became not just

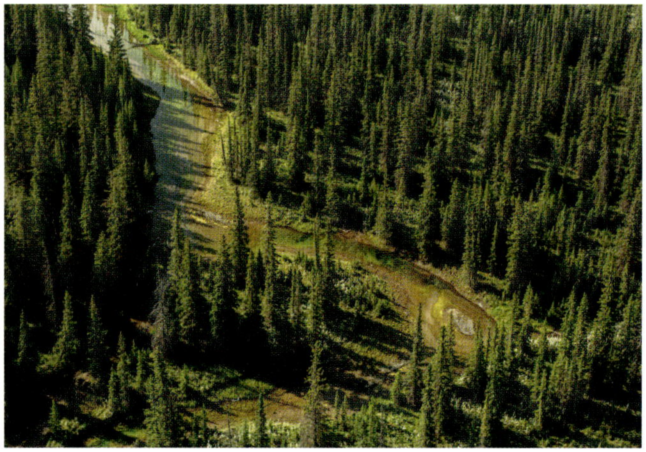

Just east of Canmore, spring flows emerging from the Bow River's floodplain sustain Bill Griffiths Creek. Its reliable year-round flow makes it an important spawning area for Bow River brown trout.

one of the most passionate advocates for the protection of this vast green valley – the only unsettled watershed remaining anywhere in southern Canada – but one of the world's leading authorities on gravel-bed rivers.

The gravel-bed rivers of the Canadian Rockies are geologically young because the landscapes they drain are recent. The glaciers that sculpted today's river valleys only melted back 10,000 to 15,000 years ago. All those millennia of crushing, grinding glacial action filled the landscape with massive amounts of broken mountain bits known as glacial till. Till is an unsorted blend of gravel, sand and silt. Streams have been at work ever since, washing that glacial till into the valley floors, sorting it, reworking it and spreading it in broad fluvial terraces. As the rivers aggrade their valleys, their floodplains become mosaics of curves, meanders and abandoned channels as the streams shift hither and thither from one spring flood to the next.

The cutbank beside our fire was carved into water-rounded gravels deposited by the Flathead River. In fact, the entire valley floor was the river's playground: at some point or another over the past few thousand years, it had flowed across all of it, depositing new gravels from farther upstream until, its channel clogged, it shifted and carved a new channel only to repeat the process of filling, shifting course and cutting new channels, again and again and again. "The thing is," said Hauer, "most people look at the active channel and think that that's the river. It's not. The river is beneath us, too. At any given moment, there is far more water in the gravels from one side of this valley to the other than in the channel where those fish are rising right now."

Friction and surface tension in the pores between soil particles keeps groundwater flowing far more slowly – thousands to tens of thousands times slower – than the water in surface channels. Although groundwater aquifers may seep through sandstone – a common medium for the most productive aquifers in Alberta's foothills – silt or even clay, the most permeable medium is gravel because of the large pores between each particle. In the active floodplain of a gravel-bed river, the flow rate of shallow groundwater can approach that of the nearby surface water where, for example, the river's action may have sorted large cobbles from smaller material before burying it under new sediment.

Hauer defines a gravel-bed river around four basic

concepts. The first is the river-continuum concept: the reality that the river is not just the water visible in the open channel at any given point but also the groundwater that continually drains to or from the river. Most of that water is in the loosely consolidated gravels that fill the valley floor. Although much of that alluvial aquifer is buried too deeply to interact with the surface stream, the upper portion is constantly exchanging water with the river above. In what hydrologists describe as the hyporheic zone – and Hauer likes to call the "under-river" – groundwater and surface water are continually changing places. The amount of water in the surface river channel can increase or decrease by as much as 40 per cent as it drains into the alluvium or re-emerges into the sides or bottom of the river.

When water engineers try to control flooding or stabilize the river channel, their successes are often short-lived because they focus only on the surface water flow; the river continuum is much bigger than the small bit they modify. Even at the surface, their work often produces unexpected outcomes because it changes the meandering movements and sediment dynamic of the river for many hundreds of metres upstream and many more hundreds downstream. The river continuum means it's nearly impossible to change just one part of a river without that work influencing, and being influenced by, all the rest of it.

Hauer's second concept, the flood pulse, relates to the fact that rivers don't flow at the same rate from one day to the next, or from season to season. Reflecting on Policeman Creek's annual changes, I nodded; of course the annual pulse of flood waters and the shrinkage of summer flows will affect the water table in the floodplain. His first two concepts had not been difficult to grasp.

But, he pointed out, that pulsing annual flow does far more than merely awaken those floodplain streams each year. Spring floods scour out deep pools in gravel beds, providing vital overwinter habitat for fish, while also flushing fine sediments out of the gravel riffles where they lay their eggs. Without that spring cleaning, there would be too little oxygen and food in those gravels to keep young fish alive.

Even trees rely on the annual flood pulse. Willows and poplars release their fluffy wind-borne seeds in early June, just as flood waters are dropping. It's perfect timing. Those seeds land on newly deposited sandbars, where they can sprout in wet ground free from competition from other plants. The lush river forests that make river floodplains so enticing for humans and productive for wildlife are co-evolved with, and utterly dependent on, the natural rhythm of spring floods. In the fall, when their leaves fall onto the windswept floodplain, many end up in the water, where they become food for bacteria, caddis flies, minnows and, ultimately, trout and the things that eat trout.

Spring floods wash out older trees while creating ideal habitat for the next generation. The old trees have a function, too: logjams become hiding cover for whitefish and bull trout.

Hauer's third concept – the vertical concept – makes sense to anyone who has already figured out why Policeman's Creek vanishes and reappears each year. Hauer described the invisible part of the river, the part that extends down through the gravel and connects to the alluvial aquifer below: the under-river.

> Where we are sitting, the alluvial aquifer is well more than a kilometre wide and extends 30 metres beneath us. The upper part of that aquifer is essentially part of the river, because it's constantly exchanging water, minerals and nutrients with the flowing channel. Groundwater cools the river and river water recharges the groundwater. It's all the same river.

It was his next statement, introducing the final concept that he uses to define the nature of a gravel bed river, that gobsmacked me: "… and it's all full of life."

Life – down in the dark gravel and secret waters beneath us?

Hauer explained that floods and rain cause water to drain down into seemingly dry gravel flats from the matted vegetation above, washing organic compounds, fragments of dead vegetation, bacteria, fungi and other material down into the under-river. As a result, an entire ecosystem of bacteria, fungi, invertebrates and other living things is able to thrive in the hidden flows below. So dynamic is the exchange between the river's water and the buried flows of the under-river that some invertebrates, like stonefly nymphs, have been found metres into the gravel and up to a kilometre away from the active surface channel. They have no trouble surviving, and travelling, in the under-river.

Spruce trees, willows and poplars that thrive in the well-watered river gravels punch their roots deep into the gravel. That's one reason Lorne Fitch refers to them as "woody rebar" when describing their function in holding stream banks together during floods. Road engineers often use willow and poplar cuttings in bioengineering: rock gabions will hold back a slope, but rock gabions with shrubs and trees sprouting out of them will hold it back even better because roots, like living anchors, eventually reach deep into the surrounding soil.

A thin strip of water is all that shows of Canyon Creek, flowing mostly through its floodplain gravels here. The stream flows on the surface both downstream and upstream of this reach, which lies just west of Powderface Trail.

It becomes easier to imagine the hidden under-river as a living stream when you realize that it flows through and around the living and dying roots of trees and shrubs – roots whose death and life add to the organic debris leaching down from the surface. "We assume all the life in a river is in the part we can see," said Hauer. "It isn't. There is a whole ecosystem in the under-river. We've even found fish living down amid the cobbles."

The idea of fish living in the under-river was a bit more than I could get my head around that evening, but a few weeks later I learned that the Flathead River isn't the only place where fish have been found in the under-river. Policeman Creek is another.

THE FLATHEAD VALLEY's hyporheic zone, or under-river, lies atop an alluvial aquifer up to 40 metres deep. The Bow River between Banff and Calgary, occupying a narrow valley that was more heavily glaciated, flows

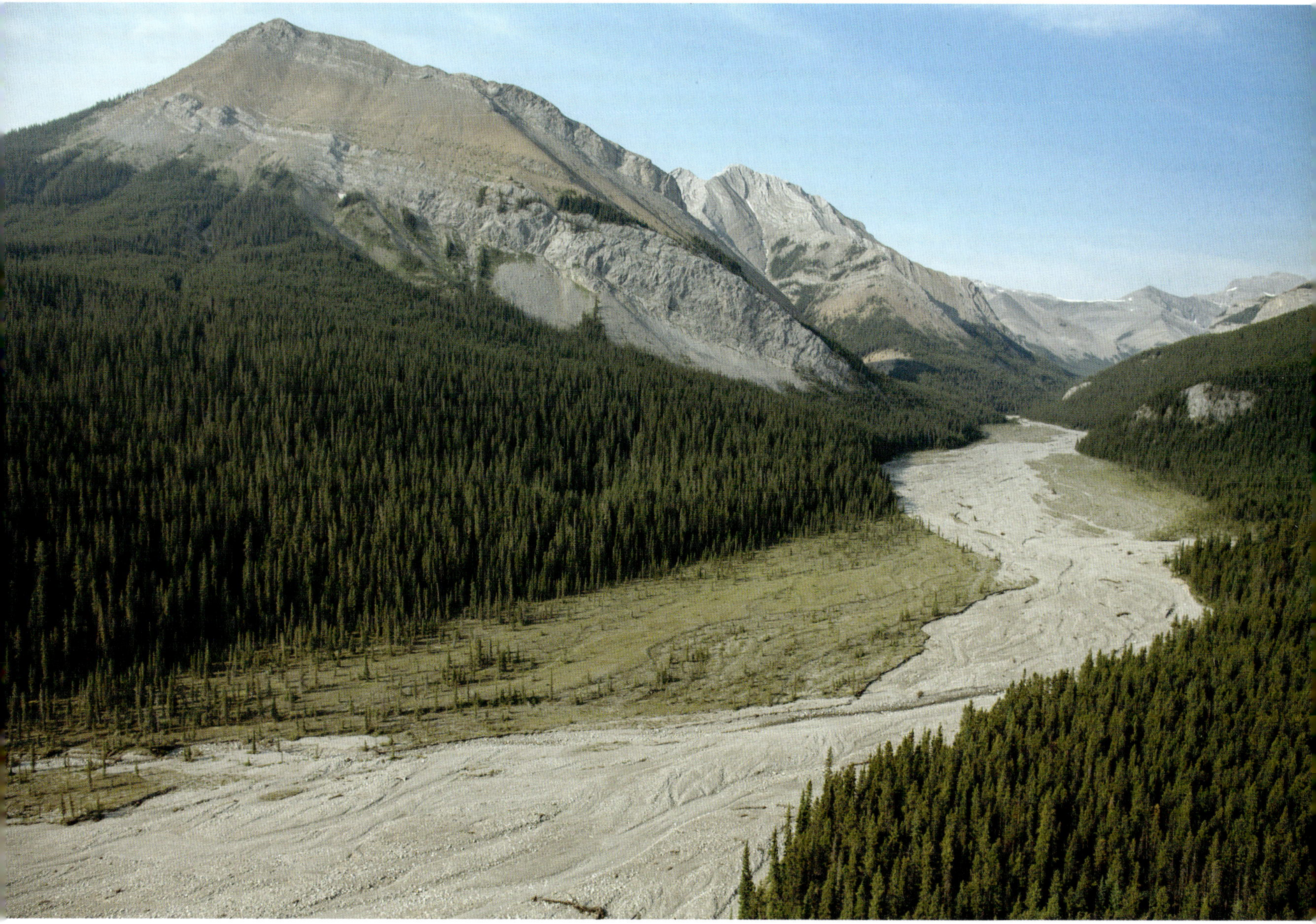

atop an unconfined aquifer of water-saturated gravel and cobbles that exceeds one hundred metres in some places.

That much unconsolidated gravel provides a lot of room for extra water. After Calgary Power dammed Lake Minnewanka in 1912, raising its level by four metres, the engineers were discouraged to find that barely 20 per cent of the additional water actually made it to the power plants at the dams near Seebe. The rest vanished into groundwater aquifers, including the buried gravels of the Bow valley. It still flowed out of the mountains, but underground. Calgary Power failed to meet its ambitions for improving the hydroelectric output of its Bow River dams, but it likely improved the flow of Policeman Creek and the many other seasonal streams that emerge along the Bow valley.

An alluvial aquifer may have excess water-holding capacity, but that's only the case where the valley's gravel deposits are deepest and during the time of year when water supply is lowest. The long river reach from Cascade Mountain through Canmore to Dead Man's Flats is one of those places where the gravels have had the chance to accumulate to great depths. Even so, during the high flows of late spring and early summer, the swollen aquifer emerges above ground as seasonal springs. All along the river's floodplain, wetlands and seasonal creeks like Policeman Creek fill and begin to flow.

Where impermeable rock bands bulge up close to the surface, groundwater has nowhere to go but above ground. The Bow River, consequently, carries more water in some reaches than in others; sometimes, where underlying gravels deepen again, river water drains into the

Unfertilizing the Middle Bow River

In the late 1970s Canadian Wildlife Service biologist Geoff Holroyd and his colleagues conducted a wildlife inventory in Banff National Park. They found that the Bow River downstream from Lake Louise had the highest density of wintering American dippers ever recorded in Canada. In their final report, they recommended that the Bow River's pristine water quality should be restored. They argued that anything that might damage dipper habitat would have far-reaching effects, since wintering dippers disperse in summer to other areas of the park.

Ironically, cleaning up the river may have had the opposite result.

Phosphorus, an element that is extremely scarce in Rocky Mountains river water under natural conditions, was the biggest challenge. Even a small amount of dissolved phosphorus over the base level had been shown to trigger big changes in river ecology, ranging from recurring algae blooms to changes in aquatic invertebrate communities. Midge fly larvae and worms increase dramatically, while stoneflies and mayflies become a smaller part of the invertebrate community. Phosphorus, essentially, fertilizes waters that aren't meant to be that fertile.

Canada National Parks Act stipulates that ecological integrity (the health, wholeness and natural functioning of ecosystems) is to be the first priority in all management decisions. Consequently, in its 1989 management plan, Parks Canada set water-quality standards for sewage effluent higher than those of any other jurisdiction in Canada and then went on to invest millions of dollars in upgrades to sewage treatment plants at Lake Louise and the town of Banff.

The final treatment plant upgrades in 2003 put Lake Louise and Banff at the leading edge of tertiary sewage treatment in Canada. Phosphorus levels dropped so dramatically that, by 2010, water-quality monitoring near where the Bow River leaves the park showed that phosphorus was back to natural levels.

And the dippers disappeared. Not completely, of course; an afternoon's walk along the snowy banks of the Bow River will still produce the occasional sighting of the little grey birds bobbing at the edge of the ice or diving in to hunt invertebrates along the river's bottom. But the large counts are a thing of the past.

Apparently dippers are not quite the discriminating wilderness perfectionists biologists had thought them to be. The high winter counts of the 1980s may well have been because effluent from the old sewage treatment plants had artificially fertilized the Bow River, producing more food for dippers.

More food for trout, too. In 1925 a fish hatchery truck broke down en route from the Banff hatchery to central Alberta, where it was to deliver a load of non-native brown trout. Rather than let the fish die, the driver released the entire load into Carrot Creek. Within a few decades, the brown trout fishing in the Bow River below Banff had become famous. Floodplain streams like Canmore's Spring Creek and the nearby Bill Griffiths Creek filled each fall with trophy-sized browns that spawned where groundwater emerged into the stream bed.

A major debris-flow flood in Louis Creek, a usually dry tributary of the Bow near Vermilion Lakes, left the river running muddy for many months in the late 1990s. Anglers complained that the brown trout fishing never recovered after that. A more likely explanation, however, is that sewage treatment upgrades, by restoring the river closer to its natural state, ended an era of sewage-fertilized fish abundance. Fishing is still good in the middle reaches of the Bow River, but it's more in keeping with the natural productivity of a nutrient-poor mountain river.

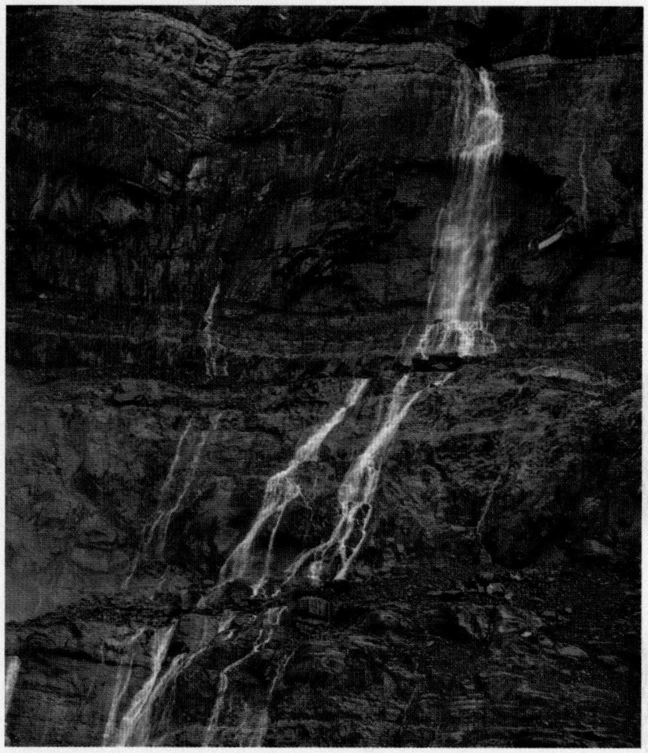

Mountain water is naturally low in nutrients, especially phosphorus.

aquifer and the river actually becomes smaller than it was farther upstream. Groundwater becomes surface water; surface water becomes groundwater. Like Hauer said, it's a continuum.

A large river like the Bow can hide those sorts of changes to its volume, but smaller gravel-bed creeks make the phenomenon obvious when they actually run dry for short distances – their entire surface flow lost to the under-river. West of Bragg Creek, Canyon Creek vanishes and reappears several times as it flows from its sources in the Fisher Range to its confluence with the Elbow River near Elbow Falls. Where Highway 66 crosses Canyon Creek near its mouth, the stream channel is often dry because its entire flow is in the gravel beneath. Only a few kilometres upstream, where impervious limestone beds lie near the surface, the channel has a substantial flow all year round. But just above where Powderface Trail crosses the stream a bit farther west, the braided gravel channel again appears dry in midsummer. Hike a couple of kilometres farther up the valley, though, and there is Canyon Creek, winking cheerfully in its channel again where the gravel deposits thin out over bedrock.

Similar disappearing streams include the North Ghost River, Wasootch and Porcupine creeks and Evan-Thomas Creek. A favourite childhood bull trout stream in the Clearwater drainage farther north was a family secret unknown to other anglers. We knew what they didn't: that a two-kilometre upstream walk on a dry stream bed would lead to a stream that actually grew larger the farther up we went. During spring runoff, the dry channel we had followed upstream would have been flowing, too. The silty flood waters would have been hard to fish, but the fish would have been there nonetheless. It's during high stream flows, after all, that young trout can slip downstream to more productive waters while big spawners forge upstream through the murk to deposit their eggs in the clean gravels of the headwaters.

IN SEPTEMBER AND OCTOBER, brook trout clean off patches of gravel in Policeman Creek, excavate shallow depressions with their tail fins and deposit their eggs where the surface stream and the under-river meet. As the stream continues to shrink, brown trout come up from the Bow to spawn in the same riffles.

Only a few short reaches of Canmore's floodplain creeks remain wet in winter. But the under-river never recedes far below the surface. One spring in the late 1990s, Trout Unlimited Canada biologists were startled to find small brook trout in a part of Policeman Creek that had been dry only a few days earlier. The stream channel above and below the emerging pool was still dry. The biologists concluded that those trout could only have survived the winter by burrowing into the under-river. They had apparently spent the last part of the winter waiting patiently in water spaces amid the gravel, rubble and cobble, a few centimetres below the apparently dry creek bed. It must have been stunningly boring for them.

When floodplain creeks drain out in response to a lower water table in late summer, only the smallest of fishes and invertebrates can work their way into the gravel far enough to survive the winter. The lack of reliable wintering habitat is one reason floodplain channels can be unproductive for larger fish. Digging a hole into the under-river is one way to help them survive.

A Canmore real-estate developer acquired property between Spring and Policeman creeks in the late 1990s and proposed to develop it for housing. The alluvial aquifer under Canmore is the source of the town's water and, in flood years, the source of the water that floods basements all through the town core. Before the developer could proceed with building his proposed condominiums on so sensitive a floodplain site, the town required that he conduct an environmental assessment. Trout Unlimited Canada brought its biologists' information to the table and left with a commitment that the developer would offset some of the impacts of his project by excavating three holes into a part of Policeman Creek that often went dry in winter even though the surface of the alluvial aquifer was just a few centimetres beneath it.

Spring Creek Development used a track-hoe excavator to punch holes as deep as it could reach into the gravel bed under the creek. They also sank several trees into one of the new pits as protective cover for any fish that might choose to move in. Subsequent monitoring showed that brook and brown trout, suckers and whitefish all took advantage of the new habitat; now, even large fish could move into the under-river for the winter. The tree-filled pool, in particular, proved popular. Biologists found 190 fish the first time they electroshocked it.

In 2012, based on the success of the mitigation pools, Trout Unlimited Canada got permission to excavate six more pools farther upstream in places where the surface creek vanishes each winter. Policeman Creek still shrinks into the Bow River's under-river each winter, but large fish no longer have to retreat down to the Bow or risk death by stranding each winter.

HAUER'S UNDER-RIVER – the hyporheic zone where groundwater and surface water interact through the seasons – is only the top of what is usually a much deeper alluvial aquifer under the gravel-bed rivers that drain from the Rockies. An alluvial aquifer is groundwater that flows through unconsolidated gravel, sand and other material and, unlike deeper aquifers, is unconfined by overlying bedrock. Gravel-bed rivers like the Bow and its major tributaries are all connected to alluvial aquifers, which are often part of more extensive groundwater networks.

Those aquifers are important sources of well water. The towns of Banff and Canmore are among several in Alberta that get their municipal water supply from wells drilled into the Bow River's alluvial aquifer. Those sorts of wells will become increasingly important in a water-challenged future.

On the other hand, sometimes we get domestic water from alluvial aquifers in places where it isn't welcome – in basements, for example.

In spring, when rivers flood, it's not just the surface water level that rises; the groundwater does, too. It's all connected, after all. That's why berms along Calgary's Bow and Elbow rivers, while keeping the rivers from spilling into floodplain neighbourhoods, can't stop basements from flooding. It's not surface water seeping into basements; it's groundwater. Floodplain homes are, in effect,

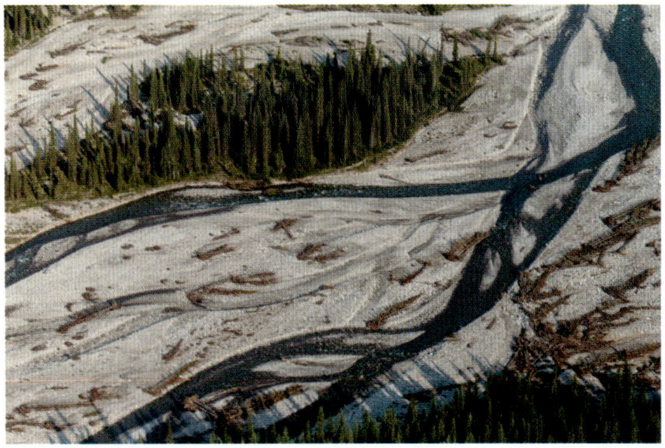

Cobble Flats, Elbow River. River water becomes groundwater, and groundwater becomes river water. The constant exchange connects the under-river, or hyporheic zone, to the surface flow in gravel-bed rivers.

built in the under-river – places where rivers and aquifers exchange water, depending on the season.

Given their importance as sources of clean groundwater, and the fact that they store a lot more water than the rivers we usually think of as our water supply, protecting the alluvial aquifers underlying the Bow, Highwood, Sheep, Elbow and Ghost rivers from drainage or contamination is not just vital to all those seasonal streams on the floodplain and to the fish and other wildlife that depend on them: it's vital to southern Alberta's water future. Deep groundwater aquifers are relatively easy to protect because they lie underneath protective bands of rock. Fracking – using pressurized fluids to shatter buried rock layers and release their gas or oil deposits – is starting to change that protected status, but even so, it's the unconfined alluvial aquifers that remain most vulnerable. And it's at the top edges of those aquifers that the constant exchange of water through the hyporheic zones of surface rivers puts those buried water sources most at risk of contamination.

Historically, floodplain land was undesirable for development, so town planners concentrated industrial activity there. Calgary's early oil refineries, junkyards, garbage incinerators and sewage plants were all located on the Bow River floodplain, on top of the alluvial aquifer. When anglers used to complain that Bow River fish downstream from the city tasted like diesel oil, they were right. Those fish lived in water that, having passed through the under-river portion of the Bow's alluvial aquifer, was full of Calgary's industrial wastes.

Fortunately, most of Calgary's worst toxic leachate sites have been cleaned up. Even so, polluted runoff water drains from the streets, yards and industrial areas of small towns and big cities alike. What doesn't go into storm sewers that deliver it straight into the nearest river or creek goes into the ground. It doesn't disappear there; it seeps into the underlying aquifers. A study of Elbow River water quality found dangerous levels of toxic metals where the Elbow meets the Bow. The pollution is the product of urban development that has not been mitigated sufficiently by, for example, diverting runoff into settling ponds designed to trap street contaminants. Since that pollution ends up in the river, some eventually ends up in aquifers, too. Those who assume that their wells produce clean water may be deluding themselves; it all depends on what is draining into their groundwater from above.

The other growing risk to the Bow watershed's alluvial aquifers is gravel, or aggregate, mining. The beds of old glacial streams are a rich source of gravel throughout southern Alberta. Many of those gravel deposits are in eskers or kame terraces well away from today's watercourses. Those are the primary, and best, source of the gravel for highway building, concrete manufacture, house foundations and other such uses. But the under-river's gravel is a tempting alternative for cost-cutting developers. It's easily accessible near pretty much any river crossing. Excavating gravel from a river floodplain, however, can lower the water table when developers dewater the pits. It can also change underground pressure gradients. Both the under-river and the intimately connected surface river can see their water flows depleted.

Stealing gravel from the floodplain of a living river has other effects too: after the 2013 flood, many trout, suckers, northern pike and other fish were stranded when the surface flow dropped off. As they always do during flood events, fish abandoned the turbulent flows of the channel for the relatively calmer flows on the floodplain. There they took shelter in low places. A lot of those low places were pits where developers had mined gravel. When the flood waters receded, the fish had no escape. Trout Unlimited Canada organized volunteer brigades to rescue over five thousand fish from 60 sites along the Bow and its tributaries. It was a small fraction of the number that had become trapped and were ultimately lost when hot weather returned and the gravel-pit pools became algae-choked and oxygen-depleted traps before draining out completely.

MY ORIGINAL INTRODUCTION TO THE CONCEPT of the under-river came as the result of an invitation by an environmentalist friend, Harvey Locke, who has been instrumental in many large landscape-conservation initiatives around the world. Having enlisted me to help with a "bioblitz" of southeastern British Columbia's Flathead valley, it was he who introduced me to Ric Hauer there and said, "You guys have to talk."

Big rivers and their floodplains are important corridors that connect landscapes. Because of their abundant water and diverse riparian habitats, they are also ecological hotspots. Most species of wildlife spend some or all of their life cycle down by the river. After that eye-opening discussion beside the campfire with Hauer, I commented one day to Locke that I had become conscious of under-rivers everywhere. What could well be part of the Spray River's under-river oozes to the surface along a mountain slope south of Canmore. The trail to Grassi Lakes, a popular picnic destination, crosses springs and hanging bogs spotted with wetland plants like butterwort and elephant head. The slope oozes groundwater from beneath the Spray River, where TransAlta has diverted its surface flow to a penstock and hydro plant at the edge of the Bow valley.

Locke later sent me an article he and Ric Hauer had co-authored as a contribution to the debate over whether to develop micro-hydro on a gravel-bed river in Colorado. They wrote:

The water in the river channel, river bed, and riparian zone are important at the scale of the entire landscape.

The river corridor composed of channel waters, river water flowing through the gravels and the floodplain surface interact to create habitats that are used by up to 85% of all the species in the landscape at some point during the year. The river corridor functions as the ecological backbone of the entire landscape.

The removal of water from a gravel bed river system affects much more than the amount of water available for things that live in the river. Eliminating floods ultimately eliminates the space for new growth; the forest simply ages and dies without being replaced. The gravels eventually tighten up leaving no room for the fish to spawn or the insects and other aquatic life. The floodplain becomes simplified, the cottonwood forest is lost, birds that use trees disappear, and the vitality of the region is diminished.

Except when their upper portions – the parts that are perennially connected to the flow of surface rivers – emerge seasonally to flood Policeman Creek and other ephemeral floodplain streams with life, the alluvial aquifers of the Bow headwaters drain invisibly through and between the valleys that connect the Rockies to the distant Great Plains. Those groundwater treasures are nearly always out of sight. They are far too important, however, for us to keep them out of mind.

Rip-Rap: Walling the River In

Following a major flood in 2005, government agencies and private property owners found that the major rivers draining to the Bow River had created new channels and filled old ones in. If they were honestly surprised, they shouldn't have been: that's what rivers do during floods. When a river spills across its floodplain, it stores water temporarily and deposits some of the sediment load it has picked up. Displacing energy into rearranging the floodplain reduces downstream damage, renews the rich soils that make floodplains such lush places, and stores both water and sediments.

For those who had built houses, barns, fences and roads on the river floodplains, the changes were all wrong. The river had left its "normal" channel. Ignoring the fact that there is no normal channel, merely the channel that a river occupies at any given time during its decades-long process of meandering about the floodplain, the bureaucrats and engineers set to work putting the river back where they felt it belonged and armouring its banks with rip-rap – berms built of large boulders – to keep it there.

Studies have repeatedly shown that rip-rap replaces productive trout habitat with near-sterile rockscapes. Fish populations drop by at least two-thirds along river reaches armoured with rip-rap. Trout Unlimited Canada, worried that the cumulative effect of multiple bank-armouring projects along southwestern Alberta's best trout streams might wipe out much of the new fish habitat the flood had created, commissioned a study by a Calgary consulting firm, Applied Aquatic Research.

The consultants floated by canoe along the Elbow, Sheep

and Highwood rivers, and mapped every place where the natural bank had been replaced with rip-rap. They found a lot of river abuse. More than six kilometres of the Elbow's banks had been armoured with large rocks or concrete. A similar amount of rip-rap lined the Sheep River downstream of the Forest Reserve boundary. Almost five kilometres of the Highwood's banks had been hardened.

Eight years later, another big flood poured off the Eastern Slopes headwaters. Ironically, some of the flood-proofed rip-rap sites highlighted by the aquatic consultants were the worst damaged by the 2013 flood. Lacking live vegetation roots to hold it together and designed for lower flow levels, bank armouring washed out along the Elbow River at Allen Bill Pond, Bragg Creek, the Highway 22 bridge and upstream from Glenmore Reservoir. Inevitably, the floodplain developments that rip-rap had been intended to protect suffered extensive damage.

Along the Sheep River, the consultants had highlighted extensive rip-rap and bank modification at Turner Valley. Sure enough, in 2013 it was that reach of the river, downstream of the town of Black Diamond, that suffered the greatest damage. The consultants had also documented specific concerns about the amount of rip-rap in High River. That town was swamped in 2013 when the Highwood washed over the bank armouring meant to protect it.

Immediately after the 2013 flood, both the federal and provincial governments rushed to announce flood recovery projects. High on the list? Replacing the rip-rap that had failed to hold the last two floods.

Nothing can stop a big flood from rearranging a river's floodplain. The best way to avoid flood damage is simply not to put anything valuable on the floodplain. Efforts to control a river with rip-rap are make-work projects for engineers and contractors that ruin fish habitat, reduce the floodplain's ability to store water and sediment during spring runoff, and create the illusion that people can stop rivers from acting like rivers.

Replacing engineered bank armouring over and over again and expecting different results is a kind of collective insanity that infects communities that won't accept a simple truth: the floodplain belongs to the river. The river will always take it back.

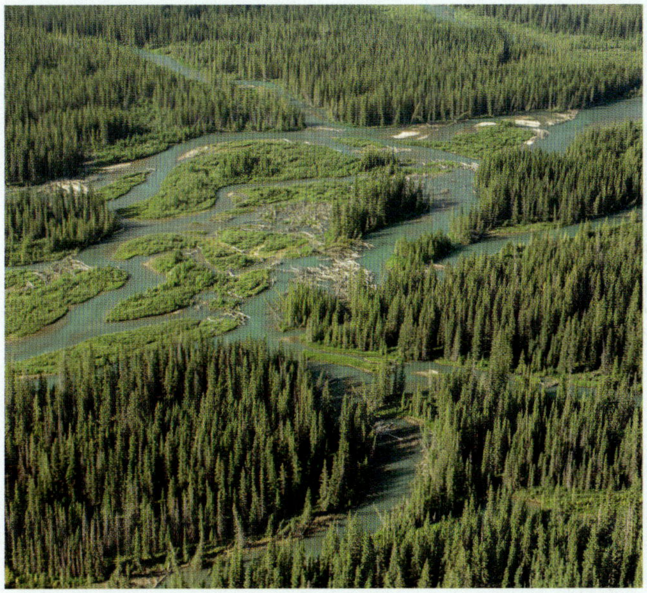

In late spring there is no room for more water in the gravels that fill the Bow River valley. Surface streams and wetlands fill again, and the floodplain pulses with water and life.

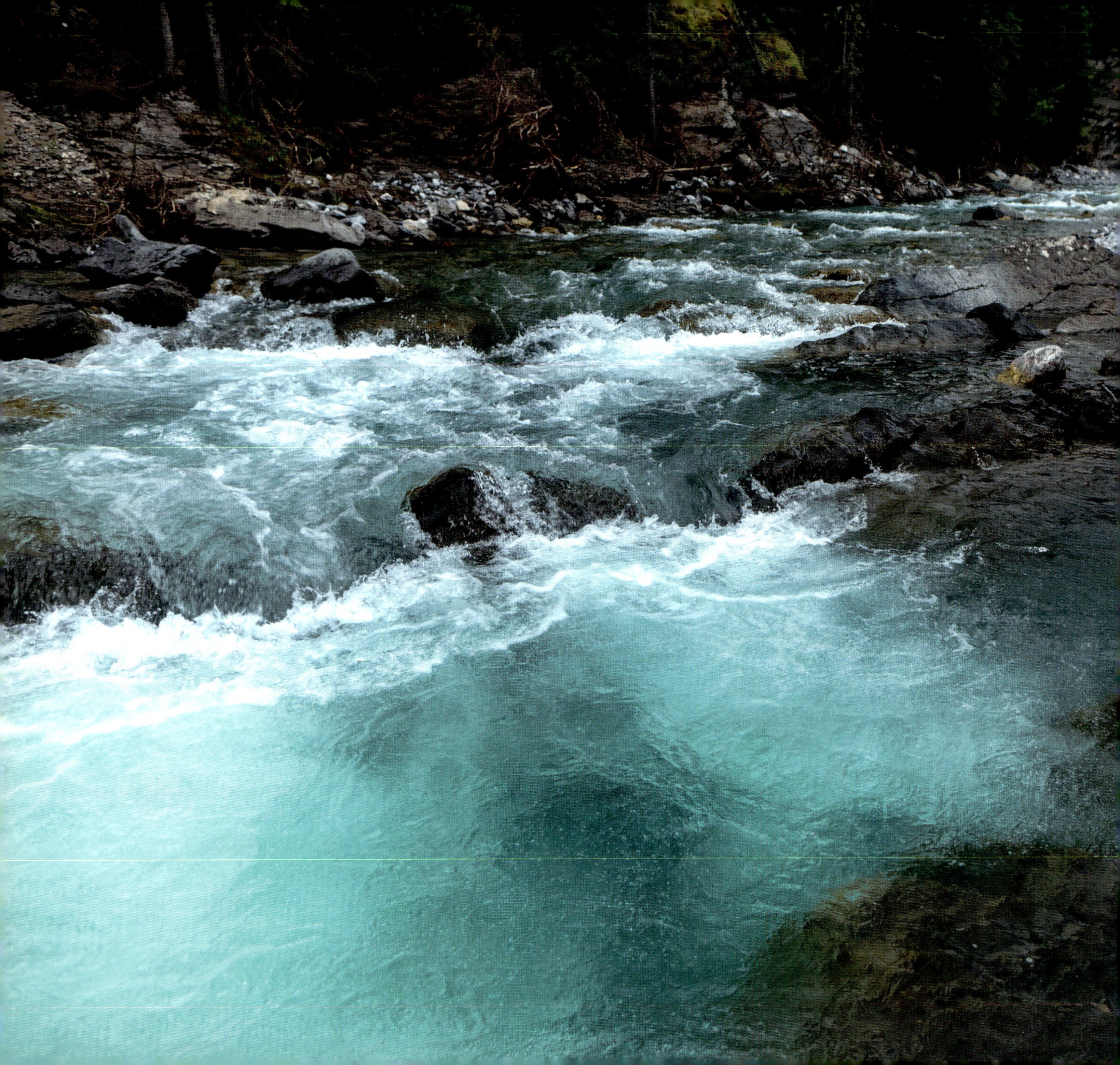

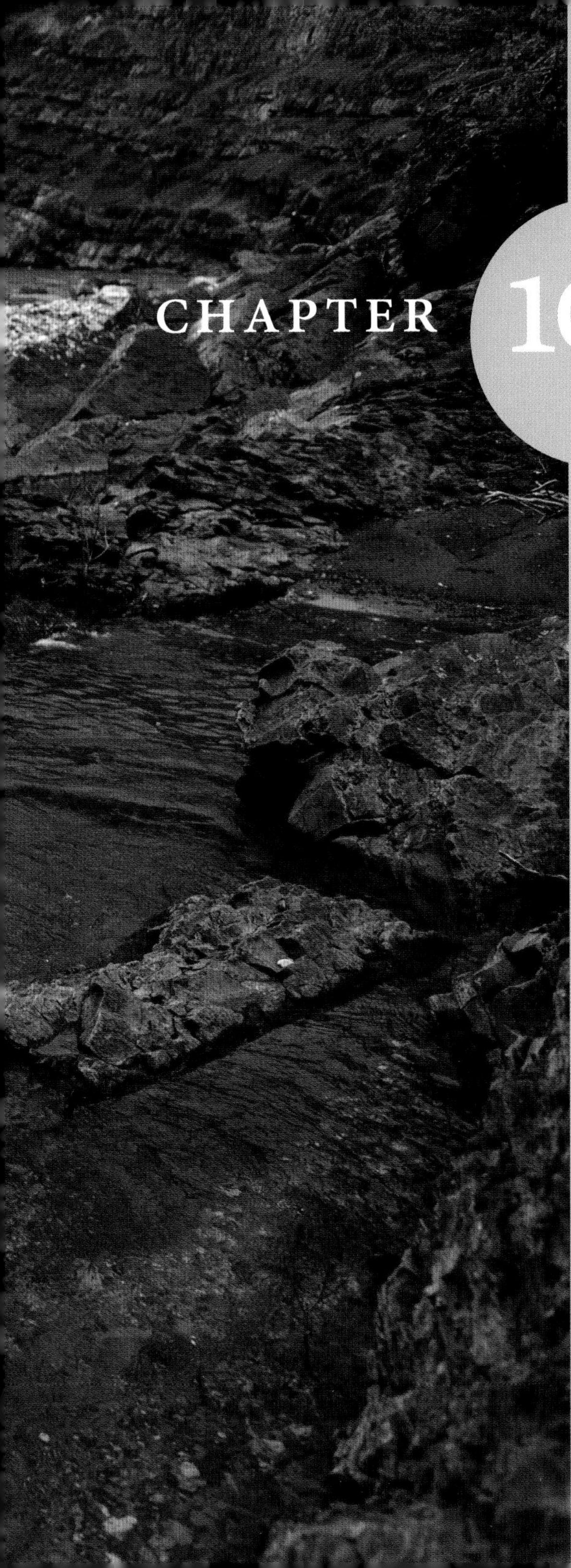

CHAPTER 10

Water and Wildness
Sheep River

THERE ARE TWO WAYS into what my family called "Seven Mile Walk Creek." Both are well worth the hike, but neither involves seven miles of walking.

From one staging area south of Threepoint Creek, at the end of the road west of Millarville, it's a gradual uphill hike of seven kilometres along a gated road now mostly grown over with grass. When I ran it one evening in 2014, it was not just gated but partly reclaimed by nature; the June 2013 flood had washed out most of the culverts. Elk, black bears, bicyclists and cougars had left their tracks on the trail, but there was no sign of motor vehicles.

The other way in is from a staging area near the R.B. Miller research station at Gorge Creek, west of Turner Valley. That's the route my father chose when he would take his offspring to fish another of his secret streams whose actual name we weren't allowed to know. It felt like a seven-mile walk to me, but it's actually only about six kilometres to where the dark little creek that had been winking at us from deep in the spruce trees below the road finally emerged and went snickering through a culvert to sneak off into the woods

Page 142: *Sheep River Falls, Kananaskis Country.*

Right: *Grizzly tracks in floodplain silt. Bears and many other species concentrate in the wettest parts of the landscape, making water and wildlife conservation almost the same thing.*

Far right: *Sheep River canyon, carved into dark shale.*

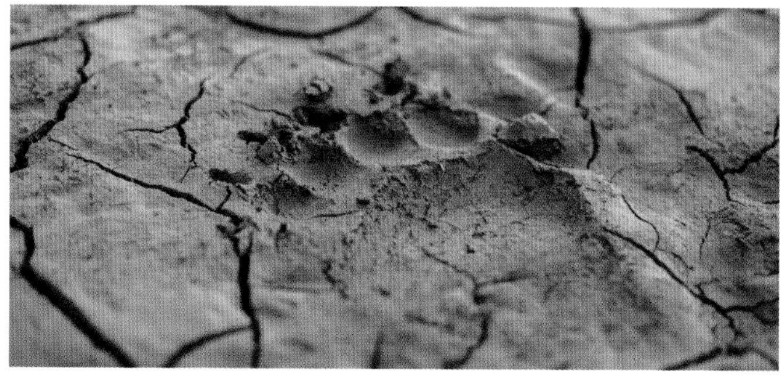

on the other side and lose itself in mystery. At least, it was mystery to me back then, as I was not allowed to follow it.

Gorge Creek, blinking through the trees for the first couple kilometres of our long walks, was a particular torment. It was closed to angling because of fisheries research. In my young mind, that meant it must be like the display pools at the fish hatcheries in Calgary and Banff, where huge trout cruised slowly around small pools, teasing visiting anglers. I desperately wanted to fish Gorge Creek. Never had I seen a stream so tantalizingly perfect and hopelessly remote. But it was not to be; instead, we caught small native cutthroat trout in the headwater pools of its neighbour, a stream named after freed African-American slave and respected early Albertan cattleman John Ware. Ware Creek is one of the major tributaries of the north fork of the Sheep, or Threepoint Creek, as it's officially known.

The little brook we fished every second year through the 1960s didn't feel like a major tributary – the stream's headwater reach was newly born from springs that emerged from the slopes of Volcano and Link ridges. It was easily small enough for an adult to step across in many places. I caught my first fish there – a 15-centimetre cutthroat trout. It was never certified by the officials of the family – my dad and older brother – because in my excitement I decided to wash the gravel and leaves off it so it would look sleek and beautiful when I presented it to them. The slippery little thing squirted out of my hand and went tumbling off into a riffle, never to be seen again. I was shattered.

It was always my lot to be left at the road, with firm instructions not to wander out of sight of it, while the older contingent went off down a cattle trail into the woods. I entertained myself watching shady pools for the little trout that cruised in and out of patches of sunlight in the mossy depths of the forest. When I tried clumsily to catch one, the trout would invariably dart off to safety. At length I would hear Dad and Gordon approaching through the timber with the much larger fish they had caught. Then we would begin the long hike back to the gate at the start of the road.

Years later, in the 1990s, my wife, Gail, and I moved to Okotoks for a brief time. Our children were close to the age I had been during those early angling excursions.

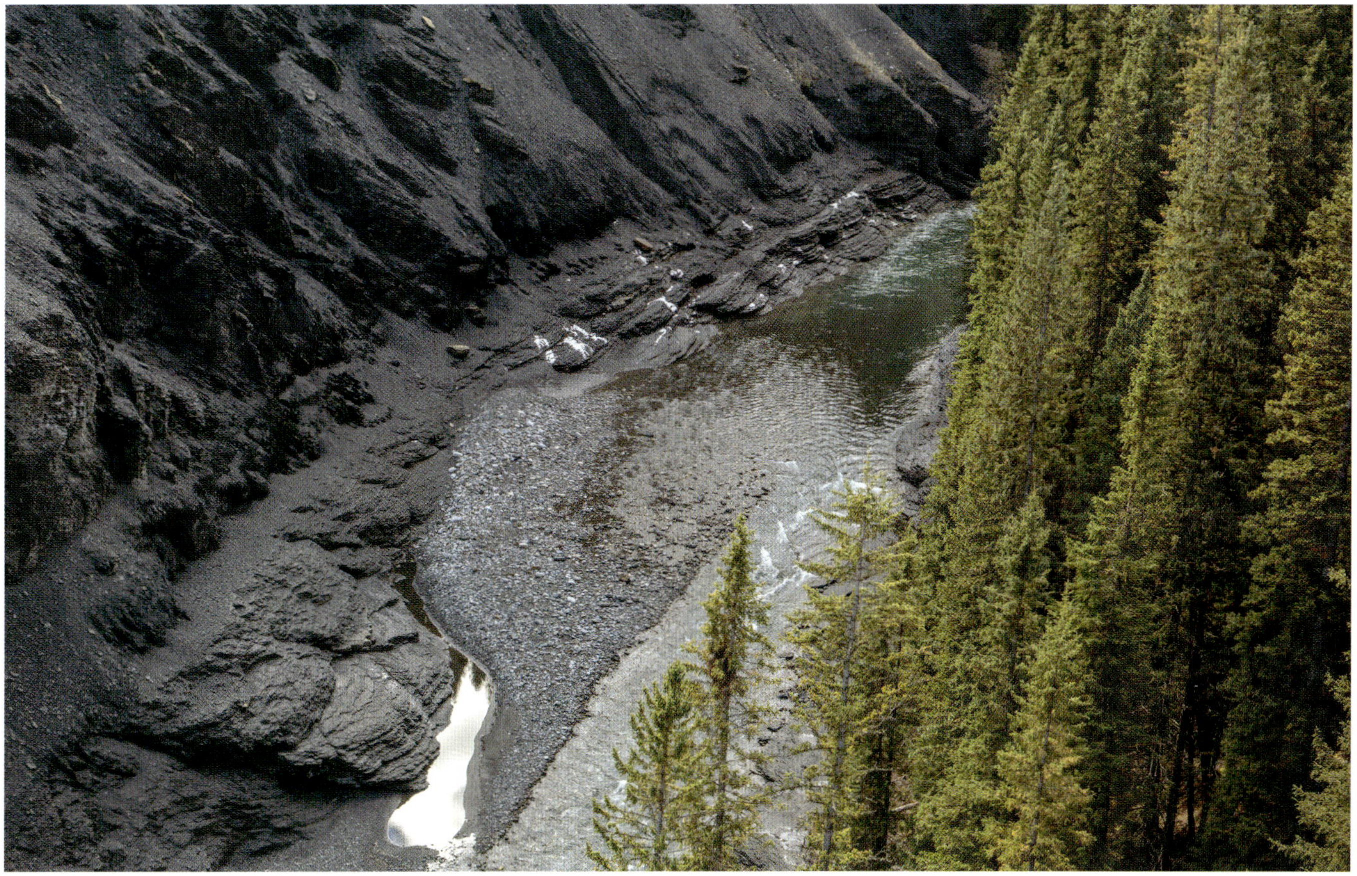

Although Ware Creek flowed through the heart of town, it was unrecognizable because its waters had merged with those of Threepoint, Fisher and the main Sheep River. I proposed to the family one weekend that we trace the creek back to its source, where I had caught my first fish. I was curious about what Dad and Gordon had been finding downstream from that culvert.

That year, the gate was open on the little road that loops from Gorge Creek over to Threepoint, so we were able to drive right to the culvert crossing. The creek seemed smaller than I remembered. Gail and I organized our troop and set off down the cow trail.

Very soon, we encountered wet, open thickets with the telltale canals and cut stumps of an old beaver pond,

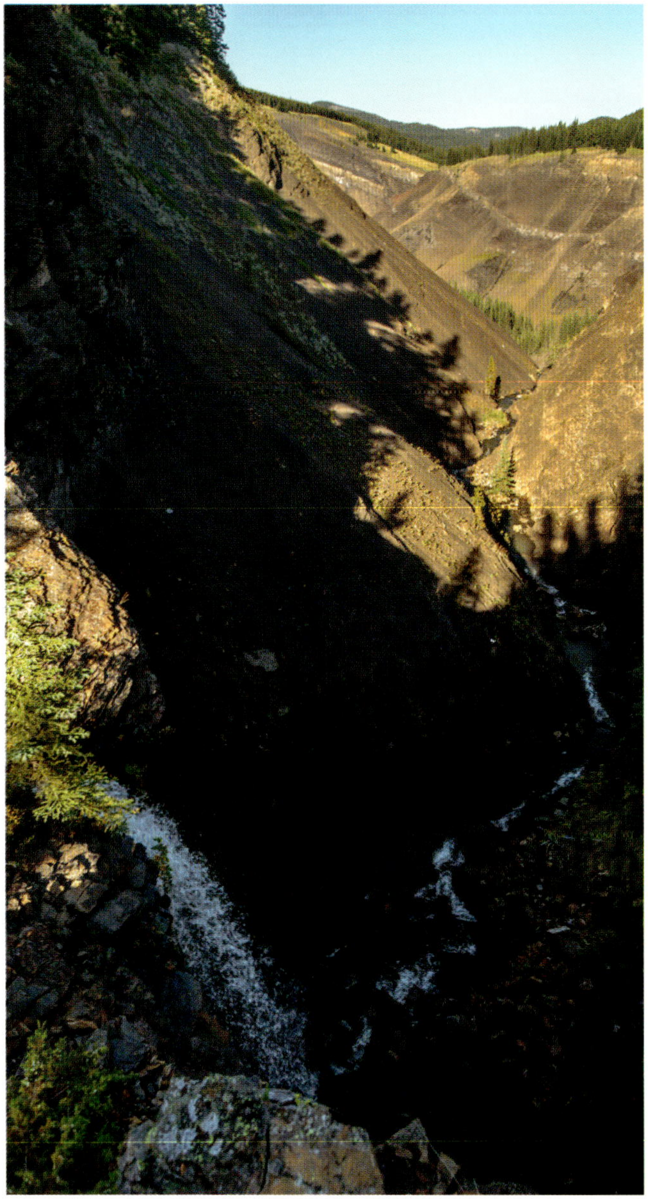

Threepoint Creek's dramatic gorge offers secure habitat for bighorn sheep, cougars, American dippers and cutthroat trout.

now abandoned and turning to meadow. The mystery was solved: Dad and Gordon had been catching beaver pond trout, which, thanks to the abundance of food wherever a fertile little creek gets turned into a sprawling wetland, tend to grow larger than those that occupy the stream above or below the pond. The ponds were gone, leaving a lush riparian mosaic of sedge meadow, spruce trees and shrubbery, pocked with moose tracks and droppings and smelling of wild mint and decay.

A little farther on we arrived at a live pond backed up by the tallest beaver dam I've ever seen. The beavers had plugged a gap where the creek tumbles into a narrow valley. It had evidently become a long-term project for the beavers to keep extending the flood waters upstream, because the dam was at least five metres high. In the deep channel above it, I landed a 44-centimetre cutthroat trout on my first cast. That was all I caught, however, before the kids began demanding relief from the mosquitoes.

I planned to return to the hidden pond the following summer, alone, so I could finally enjoy the kind of fishing I'd missed all those decades earlier, but the Sheep drainage had a major flood in the spring. The monster beaver dam blew out, likely because the upstream culvert failed, sending a massive pulse of water and sediment down the stream's swollen channel. When I arrived, I found moose droppings and bear tracks in mudflats where a few months earlier there had been deep water. The beavers will be back someday, but for now it was time for the pond marl to produce willows, sedges, moose and warblers for a few years and for the creek to erode a new channel through the accumulated silt of the former pond.

A DECADE LATER, in June 2014, I visited Seven Mile Walk Creek again, this time from the other end of the now-closed road. A year previously, the creek had once again been hit with a major flood that cut new channels and wore away the outside bends of the stream, leaving easily eroded soil exposed to the hungry water. The day I returned, the stream was running high and brown at the tail end of three days of rain. The staging area was, not surprisingly, empty. Since I was training for a race, I chose to run the old road rather than follow the creek upstream.

From the north access, the track leaves Ware Creek and swings into Link Creek valley. Like Ware Creek, to which it is a tributary, Link Creek emerges from spruce-shadowed headwater rills into gently sloping meadows whose rich silt was doubtless accumulated, at least in part, behind long-gone beaver dams. Today its valley is covered with tangles of tall willows, aspen groves, wet sedgy hollows and, on the better-drained sites, lush grassland of rough fescue, tufted hair grass, shooting stars and myriad other foothills plants. Moose droppings were everywhere, and the willows – their tops dead from drought stress only a few years earlier – were hedged and stunted from heavy winter browsing. It wasn't just moose chewing the willows down. Deer tracks were abundant and the adjacent aspen groves had fresh scars on the tree trunks where wintering elk had scraped them with their incisors to get the green inner wood.

With so much evidence of big game, I wasn't surprised to find fresh cougar tracks on the road and to see the hairy scats of wolves every few hundred metres as I huffed and puffed my way up the winding way. At length the road dropped suddenly down to my old familiar culvert. As expected, the creek had again overwhelmed the culvert during the big flood and cut a new channel through the road bed. Culverts are rarely big enough to handle extreme flood waters. Instead, they quickly plug with debris and become dams. The creek pools on the upstream side, pours over the road and in short order carves a new channel through the road bed big enough for its flood flow.

A washed-out culvert is hard on a creek; massive amounts of sediment wash downstream when the stream breaks through the road bed. Exposed to summer rains, the raw surface continues to erode sand and silt into the creek long after the diminished water flow can no longer carry the sediment away or deposit it back on the floodplain. Instead, the fine material plugs up the gravel, suffocating fish eggs and invertebrates. In reaches with slow flow, the gravel can completely disappear under muck; the creek becomes a mud-bottomed channel.

Post-flood, Ware Creek again flowed through the culvert, but the previous year's extreme flows had completed the job of turning the culvert into an impassable barrier for trout. A culvert separates the water from its floodplain and banks. Without the friction and work that normally slow its flow and absorb its energy, and constricted by the fixed-diameter width of the culvert, the stream becomes a merciless sluice, like water squeezed through a hose. It comes out of the culvert faster than it went in and promptly uses all that energy to erode the stream bed and banks below the culvert.

Ware Creek now poured over the hanging lip of the culvert into a deep hole. Even if a fish could jump straight out of the foaming plunge pool into the creek's cascading flow – a physical impossibility – the culvert itself was too long and smooth for trout. Trout can't swim fast for long distances; they dart from one eddy to another when moving upstream. There are no eddies in a culvert. Fisheries biologists describe them as velocity barriers – water flowing too fast, over too long a distance, for a fish to make it from one end to the other.

If a flood or drought should ever wipe out the cutthroat trout that occupy upper Ware Creek, they will not be back. The hanging culvert will prevent their return, just as dozens of misplaced culverts have already done on tiny headwater streams up and down the Eastern Slopes.

It was growing late. I didn't have time to wander up the creek to see whether fish still survived upstream from the culvert, so I resumed my run through the green foothills. It wasn't long before the abundant signs of wildlife once more distracted me from thoughts of floods and fish – but not of water. In the headwaters, it seems like everything is about water – even the wildlife.

IN THE LATE 1970S and early 1980s I was part of a team that did the first comprehensive ecosystem mapping and analysis in Banff and Canada's other mountain national parks. Prior to that, there had been few attempts to put soil scientists, botanists, wildlife biologists, ornithologists and herpetologists together in one place with instructions to create an integrated picture of how the natural world works.

The diverse vegetation and well-watered valleys of the Sheep watershed near Ware Creek sustain large numbers of mule deer, elk and moose, and one of the highest densities of cougars in North America.

The soil scientists mapped landforms by their origins – deposited by rock slides, glaciers, water or other forces – and the botanists described how vegetation sorted itself out on those features. The vegetation patterns were influenced by climate factors that changed with elevation and the orientation of mountain slopes, so we ended up subdividing the "ecosites" into different climate bands. The montane zone was the lowest in elevation, with the mildest winters and warmest summers. The subalpine, subdivided into a lower zone with continuous forests and an upper zone with the open, patchy woodlands of timberline, lay at higher elevations, and above that was the alpine.

My part of the team was tasked with measuring the importance of each ecosite in each climate zone for various kinds of wildlife. Unfortunately for night owls like me, the work required getting up at 3:30 in the morning in order to count songbirds during the dawn chorus. It also involved trapping dozens of small rodents and counting clumps of droppings from elk, deer and other hooved

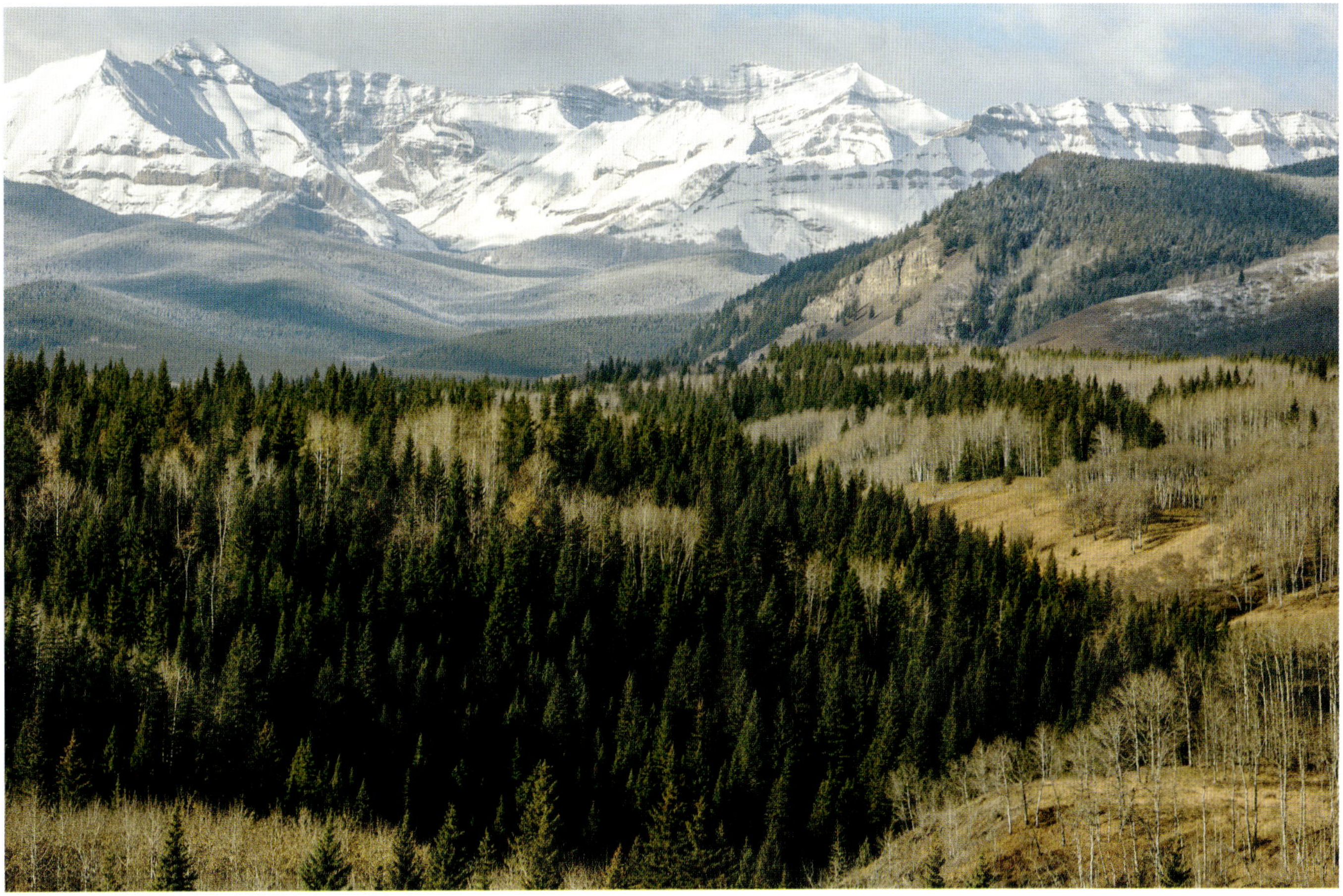

animals. A recent university graduate couldn't have asked for better work, with its long days in remote wilderness and animated discussions with colleagues about what we were seeing and learning.

When we finally crunched all the data from several years of fieldwork, it became clear that wildlife is most diverse and abundant in the parts of the landscape to which water flows, compared to the parts from which it drains. More water, more wildlife.

Two landform categories receive water from the rest of the surrounding landscape and, consequently, are exceptionally important for wildlife.

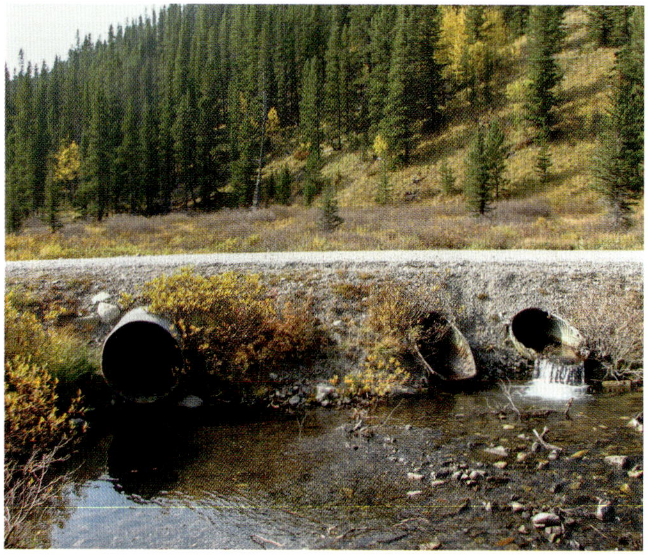

Hanging culverts completely fragment a headwater stream, isolating trout from their spawning areas and creating downstream erosion problems. Photo: Kevin Van Tighem

The first category is alluvial fans: tilting deposits of stream sediments found wherever a creek or river – issuing from a side valley into a larger main valley – slows down and loses power. Unable to continue moving all the gravel, sand and silt it has picked up farther upstream, the stream deposits it. Over the years, as new deposits gradually lift the stream bed higher, the water shifts to a different channel until it, too, is full and the stream moves again. After many decades or centuries, the shifting streams build up fans of water-deposited materials that can partially block whole valleys. Most of the sediments in Rocky Mountain alluvial fans were deposited in the first few hundred years after the glaciers melted back, because that was when the valleys were most full of unstable, easily eroded debris. Those same alluvial fans are still active, however; the difference now is that sediment deposition events are more infrequent. Usually it takes a major flood to mobilize all the material accumulated in the upper creek basin and move it downstream to the alluvial fan at the mouth of the valley. Alluvial fans in Canmore and Exshaw experienced major deposition events during the 2013 flood and will experience more in the future. It's seldom wise to build houses on the parts of the landscape where flood waters will bring massive amounts of rock, gravel, sand and silt out of side valleys during big floods – but we've done it all through the Rockies.

Riparian floodplains are the second category of landform that receives water and sediment from elsewhere. Again, it's their low gradient relative to the surrounding countryside that makes them net recipients of water and the sediments it transports during high-flow periods. Water can't drain rapidly, so it pools in seasonal wetlands or meanders onto the valley floor. Since the water isn't able to move fast, it loses power and its sediment load settles out. Unlike alluvial fans, which intercept a lot of the larger sediments, stream floodplains often get the smaller material – fine gravels, sands and silts. As a result, they have deep, rich soils.

We found that regardless of which category of wildlife we looked at – birds, grazing mammals, large predators, small rodents, amphibians or reptiles (of which garter snakes are the only example in the Rockies) – there were more kinds of them, in much higher numbers, on alluvial fans and floodplains than in any other kind of habitat in the parks.

One obvious explanation for the disproportionate importance of those habitats is the abundance of water. After most of the snow has melted, rainwater becomes the only reliable source of water for animals and plants. The more time that passes after a rainstorm, the less water that remains on hilltops and slopes, because what doesn't soak into the ground runs off. But there is almost always water to be found on alluvial fans and the floodplains of the streams, because those are the places that gather the runoff. Abundant water not only enables animals to quench their thirst when they need to but also produces lusher and more productive vegetation than drier landforms.

Vegetation is more diverse where moving water shapes the land. As streams shift course on alluvial fans or meander about their floodplains, they wash out mature forest stands, deposit new sediments that are soon colonized by young plants, dry out formerly well-watered sites and flood new sections. Inevitably, that makes for complex patterns of very different kinds of plants. Unlike the continuous pine forests that commonly clothe the surrounding hills, areas along streams are often a mosaic of old spruce stands, younger willow thickets, clumps of aspen and poplar, grassy meadows and wetlands. All that habitat diversity offers a greater variety of animals and birds places to live. It also means that food types that peak at different times of year are available in one place.

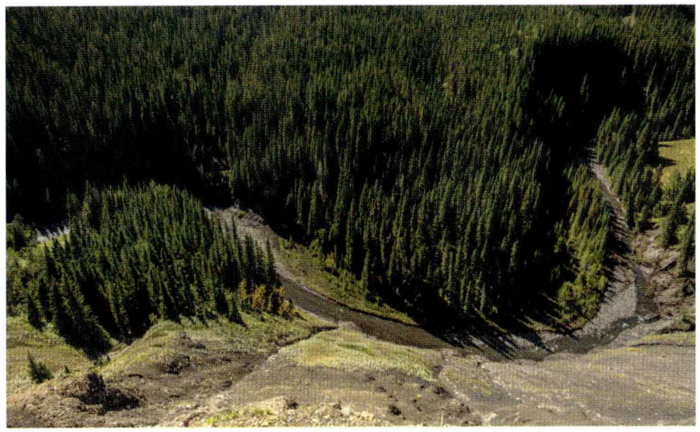

Threepoint Creek is the north fork of the Sheep River and, like the main fork, has eroded steep canyons into dark shale outcroppings. Runoff and groundwater seepage sustain rich wildlife habitat in poplar thickets and meadows along the lower slopes.

Given the reliable supply of water, high vegetation productivity and habitat diversity, it's little wonder that almost every kind of animal we looked at was more common on alluvial fans and stream floodplains. Black and grizzly bears feed on the sprouting horsetails, hairgrass, dandelions and sedges that grow there. Elk and moose have their calves on midriver islands and hide them in willow thickets while foraging in nearby marshes. Willow and alder flycatchers nest in the same willows and fly out to catch hatching insects over wetland openings or back channels of streams. Sandpipers, wolves, mink, voles, herons and garter snakes leave tracks in the mud as they travel from one food source to another. Woodpeckers excavate nesting holes in old spruce trees that have died of root rot. When the woodpeckers move out, flying squirrels, bufflehead ducks or deer mice move in. June mornings are a bedlam of birdsong, chorus frog cheeping and toad grunts wherever water flickers behind green leaves. In winter, elk, deer and their predators move like shifting shadows across the sloping alluvial fans or follow game trails that wend their way along nearby floodplains.

WHILE WE WORKED at creating a coherent picture of the ecological complexity of the mountain national parks, Martin Jalkotzy and Ian Ross were a few kilometres away, developing their own insights into wildlife ecology in the Sheep River valley. Where our studies took place deeper into the mountains, Jalkotzy and Ross focused on the outermost mountain ranges and adjacent foothills. The heart of their study area was just south of Ware Creek, in the Sheep River Wildlife Sanctuary (now part of Sheep River Provincial Park.)

The sanctuary had been established to protect a unique population of bighorn sheep that winter in the foothills. Some remain there year-round, but most migrate up the canyons of Gorge Creek and the Sheep River to spend the summer in the higher mountains to the west. Legal protection in a sanctuary was important: the same roads my family used for fishing access made it easy for hunters to get to the sheep. According to Stoney Nakoda history, bighorns once lived even farther east, on the rock outcrops and river bluffs around Turner Valley and Black Diamond. Hunters killed off that accessible herd in the 1800s.

Orval Pall had initiated a study of cougars in the Sheep River Wildlife Sanctuary in 1981 to provide a biological basis for management of cougars as a trophy species along the Eastern Slopes. The sanctuary was a good choice, because cougars were abundant and provincial wildlife managers were concerned about how much predation the area's sheep herd could handle. Unfortunately, Pall died five years into the study, at the age of 34, when a single-engine plane he had chartered for a bighorn sheep survey went down in a thunderstorm. Eleven others died in the ensuing search for the downed plane.

Jalkotzy and Ross had been working with him on the study, logging countless hours tracking radio-collared cougars across hill and dale with the help of Ralph Schmidt, a Calgary fireman and hound hunter. They continued the work after Pall's tragic death. In a sad irony, Ian Ross later died in another plane crash, this one in Africa, where he was studying that continent's wild cats.

The study wound up in 1994 – by which time it had become the longest and most exhaustive study of wild North American cats ever undertaken. The researchers captured and marked 87 separate cougars during the course of the study, and examined 368 cougar kills. They did detailed tracking of 61 cougars to figure out how they use the landscape for hunting, travel and socializing.

Their findings had a few surprises. For one thing, unlike studies from elsewhere that indicate high cub death rates, they found that 97 per cent of young cougars survived to adulthood. In addition, despite the presence of a year-round bighorn herd in the core study area, cougars killed far more mule deer – 55 per cent of all the kills identified. Even so, some cougars became sheep hunting specialists, and one individual in particular single-handedly killed 9 per cent of the sheep and 26 per cent of the lambs in the Sheep River sanctuary over the course of one winter. Moose were also surprisingly prominent on the menu, mostly calves killed by adult male cougars.

Cougars didn't appear to have any trouble using all available habitat in spite of various kinds of human use and development in the area. Seasonal winter road closures likely helped.

The Sheep River study area turned out to have one of the highest densities of cougars ever recorded in North America – between 2.7 and 3.3 cats per 100 square kilometres in 1984 and as many as 4.5 to 4.7 by 1988. During the course of the study, the total number of cougars increased from around 23 to 36, mostly because of an increase in the number of adult females and their kittens.

That many cougars need a lot of food. The Sheep River drainage produces a lot of cougar food because the habitats that we had found to be so important in the Rocky Mountain national parks farther west are more abundant in the high foothills. Valleys are broader and streams more numerous in the foothills than in the Rockies. Thousands of years of beaver activity built broad riparian valley floors. Soils are deeper here than they are farther back in the mountains – glaciers deposited a lot of material here that they had scraped out of the higher mountains, and the climate is milder than at higher elevations, giving plant roots more time to grow into glacial debris and stream deposits and work their soil-building magic. The deeper soils absorb more water.

Everywhere in the Sheep River drainage, lush aspen forests, south-facing fescue grasslands and dense tangles of willows reflect the wetness and fertility of the landscape. They also provide optimal habitat for herds of mule deer, elk and moose, and growing numbers of white-tailed deer. Springs that emerge into fen meadows and canyon walls bring dissolved minerals to the surface; in some places they are trampled to mud each year by ungulates using them as salt licks.

Water and wildlife are essentially the same thing; in the Sheep drainage, the evidence is everywhere. The same rule holds true throughout the foothills drainages that feed the Bow and Oldman rivers. Grazing and browsing animals gravitate to the same parts of the landscape into which water drains, because that's where the best forage is to be found. Their predators, consequently, do the same. If you want to find a wolf den or a cougar track in the Sheep drainage, look for the hollows and valley bottoms that hold water. In a very real way, then, abundant predators are an indicator of a healthy watershed. If the Sheep River country held less water, it would hold fewer animals.

Even the bighorn sheep that winter on the fescue grasslands along the main road west from Turner Valley owe their survival to the action of water in the landscape. Bighorns rarely spend much time far from rocky cliffs, where they can escape from predators by climbing to safety. Many of the sheep that continue to winter in the foothills survive their annual migrations to and from the mountains by following the steep canyons that Gorge Creek and the Sheep River have carved through shale. Other sheep herds spend much of the year using similar steep canyons carved into the high foothills by Volcano and Threepoint creeks to travel safely from one seasonal range to another. Water erosion has created bighorn travel-ways that keep the Sheep River's namesake animal thriving amid the unfriendly forests that cover much of its watershed.

Gorge Creek, a tributary of the Sheep River. Research at Gorge Creek proved the futility of stocking hatchery fish and the importance of conserving native trout in foothills streams.

JALKOTZY AND ROSS weren't the only graduate students delving into the relationships among wildlife, their habitats and the richly watered valleys that drain to the Sheep River. Ever since the 1950s, researchers based out of the R.B. Miller Station on Gorge Creek have examined ground squirrel ecology, bighorn sheep population dynamics, deer behaviour, grouse ecology, amphibian habitat selection and other aspects of the headwaters ecosystem.

Gorge Creek became a research stream in the 1950s, when the Alberta government was under increasing pressure from fish and game groups to stock more trout into foothills streams. Long-time anglers were complaining that fishing had deteriorated after roads made once-remote streams accessible to the masses. Many streams were already being stocked regularly, but it didn't seem to help. Department staff, painfully aware that their limited budget provided most of the funding for the expensive program, suspected it was because the fish died as soon as they were released.

The department asked Miller, a professor at the University of Alberta, to come up with a definitive answer. Miller was a fisheries biologist – a rare creature in the province before the government finally began hiring its own science expertise. Miller felt that the only way to get answers that would withstand the inevitable controversy between penny-pinching bureaucrats and eager anglers would be to do a careful, long-term study on a foothills trout stream.

His research station began in 1950 as a small tent camp at a site Miller and his wife selected near the mouth of Gorge Creek, within a comfortable distance of the nearby ranger station. Gorge Creek was ideal for his purposes. It had a good population of native cutthroat trout. Much of the upper reach is similar to other foothills streams, with a gravel-bottomed stream wandering from pool to riffle to pool through a forested valley. But where the creek drops toward its confluence with the Sheep River, it has carved a narrow canyon with pools separated by rocky outcroppings and narrow drops. The lower creek was ideal for installing fish barriers between pools so that the fates of individual trout, whether the already resident wild fish or hatchery-bred immigrants, could be monitored without risk of vital evidence swimming – or washing – away.

Miller's research involved fencing off stream reaches between one and two kilometres long and then experimenting with various hatchery-raised trout in each section. The fenced reaches each contained up to three hundred wild cutthroat trout that already occupied the best habitat. Miller found that dead hatchery trout began appearing within a day or two of their release. Within ten days of release, more than half had died. The rest failed to thrive, losing weight steadily for the first month or so and then, as

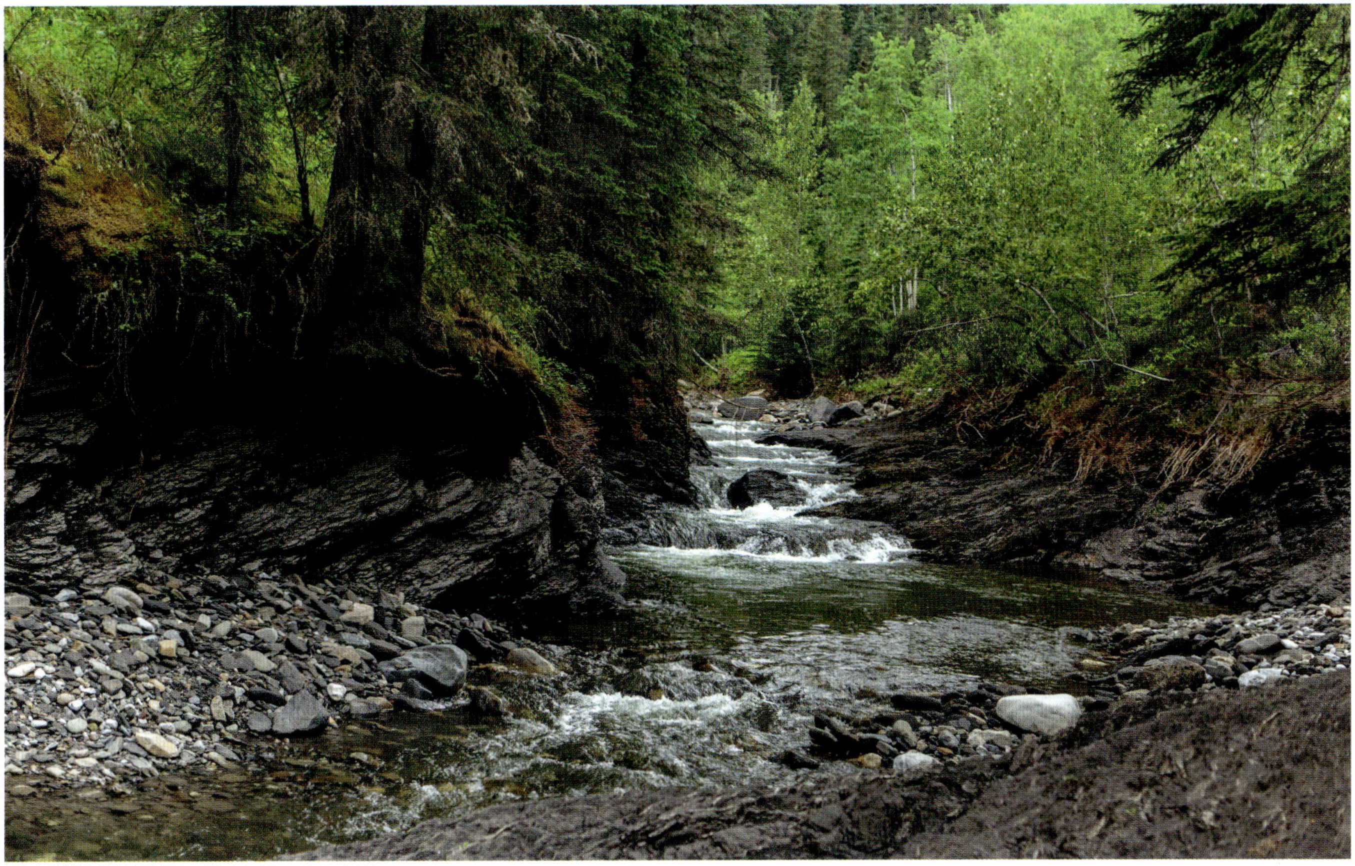

they learned how to forage for natural foods and take advantage of stream structure to save energy in resting spots, only gained weight slowly. The young fish should have grown rapidly, but most were the same weight in late fall as they had been when originally released in the spring.

Almost all the pond-reared hatchery trout died within a few months of being released. By the end of the first winter, fewer than 5 per cent survived, and by the end of the second winter, the best survival rate recorded was 3 per cent. Wild fish imported from other streams did better, with about half surviving their first winter and a bit less than a third still alive after the second.

When Miller examined the bodies of the hatchery fish that died, he found high levels of lactic acid in their muscles. The fish had died of exhaustion in an unfamiliar environment.

Hatchery-raised trout learn bad habits in the hatchery that, when transplanted to a natural stream ecosystem, work against their survival. In hatcheries, young trout are bold and aggressive feeders because they have to be. They spend a lot of their time near the tops of the hatchery pools: that's where their food is delivered, and there is little cost to them in terms of wasted energy, as the current through hatchery pools is usually very weak.

Transplanted into streams, the hatchery trout are at the bottom of the pecking order. Existing wild trout aggressively defend the best holding water and force the inexperienced newcomers to waste energy fighting the current in marginal habitat where the current is stronger and insect life less abundant. Predators, including anglers, have little trouble finding them. Wild, native trout in the same streams conserve energy by resting in the slower water at the bottom of pools and near boulders or other obstacles. The resident fish draw down their muscle glycogen levels more gradually than the hatchery fish, partly because they only feed when food is abundant and partly because they occupy the most sheltered locations.

Miller's studies helped explain why years of intensive stocking in streams up and down the foothills of the Rockies had done nothing to improve the fishing or even to slow down the rate at which fisheries collapsed. The government took a U-turn in its fish-stocking program. By the 1960s hatchery trucks had stopped disgorging cargoes of befuddled fingerlings into foothills creeks. Instead, the province began stocking reservoirs and sloughs. Hatchery fish did much better in those food-rich still-water environments, where there were no wild fish with which to compete. The stocked ponds had the added advantage, in many cases, of being closer to cities and towns and consequently more accessible for anglers.

Based on Miller's and others' work, fisheries biologist Lorne Fitch concludes that trout should only be stocked in streams under a very specific set of conditions: they should be released fully grown, immediately before or during the angling season, in streams with high angler use and only where there are no or very few native trout.

Researchers found that stocking hatchery-raised trout can actually harm the native trout already in a stream. When the Alberta Fish & Wildlife Division stocked catchable-sized rainbow trout into Jumpingpound Creek in the late 1960s, the fishing was soon worse than it had been before. Fishermen who flocked to the creek to exploit the hatchery fish also killed many of the native cutthroats and rainbow trout. When fisheries managers stocked the Elbow River in Calgary with catchable-sized rainbow trout, anglers not only caught three-quarters of the stocked trout that summer but fished out most of the river's existing whitefish population, too.

Even without heavier angling pressure, some studies showed that wild trout populations decline after hatchery fish are stocked, possibly because their stress levels increase in response to the increased competition.

Miller produced several important scientific papers before his death in 1959. The government kept the research station open and, in honour of Miller's contributions to fisheries management in Alberta, renamed it in 1989 as the R.B. Miller Station. The original purpose of the station having been satisfied, the scope of scientific investigation for its graduate students expanded to wildlife, vegetation, soils and other aspects of the headwaters environment. The station is now affiliated with the University of Calgary's Biogeoscience Institute, which is based in a former Canadian Forest Service research station near Barrier Lake, in the Kananaskis valley.

THE RELATIONSHIPS connecting water, wet places and wildlife account for the distribution and abundance of herbivores and their predators in the Sheep drainage, just as they do its trout. Humans, too, have historically congregated in the same rich habitats. For instance, the first trails and roads into the high country followed the edges of valley floors – the same places that hold the most water and wildlife. That convergence accounted for both the washed-out culverts I encountered on my run to upper Ware Creek and the abundant animal tracks along the road. It also explained the elk tooth marks on the roadside aspens, the browsed-down willows and the big, shiny bear scat I accidentally stepped in.

Landscapes with lots of water often have lots of bears, too. Bear biologist Wayne McCrory says that, fundamentally, bears are water animals. "The biggest bears and the densest populations of bears are where there is the most water in the landscape – along the salmon streams and tidal flats of British Columbia and coastal Alaska," he says. "In the Rockies, where there's less water, you still find the most bear activity in the wettest places."

Bears are omnivorous – they wander seasonally to whatever will give them the richest supply of protein, starches and sugars. That diet brings them to alluvial fans, stream floodplains and wetlands again and again through the year. In the spring, sprouting greenery and starch-rich roots and bulbs are most abundant there. Some bears become adept at finding and eating newborn elk and moose calves. That hunt leads them to the dense thickets along streams where nervous mothers most often hide their young. Later in the summer, as the surrounding landscape becomes increasingly dry, lush vegetation persists in the wet places, and the bears chow down on tufted hairgrass, dandelion flowers, horsetails and other seasonal goodies. In the fall, when human hunters arrive in the high country to take their share of its bounty of hooved animals, bears seek out the gut piles left behind, once again benefiting from the wetness that yields wildlife.

Grizzly bears range throughout the headwaters of the Bow River, including the high country and streams draining to the Sheep River. In retrospect, it might not have been such a good idea for my father to leave his little boy alone for hours on end on the lonely banks of upper Ware Creek even if, in the 1960s, grizzlies were considerably less abundant there.

The big wanderers have always been controversial neighbours because of their willingness to attack people when they feel threatened and their tendency to see livestock, stored grain, untended barbecues and garbage cans as food. The relationship between grizzlies and people became more complicated in 2004, when an analysis of DNA-based mark-recapture studies throughout most of western Alberta yielded a province-wide estimate of fewer than seven hundred grizzlies. The government designated the grizzly a threatened species. Their new legal status brought an end to grizzly hunting in 2006 and required managers to develop a recovery plan to reduce risks to the big bears.

Grizzlies generally do just fine if people don't kill them. With the institution of bear-proof garbage management systems and the end of the grizzly hunt, fewer grizzlies die at human hands today than in the past. Still, every year some do die at the hands of humans; in 2013 alone, provincial wildlife biologists tallied up 13 known roadkills and another 11 grizzlies shot by poachers. Hinton-based grizzly researcher Gordon Stenhouse has determined that poachers almost always kill bears within a few metres of a road or motorized trail. Most grizzlies avoid human activity on general principles, so even without the risk of being shot or run over, they avoid well-used roads and trails. That's why a primary focus of Alberta's 2008 Grizzly Bear Recovery Plan is to reduce motorized access into areas of prime grizzly bear habitat.

The final closure of the old forest road from Gorge Creek over to Ware Creek after the 2005 flood is aligned with the recovery plan, as is the ongoing ban on off-highway vehicle use in the surrounding Sheep River and Bluerock Wildland provincial parks. But elsewhere in the Sheep drainage – around Threepoint and Fisher creeks in particular – networks of illegal and eroding trails offer ample evidence of the determination of some poachers and motorized vandals to find their way around closures and regulations. Blown-out culverts along the Ware Creek road also show that simply putting a gate at either end of a road doesn't eliminate its impact on streams, water and wildlife habitat.

The dark shales of the Sheep River canyon erode into fine soil that sustains lush adjacent grasslands. Bighorn sheep use the canyon walls for security from predators as they migrate from nearby mountains to their foothills winter range.

Many people are ambivalent or even antagonistic toward the idea of closing vehicle access to increase the number of bears. But few would argue against the idea of improving the headwaters landscape so that it yields more and better-quality water – especially if doing so also means better fishing and more wildlife. Grizzly recovery doesn't have to be just about bears – done well, it can be as much or more about water security, flood mitigation and wildlife conservation. The bears will still benefit.

Roads bring groundwater to the surface as fast-draining springs, and their ditches channel rain runoff quickly into creeks. The result is an increase in the damaging power of spring floods and a decrease in groundwater. Instead of residing in the soil for weeks, keeping foothills vegetation green before seeping into streams later in the summer, the water drains away quickly away in the spring along with mud from soils that took centuries to build.

Access restrictions may be essential for recovering grizzly populations, but they are also essential for watershed health. Land managers would do well not only to barricade unnecessary roads and OHV trails but also to break up the compacted soil under them and restore the original slope contours where they cut into the water table

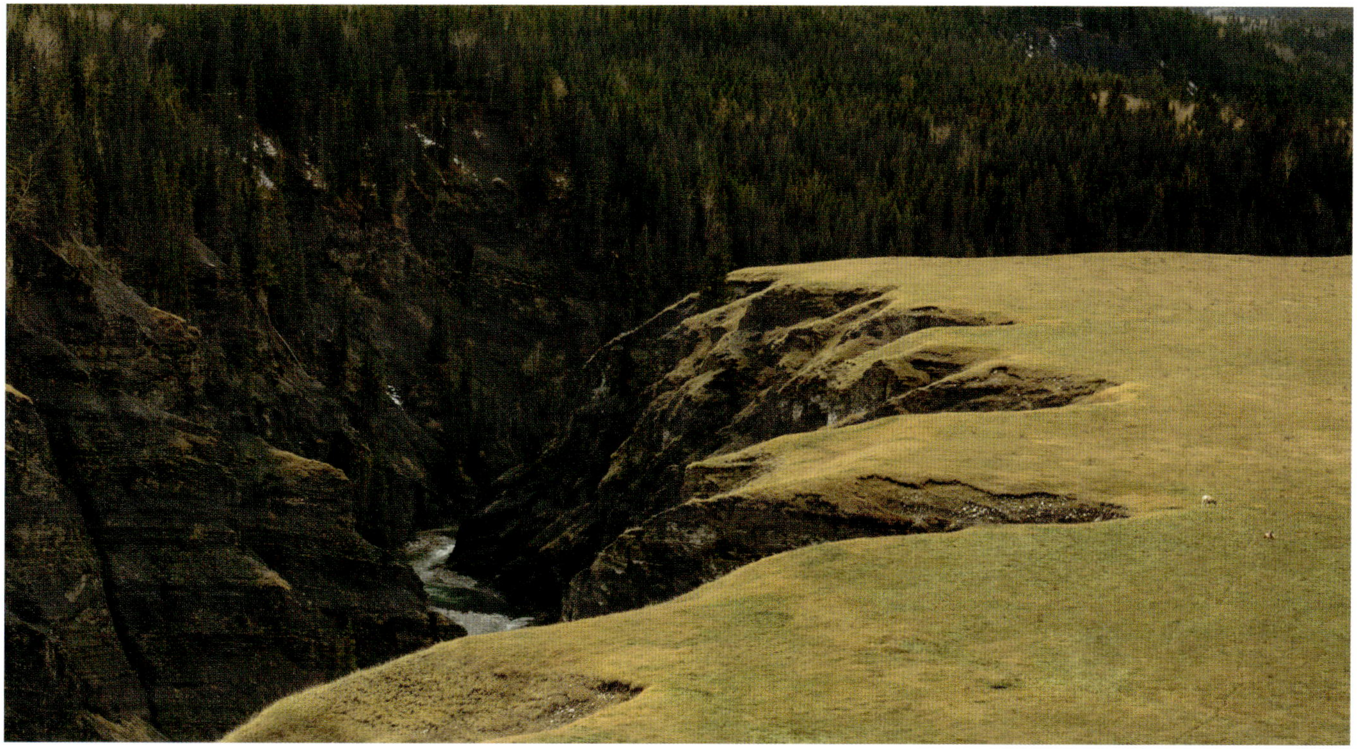

on hillsides. Breaking up and revegetating the compacted road beds reduces flood damage by removing the effect of these unnatural dams on runoff water. Aggressive rehabilitation of this sort would also discourage vandals from reopening the trails.

The old road that my family used to hike to Seven Mile Walk Creek is almost back to nature. Bringing it the rest of the way by physically removing the road bed would reduce future flood damage, retain more water in the wet places that sustain the Sheep's abundant wildlife, and reduce the risk of grizzly bears being killed or displaced from their best habitat. Parents would still be able to hike their children in to rendezvous with native cutthroat trout – not stocked fish – in the shadowed pools where Ware Creek is born. Contrary to the spectral vision of inevitable loss that sits at the heart of so many modern dialogues about nature and wild places, however, their hikes would be through a greener, healthier landscape than the one my family knew. A place like the Sheep River watershed was meant to be: one of water, wildlife and wildness.

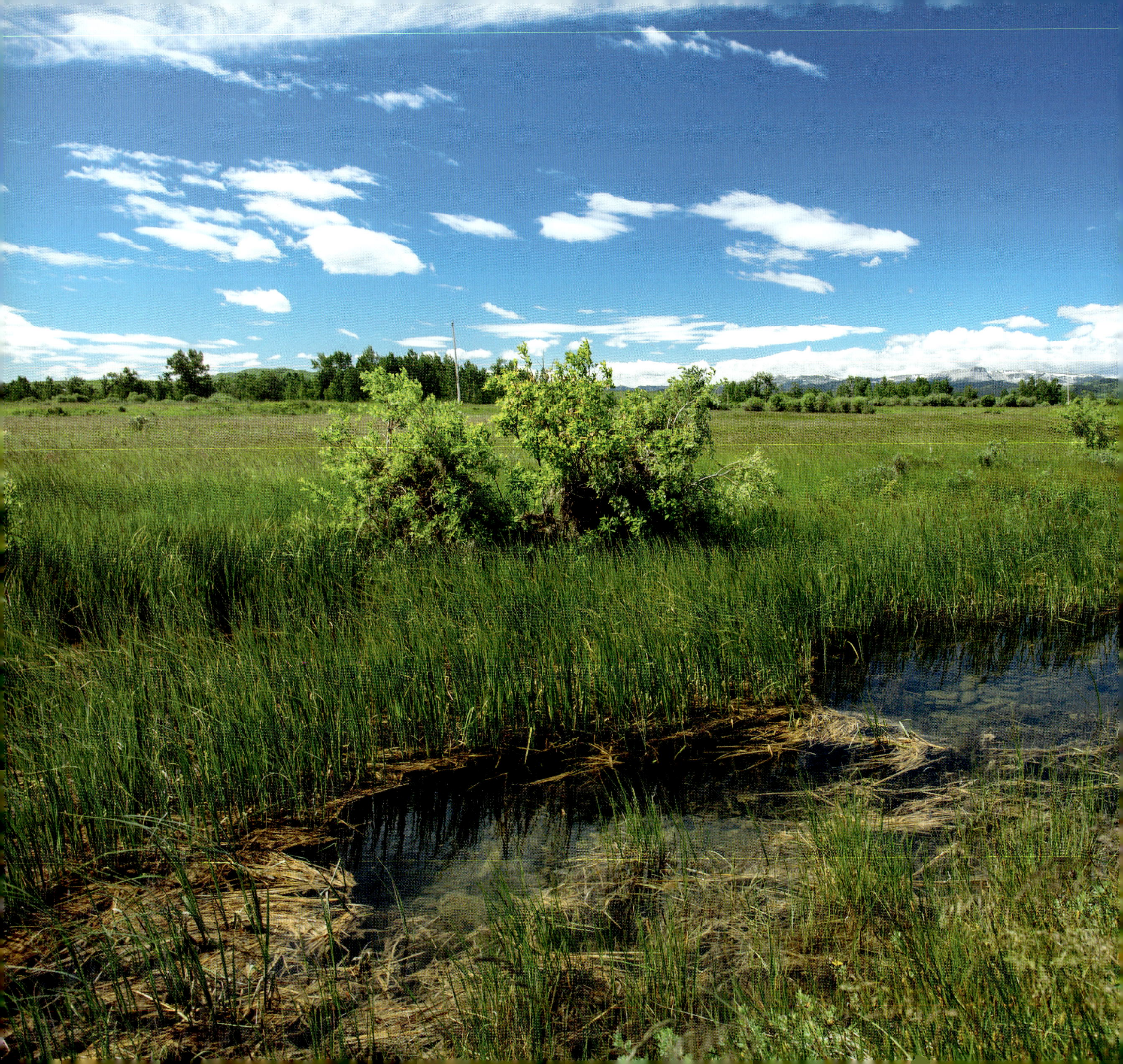

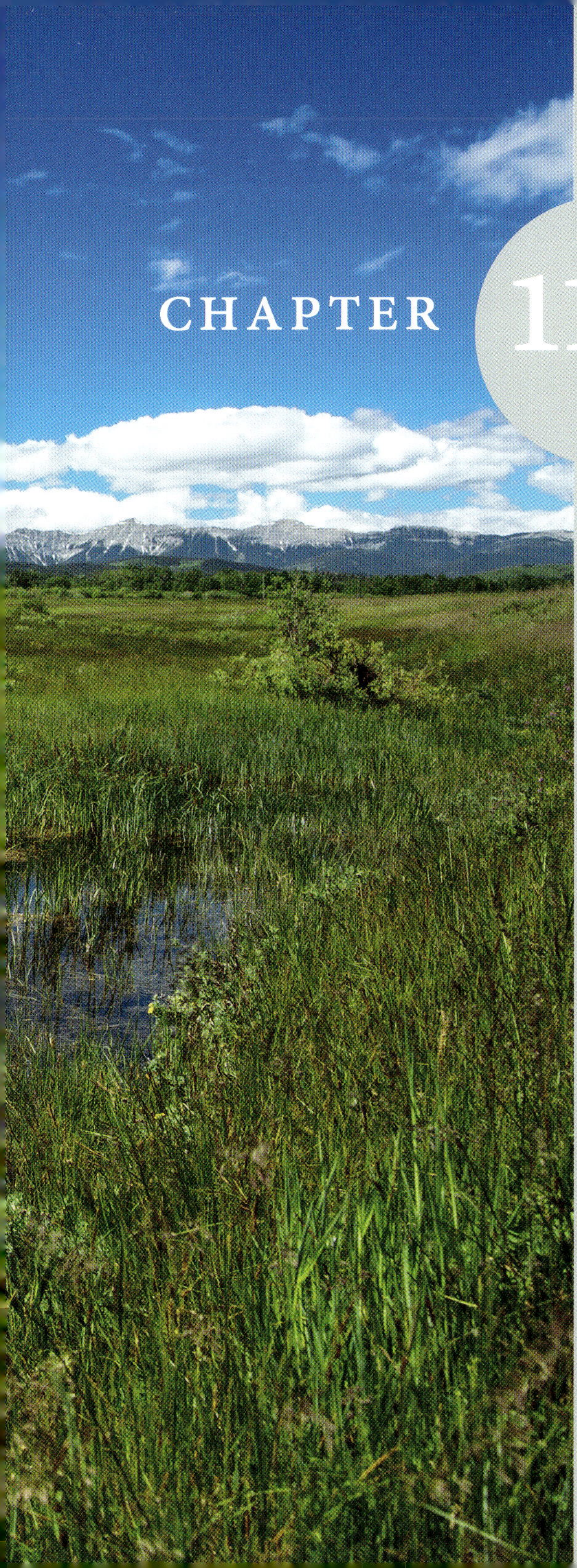

CHAPTER 11

Cattle in the Creek

Pekisko Creek

THERE'S PART of an Ian Tyson song, "Fifty Years Ago," stuck in my head this evening:

> And the sighing of the pines
> up here near the timberlines
> makes me wish I'd done things different.
> Ah, but wishin' don't make it so.

The men seated on folding chairs around me are mostly in denim jeans. Crossed legs end in scuffed riding or work boots; crossed arms end in callused hands. Ball caps and western hats frame reserved, if not downright skeptical, faces. Few of these guys look like they're wishing they'd done things different, but of course there is a lot of western maleness here this evening. Nobody's going to be the first to admit to doubts or regrets in this gathering.

Maybe Ian Tyson's song got into my internal jukebox because Lorne Fitch is at the podium now. He's telling a parable about the Longview Saloon, one of Tyson's favourite venues. With his bushy beard and wire glasses, Fitch

Page 160: *Water-loving cottonwoods form a galley forest along Pekisko Creek, and willow tangles and sedge meadows mark spring seeps that feed the creek. Well-managed ranch land.*

looks more like a poet-philosopher than like a rancher. He is neither: since retiring as senior fisheries biologist for southern Alberta, he has become a respected elder among the stream conservation community.

His deep voice firm with conviction, Fitch disarms the audience with self-deprecating humour and an evident respect for the ranchers whose stories he shares. Even so, there isn't a lot of warmth in the room yet. It's still early, though. The crowd will come around. I've seen the magic before.

Lorne's telling his Pat and Mike story. Pat and Mike are two foothills cowboys who've been enjoying the good companionship and cold beer at the Longview Saloon on a windy Saturday night. Come closing time, Mike stops in the washroom and Pat heads out to the parking lot to start up the pickup truck.

When Mike steps out into the darkness, he sees Pat crawling around on his hands and knees at the opposite corner of the parking lot from the truck, under the only streetlight.

"What are you doing?" Mike demands.

"Looking for my keys."

"But your truck's way over there."

"I know that, but the light's better over here."

Fitch is making a point about range management. More specifically, he's making a point about why, during the last century, so many of western Alberta's creek bottoms became tired, trampled and washed-out in spite of the sincere efforts of the ranchers managing them. There is a widespread ethic in cattle country that aims to leave the land in better shape than ranchers found it. If clean water, shady willows and a robust trout population are proof of good stewardship, ranching has not always lived up to those ideals. Cochrane's community history book, for example, includes many references by early settlers to the good fishing in Grand Valley, Horse and Bighill creeks. Within less than a century, all three creeks became largely fishless. Fisheries biologists assessed the main problem as being damage caused by cattle.

It's not that the ranchers along those creeks set out to damage them, or that they felt indifferent about the eroding banks and silted riffles. Many of them fenced, herded, adjusted their stocking rates and did everything that conventional range-management thinking would say adds up to good stewardship. But, as Fitch is pointing out today, even if it is easier to look for the keys to good riparian management under the light of received ranching wisdom, a century of stream deterioration has shown that they aren't there. He concludes his little anecdote with a droll punch line that gets a few chuckles: "You know, the first symptom of insanity is to keep on doing the same thing in hopes of getting different results."

Fitch is in this rural community hall tonight at the invitation of some local ranchers whose arms aren't crossed. They don't need to be convinced by his well-practised spiel about cows, creeks and restoration; they already practise what he preaches – in fact, they're his inspiration.

During the many years when he was responsible for

the productivity of southern Alberta's streams and lakes, Lorne Fitch went through a lot of unhappy soul-searching about the deteriorating condition of the fisheries until, one day, driving through a foothills valley, he saw a mile-long reach of creek bottom that was lush in willows, slough grass and sparkling water. It was completely unlike the rest of the cow-battered valley.

After gazing in wonder at a living example of what foothills streams were meant to look like, Fitch went in search of the rancher through whose land the creek flowed. At the door, once the introductions were out of the way, he asked the rancher what he was doing that kept his stream bottom in such exceptionally good condition. Buoyed and excited after a stimulating talk with a humble soul who had quietly figured out for himself how to move his cattle among pastures so that the creek bottom retained its shrubby cover and well-grassed stream banks, Fitch shared his epiphany with colleague Barry Adams, a rangeland specialist with Alberta Agriculture. They began to wonder how many other ranchers were out there with healthy creeks and a tale to tell.

Cows and Fish – the popular name for the Alberta Riparian Habitat Management Society – was born soon after. The organization promotes best practices developed in ranch country by ranchers to restore streams and their floodplains to health: things like providing off-stream watering sites, reducing the period during which cows are let into stream-bottom pastures, changing the season of grazing to when vegetation is most resilient, and resting riparian pastures periodically so that willows and grasses can build strong root systems.

I'm at tonight's Cows and Fish meeting partly to be inspired once again by the Fitch and Adams show, partly to learn what this area's most progressive ranchers have to teach me about the possibilities of creating a sustaining culture in cattle country, and partly to beat up on myself. As a writer, my early contributions to the discussion, I'm now painfully aware, were more inflammatory than helpful. That's why I'm hoping the lean, wiry men around me haven't read my essay "The Curse of the Cow" – or if they have, that they don't realize they're sitting near its author. Otherwise, there's a chance it's my teeth, rather than my keys, that I'll be looking for in the parking lot later this evening.

MY STRING OF ANTI-COW WRITINGS began in the 1980s, shortly after I returned from a long day of fishing in the Coal Creek valley, a south-bank tributary of the Sheep River, west of Turner Valley. I had taken my then-seven-year-old son Corey with me. During the long hike in from the Sandy McNabb Campground, I imagined us sharing the kind of idyllic day in the foothills that I'd often enjoyed with my own dad. When we arrived in the creek meadows, however, the valley was full of cattle. The South Sheep Grazing Association, comprised of a number of small ranchers from the nearby foothills, has a summer grazing licence for the Sheep River's tributary valleys. On that July day, it seemed like all their cows were in the Coal Creek meadows.

No problem. If you're an Albertan, cows are part of the decor.

But when Corey began to make plaintive noises about

water, I realized we did indeed have a problem. I'd counted on getting drinking water from one of the valley's many springs, but every one of them had been thoroughly fouled by cattle. What should have been lush wet sedge meadows were mucky swamps full of cow tracks. Where clean water had once seeped from hillsides into narrow, moss-lined channels, it now oozed into muddy, trampled holes crusted with cow manure. As the sun beat down on a cowed-out valley, the culprits stood in the creek, placidly twitching their tails at flies, bemusedly watching a frustrated dad try to soothe an increasingly miserable little boy.

Heading home in defeat down a trail redolent with manure, I reflected on the fact that this Forest Reserve valley is all public land that, by government policies dating back to the early 1900s, is meant to be managed primarily for watershed protection. Yet those cattle were turned out year after year with no measures to protect that watershed's springs and seeps. Cattle, unlike bison and other native grazing animals, are essentially a riparian animal whose wild ancestors lived in subtropical swamps. Their DNA consequently programs them to gravitate to wet places. Leave them alone, and that's where they'll be. And that's why so many foothills streams became sick during the 20th century – too many cows in all the wrong places.

The ranchers who owned those animals never set out deliberately to ruin creeks. They just hadn't figured out how to keep their stock from camping out there. Cows need regular access to drinking water, after all. One can only afford to put in so much fencing. And in any case, fencing on creek floodplains can be an exercise in futility, because creeks have a habit of washing out fences.

But as I returned home that evening with a miserable, half-dehydrated son, I wasn't feeling philosophical; I was downright annoyed. After the kids were in bed, I fired up the computer and punched out the first draft of an essay that I titled "Curse of the Cow." When it later appeared in print, it did not endear me to the western ranching fraternity – an awkward matter for one who relies on permission from landowners to access some of his favourite creeks and ridges, and even more awkward when a new job led to my having to work closely with ranchers in the Waterton area.

While I wrote diatribes against cows and ranching, Lorne Fitch and Barry Adams came up with a more positive and ultimately more effective solution to cow-beaten creeks. They began looking up and down the Alberta foothills for healthy streams and then approached the ranchers to find out more about their grazing systems and the thinking behind them. With Fitch's expertise in fish and wildlife habitat, and Adams's in-depth knowledge of how different kinds of plants respond to grazing, they were often able to explain to the rancher the ecology of how his or her common-sense, trial-and-error approach worked. Lights were soon going on for everyone involved in those conversations as they built upon one another's knowledge. It wasn't long before the energy and enthusiasm generated by those discoveries made them look around to see how to get other ranchers and resource managers into the dialogue.

Trout and Cattle

Fisheries ecologist Lorne Fitch has argued for many years that a simple measure of a stream's health is the status of its native trout populations. Cutthroat and bull trout need cold water, clean stream sediments and sustained flows – all of which are the products of a healthy watershed. As landscape damage and riparian abuse cause the springs to run more sporadically, floods to come down harder and mud to wash into the creek gravels, native trout disappear.

Early settlers along the north bank tributaries draining into the Bow River in the Cochrane area left glowing accounts of fishing for cutthroat and bull trout in Horse, Grand Valley and Bighill springs. For instance, Lilian Cowan-Douglas, writing about her parents' ranch in the Bighill Creek valley, said, "Converging near the house were two little creeks, full of trout."

Farther east, even Nose Creek held trout in the early 20th century.

But while those early Albertans delighted in the great fishing in their home streams, they were also trapping out the beavers whose dams helped sustain base flows into those creeks. While the settlers diverted precious water to irrigate gardens and crops, their cows were trampling the stream banks and eating down the willow shrubbery, slough grass and sedges that shaded the trout pools, enriched the stream with organic material and helped hold the banks together.

By the end of the 20th century, viable populations of native fish no longer survived in the little creeks near Cochrane and Calgary.

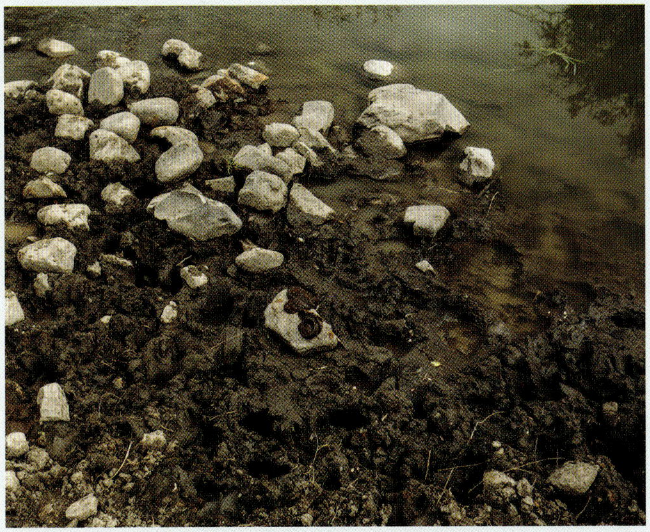

Left to their own devices, cattle will congregate near water, where they trample wet soils and reduce the protective root mass by repeatedly grazing down grasses and sedges.

Citizen groups like Trout Unlimited Canada and Cochrane's Branches and Banks Foundation, as well as individual ranchers who have adopted the enlightened cattle-management approaches promoted by Cows and Fish, are trying to restore the health of the streams and, by extension, of the watersheds they drain. The best measure of their eventual success, says Fitch, would be the recovery of native fish stocks.

Still, he cautions, "The deterioration of these creeks unfolded over more than a century, and the problems are complex. People need to understand that their recovery could well take just as long."

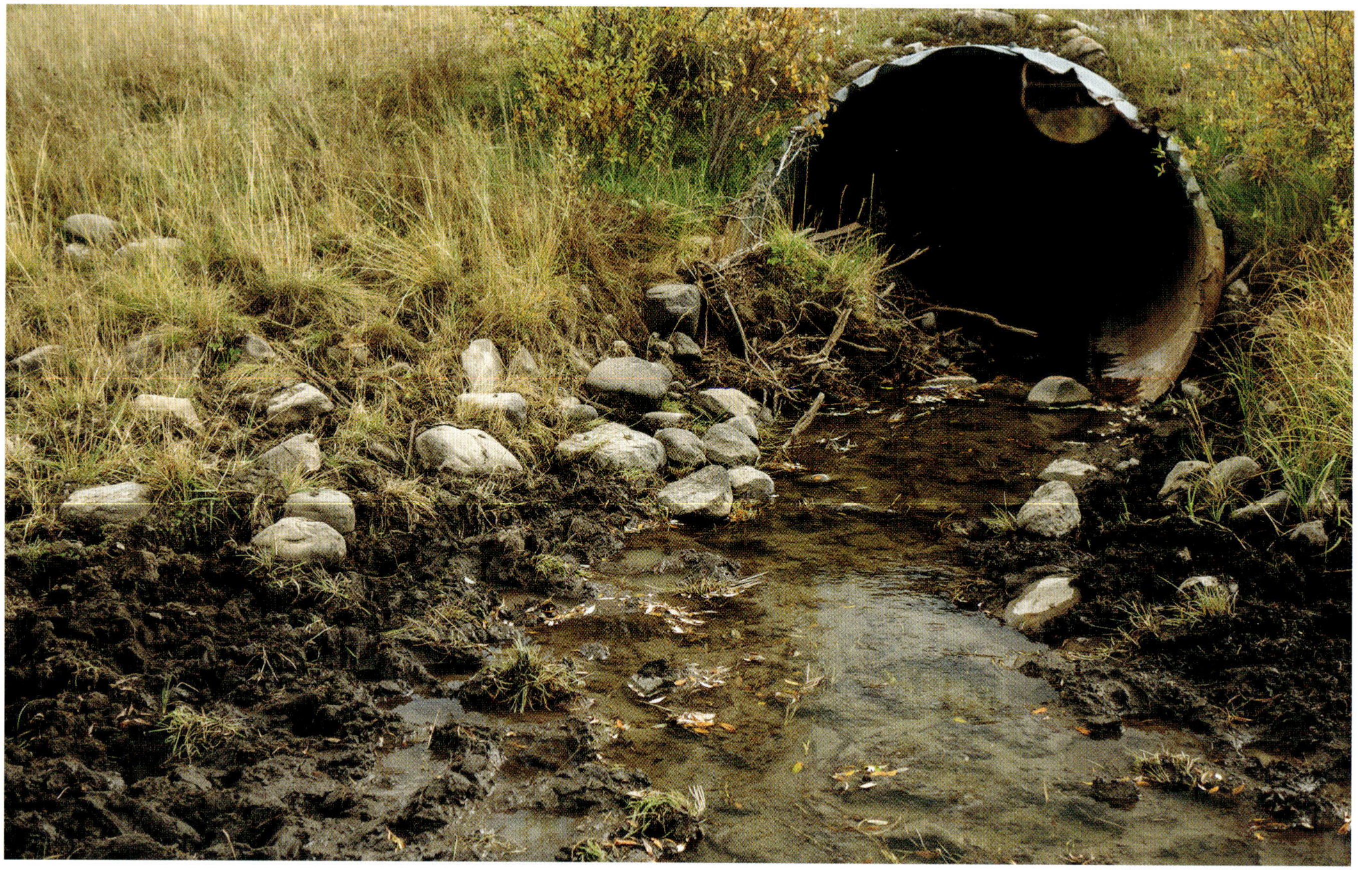

ALDO LEOPOLD, perhaps the most influential conservationist North America has ever known, once said that we have made the world safe for cows, and now the challenge is to make the world safe *from* cows. Fortunately that's possible; although domestic cows aren't native to the Alberta foothills, grazing is. It isn't a matter of getting rid of the new ruminants; it's a matter of managing them well.

The bison that once ranged in immense herds across the drier prairies to the east moved into the foothills each fall to spend the winter where chinook winds keep the fescue bunchgrass slopes open through most of the season. The grazing pressure must have been significant, because the numbers of bison were immense. Ezra Lefthand, a Stoney, told one early rancher that when he

Two ways to damage a creek: install a culvert instead of a bridge, and allow domestic cattle to graze and trample riparian vegetation during sensitive seasons.

was a very small child he was camped with his family south of Pekisko Creek in a very narrow valley between steep hills. During the night, they heard the bison migrating through the camp, and the people were so afraid of startling the buffalo that they stayed inside their teepees and wouldn't let the children cry. It took the herd three days and two nights to pass.

Ever since the glaciers retreated, grazing animals have cropped the bunchgrass hills beneath the chinook arch. Some – like mammoths and, later, deer and pronghorns – fed primarily on woody browse and forbs rather than grasses. Others, like bison, were for the most part upland grazers who visited creeks and sloughs to drink but then moved on. They grazed the foothills intensely, but for only a brief period each year before continuing their annual circuit across the plains. In the open, unfenced landscapes of pristine Alberta, animals were never confined to single pastures for long periods the way cattle are today. Even if they had been inclined to spend long enough in one spot to overgraze its vegetation, they had to move repeatedly to avoid predators like wolves, cougars and Aboriginal hunters.

Many native vegetation communities are adapted to seasonal grazing and, without it, deteriorate or give way to other types of vegetation that are of less value to wildlife and watersheds. Well-managed cattle operations are as essential to the health and productivity of the headwaters as the more poorly managed ones are harmful.

The ecological challenge with cattle grazing is to emulate, as much as possible, the kinds of grazing patterns that the vegetation and landscape evolved with – but to do so with an animal that doesn't behave like the original grazing animals, in the absence of large predators, and with a landscape that has been carved up with fences and land-ownership deeds that largely eliminate the free movement of animals across the land. Just to complicate the challenge a bit more, most ranchers don't have a large labour force or a bottomless well of capital; solutions need to be cheap and practical.

Like Ian Tyson says, "Wishin' don't make it so." True, but intelligent creativity, collaboration, information sharing and open-mindedness can. Increasingly, they do.

SOUTH OF THE LONGVIEW SALOON, Pekisko Creek drains a rolling foothills landscape of fescue grasslands, willow thickets, beaver ponds and forest. Its headwaters, just east of the Rocky Mountain front ranges, are well served with springs whose water originates in snowmelt and rainfall farther west. Farther downstream, as the creek grows into a gravel-bottomed, chattery little trout stream, the landscape opens out into row after row of grassy hills that were the location of some of Alberta's oldest cattle ranches. Those hills are the source of the creek's name: *pekisko* is "many hills" in the Nakoda tongue.

George Lane brought the first large herds of cattle into

Pekisko Creek country in 1882, trailing a herd of three thousand head in from Idaho to stock a large ranching lease acquired a year earlier by Fred Stimson, the Quebec-born cattleman who founded the North West Cattle Company. The ranch, which came to be known by its Bar U brand, was one of several large open-range leases established in the region during the late 1880s in response to incentives offered by the Dominion government. Like other large lease ranches of its day, it was characterized by absentee owners – mostly eastern-based speculators with political friends – and overstocking. Within a few years the four hundred-square-kilometre Bar U was pasturing more than 10,000 head. Elizabeth Lane estimated that over 25,000 head of cattle and at least one thousand horses were on the open range south of Pekisko Creek by 1904.

Over the years, as market conditions and land regulatory regimes evolved, the Bar U changed ownership a few times before it was finally broken up and its private land holdings sold during the early 1950s. Unlike most of the other original Alberta ranches, the Bar U's headquarters survived largely intact into the late 20th century. Parks Canada eventually bought it and, after restoring some of the buildings, opened it to the public as the Bar U Ranch National Historic Site, commemorating the history of ranching in western Canada. The ranch's once-vast land holdings now support numerous smaller ranches, but the feeling of open space and native Alberta prairie persists.

Early ranching was considerably harder on creeks and wetlands than most of today's foothills cattle operations. The large mixed herds of the frontier era were only pulled together and sorted out during annual roundups, when cowboys branded the new calves and cut out the animals that would be shipped to market. The rest of the time, the animals were more or less left to their own devices. They congregated where the forage was most lush – usually in wet places – or took shelter from wind and sun in timbered areas near creeks. In those sacrifice areas, cattle usually made short work of low shrubs, tree saplings and much of the grass. Healthy riparian vegetation holds stream banks together with its roots, helping them resist the erosive power of water and acting as the "woody rebar" that Lorne Fitch has aptly labelled it. Without well-rooted vegetation to protect their banks and shade the water, the streams grew wider and warmer. Heavy grazing of the uplands increased the severity of flooding during rainstorms, compounding the damage.

The wear and tear was often most pronounced near ranch headquarters, where the creek was treated simply as a watering site for holding pastures that got trampled by cattle and horses year-round. At the Bar U, Pekisko Creek eventually became a broad, eroded channel surrounded by dying cottonwood trees – unfortunate, since that reach of creek was, and still is, important for trout that travel upstream from the Bow River each spring to spawn in its spring-fed riffles.

The roots of mature black cottonwoods protect Pekisko Creek's banks from erosion on well-managed riparian range upstream from the Bar U.

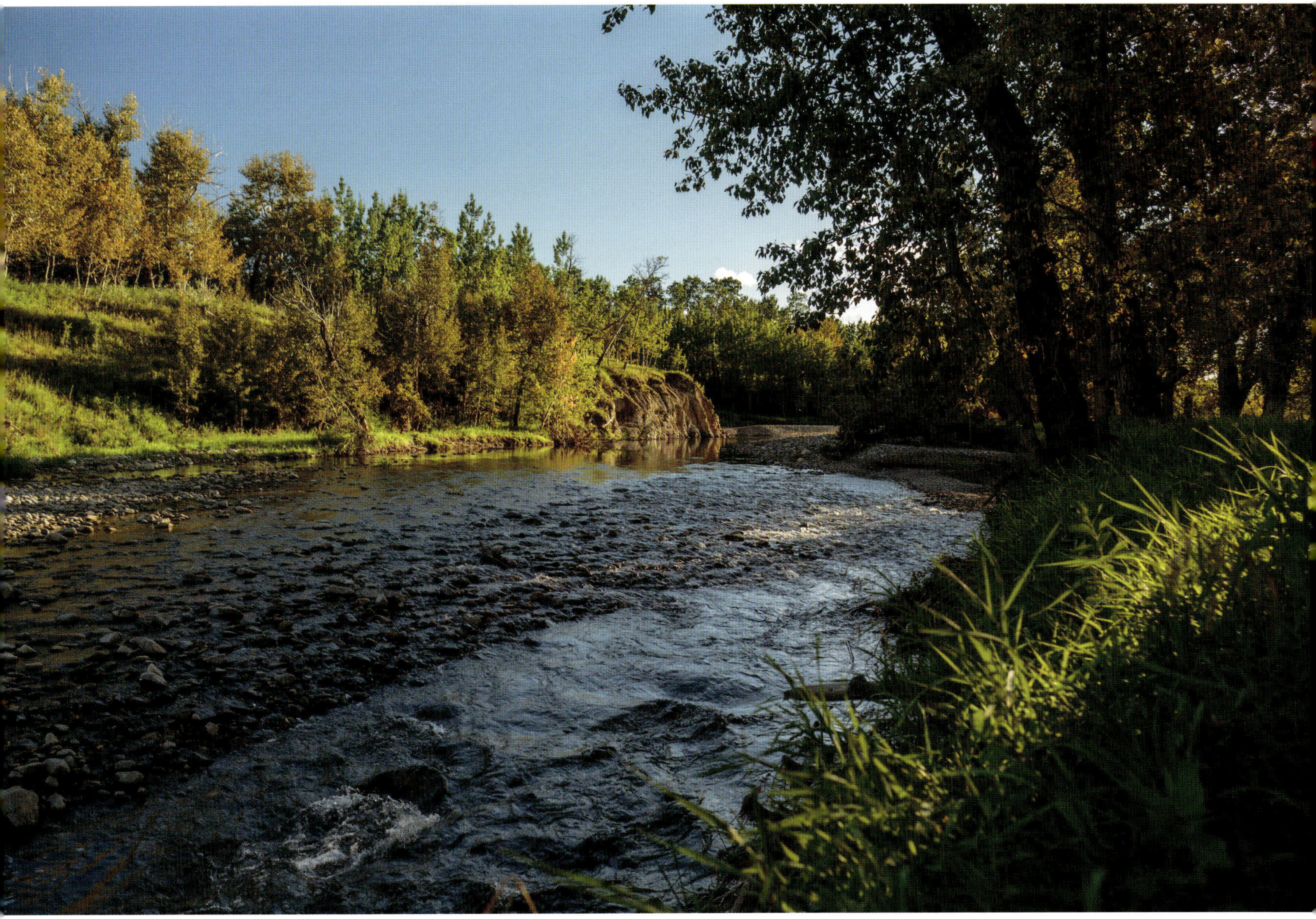

I asked Norine Ambrose of Cows and Fish if the organization had had any success working with the federal custodians of the historic site now that its buildings were no longer the heart of a working ranch. She said there hadn't been much interest lately. "I think they see their role as presenting the site as authentically as possible to reflect its historic condition."

The historic condition, unfortunately, involved a lot of trampling, manure and erosion – not a well-vegetated floodplain. Ranchers had not yet learned successful approaches to riparian management in the early days of the Bar U. They weren't particularly concerned yet either.

Even so, site managers tried to restore some of the original cottonwood forest during the first years of the historic site's operation. After a major flood in 1995, young cottonwoods sprouted on newly deposited point bars along the creek. Parks Canada staff worked with Cows and Fish to fence off some of the new growth. Spared grazing and trampling by the 1997 fencing project, the young trees were soon a carpet of greenery.

Unfortunately, spring floods hit the Bar U with a vengeance in 2005 and again in 2013. Without deep-rooted native grasses and riparian forest to stand against the roiling flood waters and protect the stream banks, the floodplain was exposed to the full erosive force of the water. Both the new fences and the resprouting trees washed away. The fencing wasn't replaced.

Those floods left even more exposed gravel and less soil and vegetation than before. Any argument that restoring a healthier riparian plant community might not represent the condition of the ranch back in the cow-blasted and horse-trampled days of the early 20th century became moot; the washed-out remains of the first big floods of the 21st century are even less historically authentic.

THE MCPHERSON RANCH IS just upstream from the Bar U. Its reach of Pekisko Creek was one of the first Cows and Fish demonstration sites. The McPhersons had for many years put their livestock into the wooded creek bottom only in winter and early spring. Cattle that are held on a forested stream bottom in winter can damage the vegetation by chewing off the protein-rich buds of trees and shrubs, but the McPhersons fed their wintering cattle hay rather than leave them to eke out a living from the riparian vegetation. They used the stream bottom to shelter their stock from cold winds and provide open water through the winter, not as pasture. Feeding hay was a practical choice – letting the cattle degrade the very vegetation that sheltered them would have made no sense – but it also protected the riparian forest's health.

The big floods that washed out the Bar U's floodplain and broke down its creek banks simply deposited a lot of silt and tore out a few old dead trees on the McPhersons' reach of Pekisko Creek. Today the creek still flows inside a defined channel through a lush gallery forest of healthy cottonwood trees and shrubbery.

Farther upstream, where Pekisko gathers up most of its flow from a network of small streams and seeps that drain a paradise of grassland, willow thickets and forested ridges, the creek is a living model of riparian health and good range management.

"MY GRANDFATHER'S PARTNER came to upper Pekisko in about 1888. He was one of the homesteaders that were prevalent on the periphery of the Bar U in those days," said Gordon Cartwright as we sat in his dining room looking out over the greening landscape one May afternoon. "His name was Dickson – that's where Dickson Coulee got its name. Another homesteader was Freddy Nash – he was the ranger over on the Highwood. Before the Burkes I think there were two other families on that place. One was Gordon McConnell that McConnell Falls is named after. They had a homestead there, and when my grandfather came to this country, that's where he went to work in 1900, after coming out to the Bar U initially."

The Cartwrights – Gordon and Wendy – had invited me to their ranch in response to an e-mail asking what they could tell me about their home stream.

Driving south from Canmore, I took the shortcut between Bragg Creek and Millarville. Highway 762 used to traverse ranching country, too, but its proximity to Calgary led to those ranches being subdivided into acreages for oil millionaires. Monster homes and gated drives flickered past as I drove through the headwaters of Fish, Priddis and Fisher creeks.

Fisher Creek, as usual, was dusky with silt pollution even though there had been no rain in the past week to muddy it. Its banks were slumped and eroding, evidence of punishing floods. Fisher Creek has the misfortune of arising in the McLean Creek off-highway vehicle area; the once-productive trout stream is now chronically sick because of oozing wounds carved into its headwaters by recreational vandalism endorsed by the Alberta Forest Service. Heavy clear-cut logging hasn't helped it either.

The grim regret that had taken over my mood after crossing Fisher Creek vanished, however, once I turned onto the gravel road that leads to the Cartwrights' isolated home. Cattle grazed quietly in lush fescue grasslands filled with shooting stars, crocuses and other spring flowers. Pekisko Creek was running high with snowmelt down in the cottonwoods. The whole surrounding landscape seemed to glisten with flowing water – clear springs emerging from draws, beaver ponds, duck-filled wetlands in the hollows. In one large slough I spotted a trumpeter swan trying, unsuccessfully, to look invisible on her nest. Newborn calves were everywhere, tugging at their mothers' teats, gambolling about with one another or staring at my car in consternation before wheeling to race off across the grass.

The road had taken me through a pair of log gates past a sign announcing that I was in the domain of "Cartwright and Sons." The left gate was marked with the EP brand, and the right with the D. Until recently, both of these ranches had been part of the Cartwright holdings, which included much of the upper Pekisko Creek drainage. Like the Bar U, however, the structures are now more a reflection of history than of the present.

The EP ranch used to belong to Edward, Prince of Wales, who, having visited the Bar U in 1919, was so taken by the countryside that he arranged for George Lane to buy a neighbouring property so that the prince could have his own foothills ranch. It proved to be an impractical purchase for the Royal family's prodigal son, however. In 1962 he sold it to Jim Cartwright, who was building up his

Right: *The lush, well-watered native vegetation of upper Pekisko Creek: proof that cattle ranching, wildlife habitat and watershed health can be compatible.*

Far right: *A Pekisko Creek feeder spring is almost invisible in the lush riparian vegetation it sustains.*

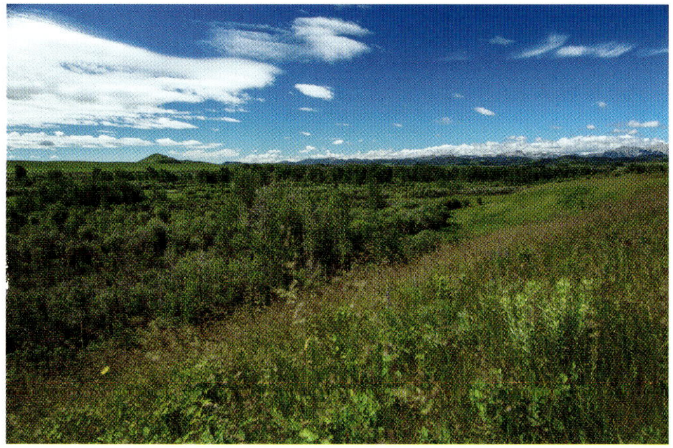

holdings in the valley. By the time I first visited the valley in the 1980s, Cartwright and his sons, John and Gordon, had the EP and D ranches and extensive public land leases attached to them.

Those holdings were built the slow way – through hard work, risk taking and careful business decisions. Gordon Cartwright's grandfather Aubrey started as a hired hand and went on to become a partner with one of the early homesteaders, John Thorpe, who grazed yearling cattle in the Cataract and Wilkinson valleys, west of the Pekisko ranges. They bought their first large cattle herd and the D brand from another small rancher who had been bankrupted by the devastating 1906–1907 winter. As opportunity arose, they acquired more cattle and land.

If good fortune and good management enabled the Cartwright family to build up their holdings in the Pekisko Creek valley in the 20th century, it was the growing challenges of keeping a ranch viable in the next century that led them to sell much of it off. Today the Cartwrights have eight sections (20.72 square kilometres) of deeded land – still a large holding by most standards but well less than during the peak years, and less than Cartwright feels is optimal for ranching in the headwaters country:

The outfits on this landscape evolved to an optimum scale. There were outfits like the Bar U that were too big. It's hard to have the same commitment out of a company-backed operation as it is where a family is investing their sense of home and their identity in what they're manifesting on the land. And then in the earlier years on the fringes there were all these small homesteaders who couldn't make it.

You need the right scale to have ecological integrity because you have to be able to set aside areas for rest and recovery and you have to have flexibility to adjust to things like drought and fire. The more cut up the country gets, the less choices you have. Last year we had about 2,500 acres of this place that was hailed badly, so we needed to adjust to the need to rest that land until the vegetation recovered. On a larger operation you have those options.

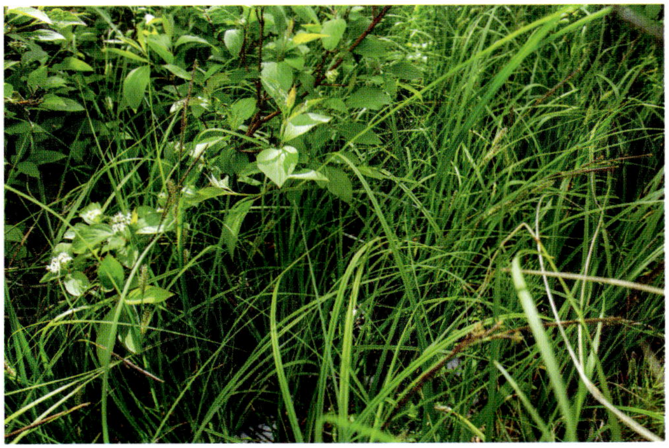

The profitability of foothills ranching has become increasingly marginal in the last three decades. Foothills ranchers have to contend not only with environmental changes that reduce carrying capacity and increase livestock losses but also with global economic trends and agricultural policies that put range-cattle production at a disadvantage relative to more intensive production, such as high-volume feedlots.

On the environmental side, the quality of native foothills rangelands is diminishing because of invasive grasses and weeds that outcompete native plants, as well as the steady expansion of forests into what used to be grassland. Early ranchers brought in timothy hay and even ploughed up native prairie to plant fields of timothy. Cut green, the introduced timothy grass makes a high-quality hay that was in heavy demand during the early 20th century for horse herds. But timothy is shallow-rooted, unlike the native grasses it outcompetes, and it has very little nutritional value once it has cured on the stem. The native fescues and wheatgrasses cure full of nutrients and protein, providing excellent winter forage for cattle and the wild elk with which they share the range. As timothy becomes more prevalent, the quality of that late-season forage declines, and so does the carrying capacity of the range.

There's less open range in any event. Dr. Art Bailey of the University of Alberta evaluated forest cover changes in the Pekisko Creek drainage in 1978 by comparing aerial photographs taken in different years. He estimated that aspen forest had expanded 3.4 per cent per year between 1950 and 1977. Elk, deer and moose benefited from aspen expansion, but it came at the expense of the fescue grassland that feeds cattle. Lack of recent fire is one factor encouraging the spread, as the buildup of understory vegetation, especially on sheltered slopes, creates cooler, moister soil conditions favoured by aspens. The aspens, in turn, change the microclimate by trapping snowdrifts that encourage the growth of non-native grasses like timothy at the expense of rough fescue and other native vegetation. Cattle graze the shrinking native grasslands more heavily by necessity, which also puts more pressure on the most palatable native forage species.

Prescribed fire could reverse some of the vegetation deterioration, but Cartwright is sensitive to the dangers of letting fires burn in landscapes where its absence for decades has allowed natural fuels to build up to unnatural levels. The frequent light fires that used to burn through the foothills regularly left soil and plant roots undamaged, but half a century of fire suppression has allowed

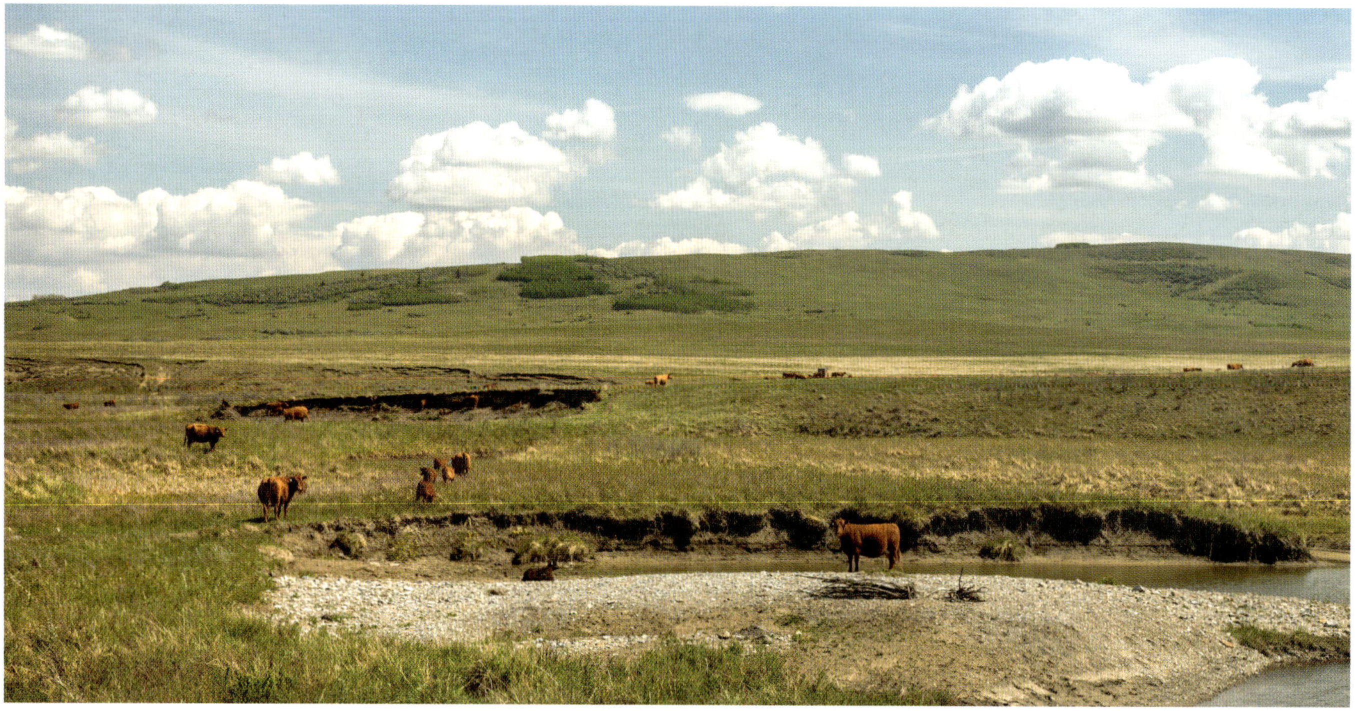

vegetation debris to accumulate, increasing the risk of intense and destructive fires well outside the range of natural variability. But, as Cartwright says,

> There's some value in more frequent smaller fires, and if you pick the right timing for humidity and fuel conditions and so on, you could probably do it in an even more benign fashion than nature would have done.

The Cartwrights and their neighbours Francis and Bonnie Gardner raised a few eyebrows among their neighbours when they teamed up with Barry Adams to experiment with prescribed fire to reduce the forest encroachment on the public land they lease for pasture. The carefully controlled burns helped, but they were too costly to be more than a one-time event; it would take regular fire combined with carefully timed grazing to knock back aspen growth in any measurable way.

The environmental changes reducing the productivity of foothills ranges at least respond to management where ranchers have the expertise, motivation, time and money to try doing things differently. But the bigger economic challenges, Cartwright says, are far more intractable:

More than a century of cattle grazing has eliminated woody vegetation from much of Stimson Creek's floodplain and left the stream vulnerable to erosion and siltation. Recent adoption of more progressive grazing strategies by some ranchers may eventually reverse the harm.

> Policies that subsidize crop agriculture have marginalized range cattle production by driving cattle into feedlot operations. Incentivizing the ploughing up of rangeland got us into the feedlot model, because there's no better way of getting rid of surplus grain than putting it through livestock. When you think of the energy flow through that system and where it's coming from and the subsidies for the fossil fuel industry, the subsidies for every gallon of diesel … as feed becomes commoditized, you're competing with that. All the economic incentives have been to introduce new forages, more intensive production, and those things undermine the economics of managing these natural landscapes. That's the crux today, is that to do it, to back off and be within the carrying capacity of the land, isn't an economic proposition. It's not self-sustaining. Some ranches get into the hands of people with lots of capital, but even with the people who bought one of our places, they had a good young manager and he was perplexed; he said to me, "How does anybody make money doing this?"

MAYBE THERE IS NO FUTURE FOR foothills ranching. There are even those who would argue that its demise would be a good thing. A couple of decades ago, I might have been one of them.

Many larger ranches rely to a large degree on public lands grazing leases that have been contentious with hunting interests and taxpayer advocates for many years. The lease rates on public land are significantly lower than what ranchers pay when leasing private land. Some public interest groups describe that as an ongoing subsidy and argue that the public should be getting a better financial return for the use of our land. That sense of inequity gets magnified when ranchers limit public access. Even though the leased land is highly valued for hunting and other recreational uses, many ranchers try to restrict access to that land as if it they actually own it. When conflicts arise between domestic cattle and wild predators like wolves and grizzly bears, the predators often lose. That in turn drives animosity against ranchers from those who feel that public land should be managed for its wildlife values, not just for a single vested interest.

Those arguments have merit. That's why there have been recurring attempts to find more elegant approaches to accommodate the competing interests. In the early 21st century the Alberta government finally found a workable compromise for the access issue that enables ranchers to protect their legitimate interests while allowing hunters and hikers reasonable access. Predator-friendly ranching has gone from an oxymoron to something actually practised by some foothills livestock producers. The Cows and Fish program has gone a long way toward addressing the issues troubling me during my anti-cow phase, although the lack of riparian forest and the frequently muddied flows of Stimson Creek, a major tributary that joins Pekisko Creek from the south, suggest that there is still some distance to go before some cow-degraded headwater streams can be considered healthy again.

But the critical question for those who think public lands ranching is an anachronism, and that its economic extinction is not just inevitable but desirable, is the one asked too seldom in resource management debates: "And then what?"

If ranchers give up, someone else will find a way to profit from those foothills watersheds. They are already lined up, wanting in – oil and gas developers, real estate promoters, off-highway recreation groups. As long as ranchers are on the land and keeping the banker at bay, those others are going to have to either wait or negotiate with a deeply entrenched community that actually cares about vegetation, water, and landscape health. The fragmented landscapes closer to Calgary, after all – full of weed-lined roads, trophy homes, overgrazed horse pastures and ruined wetlands – used to be ranchland too.

"What worries me is a lack of vision for stewardship," Gordon said when I asked him his biggest concern for the future.

> We live in an era where everything is driven by short-term economics without any appreciation of the underlying natural capital. In all the years that I've ranched here, there were periods of intense feelings about public lands and access to grazing leases, but it's like everybody missed the point. The value here is in holding those watersheds together and maintaining the health of those landscapes. It's a suite of benefits for society that is many times what you can produce from a pound of beef. It's the stewardship that maintains a balance of cover on the watershed and the integrity of the native plant communities that provide the resilience and the regenerative capacity.
>
> It's like stewardship is a non-concept in this province. Everything is about liquidating assets. That's where the focus has been. In the long run, when those are depleted, it's the regenerative assets that underlie society's wealth.
>
> The major asset here is the watershed. It's one of the more productive watersheds and one of the more effective ones in terms of the balance of cover types. If you go north of Calgary in the heavily forested areas, the yield to aquifers and rivers is probably around 40 per cent because of transpiration losses, whereas it's more like 60 per cent on this landscape. If you look at the long-term average of precipitation in the collection area in this area, the 50,000 acres above the EP bridge here, at $1.16 a cubic metre it's yielding $94 million worth of water every year.
>
> If you have a long-term plan, you can change that number. If you leave it status quo with no plan, that number goes down over time. You're depleting the resiliency of that watershed; you're putting it at risk

A foothills cattle herd. As long as public lands ranching remains the dominant land use in the foothills, watershed protection will remain possible.

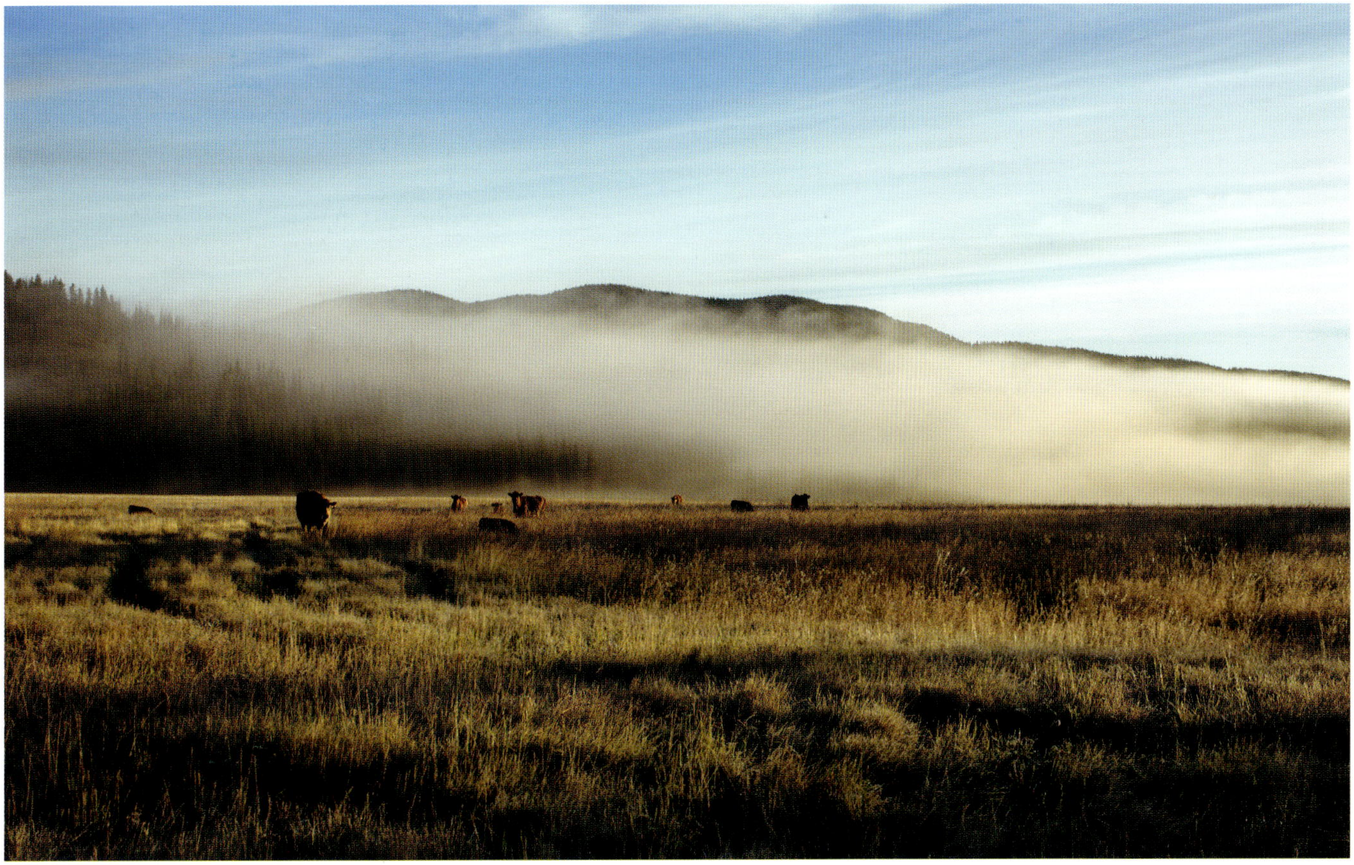

of big fires and the spread of invasive species in the system. The native plant communities are effective at capturing energy and water and also resilient to the effects of climate change and drought or fire or other impacts.

If you have well-adapted rangelands where you're able to maintain enough litter and cover, that helps minimize the runoff and maximize infiltration. The range doesn't trap the snow so well as the forest, but it does effectively take moisture into the soil more than the forest. The grass and litter impede the runoff so when it rains it soaks in, and of course grassland doesn't have the transpiration losses of forest, so a lot of it stays as groundwater.

Gordon Cartwright is as much a hydrologist and applied ecologist as he is a guy who raises cows. He thinks about water a lot – not just because of its importance to cattle production but because of the many ways in which his management of land and vegetation influences watershed processes. A careful, pensive speaker, he became most passionate when describing the importance of native rough fescue grassland and other range types in turning rainfall into groundwater, reducing flooding caused by overland drainage and conserving water.

> Ideally on the landscape you're going to be looking at how do you get the right balance of controlled fires and forestry – most of the forestry is going to be on the north slopes, in the colder sites, because you want the snow capture and you want to minimize the transpiration losses to the forest, because that's a huge loss to the watershed when it becomes overly forested. Trees and shrubs play a valuable role in trapping snow … but trees also breathe considerable volumes of water to the atmosphere. We can see this in the fall, when the water levels of springs rise after the aspens lose their leaves.

Based on the hydrologists he's consulted, Cartwright says that forest losses to evaporation, snow sublimation and transpiration can be as high as two-thirds of the available moisture.

> While grasslands reduce transpiration losses, range health affects infiltration. Plants and litter protect bare soil from being sealed by raindrops, which fall at terminal velocity. Litter and standing material also cool the soil surface and reduce evaporation. The structure and organic component of healthy grassland soils allow water to filter into aquifers. The better the health of the grassland, the greater is its ability to reduce flooding and charge aquifers. The health of grassland depends on managed grazing.

DURING OUR CONVERSATION two things became clear to me.

One was the degree to which the public benefits from what is essentially unpaid work by dedicated volunteers. A lot of the Cartwrights' work has less to do with producing beef than with keeping the land healthy. It was Gordon's parents who reintroduced beavers – extirpated decades earlier by trapping – to rebuild wetlands and restore the flow to creeks that had gone dry. The family pulls weeds, fences their own cattle out of wetlands, fought a successful battle to keep a major gas pipeline from slicing across the head of the valley and developed a system to let hunters and anglers enjoy the ecological wealth of the valley without constantly bumping into one another or disrupting ranch operations. They police the drainage against off-road vandalism and monitor the health of its wetlands constantly.

Alberta is today, to a great degree, a place of former glories and lost natural wealth. But the Pekisko Creek watershed is an exception. Wallace Stegner wrote of the "geography of hope." That geography survives in the green hills that drain to Pekisko Creek because – not in spite – of ranchers like Gordon and Wendy Cartwright.

Ironically, while the people of Alberta paid taxes to cover the wages and expenses of the bureaucrats who spent the last century mismanaging the adjacent forest reserve, the public treasury contributed little to cover the costs or reward the efforts of people who have made the care of our public lands, watersheds and streams a labour of lifelong love.

We, the public, don't subsidize progressive foothills ranchers like the Cartwrights. Just the opposite: they subsidize us.

The Cartwright's land has plenty of the kind of sweet, clean springs that I could have let my thirsty little son drink from back in the days when I developed my original antipathy toward ranching. It wasn't independent foothills ranchers but the taxpayer-funded Alberta Forest Service that allowed valleys like Coal Creek to be ravaged by negligent cattle grazing through the late 20th century – not to mention clear-cut logging, unregulated OHV use and poorly reclaimed oil and gas development.

"The forest service used grazing to remove fuel to protect forests from fire," Cartwright said. "In fact my father told me that his father had urged the government to reduce stocking rates but had been told to stock at the prescribed rate or forfeit his allotment to someone else who would."

Some livestock groups have lobbied for the Forest Reserve lands, where grazing is managed under an annual permit system, to be converted to long-term grazing leases like those in Pekisko Creek valley and elsewhere in foothills. They say that improved security of tenure, by giving lessees a greater sense of ownership and responsibility, would lead to better stewardship than the current permit system promotes. From where Cartwright and I sat talking, I couldn't see anything out the window to suggest that they might be wrong – as long as the leases go to ranchers as committed to good stewardship as the Cartwrights and some of their neighbours.

THE OTHER INSIGHT I brought away from our conversation was the degree to which public lands ranchers struggle to keep at bay a profound sense of hopelessness.

"We've lost so much knowledge and experience in the last few years," Cartwright said, looking pensively out at the rolling rangelands. "So many good, talented young ranchers just packed it in because of the BSE [mad cow disease, which depressed Canadian cattle prices for a decade] crisis. They couldn't make a go of it. Where are we going to get that kind of expertise when we need it? There isn't another generation coming in."

Foothills ranches are based on private land holdings, regardless of whether the rancher also has a public lands grazing lease. Historically, much of the private land ended up along the permanent streams in the area, so its importance for biodiversity conservation and watershed health is often disproportionate to the area it occupies.

Unlike the public land areas, whose use or abuse is largely a matter of public policy, what happens on private land is at the discretion of individual owners. Many choose to cash in on the amenity value of their land rather than keep on raising cattle. In some areas closer to Calgary, that's resulted in extensive subdivision and development: fields are full of houses now, not cattle.

Small acreages can be hard on nearby streams when they are overgrazed by horses, mowed into lawns or full of roads and disturbed soil. Water runs off too rapidly, carrying soil into the nearby streams instead of soaking into the wild prairie to replenish the water table. Stream flows are more volatile and creeks more muddy-bottomed than when ranching was still the dominant land use.

The problems become most severe where subdivision is most advanced. The Town of Cochrane and neighboring Municipal District of Rocky View have allowed high-density housing subdivisions on what used to be the rolling fescue grasslands of the historic Cochrane Ranche. Cochrane's Fireside development and a housing subdivision at nearby Cochrane Lake are two examples where once-healthy wetlands now overflow with stormwater runoff from driveways, streets and patios. The former ranchers and developers who converted the land into real estate have already pocketed their profits; local governments now have to foot the bills for diverting the runoff into Bighill and Horse creeks and the Bow River. In response, those creeks flood more frequently now and are increasingly polluted by fertilizers, herbicides, pet waste and street contaminants.

The growing threat of land subdivision led Gordon Cartwright, with several of his neighbours who ranch along Alberta's "Cowboy Trail" (Highway 22), to found the Southern Alberta Land Trust Society. SALTS works to protect native foothills landscapes from subdivision and development, primarily by putting permanent development restrictions on private land by way of a legal instrument called a conservation easement. The Cartwrights have placed a conservation easement on part of the D ranch, forgoing the possibility of cashing in on its future real-estate development potential. A permanent codicil on the land title now prohibits new roads and developments. SALTS paid them, on a one-time basis, for that easement. The problem with that sort of conservation, however, is that the costs involved in stewardship go on into the future, and the financial needs of a ranching family don't end with the sale of a conservation easement.

Cartwright would like to see a new form of conservation agreement that provides a recurring flow of money, something like a five-year renewable easement. It would provide a sustainable revenue stream for ranchers who practise stewardship of wildlife habitat and water quality, and they would no longer have to rely solely on beef sales. Without some kind of diversification of farm gate income, the days appear increasingly numbered when there will be ranchers willing and able to keep these places wild, green and laced with healthy springs and creeks.

LARRY SIMPSON works for a land trust, too. The Nature Conservancy of Canada (NCC) is the biggest private land conservation group in the country and one that has, in recent years, worked with ranchers to protect vast swaths of land in the Oldman River drainage from development. The NCC bought ranchland outright in the rich aspen parkland country surrounding Waterton Lakes National Park and, more recently, paid over $15 million to buy conservation easements on the 12,150-hectare Waldron Ranch a few kilometres south of Pekisko Creek. Some of the SALTS members are a bit wary of the NCC because its board is comprised mostly of people connected to large corporations and institutions, rather than landowners. Even so, the two organizations have common values, and their work tends to complement each other's.

Simpson left his job as a land man for an oil and gas company back in the 1980s, when he realized that his work wasn't aligned to his core values. He is as quietly passionate about the need for private lands conservation as he is respectful and understanding of the issues facing the families owning that land:

> We are in the middle of one of the largest changes in land ownership in Alberta's history. There is a whole generation of ranchers who are getting too old to carry on ranching. Many of them don't have family to pass the place on to, as might have happened in the past, because their children see better financial rewards in jobs they can get elsewhere. Real estate values have been climbing, and returns from livestock production have been dropping. There is a real threat that the most productive native grasslands in Canada – the last five miles of mostly intact prairie at the western edge of the Great Plains – could be lost in our lifetimes.

Native grassland – the vegetation that, as Cartwright points out, is so vital for trapping rainwater and moving it down into the soil – is one of the world's most endangered ecosystems. Many grasslands have been ploughed and converted to crop agriculture. In Alberta, more than 75 per cent of parkland fescue grassland and well more than half of the dry mixed prairie east of Highway 2 have been lost in just this way. The foothills fescue grasslands have fared better because of a short growing season that kept the plough at bay during the frontier era, and the ability of those grasslands to produce good economic returns through range livestock production during most of the 20th century.

Simpson's vision is that those fescue foothills – the "last five miles" of prairie before the Rocky Mountains – will be saved by private conservation initiatives that not only help keep watersheds healthy and nature intact, but make it possible for ranchers to stay on the land in changing economic times. The biggest obstacle to success is money: the cost of buying development rights over so large a landscape runs to the millions of dollars. Just two large NCC projects in the Oldman watershed – the Waterton Front initiative and the Waldron Ranch – cost almost $40 million, much of it donated by family foundations and individuals.

The efforts of rancher-driven organizations like SALTS and national conservation organizations like NCC may go a long way toward retaining the best characteristics of the foothills headwaters. It will depend mostly on the support of donors who share their sense of urgency. Public policy changes that pay ranchers for the ecological goods and services that flow from good stewardship of the Bow River headwaters would help, too.

It could happen. In the peaceful green stillness and beauty of the upper Pekisko Creek drainage, optimism and hope spring as eternal as its clean, sweet water.

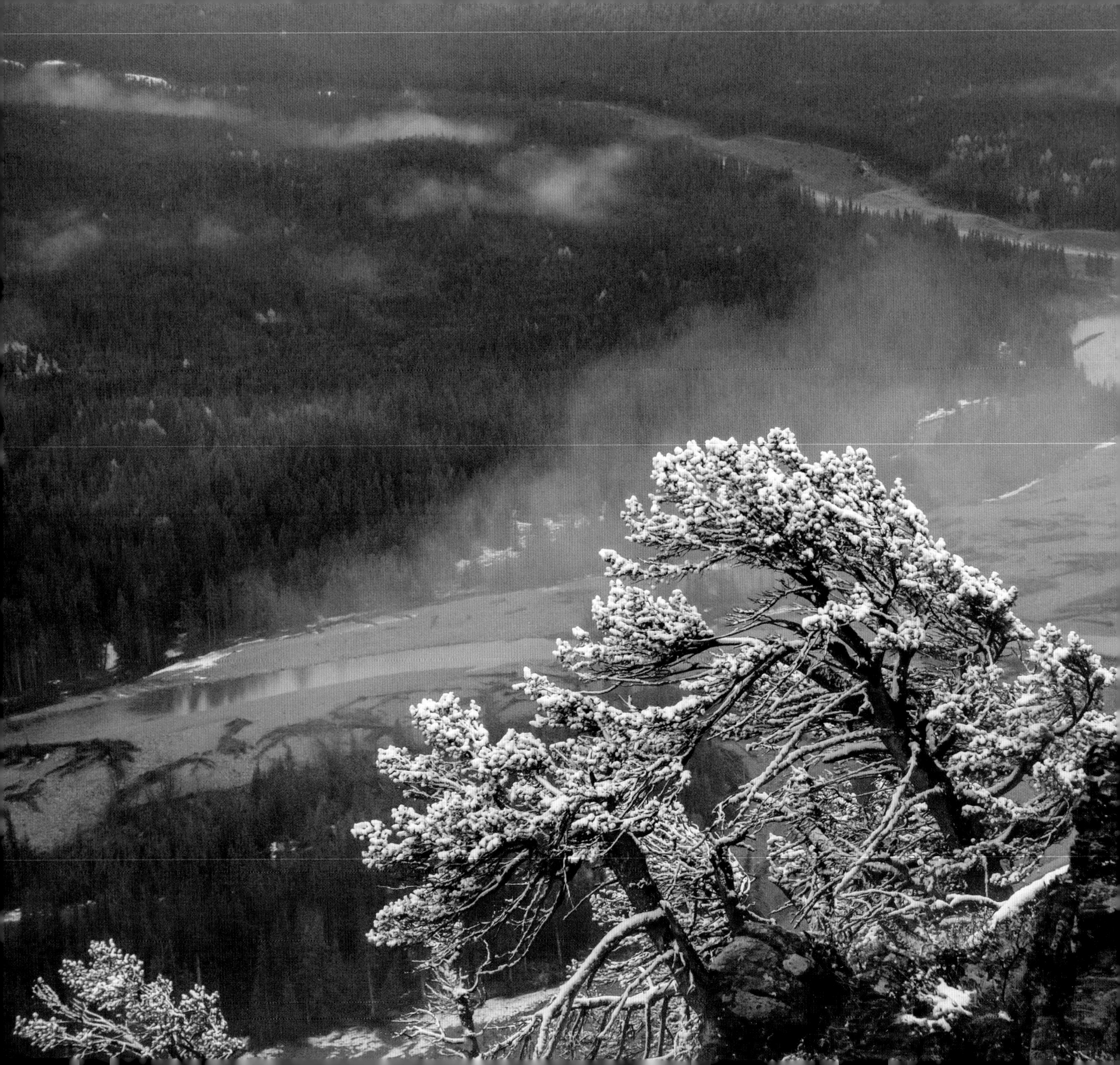

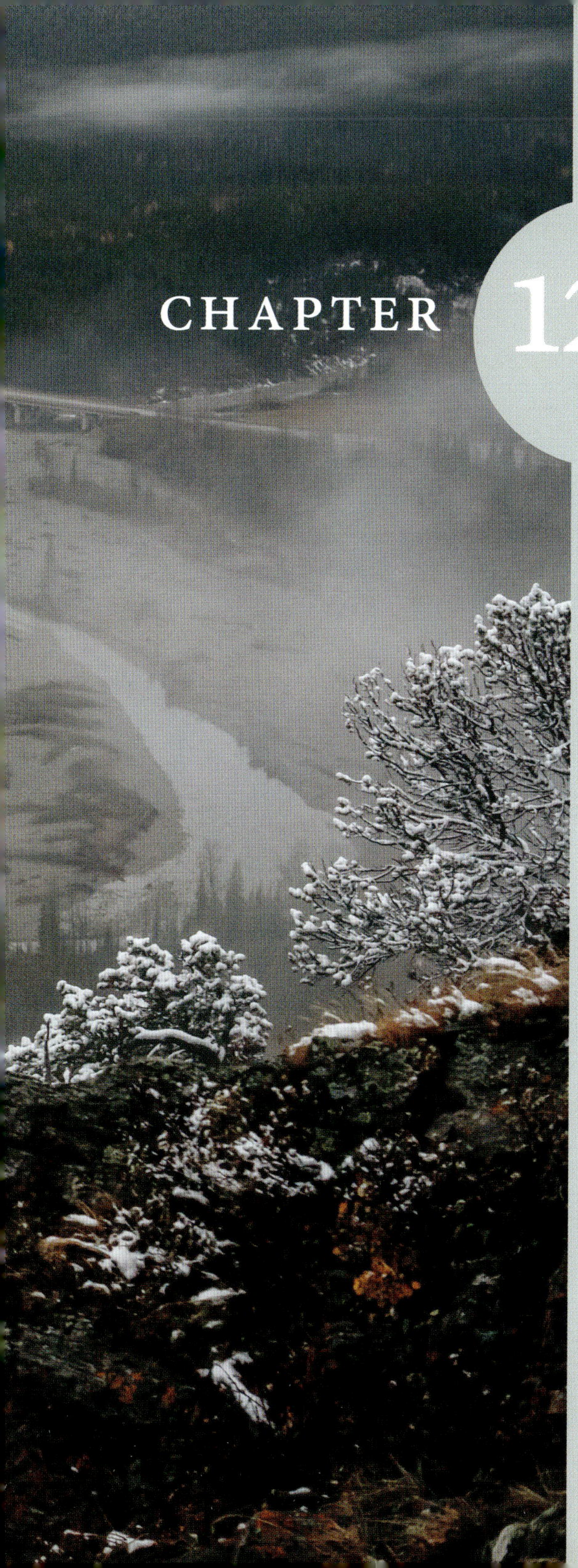

CHAPTER 12

Mountains Breathing

Highwood River

IF YOU PUT A CHILD INTO A SLEEPING BAG in the upper Highwood just as the last robin has ceased to sing, chances are that child will soon become aware of a far rushing sound that fills the outside world. Its soothing resonance has bemused many a sunburned young adventurer trying to figure out what he or she is hearing as tent walls grow dark against the outside night's mystery. At times, it might be the roar of the nearby river, but then it fades until it sounds like the hissing of zephyrs in a thousand timberline treetops or, perhaps, even the sound of mountains breathing.

It is a sort of rushing hush, a living sound that fills the spreading dark spaces between mountain ranges where streams with names like Cat, Picklejar, Fitzsimmons and Mist pulse cold, clear and newborn from alpine meadows and timbered draws. It is a sound rich with imagined possibilities for children who, still wondering, fade to sleep at last beneath the silhouetted peaks of timeless ridges.

Mountains line both horizons in the Highwood valley. The river runs south for many kilometres from its origins in the Misty Ranges before finally

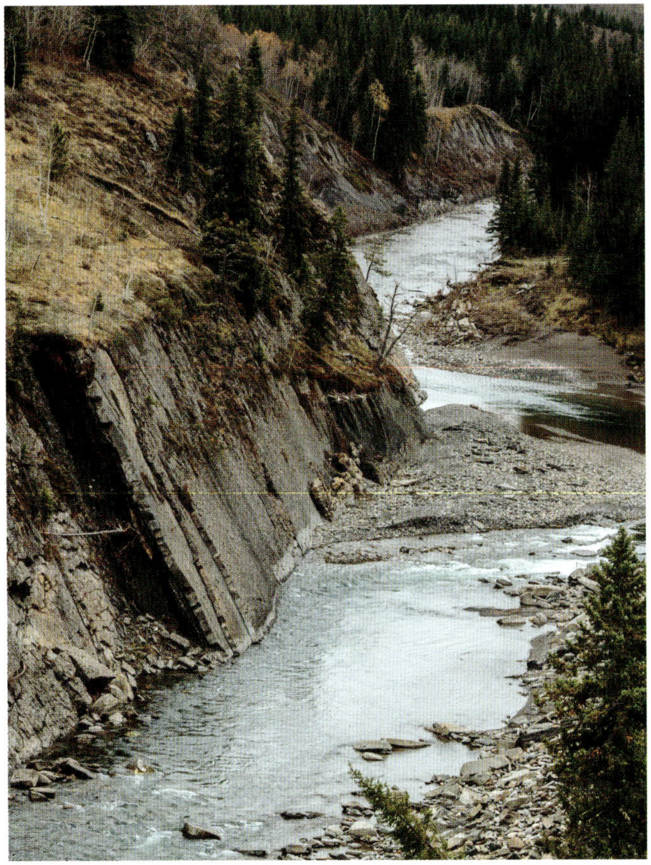

Page 182: *Another mountain evening settles over the upper Highwood River.*

Left: *Highwood River, near Eden Valley.*

doglegging east and tumbling its cobbly way through Eyrie Gap, gathering the clean, sparkling waters of Cataract Creek into itself and then spilling out through the last limestone ranges. There it tumbles into the shallow canyon it has carved out through the famous ranching foothills country west of Longview, and leaves the Rockies behind.

To the west are peaks of the Elk Range, an almost continuous wall of dark rock from Mount Farquhar in the south to Mount Tyrwhitt in the north. Spur ridges, heavily forested with lodgepole pine, separate tributary drainages that drop from the talus slopes and open larch forests lining its flanks.

East of the river, grassy hills crowned with limber pine ascend to the sloping limestone faces of the Highwood Range. In April, when clumps of prairie crocus begin to emerge from the coarse tussocks of fescue on the hillsides, and the deep hoots of courting blue grouse roll down off the ridges, circling black specks appear above the Highwood Range. Hundreds of golden eagles are tracing their way north along an ancient eagle highway.

Not all those eagles continue north to Yukon, Alaska and eastern Siberia. Some eddy out of the stream of fierce-eyed wind-riders to return to traditional nest sites in the cliffs below. Eyrie Gap gets its name from one such ancient golden eagle nest. For many years another famous nest overlooked the forestry road near the Sheep River, farther north.

Those eagles, of course, harbour no doubts about the fitful hush that fills the valleys below. They ride its source: the winds that spill over the Elk Range and trace the topography, teasing treetops and tickling the glassy surfaces of beaver ponds before being funnelled through Eyrie Gap or squeezed across the Highwood Range. It is those reliable updrafts, where chinook winds break over the Highwood Range, that have made this an eagle highway. Hundreds of birds – not just eagles but hawks and falcons – travel it twice yearly between nest sites in Canada, Alaska and eastern Siberia, and wintering grounds in the southern US and Mexico, and back again.

The upper Highwood is the heart of chinook country. Frequently, in winter, ranchers looking west to see what kind of day is shaping up see the grey wall of the Highwood Range etched hard against a thin band of pale sky beneath a long arc of cloud. That chinook arch is a promise of mild temperatures and strong winds in the foothills country around Longview, but it also indicates snow on the British Columbia side of the Continental Divide, and howling gales along the summits.

The prevailing westerly winds at the latitude of the Bow River headwaters have shaped the landscape for millennia and from time to time coloured that landscape's history with drama. Before they spill over the continental divide into Alberta, the weather systems that bring those winds have crossed multiple mountain ranges and lost most of their original moisture. Even so, they often deposit more rain and snow in the headwaters country. But then, descending the east side, the air warms and becomes denser. Humidity drops, turbulence increases, and another chinook comes roaring out of the Alberta Rocky Mountains into the foothills below.

Back behind the first range of mountains, the Highwood River courses across its cobbly floodplain, adding its rush and chatter to the overhead roar of wind seething through the crowns of millions of pine trees.

THE HIGHWOOD IS NAMED AFTER TREES, but its forests have come and gone over the years.

In the early 20th century, loggers did their part to change the river and its forests, cutting large swaths of timber along the lower valley.

Lineham Creek got its name from the man who brought logging to the upper Kananaskis valley. John Lineham started out logging near the Sheep River and milling his lumber in Okotoks until 1903, when he set up a mill and lumber yard adjacent to the CPR line in High River. Having persuaded the Dominion government to grant his company seven timber berths along the Highwood, totalling about 230 square kilometres, he wasted no time in sending crews upstream to the forests that lay behind the Highwood Range.

The first logging camp was near Lineham Creek, but camps moved from year to year to remain close to the woods operations. The camps held up to hundred men, many of them homesteaders new to the country and looking to get some cash money before they settled down. They earned $12 to $20 a month, and each two-man team was expected to cut 140 logs each day. The final tally was up to 90,000 logs for each camp's winter season.

Each winter, the crews worked with hand tools to cut the logs to length, skid them out behind horses and stack them on rollways overlooking the river floodplain. When the water came up during spring floods, the crews released the logs and rolled them into the roiling brown water. The logs then floated almost 161 kilometres downstream to a mill at High River, where they were trapped in a log boom and hauled out for milling.

Massive logjams sometimes formed, and if the most experienced log drivers couldn't release the jam, they would use dynamite to blow the logs loose again. Charlie Fitzsimmons, after whom Fitzsimmons Creek was named, was noted for his ability to dynamite logjams loose. Certain notorious spots like the Cauldron, near Cataract Creek, required the crews to build ramps or aprons to keep logs from getting hung up in eddies and boulder jams. Other times, if the river dropped suddenly, logs would be stranded all along the river, and crews would have to use horses to snake them back down to the water and set them adrift again.

Similar log drives took place along the Sheep, Kananaskis, Ghost and Bow rivers during the early 20th century. The biggest operation was the Eau Claire and Bow River Lumber Company, which began logging its timber berths in the Kananaskis, Spray and Bow River valleys as early as 1886, floating the logs all the way downstream to their mill at what is now Prince's Island Park, in Calgary. Early Calgary was a city of wooden houses, almost all built with Eau Claire lumber. In the same way, early High River homes, and the houses of the farmers and ranchers busy populating the surrounding landscape in those early years, were built with wood milled out of the Highwood River's spruce and pine stands.

In spite of the log drives, with many hundreds of large timbers gouging the riverbed and jostling through the gravelly riffles, the Lineham company's activities likely had little lasting effect on the Highwood River. The logging was done in winter, and the logs were skidded across snow or frozen ground by teams of horses, so there was little damage to the soil. Big spring floods rearrange the riverbed with or without a cargo of logs, so the log drives were just a little more woody debris added to the usual flotsam and jetsam of a headwater river in spate. The most lasting effects were likely from the use of dynamite to widen rocky bottlenecks, which would have changed some of the floodplain processes immediately upstream and downstream as a result of the reduced resistance to the river's flow.

The most immediate effect that three decades of logging had on the river was probably the large number of fish that ended up in loggers' bellies. At the downstream end, the log boom in High River became a popular place for boys to catch spawning mountain whitefish in the fall, either snagging them or angling with bait. Logging drained fish, not just trees, from the headwaters.

Lineham died in the spring of 1913, and the company was sold, becoming the Wilson Lumber Company. It continued to log the upstream berths for milling lumber, telephone poles and firewood, but the logging era was pretty much over by the late 1930s. It was doomed by market forces that made the cost of wood from old-style intensive logging operations more expensive than wood brought in by rail from the larger industrialized operations in British Columbia.

The company's final death knell was in 1936, when the west wind brought fire, rather than water, to the forests of the upper Highwood.

FIRE HAS SHAPED THE VEGETATION of the Bow River watershed since the glaciers retreated. It has been influencing ecosystems for much longer than that – so long, in fact, that many of the common plant species of the headwaters country have evolved to depend on it. The seeds of lodgepole pine, for instance, are sealed under a nearly impervious layer of natural lacquer that needs the intense heat of forest fires to remove it. Young pines thrive in the phosphorus-rich burned soils after fire and require direct sunlight to grow. Lodgepole pines are, in effect, fire trees. They would be a rare novelty, rather than the dominant tree type of most mountain valleys, if fires didn't burn through on a regular basis. It's likely no evolutionary accident that green, growing lodgepole pines are highly flammable.

Lightning storms play a role in keeping fire an active part of the landscape, but human beings have always done their part too. The Nakoda, Piikani and K'tunaxa peoples, who at various times occupied or travelled through the headwaters country, lit fires deliberately to stimulate the growth of medicine plants and to concentrate animals like sheep, bison and elk that are attracted to the fresh greenery that sprouts after a burn. As European settlers began to flood into the country in the late 1800s and early 1900s, accidents and vandalism became another cause of fire.

The Highwood's logging crews watched smoke roiling into the valley in 1910, when fires burned to the south and west through most of the summer. In fact, a fire broke out in the Highwood valley itself when a survey crew camping at the mouth of Picklejar Creek lit a smudge to keep flies off their horses. It was a windy day, and the fire escaped into dry grass. To the relief of Lineham and his crews, that fire spared their valuable timber berths. It burned downstream along the south-facing slopes and flats north of the river, jumping to the more forested south side of the river near Eyrie Gap before it burned eastward out of the mountains.

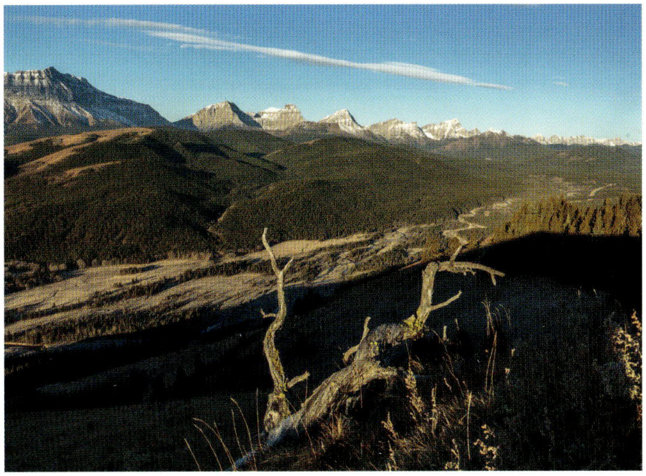

The lodgepole pine forest that carpets much of the Highwood valley dates back to the 1936 "Phillips Fire."

By the time a late-August snowstorm finally put out the 1910 fires, they had burned over eight hundred square kilometres of forest and grasslands in the Elbow, Sheep and Highwood valleys. In fact, this was just a small portion of the total area burned in western North America that year, one of the most dramatic fire years in history. Estimates in Montana and Idaho put the area burned in the US mountain States at 7500 square kilometres.

The 1910 fires spurred the Dominion government to put more resources into fire protection and also led, the following year, to a reversal of the policy that had discouraged grazing domestic livestock in the forest reserves. Cattle and horses were now welcomed as a means to keep grass from growing dense enough to pose a fire hazard.

Other fires burned through the Highwood country, including a large one in 1919, but it was the 1936 "Phillips Fire" that really changed the landscape. When the wind plays in the treetops today in the upper Highwood, most of those are trees that sprouted out of that fire's ashes.

The Phillips fire began in British Columbia's Elk River valley. Once it escaped initial attack, fire crews had to back off, as it was unsafe to work in front of the spreading wall of flame burning north into the Elk River headwaters. Those watching from the Alberta side of the Rockies saw a massive thunderhead-like cloud form behind the mountains each afternoon, towering far into the sky before tilting over and settling eastward late each evening, filling the mountain valleys and foothills with resin-scented smoke.

Freddy Nash, the forest ranger in the Sheep Creek district north of the Highwood, grew sufficiently concerned that he placed a phone call to the Alberta Forest Service headquarters in Calgary, seeking permission to take a fire crew into the Highwood and try to stop the fire from coming through the forested Weary Creek Gap. Instead of an okay, he got a scolding for wasting money on an expensive long-distance call. It was only a second, considerably more urgent call from the Highwood valley's forest ranger in mid July that finally got crews moving. By then it was too late.

Mist and snow bring more moisture to the upper Highwood River valley.

On July 23, the fire roared through the Weary Creek Gap. Driven by chinook-force winds, spot fires broke out behind the fire fighters who had finally arrived in the Highwood River valley. There was nothing they could do to stop a fire of this magnitude. According to R.M. Patterson, who ranched east of the forest reserve boundary, 1936 was the driest summer in 50 years of record keeping. The chinook winds, normally confined to the winter season, blew through much of the summer. He wrote that the main Highwood River was dry in its bed upstream from the Highwood Ranger Station that summer, and Threepoint Creek was dry near Millarville.

In one day, the fire ran 24 kilometres from Weary Creek Gap in British Columbia to the Sheep River in Alberta. It burned on into August until most of the west side of the Highwood River valley had been blackened, except for a few sheltered draws and parts of the Mist and Storm Creek valleys. A lightning storm started yet another fire above Flat Creek, on the east side of the Highwood Range, and still the wind blew. There was nothing soothing or benign about the far rushing sound that year.

Rain finally came in August, and the fires died out. Not long after, the High River lumber mill shut for good, although logging continued – only now it was salvage logging of the grey spars of dead pines and spruce.

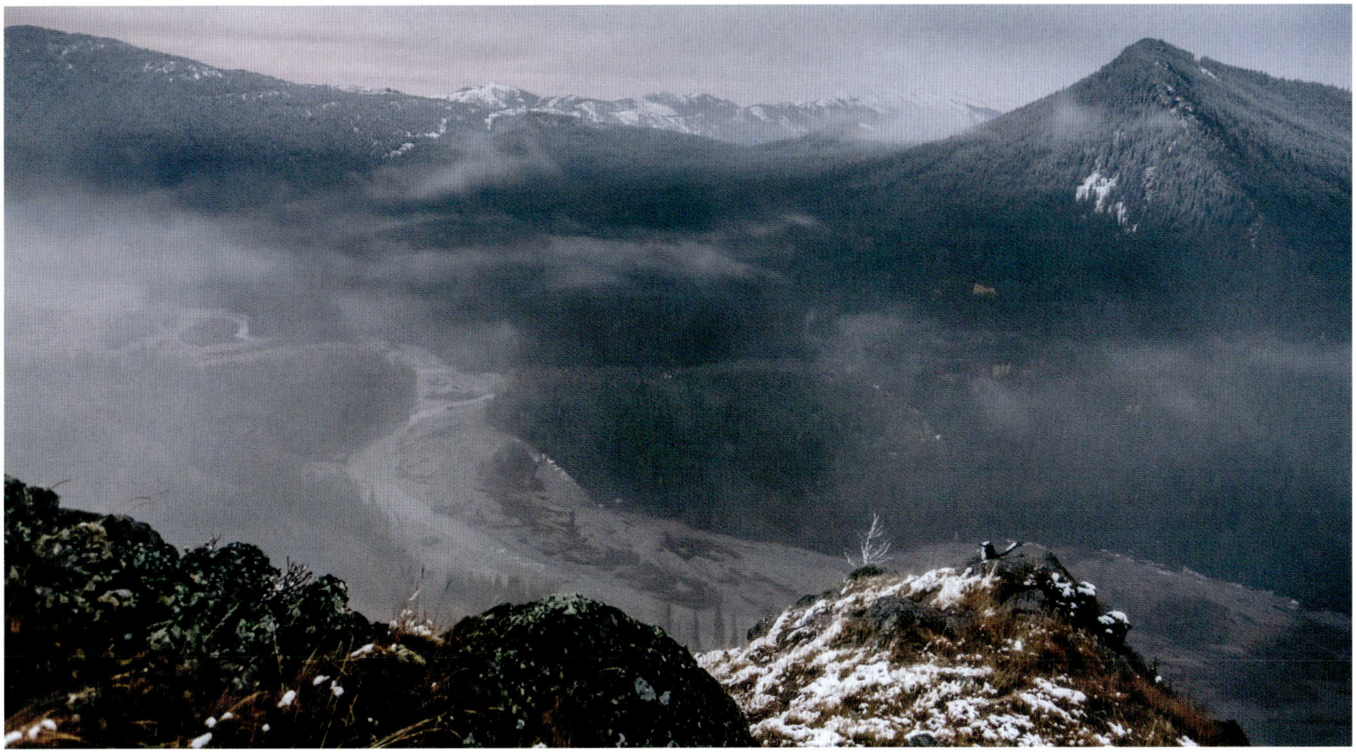

For many ranchers like R.M. Patterson, with wooden ranch buildings, miles of wooden fence posts, and most of their capital tied up in domestic cattle not noted for making intelligent choices when surrounded by smoke and flame, forest fires are among the worst of their fears. Logging companies, whose cash flow and dividend payments rely on trees becoming two-by-fours, not ash, consider fire no less loathsome. Even today, when park wardens and foresters often light fires deliberately to reduce fuel loading or restore wildlife ranges, wildfires get a lot of bad press. When the smoke clears, the headlines are about how much was "destroyed" – not how much forest and rough fescue grassland was renewed.

For natural ecosystems, fires are as much, or more, about renewal as they are about destruction. Patterson wrote of his surprise at the lush growth of hairy wild ryegrass that erupted all through the Highwood country within a year of the 1936 fire. After a couple years more, discriminating eyes would have seen billions of small pine trees sprouting out of the charred soils early

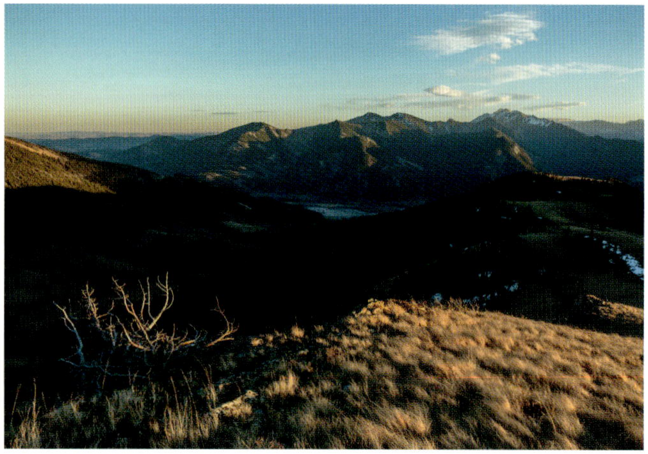

Headwater valleys and the "eagle highway" of the Highwood River drainage.

in the summer. By later in the summer, the new tree seedlings would be obscured by an explosion of fireweed in full bloom. Today's Highwood valley is again the green, breathing place the loss of which Patterson mourned in his book *The Buffalo Head.*

THE RIVER REACTED TO THE 1936 FIRE far more than to the small-scale logging that had preceded it. For the first few years after a fire, without a forest canopy to intercept it, more of the winter snowfall accumulates on the ground. The larger snowpack yields a lot of water. Burned spars and clumps of living trees that the fire missed help shade that snowpack, but the spring melt still comes off more quickly than it did previously, under the shade of a live tree canopy. In the most severely burned sites, erosion rills form where long tree roots burned out, leaving hollowed surfaces in the soil, or where the fire exposed mineral soil below the surface layers of litter and moss. When the sustained rains of late May and June arrive, they run off quickly, too, increasing the erosion. If forest companies move in to salvage the standing dead trees after a burn, as happened in the most accessible parts of the Highwood drainage, erosion can become particularly severe both because the loggers remove the last remaining shade when they cut the standing spars and because compacted logging roads expose raw soil, concentrate runoff water and bring groundwater to the surface.

The river in a burned valley becomes more prone to flash flooding in the first few years after the fire. Runoff arrives in the river fast, carrying a lot of sediment. When the snowmelt ends or the rains stop, the river flow also drops quickly. During the flooding phase, the river has more erosive power but, since it is moving a lot of sediment, that power is displaced laterally rather than down into the existing riverbed, as would happen if the water were clearer. The river attacks its banks, not its bed. The result, for the Highwood, was that many reaches of the river became wider as the river washed out its banks and scoured the floodplain soil down to the underlying gravel.

In *The Buffalo Head,* Patterson wrote:

> There was one beautiful flat on the upper Highwood from which the river washed away three and four feet of the finest black loam. Nothing remained but a waste of shingle – and that was all due to the river overflowing its banks in high floods which were the result of fires, and

then flowing down a deeply cut cattle trail. The old mat of grass that might have partly saved the meadow had already been destroyed by overgrazing.

Had Patterson chosen to stay in the area, he would have seen those gravel flats soon recolonized by pioneering plants like yellow dryas, shrubby cinquefoil and locoweed. Those early plant colonizers formed shallow root mats and thin covers of dead leaves that soon enabled willows, grasses and other meadow plants to colonize. Within a few decades, the stream channel had narrowed again as meadow and shrubs reclaimed the floodplain. When old burned spars eventually succumbed to root rot and carpenter ants, many fell into or across the river, creating turbulent eddies that scoured new holes out of pools that had partly filled with sediment during the early post-fire years.

Trout and whitefish thrive in those pools. Elk and grizzly bears forage in the renewed floodplain meadows. Overhead, the wind whispers in the tops of a billion aging pines, just as it did in Patterson's day. And someday, sooner or later, the wind will push another fire through the valley and the cycle will begin again. That's how the headwater forests work.

GOVERNMENT BUREAUCRATS, however, chose to fight the forces of forest renewal rather than adapt to them. They wanted trees converted to lumber. Fire and insects have been anathema to would-be forest protectors since the late 1800s, even though logging has usually proven a lot more harmful to forested watersheds.

The war against fire began at least as early as 1882, when William Pearce was appointed inspector of Dominion land agencies, with responsibility for land matters between Manitoba's Red River valley and the Rocky Mountains. He saw green forests as watershed protection, and he knew that nothing mattered more to the future of the West than water.

Pearce felt that the newly opened western lands should be settled in an orderly manner and in keeping with their highest and best uses. This was consistent with the thinking of most of those charged with helping implement John A. Macdonald's National Policy. Canada's first director of forestry, Elihu Stewart, said in the 1901 annual report of the Department of Interior:

> The Dominion government should know in advance of settlement the character of the unsettled districts, so as to direct immigration aright; so that mineral land might be set aside as such, agricultural land developed to the agriculturalist and land unsuited for agriculture but on which timber is growing reserved permanently for timber.

While Pearce accepted the views of earlier surveyors, like John Palliser and John Macoun, that much of the prairie west was too arid for crop agriculture, he felt this could be remedied by tapping into rivers like the Bow for irrigation water. In Pearce's view, consequently, the best use of the forested Eastern Slopes was as a water source for irrigation, and to that end he supported national park establishment at Banff and the reservation of other forests for purposes consistent with watershed protection.

Logging in the headwaters may have been a necessary evil, as settlers would need wood for construction, but Pearce was concerned with the potential effects of too much logging on the watershed values of the mountains and foothills. By the late 1800s, experience in eastern Canada and the forests of the northeastern US had already shown the devastation that could result if frontier capitalists were allowed to cut and run. Government agencies overseen by Pearce imposed strict conditions on John Lineham, the Eau Claire Company and others who were allowed to extract timber from the headwater country.

Pearce and his colleagues saw the 1910 fires in the Highwood, Sheep and Elbow drainages as threats to the water supply. Forest protection became an urgent priority.

The Dominion government hired fire and wildlife guardians, precursors to today's national park wardens, to protect the forests of the Rocky Mountains Park. A 9.52-million-acre Rocky Mountain Forest Reserve, in which permanent settlement was prohibited, covered the rest of the headwaters region along the Eastern Slopes. The authorities hired rangers to protect those forests, too.

The forest rangers were tasked with protecting their assigned districts from fires and illegal logging, maintaining a system of trail access and telephone lines, and monitoring any approved logging operations to ensure the operators were complying with the conditions of their permits. Their rudimentary motor trails often followed existing horse trails originally used by Aboriginal peoples. Many evolved, in the fullness of time, into gravel forestry roads.

In those early years, timber production was always

Chinook clouds form over the upper Highwood valley.

the highest single priority for forest reserves, as it was considered compatible with watershed protection. Although recreational camping and cattle grazing were both allowed, forest rangers viewed them more as fire-prevention measures than as legitimate primary uses of the area. The earliest campgrounds were seen as necessary evils, intended to concentrate campers in places where the undergrowth and lower branches of trees had been cleared. That way there was less risk of campfires setting the forest ablaze. By the same token, one of the rationales for licensing ranchers to pasture their stock in the forest reserves was that grazing would reduce the accumulation of dry grass, which might otherwise carry fires from one patch of timber to another.

THE PROVINCE OF ALBERTA took over management of the forest reserves in the early 1930s, after ownership of resources finally passed from the federal to the provincial governments in western Canada. Alberta passed its own legislation to perpetuate the forest reserves and to establish its own forest service. Barely two years after the new Alberta Forest Service came into being, the Phillips Fire burned through the Highwood. Initial delays in detecting and reporting the fire, followed by logistical difficulties getting crews into position to fight it, led the Forest Service to put a priority on improving the rough tracks into the headwater valleys to a road standard better suited for truck traffic.

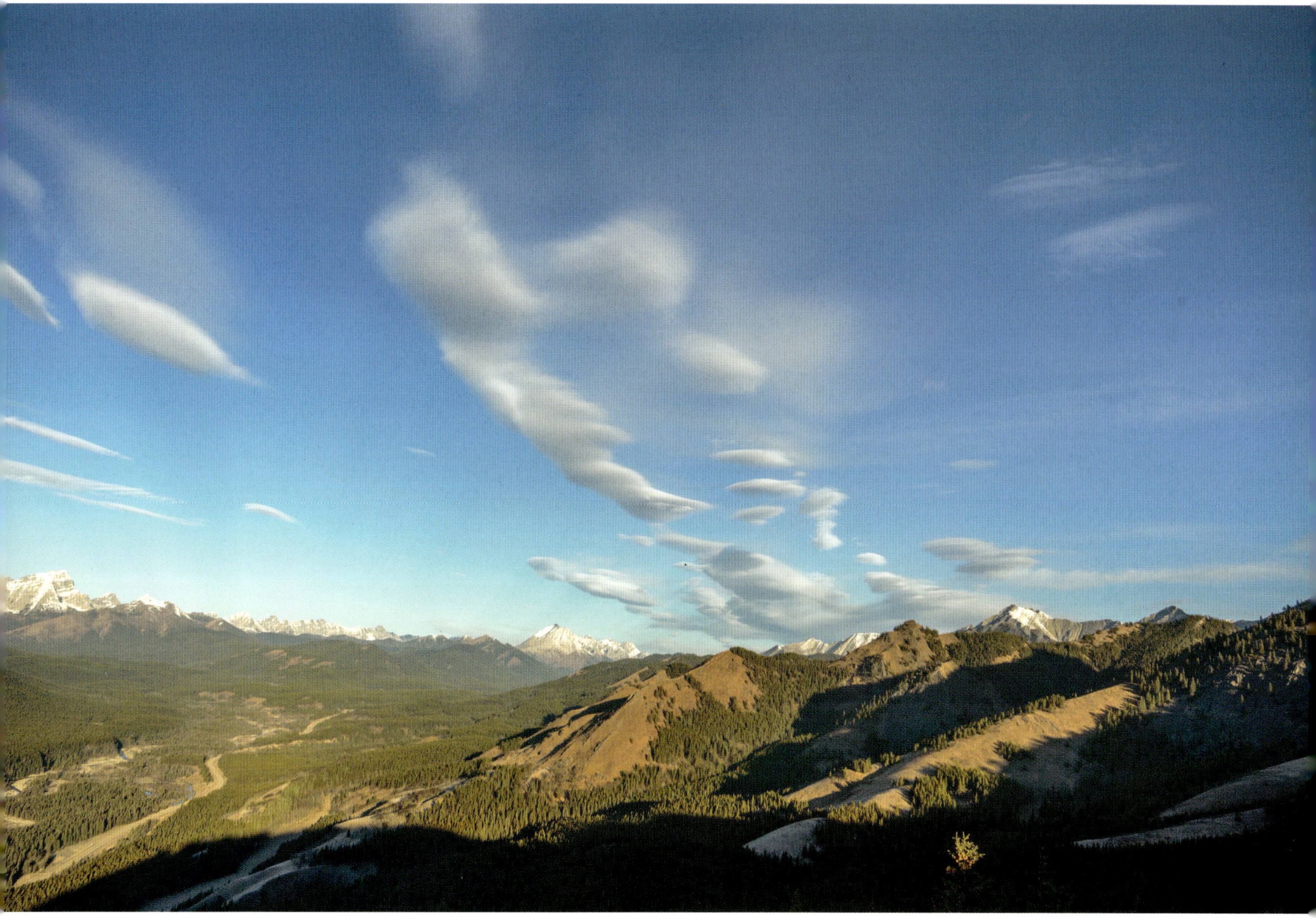

Eastern Rockies Forest Conservation Board

Alberta was not yet a wealthy province during the dust bowl years of the Great Depression. As the desperate 1930s gave way to the economic demands of the Second World War, it soon became apparent that the province was faced with forest protection costs it couldn't afford. Alberta turned to the federal government for financing to build new forest roads into the headwaters country. The federal government was receptive to the idea because, in the wake of a drought that had devastated economies right across the prairie provinces, it seemed clear that protecting the prairie headwaters was a matter of national importance.

The Eastern Rockies Forest Conservation Board (ERFCB) was established in 1948 by acts of both the province and the federal government. The conservation area under the legislation was about 14,484 square kilometres – only about 10 per cent of the total Saskatchewan drainage basin but the source of an estimated 87 per cent of its water. The headwaters would now be jointly managed by the federal and provincial governments; the feds provided the money and the province arranged for the necessary work to get done. Over the next three decades, the ERFCB represented a major transfer of wealth from the federal government to the Province of Alberta – a part of history conveniently forgotten by western isolationists.

In setting up the new management board, the governments were unequivocal about the single highest management priority for the forested headwater landscapes of the Bow and other rivers draining east into Canada:

> The construction of dams to store water and to give a greater control of the flow in the Saskatchewan River and its tributaries is important in meeting the demand for water but, over and above, it is essential to protect and manage the headwaters of this great river for its yield of water.

One of the three primary purposes of the ERFCB was to

> conserve, develop, maintain and manage the forests in the Area with a view to obtaining the greatest possible flow of water in the Saskatchewan River and its tributaries.

In a 1972 paper presented to the United Nations, chief forester W.R. Hanson said that the board subsequently moved to the idea of "optimum" rather than "maximum" water production in light of the flooding and stream damage that would arise if they just managed for the maximum amount of water. He described the program as built around protection and maintenance of watershed values, restoration where damage had occurred and improvement over pristine conditions where that was possible.

The ERFCB proved to be a remarkably enlightened and progressive organization. It not only built the Forestry Trunk Road and other key forest access routes but also conducted research into forest hydrology, experimented with ways to reduce cattle impacts and improve range health, conducted detailed forest mapping and protected areas of high water-yield values from commercial logging. Its aggressive protection of landscape health wasn't popular with some local politicians and senior provincial bureaucrats, however; they

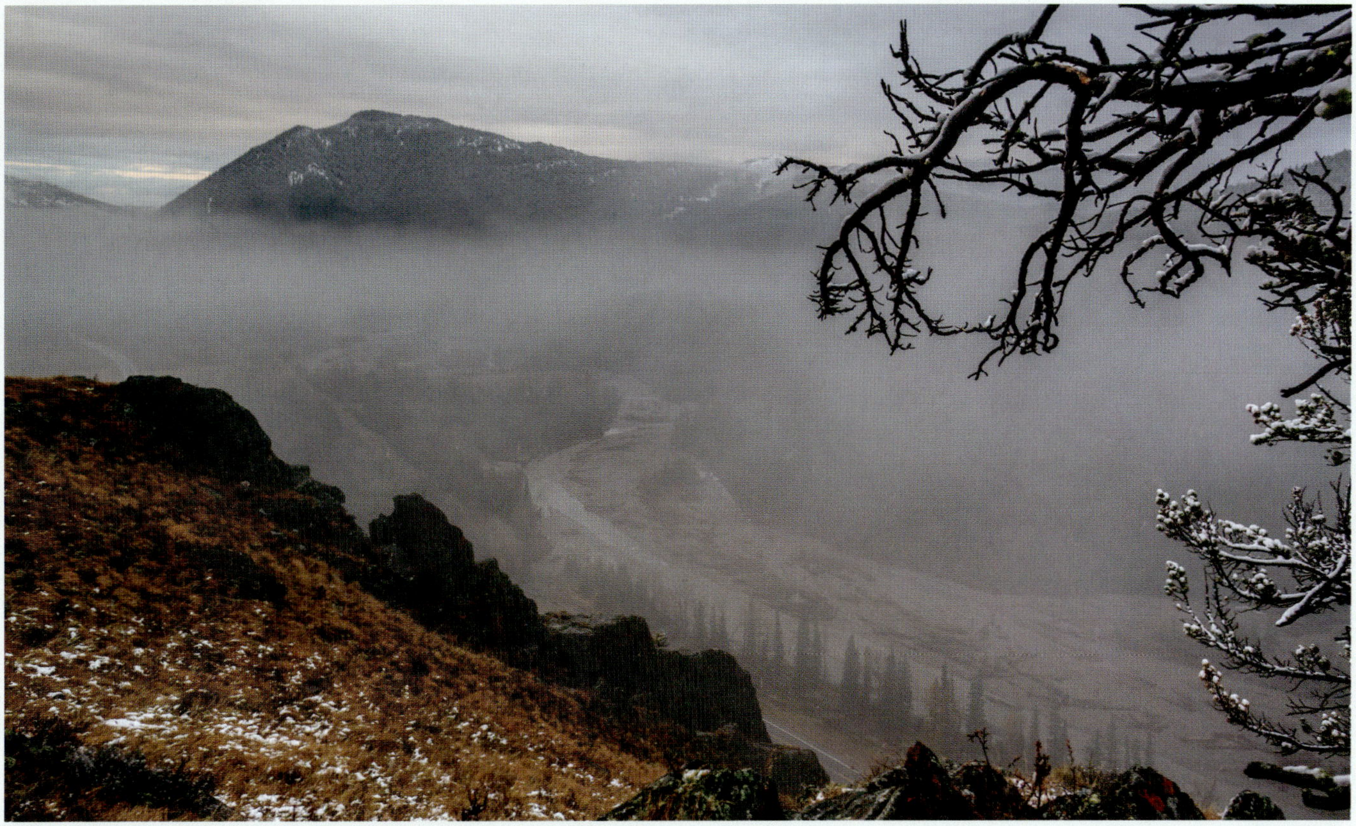

were happy to accept the federal money but also wanted to profit from more aggressive resource development. When the original 20-year agreement expired in the late 1960s, oil and gas revenues were beginning to pour into provincial coffers and supplant the need for the federal subsidy. The ERFCB was formally disbanded in 1968, and resource exploitation took over from watershed protection as the de facto priority for the headwaters.

Those federally funded roads built over the previous two decades made access to timber, oil, gas and coal resources a lot easier. Unfortunately for the health of foothills streams and the once-pristine landscapes that yield their water, the provincial agencies that took over management of the headwaters were soon more concerned with developing those resources – especially oil and gas – than with protecting watershed health.

Improved roads meant more motor vehicles and strangers in the headwater country. The peace and solitude of the once-remote Highwood River valley was further reduced when, reacting to the flush of new grass growth in the burned area, which seemed both a wasted resource and a new fire hazard, the Forest Service opened the valley to heavier cattle grazing. R.M. Patterson and his wife, Marigold, could see the end of their golden era – the perfect decade before fire and cattle, when the forests and streams of the upper Highwood country were intact and those willing and able to travel by horse pack train could have paradise to themselves. In the fall of 1945, having sold their Buffalo Head Ranch, they loaded their belongings onto pack horses and headed west into the wind, seeking new pastures in British Columbia.

THE WIND REMAINED, as did the mountains and the river and the long, slow processes of change and renewal that pulse through this headwaters ecosystem on a time scale more measured and patient than ours. Although the Pattersons may have felt they had lost their paradise, the renewed forest grew to maturity, the ancient cycles of flooding and retreat restored the river to a state not far different from how they had known it, and the snows and spring flowers and lush summers and golden autumns continued their timeless cycle in all the quiet places where springs still emerge from the ground and chatter their way down to the Highwood River.

And the road, of course, remained. Today it's even paved. New generations of Albertans, following that road, discover their own version of paradise in the Highwood country, just like the Pattersons and so many others before them. Some of those newcomers have sense enough to stop and spend a night or two camped beneath the serrated silhouettes of the Elk and Highwood ranges. Their children listen to the soughing of the western wind through the branches of trees born out of fire. Sometimes it lulls, and the muted voice of the Highwood River seems to rise, down there in the shadowed valley, to become a part of the rushing calm that pulses, like life itself, in the darkened valley. Tired children wonder, briefly, what makes that endless soothing sound they hear around them.

It's the slow, patient sound of mountains, breathing.

Another mountain evening settles over the upper Highwood River.

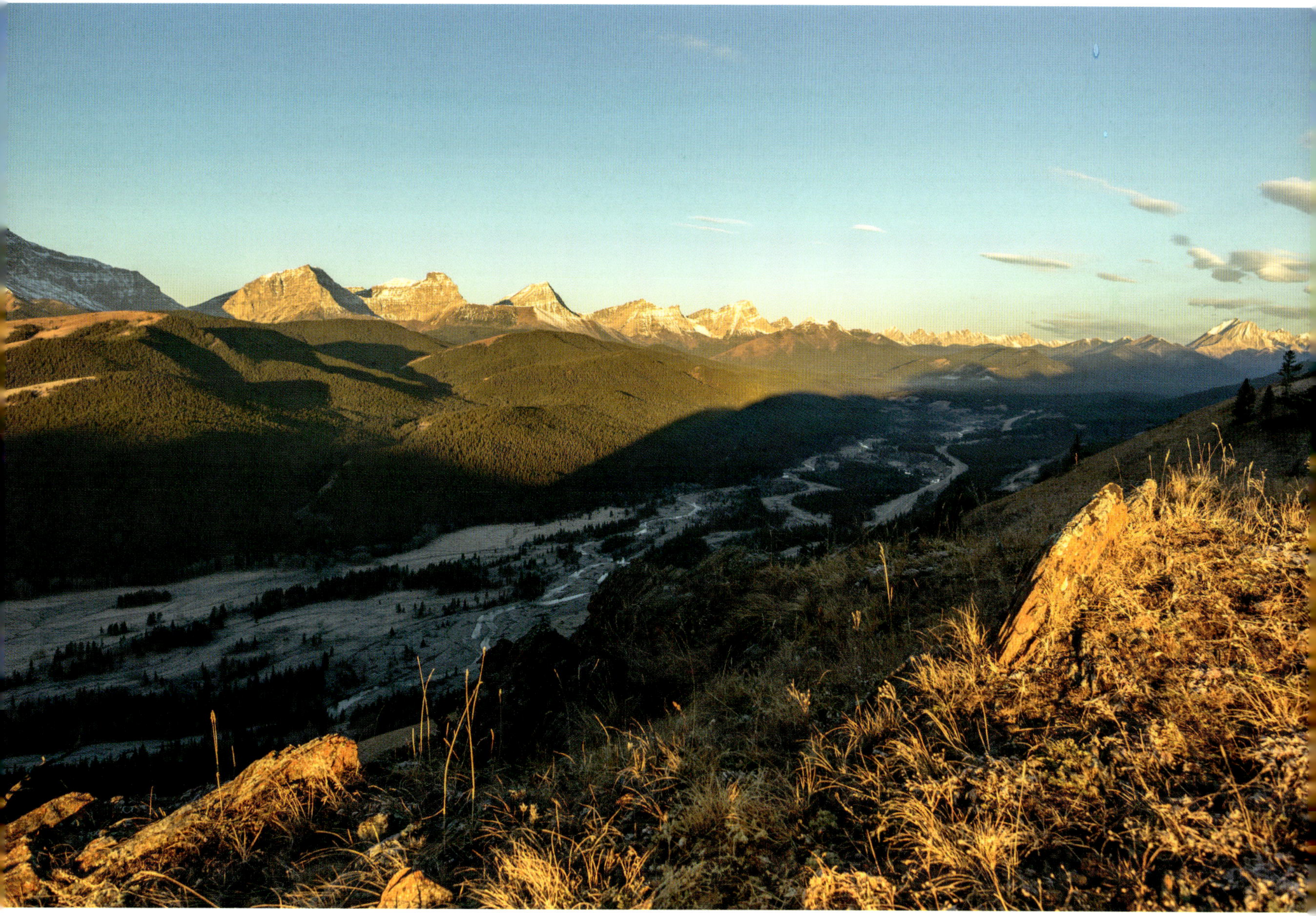

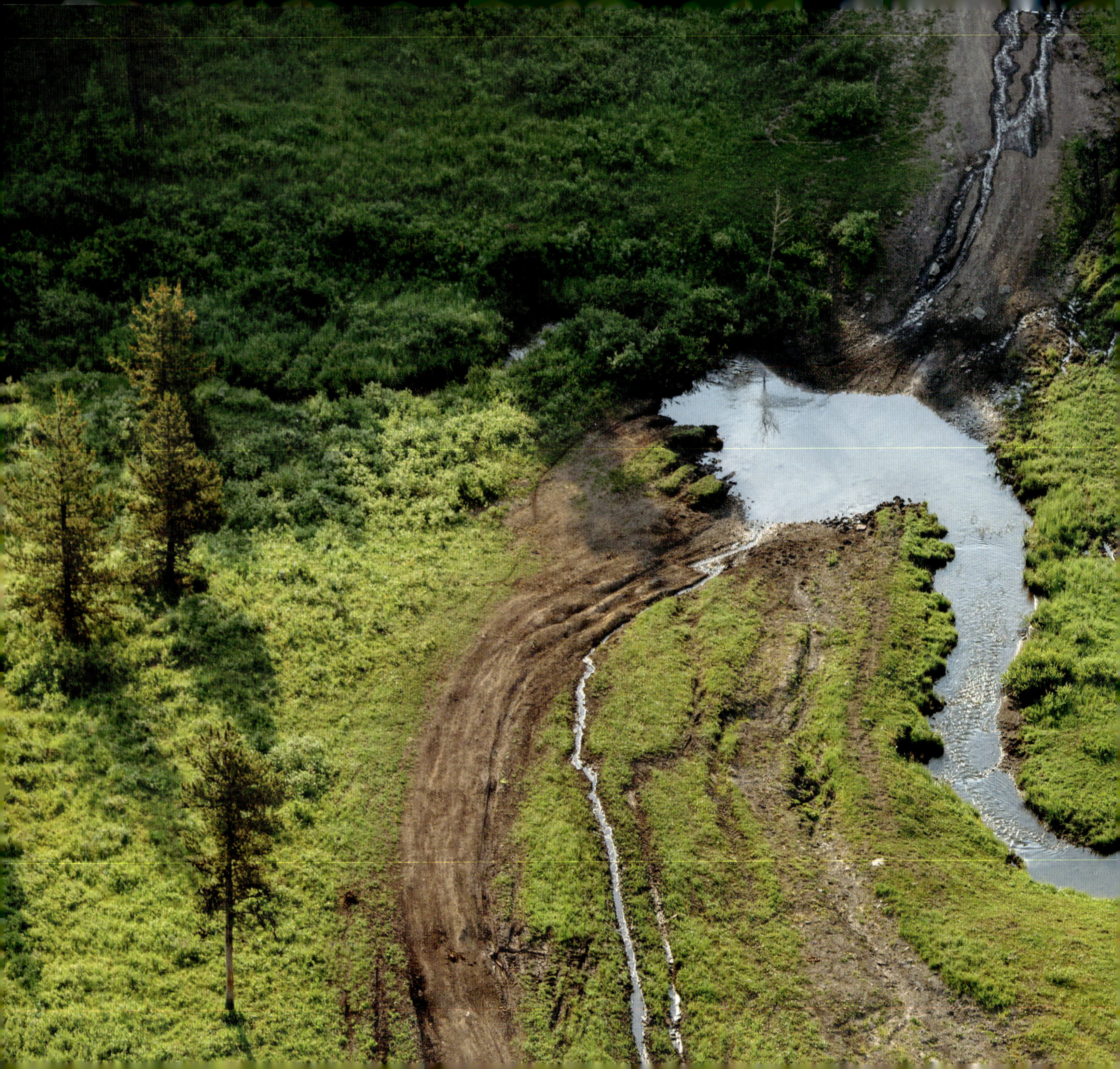

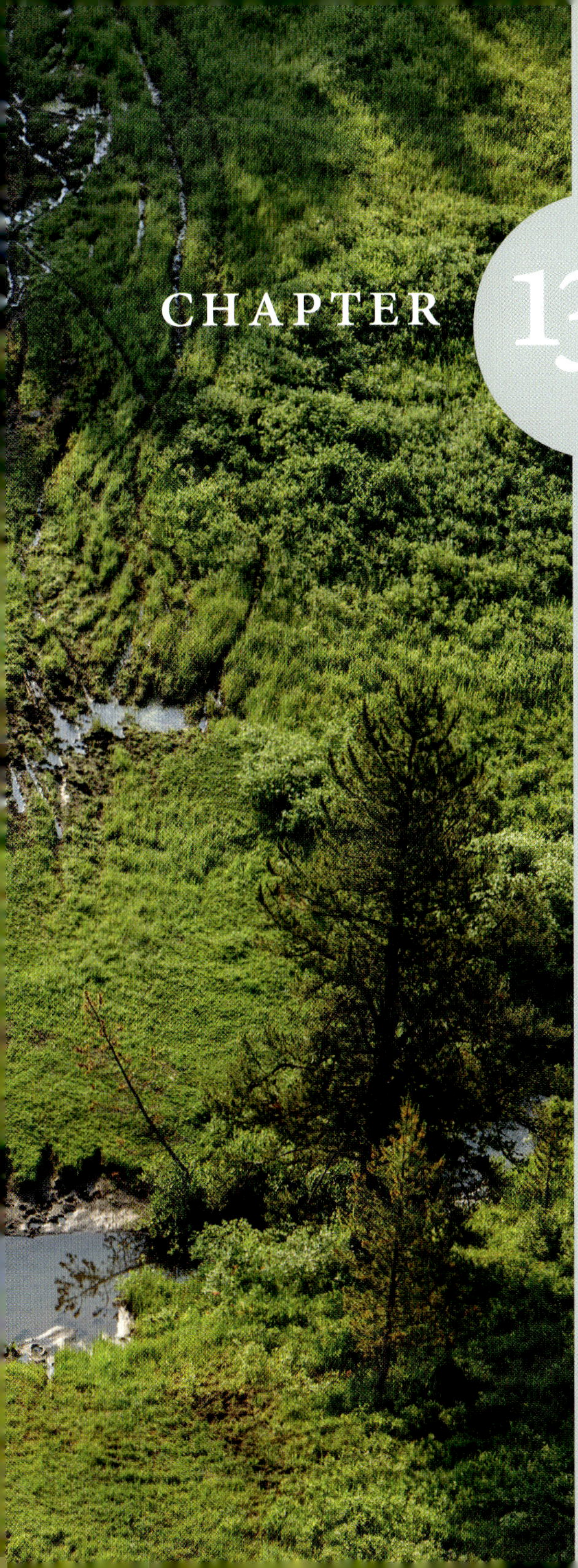

CHAPTER 13

Healing the Headwaters

THE BOW RIVER'S WATER comes almost exclusively from streams that drain the Rocky Mountains and their foothills, but its flow is diminishing. Monitoring on the South Saskatchewan River, of which the Bow is a major tributary, shows a 12 per cent decrease in the amount of natural flow over the past three-quarters of a century. The Bow and Oldman rivers are so tapped out that the Province of Alberta has denied all applications for new water licences since 2006.

Water is running low in a part of the province that supports more than a third of its population and two-thirds of all the irrigated agriculture in Canada … and whose population is projected to double within the next quarter century. Most Albertans alive today have lived through more wet years than dry, during a period of unprecedented climate stability. Few remember the devastating multi-year drought of the 1930s; fewer yet have looked at the historical record compiled by climate scientists that show longer, deeper droughts in the 1700s and 1800s. Even the historic range of climate variability threatens us with extreme droughts – but our future climate will not be the same as the past. A slowing jet stream and a warming global climate increase the threat of future droughts.

Ironically, even as we face a future of water scarcity, spring flooding is becoming more frequent, more damaging and increasingly costly to recover from. Climate models are in general agreement that more winter precipitation will fall as rain than as snow in the future, and that extreme weather events of long duration are increasingly likely. Big floods, as well as big droughts, are virtually guaranteed in this already water-short region.

Alberta's water crisis is upon us.

A LOT OF PEOPLE over the years have seen the crisis coming. Many have tried to figure out how to produce more water, but to do so we'd need to be able to control the weather. That's been suggested. Grant MacEwan, a well-respected former Calgary mayor and, later, Lieutenant Governer of Alberta, used to advocate for the use of airplanes to seed clouds with silver iodide crystals, which would encourage water vapour to condense into rain. It's a dicey and expensive business, however, trying to modify entire weather systems. Although cloud seeding is used to reduce hail damage from summer storms, nobody seriously considers it a real solution to the bigger water crisis.

In any case, there is no need for a solution, because there is no problem. Or at least if there is a problem, it's not a lack of water. Except after the very driest of winters, far more water falls as snow and rain in the high country west of Highway 2 than we could ever need. It's more a matter of timing.

Most of the snow in the high country melts out in May and June. Rainfall peaks in spring, too, often hastening the melt. Sometimes – as happened in 2013 – a heavy winter snowpack and a cool spring combine with heavy June rains to send most of the year's water supply pouring down rivers over a few short days. Even in ordinary years, the Bow River's early June flows range from three to five times greater than in midwinter, and nearly twice as high as in August.

So there's plenty of water; it's just that most of it leaves the province a month or two before it's needed. A changing climate may increase that imbalance if, as appears likely, it increases the early-season runoff. That's why some engineers see the solution as more dams. If we can't squeeze more water out of the sky, they say, let's trap it in reservoirs.

Eleven large dams already plug rivers upstream from Calgary, but they were built to produce hydropower, not to save water for irrigation, domestic use and thirsty summer streams. Hydro dams don't increase the summer water supply; just the opposite, in fact. The Bow River at Calgary now carries less water in summer and almost twice as much in midwinter as it would under natural

Page 198: *Recreational mismanagement in the headwaters: A badly gullied OHV trail increases spring runoff while drying out the water table later in summer. Worse floods; less summer water.*

Right: *Ghost Dam is one of several hydroelectric dams upstream from Calgary that reduce summer flows in the Bow River by storing water for winter release. Restoring more natural flow patterns could make the dams part of the water solution rather than forces of ongoing river destruction.*

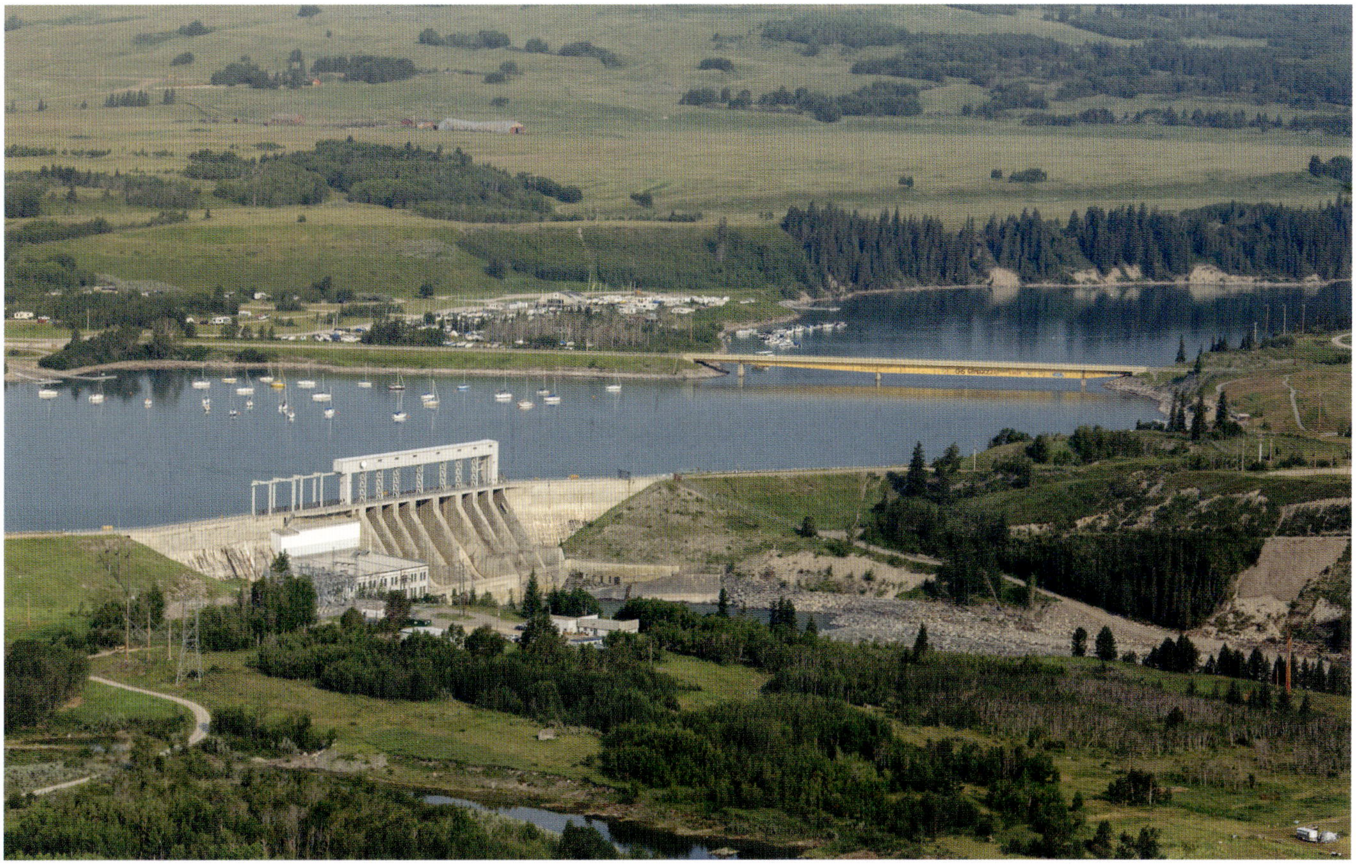

flow conditions because TransAlta holds back the runoff to produce electricity in winter. Little wonder that irrigation advocates and water engineers continue to pore over maps in search of good places for new dams to store water for summer use.

The Western Irrigation District weir in Calgary, and two other weirs farther downstream at Carseland and Bassano, divert water from the Bow River into canal systems that feed it to off-stream reservoirs. But the big on-stream irrigation dams are elsewhere in the South Saskatchewan drainage. The Province of Saskatchewan built the Gardiner Dam on the South Saskatchewan River in 1967. Alberta followed in 1975 with the Dickson Dam on the Red Deer, and in 1989 with the Oldman Dam. Still, those dams don't make water; they simply hold back some of the spring runoff. In fact, leakage and evaporation from the wind-whipped reservoirs actually reduce the water supply.

Evaporation takes more water from Lake Diefenbaker, the reservoir behind the Gardiner Dam, than all its human users – even though the reservoir serves more than three-quarters of Saskatchewan's population. Alberta's irrigation reservoirs lose, on average, a metre of water each year. Monitoring studies on the Oldman Reservoir showed that it loses a litre of water to evaporation for every one hundred litres flowing into it.

Dams waste water. They devastate rivers, destroy native fish stocks and cost a fortune to build and maintain. And even the largest of dams hold back only a small portion of the available spring runoff.

A far more elegant solution to the water supply conundrum is simply to store the water in the headwaters landscape itself: in forests, fens, beaver meadows, soil and their underlying groundwater aquifers. That's what the headwater landscape is: a living reservoir capable of storing far more water than any number of man-made dams ever could. And the advantage of storing water in the landscape is that it's not just downstream water users who benefit. Everything does: trout, creeks, anglers, bears, elk, otters, songbirds, hikers, hunters, trees and waterfowl.

The solution to Alberta's water-challenged second century is to reverse the mistakes of our first century, when pretty much everything we did in the headwaters of the Bow River reduced their capacity to produce abundant, clean water. To an objective viewer studying Alberta land use, in fact, it might look like we spent the last few decades trying to drain the high country as fast as possible rather than steward its water-holding capacity. If the landscape itself is our best and largest water reservoir, most of our land-use practices reduce its holding capacity and fill it with leaks.

It's not like William Pearce didn't warn us – before Alberta was even a province.

WILLIAM PEARCE arrived in Calgary in 1884 determined to make sure Canada didn't mess up its west. Farther south, waves of eager Americans were fighting over water holes, shooting at the Indigenous people, laying waste to forests and overgrazing the plains. That kind of chaotic settlement was not, in Pearce's opinion, an option for western Canada.

His opinion mattered. As the young country's superintendent of mines for the CPR "Railway Belt," Pearce controlled most land-use decisions west of what is now Winnipeg. Appointed by the deputy minister of the interior in faraway Ottawa, Pearce soon became known as the "Czar of the West." He established new parks, settled land disputes, allocated mineral rights and recommended settlement and development policies.

William Pearce had spent his youth in well-watered southern Ontario. He was struck by the scarcity and small size of our western rivers, as well as their unfortunate habit of shrinking each summer, when water demand peaked. He knew that the West's agricultural potential would be limited by the available water. It didn't help that the 1880s had been marked by drought; if the skies couldn't always be relied upon for water, he reasoned, the rivers must provide it.

Pearce consequently became a keen champion of irrigation development. But even as he explored the potential for dams and canals to carry water to prairie farms, he looked west to the Rocky Mountains and foothills. That was where the water came from. Nothing, he decided, could be allowed to diminish or threaten the headwaters.

Pearce helped persuade the government to set aside Rocky Mountains Park in 1885 – the world's third national park. He went on to arrange for the rest of the forests along the edge of the Rocky Mountains to be reserved as public land in 1898. Settlement and development were prohibited. Determined to lock in protection of those headwater forests, Pearce persuaded Ottawa to enlarge the park to 12,691 square kilometres, twice its modern size, in 1902. Even when later governments shrank the park to exclude valuable natural resources and potential dam sites, they retained the deleted land in the forest reserve.

The reserve included the forested headwaters of the Oldman, Bow, Red Deer, North Saskatchewan and Athabasca rivers. The Department of Interior's 1911 report described it as

> a timbered area lying alongside of a prairie country hundreds of miles in extent ... it forms the watershed for the river systems which water the great plains to the east where water supply is practically the only limit to anticipated settlement and development.

Real-estate speculators, cattlemen and loggers had ambitions for that land. But Pearce's vision won. The undisturbed forests, beaver meadows, relict glaciers and deep winter snows were reserved to gather and store water from winter snow and spring rains. That way they could always be relied on to release good water in a timely way to the cold springs and creeks that feed the downstream rivers. Watershed protection trumped all.

In 1930, when the National Resources Transfer Acts gave natural resources over to the control of the prairie provinces, one of the Alberta government's first actions was to establish its own forest service and reaffirm that the forest reserves in the headwaters of its prairie rivers were to be managed to protect water supplies. The Eastern Rockies Forest Conservation Board, during its two decades of federal–provincial collaboration, in turn made headwaters protection its top priority.

The return of Alberta's headwaters to full provincial control seemed promising at first. A new Progressive Conservative government, led by Calgary lawyer Peter Lougheed, had won the 1971 election. Faced with competing views about the highest and best use of public land, Lougheed's government launched a public hearing process in 1973. The following year, based on those hearings, the newly established Environmental Conservation Authority released recommendations for land use and resource development in the Eastern Slopes that, yet again, emphasized watershed values. The government responded to the recommendations by setting up a Resource Evaluation and Planning division in 1976 and issuing the landmark *Policy for Resource Management of the Eastern Slopes* a year later.

That policy again put watershed protection first in

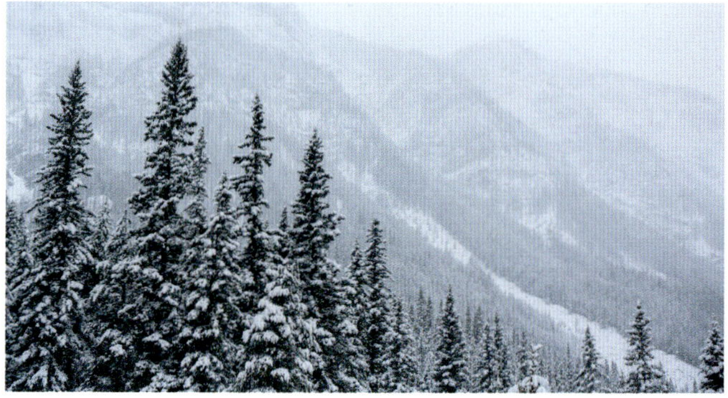

Right: *The "snow forests" of the Rocky Mountain Front Ranges and foothills produce up to 80 per cent of the annual flow in streams draining to the Bow River. Their management will determine our water future.*

Far right: *Tree canopies intercept snow, much of which can be lost back to the atmosphere during chinooks. Logging that creates gaps and small openings in the canopy can improve snow capture while providing enough canopy shade to slow the spring thaw.*

priority above all other uses, aggressively prescribing the kinds of activities and development permitted in each land-use zone. When provincial department heads and business lobby groups demanded fewer restrictions, the business-oriented Progressive Conservatives released a more development-friendly version of the policy in 1984. Even with new loopholes for exploitation of wood, gravel, oil, gas and other resources, the revised Eastern Slopes policy once more affirmed watershed protection as the highest policy priority.

Thirty years later, the *South Saskatchewan Regional Plan* replaced the Eastern Slopes Policy, but not its priority for watershed health.

With so much emphasis on watershed values over most of the last century, one might expect the headwaters of our prairie rivers to be in good condition and our water future assured. One would be wrong.

For decades, resource managers have known that the key to improving the water supply from Alberta's foothill and mountain headwaters is to enable the landscape to capture as much of each winter's snowfall as possible and to delay the release of snowmelt and rainwater from the high country until well into the summer. Contemporary logging practices, recreational use, trapping, forest grazing allotments and hydropower dam operations, however, do just the opposite. Ironically, those land uses are all regulated by government agencies whose policy priority, for more than a century, has been to put watershed health above everything else.

They just don't actually do it.

Snow Forests

Marmot Creek basin, just north of the Mount Allan ski area, lies in the heart of those headwater forests. I visited its research watershed in 2012 with University of Saskatchewan hydrologist Dr. John Pomeroy.

Why would a Saskatchewan professor be interested in Alberta's high mountain forests? Pomeroy had no difficulty answering that one: almost all the water in the

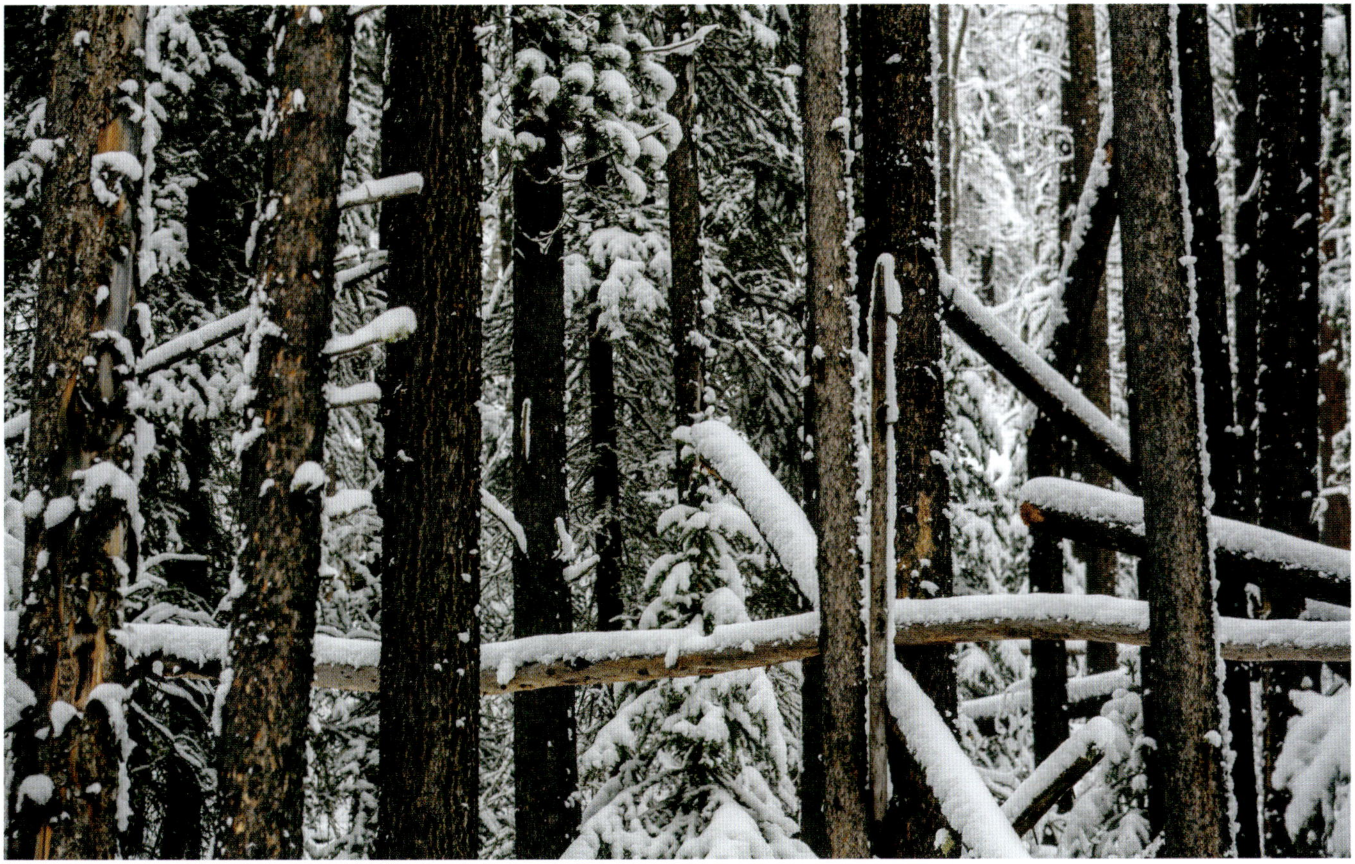

Saskatchewan River comes from Alberta's Rocky Mountains. In fact, more than 90 per cent of all western stream flows in North America come from the mountains west of the Mississippi River – mostly from melting snow. If you're concerned about prairie water, you need to pay attention to what Pomeroy describes as the "snow forests."

River flows in the Saskatchewan River have declined more than 40 per cent in the past century. Although diversions of water to irrigation farming districts explained some of the losses, about a third of the missing river flow remained unaccounted for. It was that missing water that led Dr. Pomeroy to the headwaters of his river, in Alberta.

Pomeroy isn't interested in cloud seeding or dam building. He studies the hydrology of the headwaters to find out what has changed that might account for the decline in downstream river flows. Identifying the problem is always the first step to finding a solution. Based on monitoring and research at Marmot Basin and other study sites, Pomeroy and his students have generated some likely ideas about where the water went, and how to get it back.

Part of the explanation for the diminished flows goes to climate change, and it may be too late to fix that, given our addiction to hydrocarbons and the feedback loops that we've already set in motion. We might be able to mitigate its impacts to some degree – we'd be fools not to try – but we dithered too long to avoid the changes already underway.

Even if there were such a thing as a stable climate, burgeoning human populations alone would demand that we look west, as William Pearce did a century and a quarter ago, and ask ourselves what are the right things to do in the green sliver of land that produces all the water we will ever have. There have been droughts longer than those of the dirty thirties and floods at least a third again more intense than the 2005 and 2013 ones that swamped Calgary and High River. Climate change is just an added level of uncertainty about future water supply, in a region already squeezed to meet its basic needs.

Researcher Mike Demuth used satellite images to map changes in western Canada's mountain glaciers. He found that ice cover in the headwaters of the Bow and Oldman rivers has shrunk by almost a third over the past quarter century, and the shrinkage continues. On the Haig Glacier, south of Kananaskis Lakes, another glacier researcher, Shawn Marshall, found no snow remaining in late summer in five out of the first 11 years of the 21st century. Instead of the previous winter's snow adding to the bulk of the glacier, it had melted completely away, exposing the dark inner ice of the glacier to summer heat. Like most Rocky Mountain glaciers, the Haig is losing ground to a warming climate.

Glacier meltwaters can be particularly important in late summer, when rivers, deprived of spring runoff, would otherwise shrink. In fact, the current accelerated rate of glacier melt may be masking the effects of climate change by releasing stored glacier water faster than it's replaced. Once most of the glaciers are gone – quite possibly by the end of this century – that subsidy will fizzle out. Floodplain streams like Canmore's Policeman Creek will go dry, and the Bow will be a much smaller, warmer stream. Already, according to John Pomeroy, the Bow River at Banff carries only three-quarters as much water as it did a century ago.

Overall, glaciers actually contribute very little of the water in prairie rivers – barely 2 per cent of the Bow River's annual flow. The North Saskatchewan gets less than 5 per cent of its water from glaciers.

Glacial ice retreat, however, is a proxy for a far more important water source: snowfall. With warming temperatures, more winter precipitation falls as rain, which runs off instead of being stored by mountain snowpacks until spring. Snow melts out of the foothills one to two months earlier than in it did when I was a boy – a startling change over so short a period. Reductions in snowpack translate directly into less river flow and groundwater recharge –

in short, a reduction in the water upon which people and ecosystems depend.

Changes to forest cover provide another part of the explanation for the missing water. Unlike climate change, this is one that offers hope for local solutions. It just requires that we do almost the exact opposite of everything we've traditionally done in managing headwater forests.

Aggressive forest-fire control increased the amount of unburned forest steadily through the 20th century. Even with more recent programs of prescribed fire, and with climate-change-induced outbreaks of tree-killing insects like the mountain pine beetle, the amount of old forest in the headwaters far exceeds the historic norm. Dense, continuous forests are neither natural nor good for water production.

To show us why, Pomeroy led us through a mossy glade into dark woods redolent with the scent of resin and hushed by the wistful whistles of varied thrushes. There he showed us a dead spruce tree hanging from a cable. Its sawed-off trunk ended just a few centimetres from the ground. Cables and posts held various instruments at different levels of the surrounding forest canopy, as if a mad arborist were conducting bizarre experiments.

Pomeroy was quick to explain the tree-lynching – he'd probably noticed some sidewise glances from our group. To determine how much snow gets intercepted by the tree canopy each winter, the researchers hang a sawed-off tree in its normal growth position and then weigh it periodically as the winter progresses. The technique has yielded some startling findings. Thanks to our chinook winds, more canopy snow is lost to sublimation – the evaporation of water from solid snow directly to gaseous water vapour – in Alberta's headwater forests than anywhere else in the world.

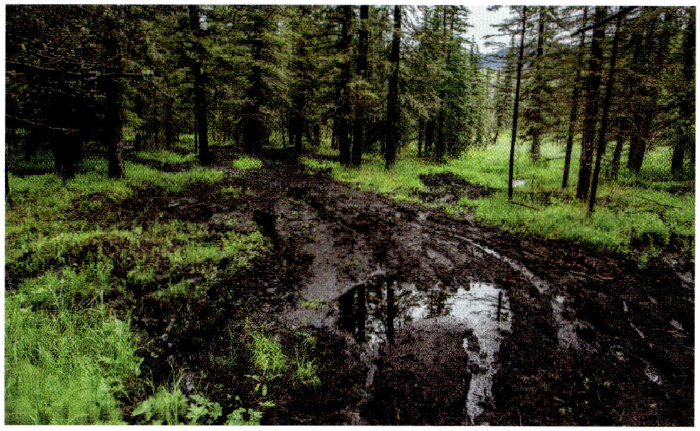

Illegal "mud-bogging" is widespread in foothills wetlands. Off-roaders turn once-productive wetlands and riparian forests into eroded morasses.

Consequently, very little canopy snow becomes meltwater in the spring; it goes aloft again and vanishes into distant weather systems. In Alberta's chinook belt – which includes most of the Bow River headwaters – sublimation can remove as much as 60 per cent of the annual snowfall, mostly from snow held on the branches of trees, each winter. That's a big loss.

Naturally, the denser the forest canopy, the more snow gets trapped in the branches of trees rather than settling to the ground. Where snow accumulates on the ground, especially if shaded from sun and sheltered from wind, much less sublimates. Instead, it melts out in the spring

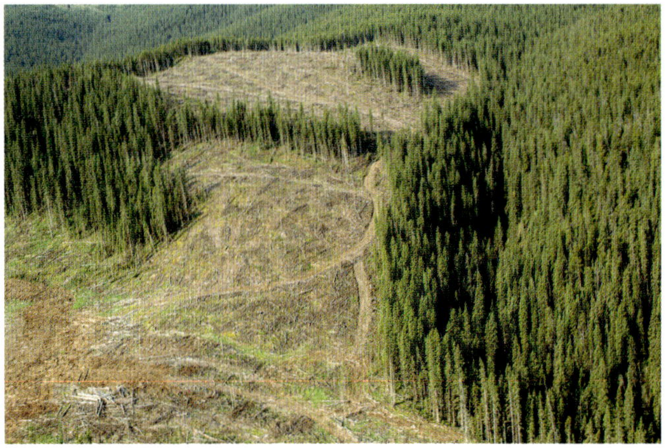

Clear-cut logging in the Elbow River headwaters. Clear-cuts trap more snow than dense forests, but the lack of shade means that the increased snowpack melts faster, causing worse floods.

to feed groundwater and streams. The tree canopy isn't all bad, though: the shade cast by trees shelters the snowpack so that it melts gradually in the spring rather than releasing all its water at once.

Clear-cut logging can increase the winter snowpack as much as 40 per cent. Snow holds a lot of air, so when the enhanced snowpack melts, it produces only a 12 per cent increase in the stream flow. That still amounts to a lot more water. Unfortunately, that water comes mostly in the form of more intense spring floods, since the unprotected snowpack melts quickly. An unlogged forest yields less water, but the extended thaw gives that water more time to go into groundwater and sustain stream flows than the flash floods that drain from clear-cuts. Forestry in a vital watershed, then, should lie somewhere between clear-cutting and total protection.

The research findings from Marmot Basin suggest that, rather than clear-cutting, it makes more sense to thin the forest or log small patches. Opening the canopy, rather than eliminating it, reduces sublimation losses in winter without sacrificing shade in late spring. The optimal amount of thinning – the size of the patch-cuts – depends on tree type, slope aspect and slope steepness. In a forest managed for water yield, the only place for small clear-cuts might be on steep slopes sheltered from direct sunshine or wind, but Pomeroy warns that those large clearings might make flooding worse during rain-on-snow events. Increasingly, he believes that "Natural disturbance [like fire] and varying clearing size and forest height and density is the ideal."

Traditional forestry replaces logged forests with dense-canopy stands of conifers like spruce or pine that produce good lumber. Logging for optimal water, however, would strive instead to keep the canopy open and increase the cover of less-valuable deciduous trees. Aspen and poplar trunks reflect about 20 per cent of incoming sunlight, whereas conifers reflect 8 per cent at best. Absorbed by the dark trunks and foliage of the coniferous trees, the rest of that sunlight becomes radiant heat that melts snow or, in summer, heats up the atmosphere and contributes to storm formation.

That's not how forest companies log headwater forests. They follow government guidelines designed to optimize the supply of wood, not water even though it's water we will need most in the future.

Rain in the Forest

Snow may provide most of the water that fills the headwater streams that drain to the Bow River, but rain plays a role, too. Not only does rain often influence the rate of snowmelt, but it contributes at least 15 per cent of the base flow to streams. Intense rainstorms can cause rapid flooding if soils are already saturated and the landscape unhealthy. A major flood that hit the Bow River in 2005 was caused by heavy, sustained rain falling on a foothills landscape badly degraded by extensive clear-cut logging and off-highway vehicle vandalism.

It was concerns about mountain pine beetles, not flooding, that led researchers in central Alberta's Foothills Model Forest to put measuring instruments all through a lodgepole pine forest and start manipulating the forest cover. Their findings reinforced the kind of forest management prescriptions that logically flow from the earlier research at Marmot Basin.

University of Alberta professor Uldis Silins and his student Pablo Piña Poujol found that, in a healthy, mature pine forest, around 70 per cent of the summer rainfall never makes it into the ground during storms. As much as 40 per cent is intercepted by the tree canopy and re-evaporated. A further 30 per cent gets held in the litter layer in the forest floor. Because the trees have usually already sucked up a lot of the pre-existing soil moisture, the rest of the rainfall goes to replace soil water; very little runs off or soaks into the deeper water table.

Silins and Piña Poujol used herbicide injections to kill trees in an effort to mimic the effects of mountain pine beetle. They found that the soil beneath the dead trees remained wet well after the snow had melted because the trees no longer drew moisture out of the soil for growth. Without live canopies, more rain reached the ground than in adjacent healthy stands, and more of that water then had to run off overland because the soil was already too wet for it to soak in. Killing most of the trees increased flooding due to overland runoff.

The exception was where the researchers killed only about half of the trees. Surviving trees were able to take up much of the extra soil water because, under natural conditions, competition among the trees meant that none had been getting as much as they needed. Silins's students found a 9 per cent increase in transpiration rates in trees whose neighbours had been killed. That, in turn, provided more room for the soil to soak up water from subsequent rains.

Overall, where only about half the trees in a stand were killed, the researchers found a 50 per cent increase in the amount of rainwater that either ran off overland or soaked into the soil to become part of the groundwater. Where all the trees were killed, however, runoff and saturation increased by 255 per cent during the first couple years, before the dead needles fell from the trees. When the needles were gone, more than five times as much water drained out of the stand.

As with snow, the Foothills Model Forest research suggests that partial-retention logging – cutting some of the trees while leaving enough behind to intercept some rainfall and keep the soil absorbent – is the best way to log for water. Both for improving water supply and reducing flood risk, thinning makes more sense than either letting

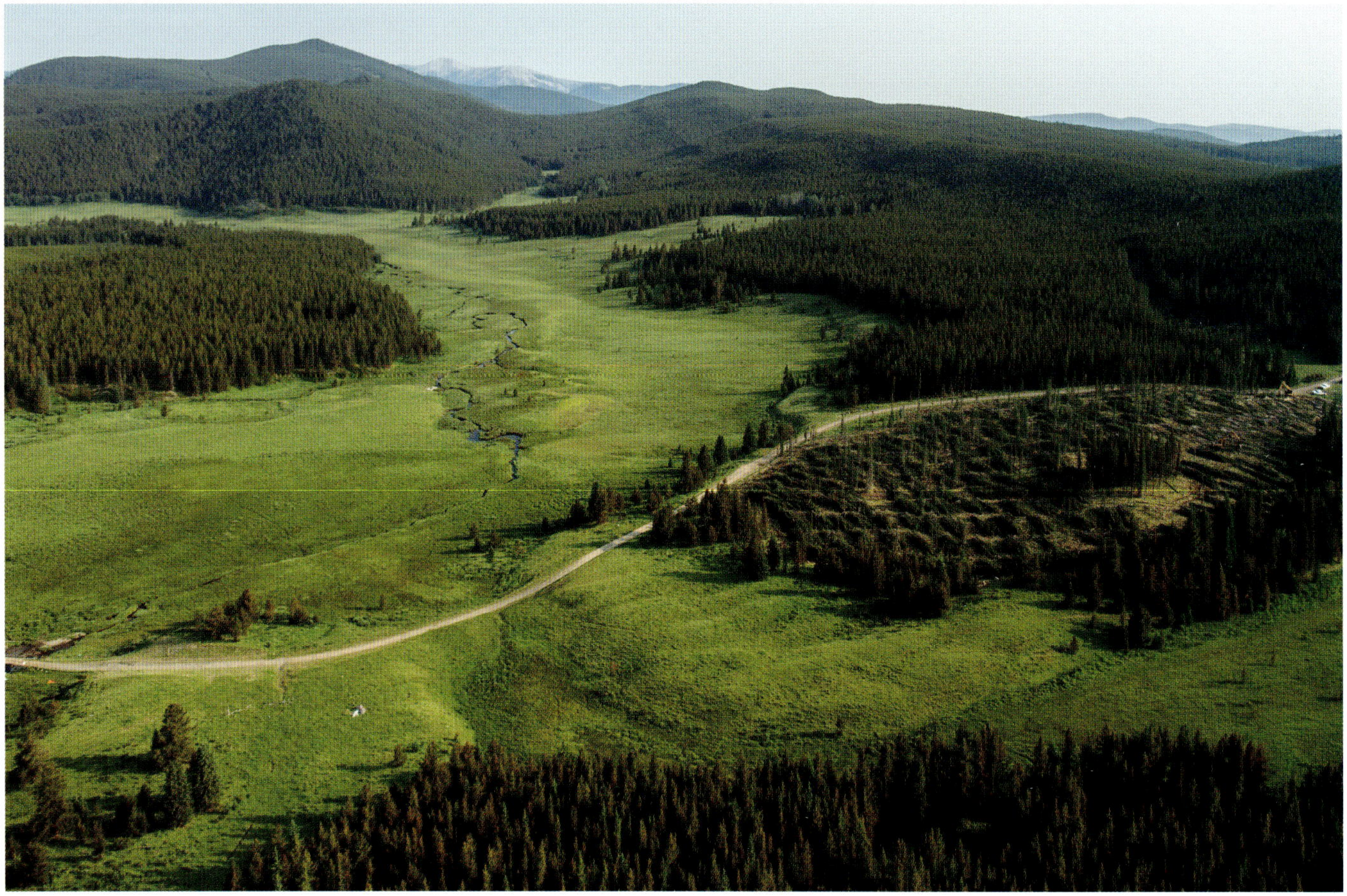

the forest become dense and old or clear-cutting it so that all the water runs off rapidly.

Logging for Water

I asked Gord Lehn what he thought about the idea of logging for optimal water yield rather than for wood fibre. At the time, he was director of communications and ecological goods and services for Spray Lake Sawmills; if anyone would have an informed opinion, he should.

Many governments prohibit logging in the headwaters of major cities, but Spray Lake holds cutting rights

A new clear-cut in upper Quirk Creek. Spray Lake Sawmills employs progressive logging techniques to minimize harm, but clear-cutting can damage watersheds by its very nature.

upstream from the city of Calgary and in almost the entire Oldman drainage. I was curious about what Lehn's company was doing to protect the water-holding capacity of so critical, and limited, a landscape. A few days after visiting Marmot Creek, I called him with an offer: I'd bring lunch if he'd show me what Spray Lake was doing for the watershed.

One late-September day we headed out into the golden beauty of a foothills autumn to look at cutblocks – both old and currently active ones – in the headwaters of Jumpingpound Creek and the Elbow River. I soon concluded that Lehn's company has good reasons for taking pride in its forestry practices.

Logging isn't a pretty sight, and it is, inevitably, a violent way to treat a forest ecosystem. Even so, there are ways of doing it that respect the patterns and processes that those forest ecosystems rely on for their continued health. The most progressive forest companies are careful to leave streams and riparian areas undisturbed, design their cutblocks so that they look like natural, fire-created disturbances and retain abundant woody debris and standing timber patches as habitat for wildlife and protection for the watershed. They minimize road building while eliminating all trace of roads when they are done. The best of the best can actually earn certification by environmental groups. The gold standard is Forest Stewardship Council (FSC) certification – awarded only to companies whose operations pass detailed performance audits by independent forestry experts. The audits are subject to peer review that includes skeptical local environmental groups.

Having seen a lot of destructive logging in Alberta, I was impressed with Spray Lake's work. It was little surprise when, a few months later, I learned that the company had finally obtained FSC certification for its operations in the headwaters of the Bow River.

FSC certification is still rare among companies operating in Alberta's headwater drainages. Government rules and market imperatives require companies to remove as much wood fibre as possible before scarifying the logged-off areas and replanting them with new spruce or pine. They bulldoze haul roads across easily eroded slopes; they force small creeks into culverts that destabilize stream floodplains and block fish from spawning areas; and they clear-cut trees from large cutblocks.

Roads increase runoff and erosion both by stripping away the vegetation that would otherwise intercept rain and snowmelt and by creating new drainage routes that enable runoff to erode the exposed soil. Where logging roads cut into steep banks, they often bring shallow groundwater to the surface as new, temporary springs. As surface water, it drains out of the landscape faster than if left to seep slowly through undisturbed soil.

Lehn reassured me more than once during our day in the woods that logging increases water yield; however I already knew from the research at Marmot Creek and the Foothills Model Forest that it's not that simple.

More snow accumulates in clear-cuts than in mature

forest. That increases water yield but most of the water comes in a rush during the spring thaw. The water pours off the landscape, eroding muddy gullies before hitting downstream creek channels with punishing floods that destabilize their floodplains. Then the water's gone. There's more water – but it does more harm than good because of its timing.

Where shady forests used to soak up snowmelt over weeks and gradually release shallow groundwater into springs and seeps through the summer, keeping creeks cool and well-watered, the open clear-cuts bake in the summer sun, their soils now deprived of moisture that ran off too soon. Creeks become shallow and sun-warmed. Downstream water users complain of increasingly intense spring floods and more frequent summer droughts – both signs of a sick watershed.

A 2014 Global Forest Watch study measured just how sick Alberta's foothills watersheds have become under the province's wilful neglect of stewardship principles. Based on air photo analysis, the authors found that forest cover has been disappearing from the Eastern Slopes of the Rockies at twice Canada's national average, well above the rate of deforestation in the US, Russia or Brazil. Almost 7 per cent of Alberta's headwater forests were clear-cut between 2000 and 2013. The oil and gas industry's aggressive forest clearing for well roads, pumping stations and pipelines accounted for some of that loss, but forest companies accounted for most.

Foresters are quick to respond that they replant the areas they cut. Restocking standards in Alberta, however, are designed around wood production, not water conservation. From flood-producing clear-cuts, the logged areas go to dense young stands that again waste winter snows to canopy sublimation while also consuming large amounts of rainwater for their own growth. Smaller patch-cuts and stand-thinning – by capturing snow in forest openings while retaining the shade effects of standing timber – would help end the boom-bust water cycles caused by clear-cut logging. Retaining more old forest would be a good idea, too.

Logging in the Elbow River headwaters. Retaining a live canopy of trees to shade the spring snowpack and removing all trace of roads are two techniques that can enhance watershed health while still allowing some timber harvest.

Dr. Ralph Cartar, an ecologist at the University of Calgary, says that no matter how carefully Spray Lake Sawmills logs, the long-term result is to create a landscape with far less old forest – the kinds of shady, gap-filled stands that yield the best water and that are also vital to biodiversity conservation – and far more dense young forest. In an e-mail, he told me:

> Current practices take a landscape that is primarily structured by fire, and add logging to the disturbance mix (without removing fire, despite frequent claims to the contrary). Using the current fire return interval of 178 years in Jumpingpound forest … and applying van Wagner's 1978 conceptual model [a standard model to calculate forest age class structures], we roughly expect about 57% of the forest cover to be

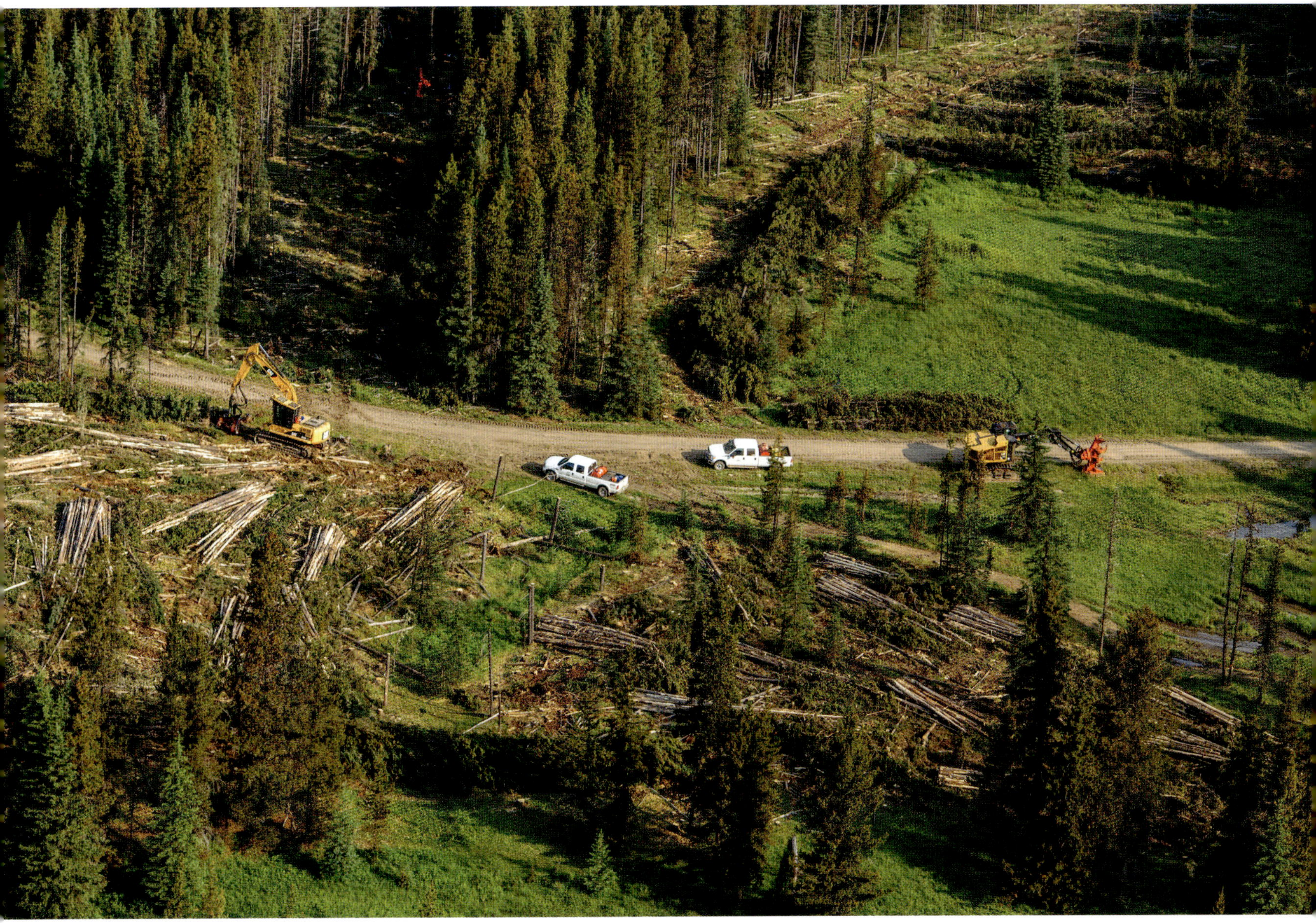

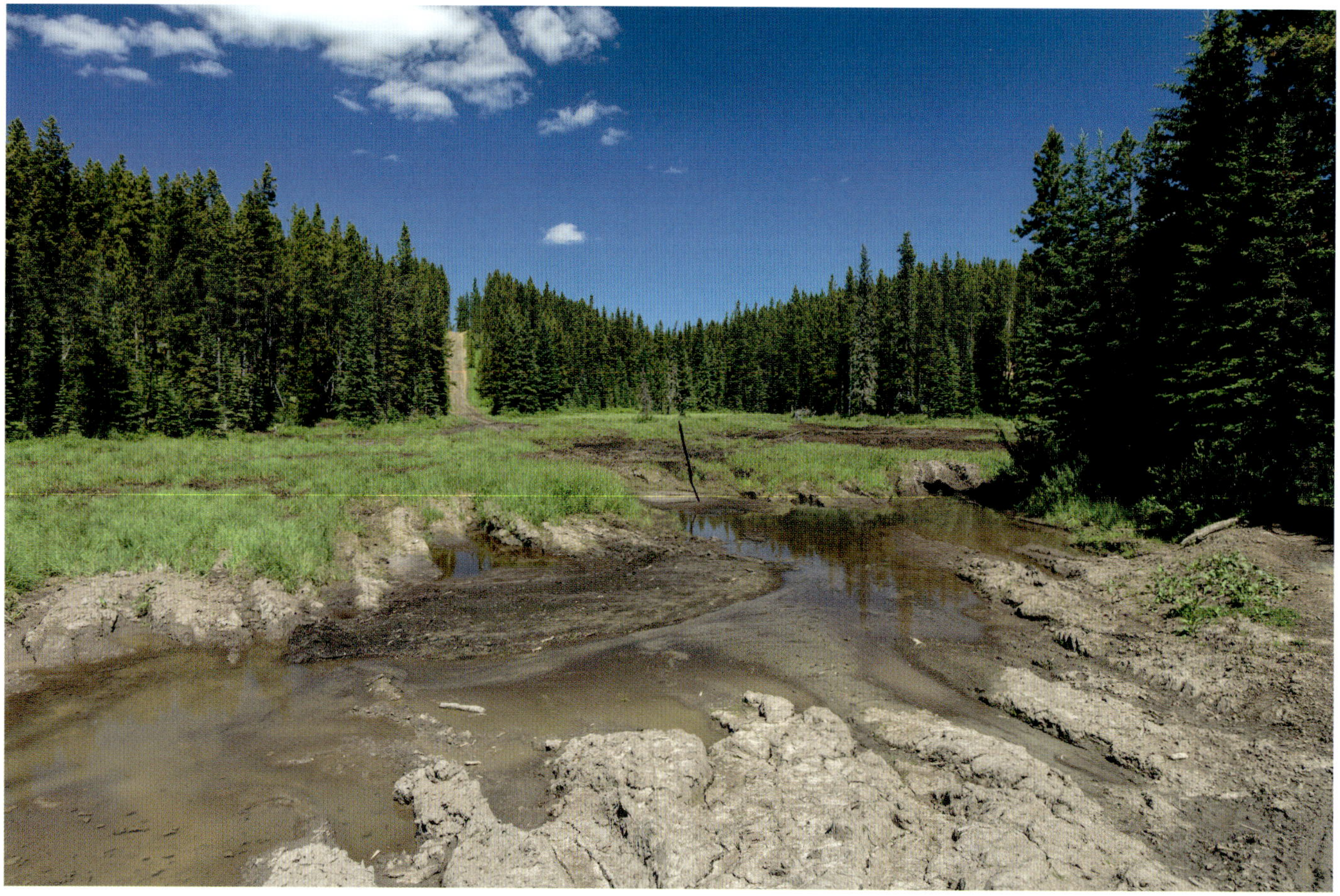

stands older than 100 years (95% Confidence Interval: 40% to 82%).

In the Spray Lake Sawmill forest plan the only bits to escape the feller-buncher will be the 6% that's too steep, and the 2% that's riparian.

So we're converting a forest landscape whose expected fraction of older-than-SLS-will-allow trees is more than half of the landscape, to one where old forests cling to steep slopes and along rivers.

Spray Lake Sawmills employs some practices that reduce the risk to the headwaters. For example, I could

Off-road vehicle vandalism in a Waiparous Creek wetland destroys wildlife habitat, hastens spring runoff and causes soils to erode into nearby streams.

find no culverts on any of their temporary roads. Lehn explained that, although Alberta's forestry rules permit culverts on smaller channels, Spray Lake's own standards prescribe a bridged crossing over any stream channel, even if it only flows for part of each year. Bridges keep streams connected and healthy.

The logged areas we visited were too large and had been clear-cut, but they were well laid-out, with uneven edges and patches of uncut trees. Spray Lake processes each tree right where it's cut, leaving the branches to help shelter the soil from rainfall and contribute to vegetation regrowth. Once finished, the company pulls out its bridges and recontours the roads, reconnecting shallow groundwater flows rather than leave them bleeding out of side-hill cuts.

But none of that seems to help their reputation. Operating in scenic areas that attract thousands of hikers, bicyclists, anglers and hunters every year, they are under attack on all sides. Aesthetic, wildlife and water concerns continually threaten the company's social licence to operate. Gord Lehn's job title reflected Spray Lake's need for more friends; logging for "ecological goods and services" sounds nicer than "clear-cutting the headwaters" – even if the latter is a more accurate description of what they currently do.

Lehn agrees that Spray Lake Sawmills could log for watershed restoration and optimization, but not under traditional wood-fibre-based business models.

Water shortages farther downstream might, however, offer new revenue options. Okotoks, for example, established a population growth cap in the 1990s due to its limited water supply. A decade later the town set that cap aside because development outside the town boundaries had rendered it moot. Removing the growth cap, however, didn't solve the water problem – it worsened it. Some town councillors want a dam on the Sheep River.

A more progressive approach than building another expensive and environmentally harmful dam, however, would be to use the money to pay for more ecologically based forestry that enhances watershed values. Reinventing forest management, based on lessons from Marmot Creek and other forest hydrology research sites, could increase water yield and the timing of water flows at far lower costs – both economic and ecological. Spray Lake's decision to assign a director responsibility for "ecological goods and services" suggests that the company may be ready to discuss that approach. But it appears not to be a discussion that seriously interests the old-guard wood-fibre foresters who occupy senior positions in government agencies responsible for the headwaters.

That's unfortunate, because the benefits of such an investment wouldn't just flow down the rivers. Opening up the forest canopy with small clearings, ensuring that no roads remain when cutting is completed and keeping the headwaters landscape moist and shady well into the summer are practices that also benefit grizzly bears, elk, trout and other species that thrive in sheltered, green places. Like us.

Officially Sanctioned Vandalism

Neither grizzly bears nor elk nor trout nor clean water, however, can thrive amid busy networks of muddy, eroding trails. The last part of my tour with Gord Lehn took us into the McLean Creek watershed, a shameful example of recreational mismanagement.

Dirt bikes, snowmobiles and all-terrain quads began to appear in Alberta's headwaters in the 1970s. Initially, it was hunters, anglers and climbers who used the new OHVs. Most of them simply wanted to drive a bit deeper into the wilds before getting off to walk. It wasn't long, however, before others began to look at the foothills as a playground for machines they saw as powerful toys.

OHV users quickly spread a web of eroding motor trails all through the landscape. Many of those tracks cross streams repeatedly, muddying them with runoff. Worse, many OHV users are not content with improved access that saves them having to use their legs like the rest of us: they like to tear land up. Mud-bogging has turned once-lush wetlands into muddy sumps. Some creeks have become de-facto racetracks. Hillsides are scarred with multiple vertical tracks that funnel rainwater and mud into the streams below after every rainstorm.

Faced with motorized anarchy in the woods, the Alberta government decided to try and regulate use by establishing sacrifice areas. In 1979 the McLean Creek watershed, along with the Ghost-Waiparous farther north, were turned over to the OHV crowd as "Forest Land-Use Zones" (FLUZ).

The idea was to provide a network of authorized woods trails for motorized vehicles. The rest of the landscape would be out of bounds. It didn't work; it had the social effect of legitimizing recreational vandalism. Long weekends in the off-road areas have become famous as three-day drunken mud-fests. It didn't help any that the government put next to no resources into laying out a proper trail network with moderate hill grades, erosion protection, bridged stream crossings and protection for wetlands and riparian areas. Instead, they simply let OHV operators take over abandoned seismic cutlines, cattle trails, open meadows and partly reclaimed oil and gas roads.

Gord Lehn showed me logging haul roads that Spray Lake Sawmills had recontoured and restored only to see irresponsible off-roaders develop new trails there. In one clear-cut, based on Alberta government guidelines, the company had to leave an unlogged buffer along a pre-existing OHV trail. The trail is a deeply eroded gully straight up a hill – a former seismic cutline – that funnels sediment and runoff directly into a once-healthy trout stream. Spray Lake, whose operational guidelines are designed to minimize their impact on the stream, was required to protect an OHV trail that functions as an open wound.

Out-of-control OHV use is a problem all through Alberta's headwater forests. Dr. Dan Andrews did a water quality study of the Waiparous River, a tributary of the Ghost, for Alberta Environment in 2006. He found that the Waiparous, which drains an OHV-riddled FLUZ, receives seven to ten times more sediment loading than the very similar Elbow River because of erosion from vehicle trails.

The Ghost Watershed Alliance Society, a stewardship

group of local ranchers and acreage owners, commissioned the consulting firm ALCES to evaluate the entire Ghost drainage. Their 2010 report revealed that the Ghost watershed has 2780 kilometres of cutlines, roads and other linear features, of which 93 per cent are used by OHV riders. This is almost four times more than Alberta Environment and Sustainable Resource Development, which ostensibly managed the area, had previously identified. In fact, only 189 kilometres of trail were officially available for OHV use; all the rest were used illegally. Riders were disturbing 14 times as much ground as they are allowed to.

The average OHV trail has an unvegetated surface up to three metres wide. Cumulatively, as much as 775 hectares of bare ground is exposed to erosion every time it rains in the Ghost drainage. If all the illegal trails were closed and re-vegetated and only the authorized trails left exposed, almost 720 hectares of new vegetation would hold snow and absorb rainfall. That would go a long way toward eliminating the erosion that turns the once-pristine Waiparous muddy brown after each foothills rainstorm. And it would yield more, and better, summer water.

Given that the study area covered only a small part of Alberta's trail-riddled headwaters, the potential for watershed restoration by closing and restoring illegal OHV trails is enormous.

Good trail planning can keep off-roaders out of fens, wetlands and creeks. Recreational trails don't need to trap overland water flow and create erosion gullies. Well-built bridges can eliminate muddy fords. But government agencies responsible for protecting the headwaters have never bothered to build good trails: they simply let off-roaders take over any linear disturbance they could find. Lehn recalls several cases where the Alberta Forest Service asked Spray Lake Sawmills to leave haul roads unreclaimed because it was a cheap and easy way to give off-roaders new places to play. This kind of benign neglect and opportunistic development carries a social cost: a culture of exploitation and abuse has developed where, in the past, users of the same valleys – now mostly displaced – had a strong stewardship ethic.

The resulting damage horrifies those who see it for the first time. Off-roading has become the most extreme and widespread cause of landscape deterioration in the

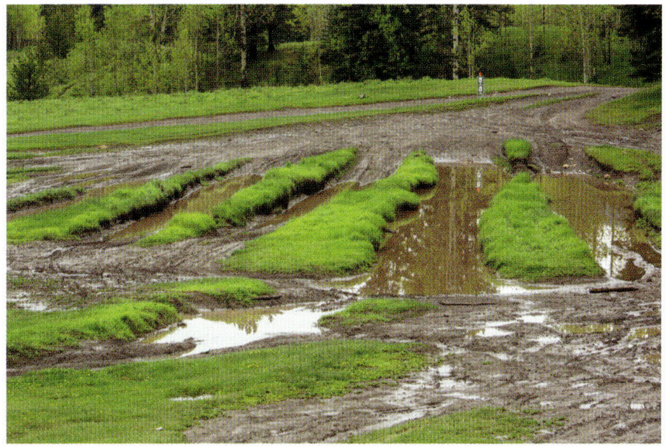

Government-sanctioned vandalism by off-roaders in the McLean Creek area has severely impaired the watershed, stripping protective vegetation from slopes and ruining creeks with more intense floods and heavy siltation.

headwaters region. Each rainstorm washes the gullies deeper – especially because the Alberta government doesn't restrict trail use during wet weather. Instead, many off-roaders look forward to rainy weekends when they can play in the mud. That mud is meant to hold plant roots, water and life – not wash into creeks or go home caked on quads and dirt bikes.

Reclaiming the current network of eroding scars with a properly designed trail network could also help balance Alberta's carbon dioxide emissions. The US Environmental Protection Agency estimates that reforestation of bare land to conifers sequesters up to 2.1 tonnes of carbon per acre each year. Fens – the open meadows through which headwater creeks like McLean, Fisher, Lesueur, Meadow and Johnson flow – store even higher amounts of carbon because of the continual accumulation of undecomposed peat. Even taking the EPA value for coniferous forest, re-vegetating the Ghost watershed's unauthorized OHV trails alone could pull more than seven thousand tonnes of carbon out of the atmosphere annually.

That might be a good use for some of the cash that industry pays for carbon credits. But it's not where the carbon money is going – most goes right back as subsidies to the oil and gas industry for research the companies should pay for themselves.

Rethinking Hydro Dams

The Waiparous joins the Ghost River west of Cochrane and, shortly past that point, its muddy waters vanish into the reservoir behind TransAlta's Ghost River Dam. There, the silt settles to the bottom of the reservoir. The 2006 Andrews study found that, in spite of the elevated levels of mud washing into the Ghost from off-highway trails farther upstream, none of that mud made it into the Bow downstream from the Ghost Dam. The value of a reservoir is measured by how much water it stores, not how much silt; the Ghost Reservoir's useful life is being dramatically shortened by OHV landscape abuse farther upstream.

That's too bad, because another part of the solution to southern Alberta's water supply crisis may lie in hydropower reservoirs like the one behind the Ghost Dam. Those who persist in seeing dams as the answer to water shortages frequently point out that the Bow, unlike the Oldman and Red Deer rivers, has no large water storage impoundments. They are wrong. TransAlta manages almost a dozen dams upstream from Calgary, with a total storage capacity exceeding half a million acre-feet. That stored water is used to generate electricity during peak demand periods, mostly in the winter, rather than to sustain river flows and meet peak water demands in summer. TransAlta is in the power business, not the water business. Electricity prices are highest in the dark and cold of winter; we need water most in summer.

TransAlta could be in the water business, though. But, as with Spray Lake Sawmills, that would require a new business model with new revenue streams – either public investment or, possibly, some of that carbon cash. Healthy riparian systems, after all, sequester carbon in the root systems of vegetation that also stabilizes and protects stream banks.

A 1990s modelling study by Golder Associates for a

Fisheries and Recreational Enhancement Working Group coordinated by TransAlta looked into how hydropower operations might be changed to restore the lakes and rivers they damage. The study showed that "repurposing" just one dam, at Lower Kananaskis Lake, could triple the lake's biological productivity, restore the Kananaskis River's once-famous fishery, reduce winter ice jams and increase summer water levels in the Bow through Calgary. TransAlta would produce less electricity during the most profitable peak-demand winter period, a change that would reduce the company's revenues.

Given the massive harm TransAlta has inflicted on the headwaters of the Bow River over the past century, it could be argued that the company should simply swallow that loss as partial compensation for ecological damages. But there is also a case to be made for public subsidy. The Oldman Dam cost almost $800 million in today's dollars. Where water is concerned, money can be found, at least for non-solutions. The next on-stream dam, should there be one, will certainly cost in excess of a billion dollars. That's ten times what it would take to compensate TransAlta each year for the next century for restoring the Kananaskis. Similar improvements in summer flows are possible from hydro dams on the Bow, Cascade, Spray, North Saskatchewan and Peace rivers.

Volunteer Dam Builders

There is at least one way to put a lot of dams into the headwaters at no cost to the public treasury. All that's needed is a restricted quota or a total ban on the trapping of beavers in Fur Management Zone 6, which includes all the Bow River headwaters. Beaver trapping bans have been in place for years in parts of Idaho, Utah and Nevada, where land managers and local communities have come to value the role of the rodents in restoring stream flows and conserving water. Licensed trappers in Alberta's headwaters, however, can kill all the beavers they like. Because beavers are trapped in winter, each trapping season is followed by a spring flood that washes out many of the abandoned dams.

Beaver ponds evaporate water, too, but in the sheltered headwaters where air and water are cooler and the reach of the wind limited by standing live and dead trees, the losses are much less than from vast sheets of reservoir water spread out beneath the sun and wind of the outer foothills. Besides, beaver dams store much more of their water underground in riparian aquifers and wetland fens. The stored water drains slowly from the landscape, feeding cold water into streams well into summer and fall, or even into subsequent years.

If water matters, it makes little sense to continue trapping so valuable an animal – one that builds and maintains dams for free. Its ecosystem services are worth far more than its fur.

Healing the Land, Restoring the Streams

The Bow River's headwaters, for all their beauty, are unwell. Too many of the things we're doing there increase runoff, damage streams and reduce water quality – even though the public policy priority for well more than a century has been to protect watershed health in this small, precious region. The only way to make more water is to optimize the ability of the headwaters to do their job. Research and experience have shown the way; what's needed is a renewed commitment to conservation and restoration.

Logging for water would restrict clear-cuts to slopes sheltered from wind and direct sunlight. On more exposed slopes, loggers would open the canopy enough to reduce snow losses from the sublimation of canopy snow, while retaining enough shade to ensure the enhanced winter snowpacks linger late. They would aggressively reclaim roads to eliminate the side-hill cuts that bring shallow groundwater to the surface. Where possible, they would promote the regrowth of aspens and poplars rather than conifers.

The operating costs for this kind of logging would be higher and profits from wood production lower than from traditional forestry. If companies like Spray Lake Sawmills can't make money from watershed enhancement, they won't do it. Still, those companies have the skills, equipment and, in some cases, corporate cultures that suit them for the work. What they need is new business models that will replace reduced fibre profits with new revenue streams for ecological goods and services. Public investment seems like the most logical solution; we've never shied away, after all, from taxing citizens for non-solutions like dams.

Public investment – possibly carbon tax revenues – could also compensate TransAlta for lost hydropower profits and enable them to restore stable water levels and summer stream flows in the Kananaskis, Spray, Cascade and Bow rivers. They've got the dams; they just need to change the way they operate them. After a century of lake destruction and river abuse, it's past time for them to help rivers heal from hydraulic abuse and to start providing water users with improved summer flows rather than pulsing winter floods and ice jams. Better dam management would save millions of dollars for downstream water users – diverting some of those dollars to TransAlta seems like an obvious solution.

No amount of careful resource stewardship and business innovation can restore Alberta's headwaters to their full potential, however, if every seismic cutline, cow trail or abandoned logging road is open to abuse by OHVs.

If off-roaders stuck to well-planned and well-built trails, their reputations would improve, even as those shredded watersheds began to heal. A more effective regulatory regime and more enforcement officers might also begin to address the bad attitudes too many vandals have developed in the absence of responsible recreational management by the Alberta Forest Service. A limited number of off-highway trails laid out to minimize watershed damage makes sense; allowing continued recreational anarchy to turn more wetlands into mud bogs, scar hillsides with erosion rills, and choke streams and reservoirs with silt does not.

Riding an OHV is fun for a few; water is life for all.

THE LARGEST AND MOST IMPORTANT reservoir in the entire river system is the headwaters landscape, where the snow and rain falls. Its soils and wetlands have the capacity to hold far more water than any number of dams farther downstream. The most important water management decisions are made by those who determine whether and how to log the headwater forests; how many roads and OHV trails to run across the landscape and how they will be built; how to manage cattle; whether to trap the beavers; and whether to drain wetlands that impinge on new subdivisions and old farm fields. Those decisions determine how much water that immense green reservoir stretching west of Highway 2 to the Continental Divide will capture and how long it will hold that water before releasing it to the streams below.

When foothill streams go murky for days after a summer rain, they are telling us our decisions haven't measured up. Healthy streams don't do that. When floods punish us with damage and destruction, we need to look beyond the river's brown flow to the hills that shed all that water, and ask what we could have done differently there. When water rationing returns and crops wither, we won't find answers in half-filled reservoirs; the questions lie farther upstream, in once-vital headwater landscapes where water now escapes too fast, too soon, because of choices we could have made differently.

William Pearce had good instincts and an inspired ability to identify strategic priorities when he argued for the protection of Alberta's headwaters. He did not have the scientific knowledge that places like the Marmot Creek research watershed have generated in subsequent years, nor the insights that come from analysis of resource management experience. We have what he lacked, but we seem to have lost his clarity of vision. Were he here today, he would doubtless be exasperated by the degree to which Alberta has allowed so much of its headwaters to be degraded, and by our reluctance to put to practical policy use the things we now know about their functioning.

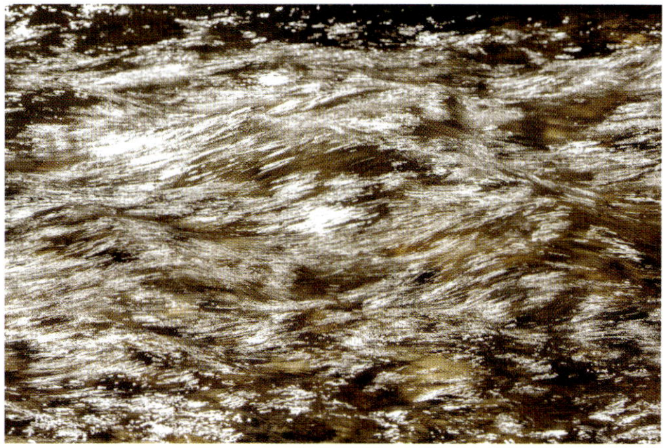

Water doesn't happen by accident or by default. Its abundance, quality and seasonality are reflections of how well the headwaters landscape is treated by resource managers and recreationists.

One thing's certain: he would have no illusions about which public value should take precedence in managing the water-generating parts of our prairie watersheds. Nor would he dispute the value of investing public funds on enhanced stewardship of those headwaters.

And at a time like this – when the region's natural water scarcity has converged with degraded watersheds, booming population growth and a warming climate to create a real-time water crisis for Alberta – nor should we.

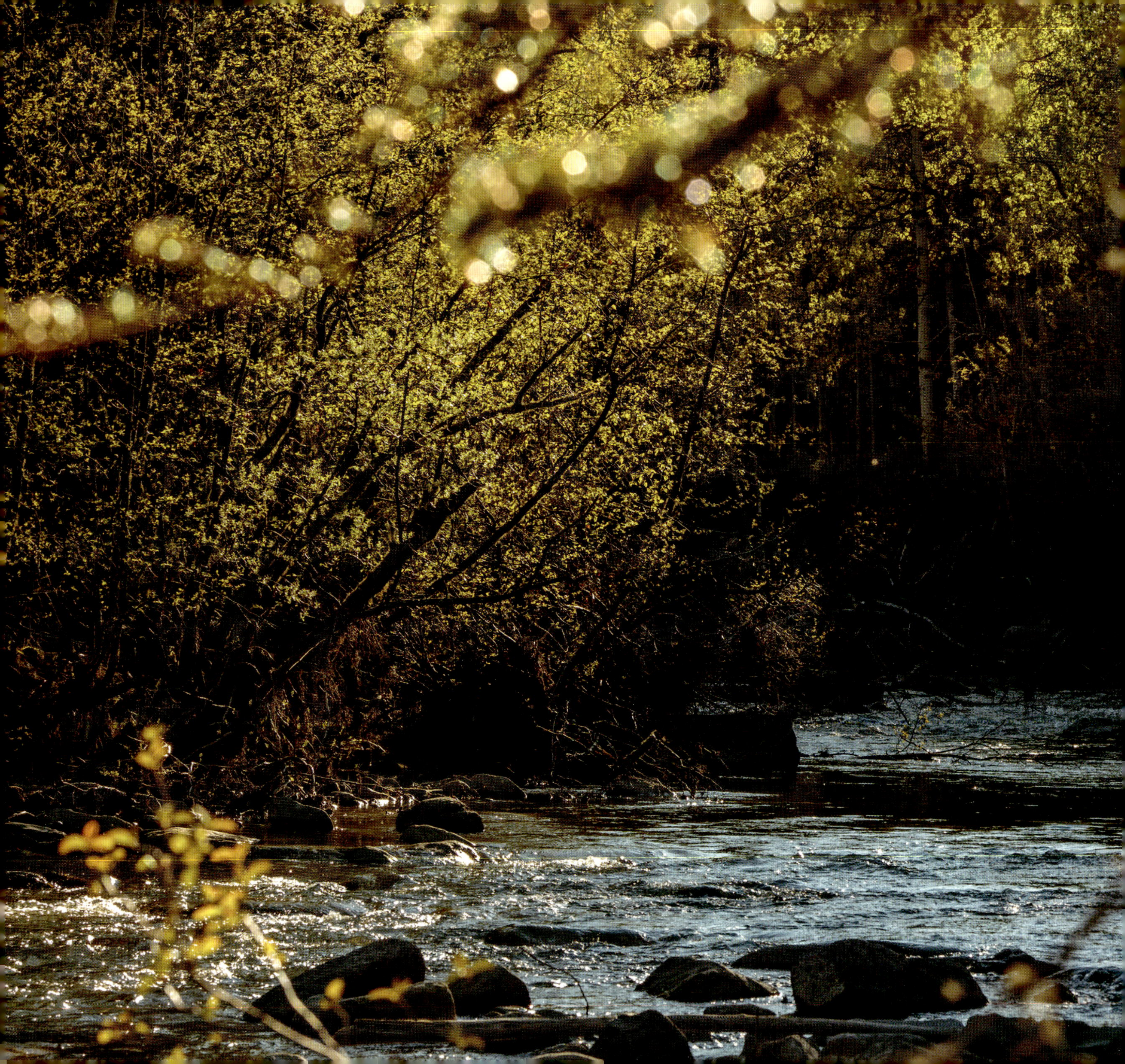

CHAPTER 14

Home and Heart Waters

WRAITHS OF MIST HANG ABOVE the wet meadows of cottongrass and sedge, the exhalations of a water-saturated foothills valley made visible by condensation in the coolness of early morning. A snipe winnows overhead, and somewhere back among the dark spruce trees that fringe the beaver pond, a ruby-crowned kinglet has added its cheerful chatter to the thrush chorus already welcoming another headwaters sunrise.

Water bubbles and seethes through the willow tangle that marks the curve of an old beaver dam, its cheery gabble going dark and resonant as it gurgles into the deep pool at the foot of the dam. Emerging from foam, current lines converge, and the stream burrows under an overhanging bank where roots trail in the current. That is where I send my muddler fly.

A solid tug tells me I have a strike. Grasping the line as I pull the rod sideways to set the hook, I feel the throbbing resistance of a good-sized fish. To my relief it doesn't take the fragile leader deeper into the tangled roots of its hiding shelter, as a cutthroat might, but goes instead to the bottom of the pool, where it tries to hold, tugging sullenly against the pressure of the line.

Easing down carefully to a small point bar of clean-washed stream gravel, I slide the fish up beside me. It is grey as the dawn itself, sleek with wetness, cold as the lingering touch of the creek. The fly hangs from the side of a gaping mouth as the fish tries to extract oxygen from an unfamiliar medium.

So there is still at least one bull trout in this stream, I muse, kneeling to grasp the slippery sides of the fish carefully with one hand while I tease the hook loose with the other. The fish twists in my grasp, still trying to escape, desperate with its need for freedom. Its flaring gills are designed to extract oxygen from water; the fish is drowning in the air. Even so, I hold it briefly to examine it before releasing it back into the security and comfort of its home stream.

Its body is sleek and long, flattened at the head. That profile doubtless helps it resist the surge of mountain waters with little waste of energy. The gape of its mouth and double array of small, inward-pointing teeth mark it as a predator on smaller fish. Its coloration is as pale as river gravel, spotted faintly along the sides and back, rendering it hard for watchful ospreys or eagles to spy from above.

The shape and colouring of this fish evolved in response to the nature of the river headwaters in which its kind has always spawned, grown and died. Ancestors of this bull trout lived in glacial Lake Calgary and hunted ancestral whitefish in the ancestral Bow River. The DNA in each of its cells is a record of natural selection sculpting a creature that belongs uniquely, and perfectly, in this place – in these waters.

Glancing up from where I crouch with a fish that has found itself on the wrong side of the stream surface, I see that sunlight has begun to flood the forested hills around us. The water running off the sides of this trout came to the creek from winter snows held by those hills, filtered through glacial debris beneath those forests, to springs that rise into the water-rounded gravels of the creek riffles.

Even though this fish's near-glacial predecessors lived in a landscape configured differently from today's, their tissues almost certainly had not only the same DNA but the same chemical composition as the fish I now hold in my hands. Scientists have only recently learned to use the chemical isotopes in plants and animals to tease out the chemical signatures of places. Every chemical in this bull trout's body, as in its ancestors', came from the stones of the eastern Rocky Mountains, the residual tills of continental glaciers, and the deep places from which groundwater emerges. Unlike my body – which contains isotopes derived from Central American coffee, California vegetables and Pacific Ocean salmon – nothing in this bull trout's body came from any place on Earth but here: these headwaters.

The trout is one with its valley: steeped in and comprised of the solutes released from limestones and shales in the upper headwaters, the tannins in swamp birch leaves and the organic hydrocarbons exhaled by summer pine forests and brought back to the earth by thunderstorms. The chemical composition of this place finds its way into the water through natural processes that have

Page 222: *We have yet fully to prove that we are worthy stewards of the green places and living streams that are the sources of our heart waters.*

Right: *Jumpingpound creek.*

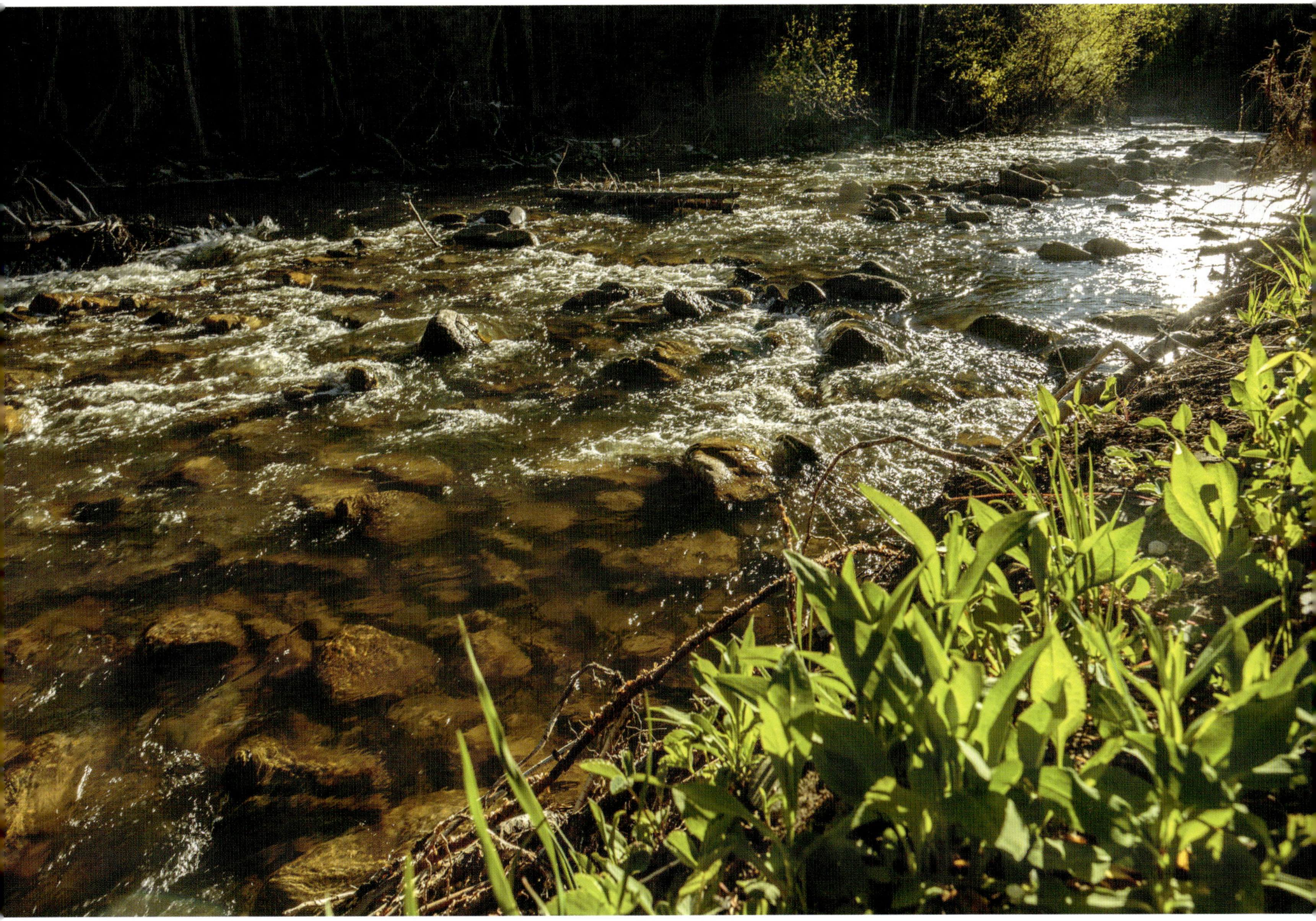

been at play here for centuries and, distilled by living waters, become the chemistry of the things that live there: the bacteria and algae, the midges and mayflies, the little fish, the big fish that eat the little fish. And this trout: this live creature in my hands at this moment in time, at this place on Earth.

The ancestors of this fish had the same chemistry and the same DNA because they evolved in this place. The behaviour, seasonality and ecology of these streams selected for the genes expressed in my bull trout and left other less useful genes behind in unsuccessful breeders. The trout, whose life is literally in my hands, is completely, unequivocally of this place.

Unlike me.

The bull trout's eyes stare at me, unblinking. Is it studying me too? What does it see? I can sense none of the kind of awareness and recognition one gets when gazing into the eyes of another human, or a dog or horse. I am looking into eyes with which I can't connect: eyes attuned to an underwater world I can only imagine. Those eyes are exquisitely evolved to see everything they need to see, but the times and processes that gave shape to them were entirely unlike those that shaped my human eyes.

I return the fish to the stream where it belongs, steadying it upright in the flow to help it recover. For a moment it rests against the bottom of the riffle, body swaying slowly in the current as its gills pull oxygen into its body from water that, in a few days' time, will flow through the city of Calgary. Then it slides into the shadows and vanishes back into its home in the headwaters of the living stream we call the Bow River.

A headwaters stream in the Waiparous Creek drainage.

STRAIGHTENING UP, I become aware of another presence nearby. Other eyes are watching me. The mist is gone now, burned off by the wakening warmth of a foothills morning. The world looks fresh and new, but the meadows are empty as far as I can see.

Still, the sensation won't go away. Then I catch a flicker of movement in the shadows beyond the edge of the pines. I see nostrils flare, then an eye. Near-motionless, three horses watch from behind the edge of the forest.

These are what Alberta Environment and Sustainable Resource Development calls feral horses: unshod, untamed descendants of ranch horses and working stock that escaped or were turned loose into the foothills early in the 20th century, when internal combustion replaced animal muscle power for human transportation and work. Their eyes and their behaviour, the long motionless inspection of a potential predator, the muscles poised for thunderous flight, the knowledge of landscape and intuitive sense of where their flight – should my behaviour tell them it is warranted – will take them, are as much an expression of their DNA as the aggressive way the bull trout attacked my fishing fly and then took shelter at the bottom of the pool.

My friend Maureen Enns and others who share her fascination and love for these horses call them wild, not feral. They are convinced that these wild-born creatures share the same genetic material as the long-extinct Pleistocene horses that used to graze here in the shadow

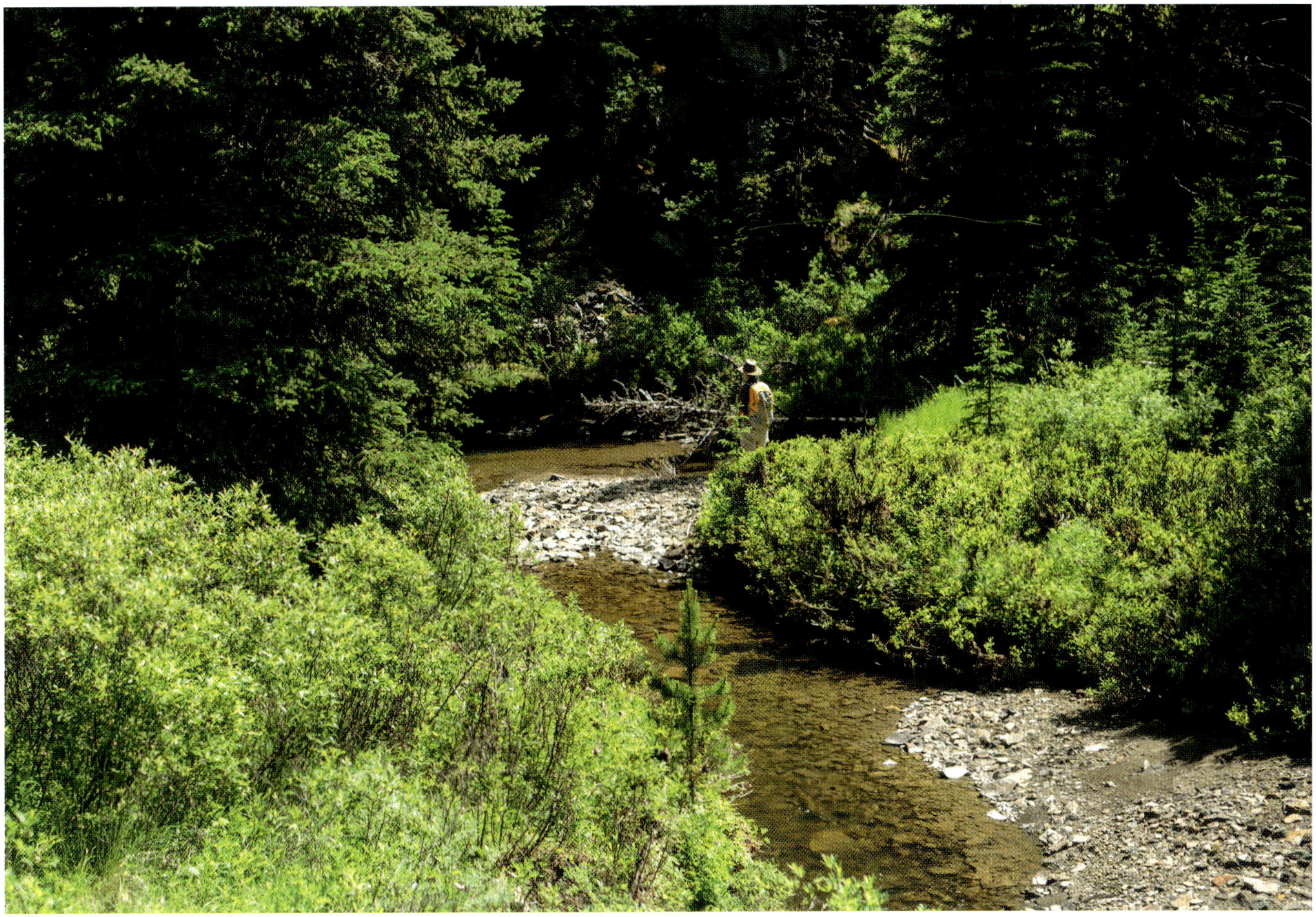

of melting glaciers. Maureen believes that generations of exposure to winter snow, spring rains and summer droughts, to wolves and bears, and to the landscape itself have selected from that genetic potential an animal that now belongs here almost as much as bull trout. She points out that these wild horses seem to float through the fens, leaving only the faintest of tracks in soft, spongy soils that shod horses and domestic cattle pound to muck. They occupy the place without harming it.

The muscles of these horses, like those of the bull trout

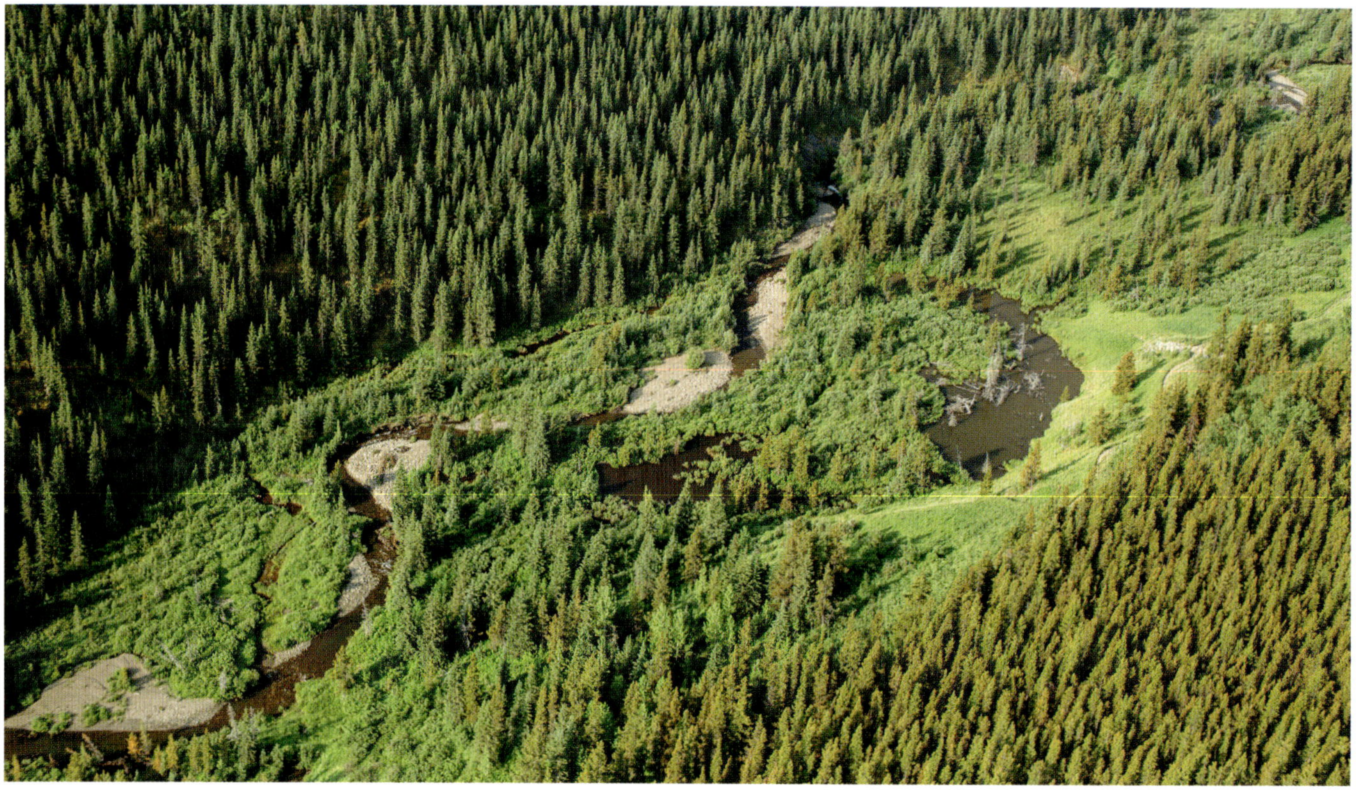

I just released, are built of amino acids derived from chemical precursors that they take up out of the hairgrass, bluegrass and fescue growing from the old beaver pond marl, fenland peat and glacial till of this landscape; and from the water they drink from this headwater stream. They may be descendants of farm horses but, 10 or 15 generations on, they are almost home again: almost native to this place.

It's a debate that divides the horse lovers from those who feel these animals are aliens that compete with native wildlife, like elk. It's as much a philosophical question as an ecological one: how long does an animal have to live in a place before it can be considered to belong there? When does it stop being an outsider?

That same question, of course, applies to us.

In some ways these horses have done better than us at making themselves at home in the headwaters. Their bones and sinews, unlike mine, are comprised of the same isotopes and elements that made up the bull trout I held

A healthy stream, sustained by responsible land use decisions, flows into a water-scarce region's future.

only a few moments ago. Their eyes have become no less wary of what they see in me.

And what of my eyes? What do they recognize when I sojourn into these valleys? My DNA is derived from European stock, but there have now been three generations of my family born and raised in the Bow watershed. Natural selection works slowly in a long-lived species like ours, but it must be working on us nonetheless. At least some of the chemical isotopes that link this land and these waters to that bull trout are part of the makeup of my body, too. I won't be eating the bull trout, but I eat elk and berries and mushrooms from this landscape, incorporating that much of its chemical nature into my own tissues.

Like most of the others who use these headwater places today, I call myself an Albertan and by doing so assert some degree of nativeness. So how much of what makes this place unique on Earth defines me now? Or am I just appropriating the name of the place while occupying it as an outsider? Am I a mammalian weed or a part of the natural community that surrounds me?

What would it take – in my human context as a keystone species, an animal with imagination, emotions and reasoning powers – for my eyes, my tissues and my very being to be defined by this green and breathing watershed? For me to belong as wholly as this bull trout, now safely back in the flickering shadows beneath its stream bank, newborn waters washing cold and clean through its gills? For me to be a part of this place even as much as those horses motionless in the deep broken shade of a pine forest, watching and waiting for the next move of a human being who has entered into their dream world on a summer morning full of resin and the scents of sweet green things?

What would it take? And what might it mean for the future of the Bow River if its headwaters again had only native creatures, because we latecomers had finally come to be counted among them? Might our eyes finally be able to see these birthplaces of water for what they are, what they were meant to be and what – if we care enough and try hard enough – they could yet be in the future? Might we begin to understand at last the voices murmuring amid the rush and rumour that rise among these headwaters – to know the stories they tell as our own, as the legend of a people who came home at last to heal their heart waters?

We could belong here, too. We could be like the bull trout, the willows, the wary horses: like the river that continually arises from these fine green places where the waters are born. We could find our best selves in the stories of those living waters and the river that gathers them together.

Ultimately, after all, we are that river.

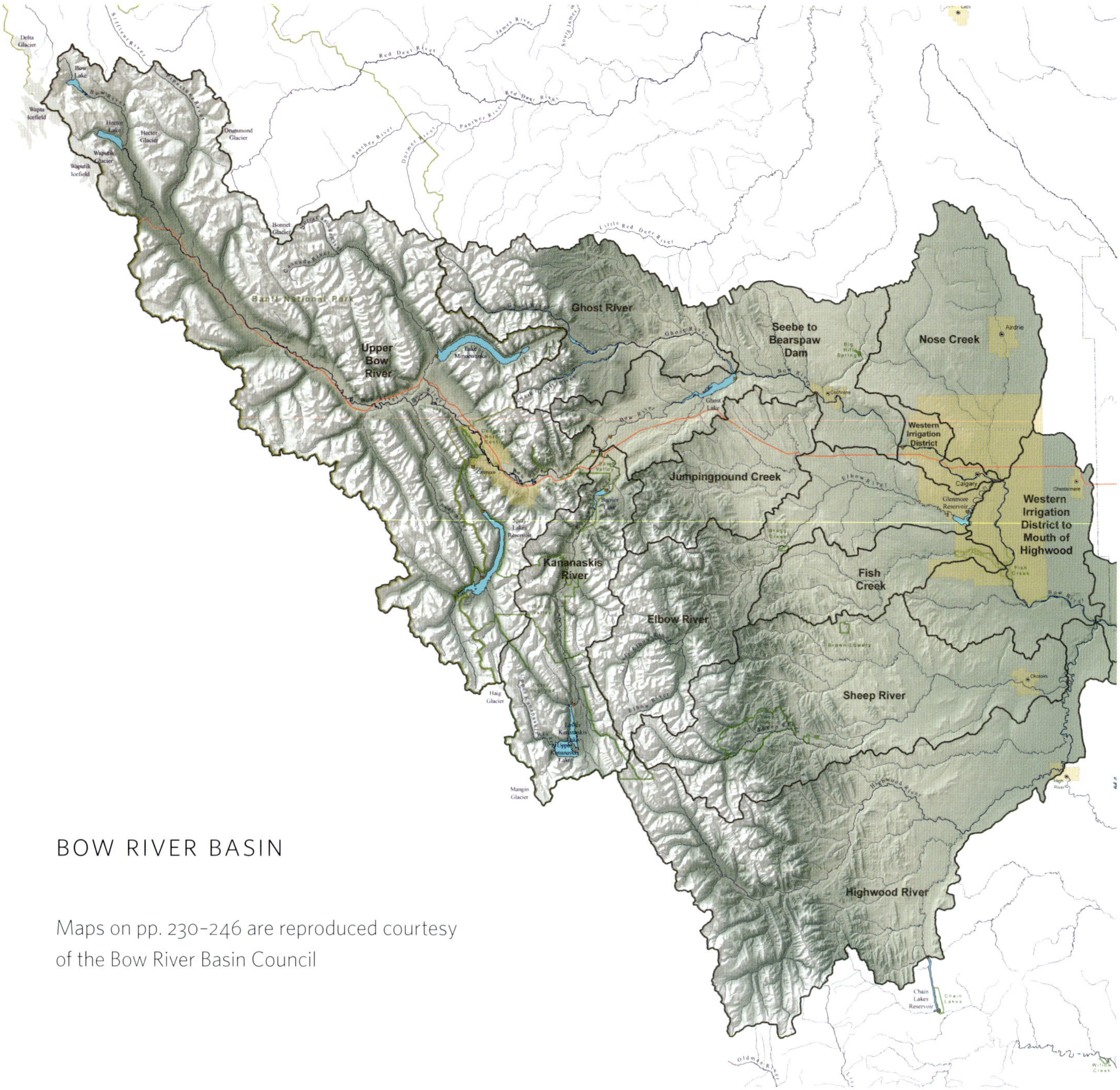

BOW RIVER BASIN

Maps on pp. 230–246 are reproduced courtesy of the Bow River Basin Council

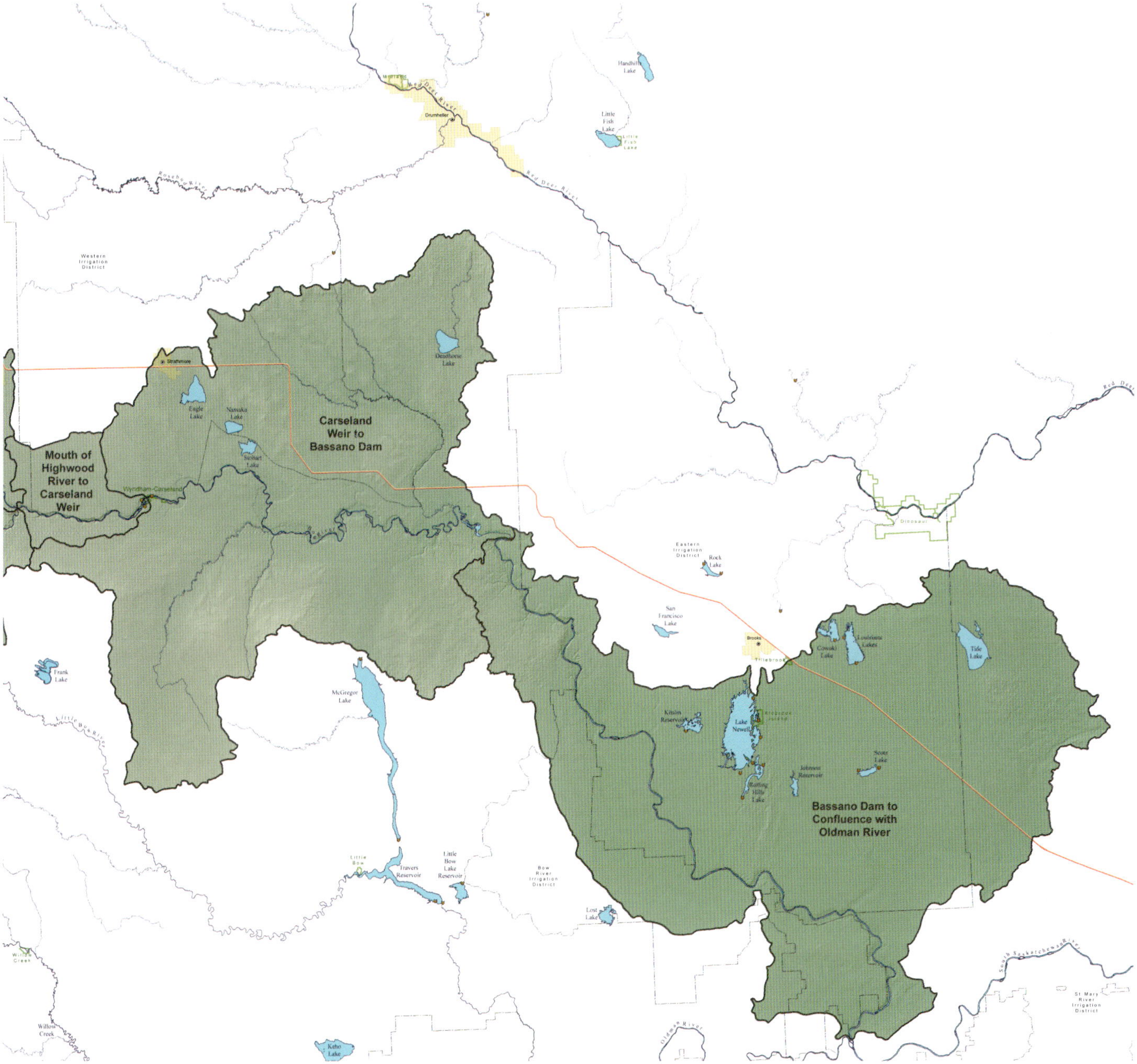
Mouth of Highwood River to Carseland Weir
Carseland Weir to Bassano Dam
Bassano Dam to Confluence with Oldman River

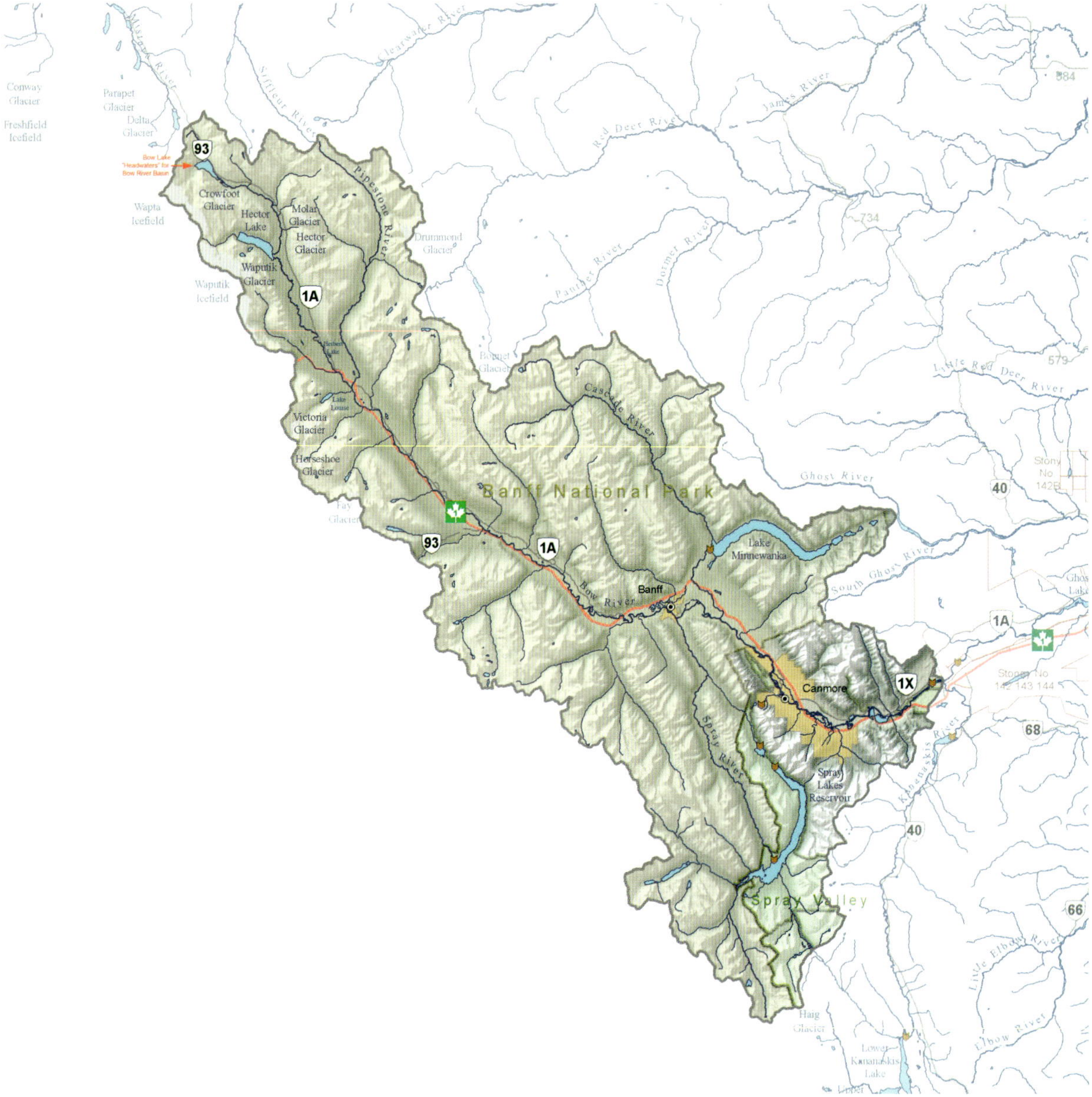

Bow Lake "Headwaters" for Bow River Basin
Conway Glacier
Freshfield Icefield
Parapet Glacier
Delta Glacier
Wapta Icefield
Crowfoot Glacier
Hector Lake
Molar Glacier
Hector Glacier
Waputik Glacier
Waputik Icefield
Pipestone River
Drummond Glacier
Siffleur River
Clearwater River
Red Deer River
James River
Panther River
Dormer River
Bonnet Glacier
Little Red Deer River
Cascade River
Victoria Glacier
Horseshoe Glacier
Fay Glacier
Banff National Park
Ghost River
Lake Minnewanka
South Ghost River
Banff
Bow River
Canmore
Spray River
Spray Lakes Reservoir
Kananaskis River
Spray Valley
Haig Glacier
Lower Kananaskis Lake
Little Elbow River
Elbow River
Stony No 142B
Stoney No 142 143 144
93
1A
1X
40
68
66
584
734
579

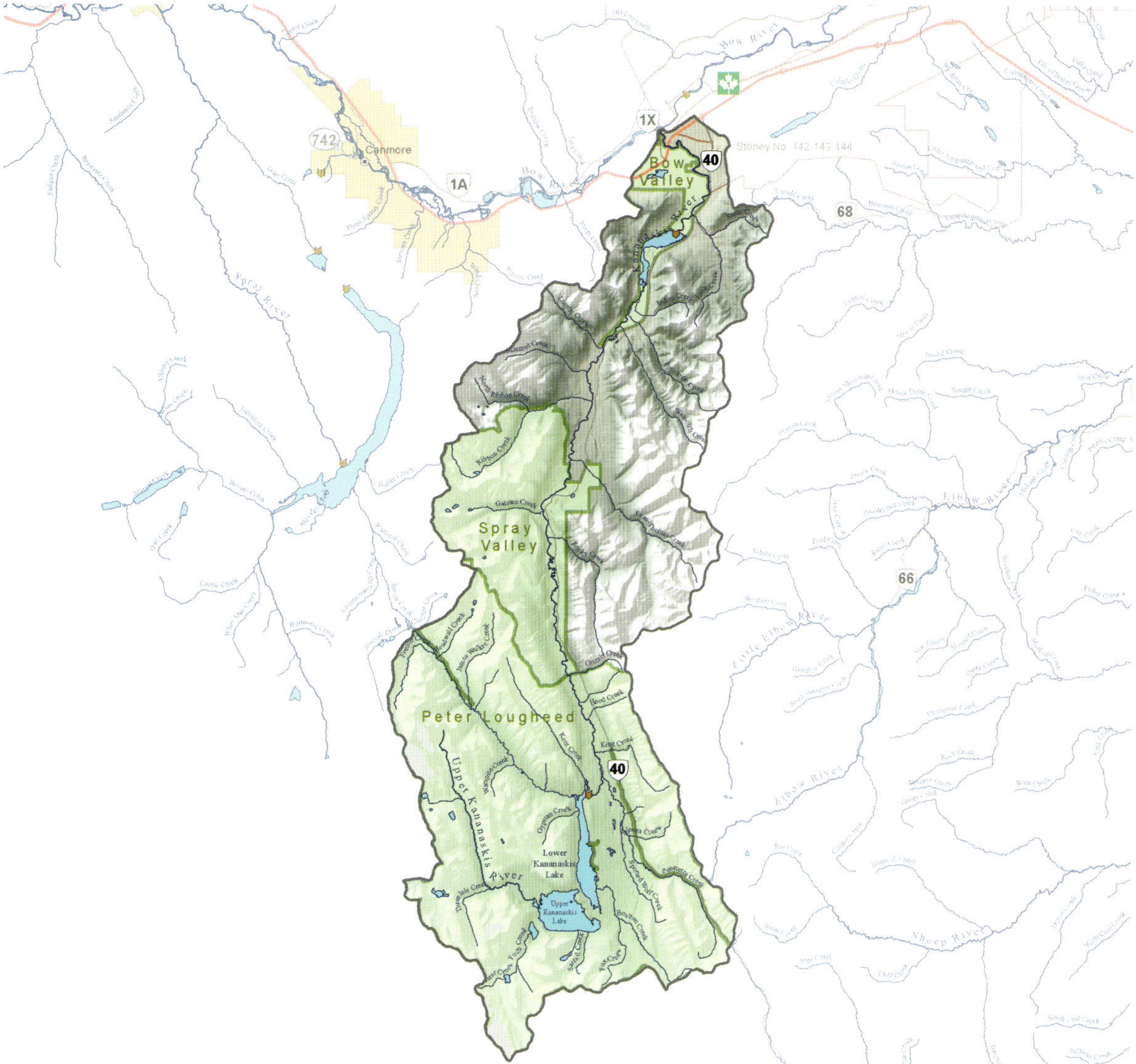

Bow River
1X
742
Canmore
1A
Stoney No. 142 143 144
40
Bow Valley
68
Spray River
Spray Valley
Elbow River
66
Little Elbow River
Peter Lougheed
Upper Kananaskis River
Lower Kananaskis Lake
Upper Kananaskis Lake
Sheep River

MIDDLE BOW RIVER SUB-BASIN

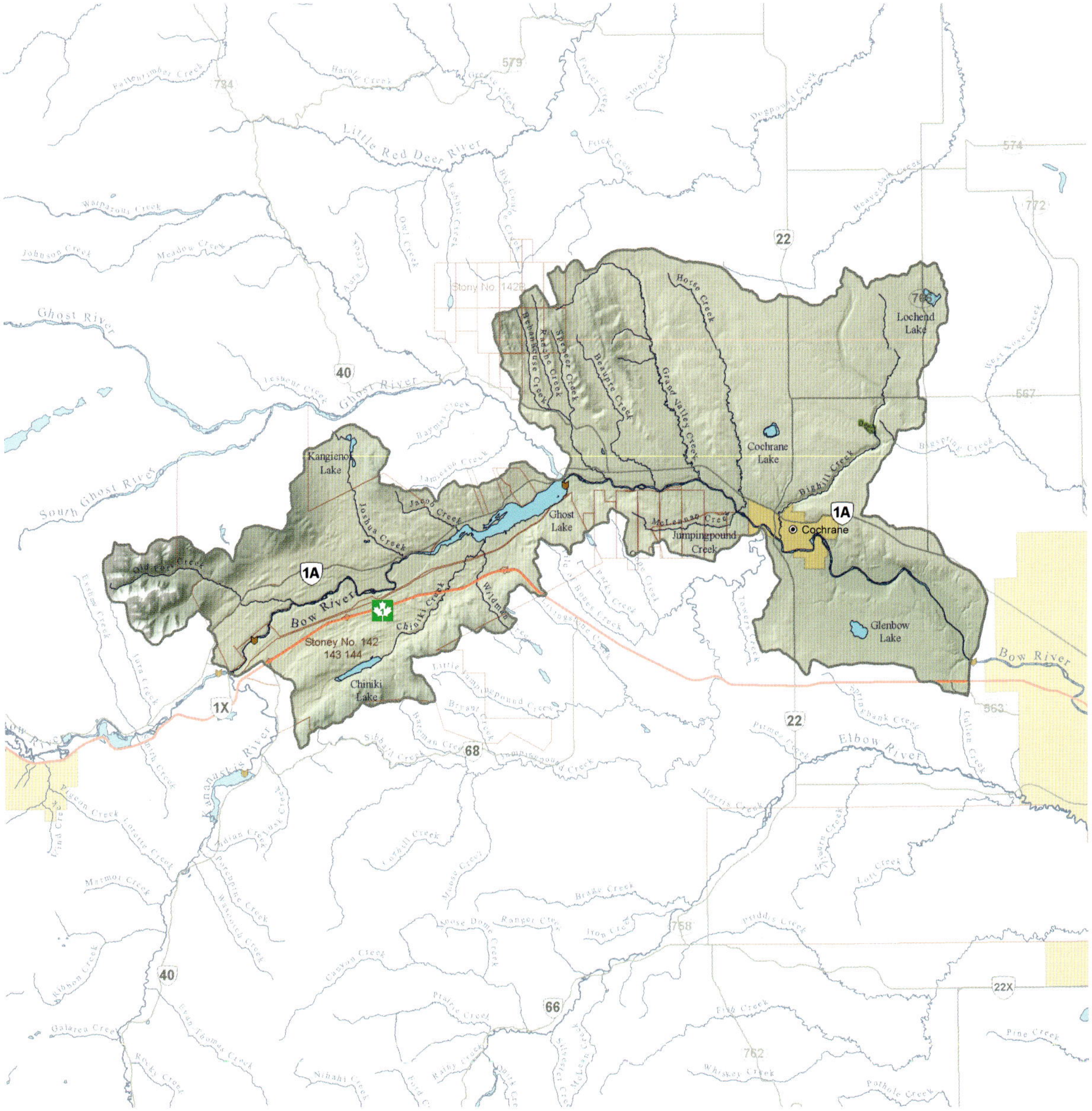

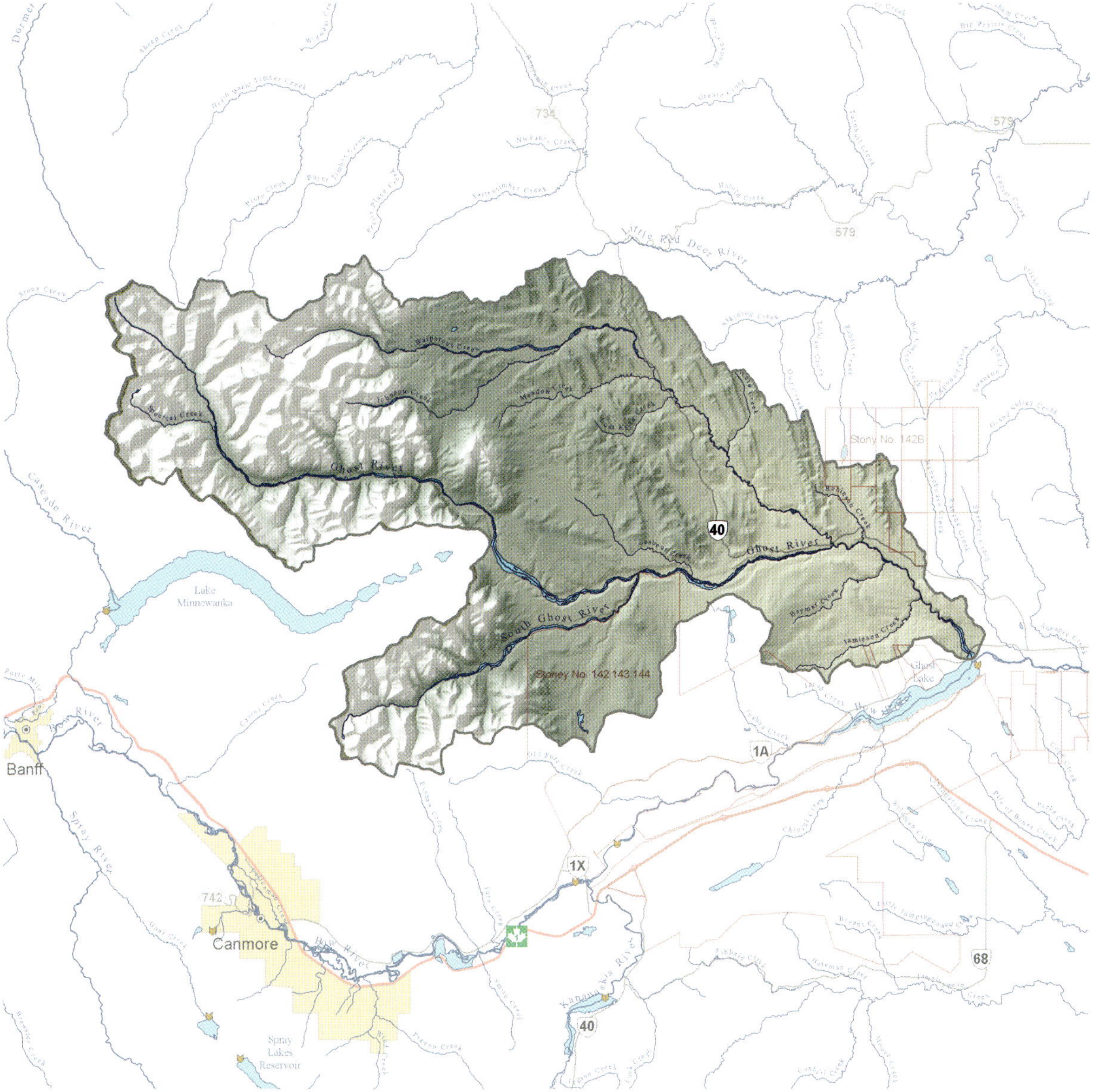
Ghost River
South Ghost River
Little Red Deer River
Cascade River
Lake Minnewanka
Banff
Canmore
Bow River
Spray River
Spray Lakes Reservoir
Ghost Lake
Stoney No. 142 143 144
Stony No. 142B
40
1A
1X
742
579
734
68

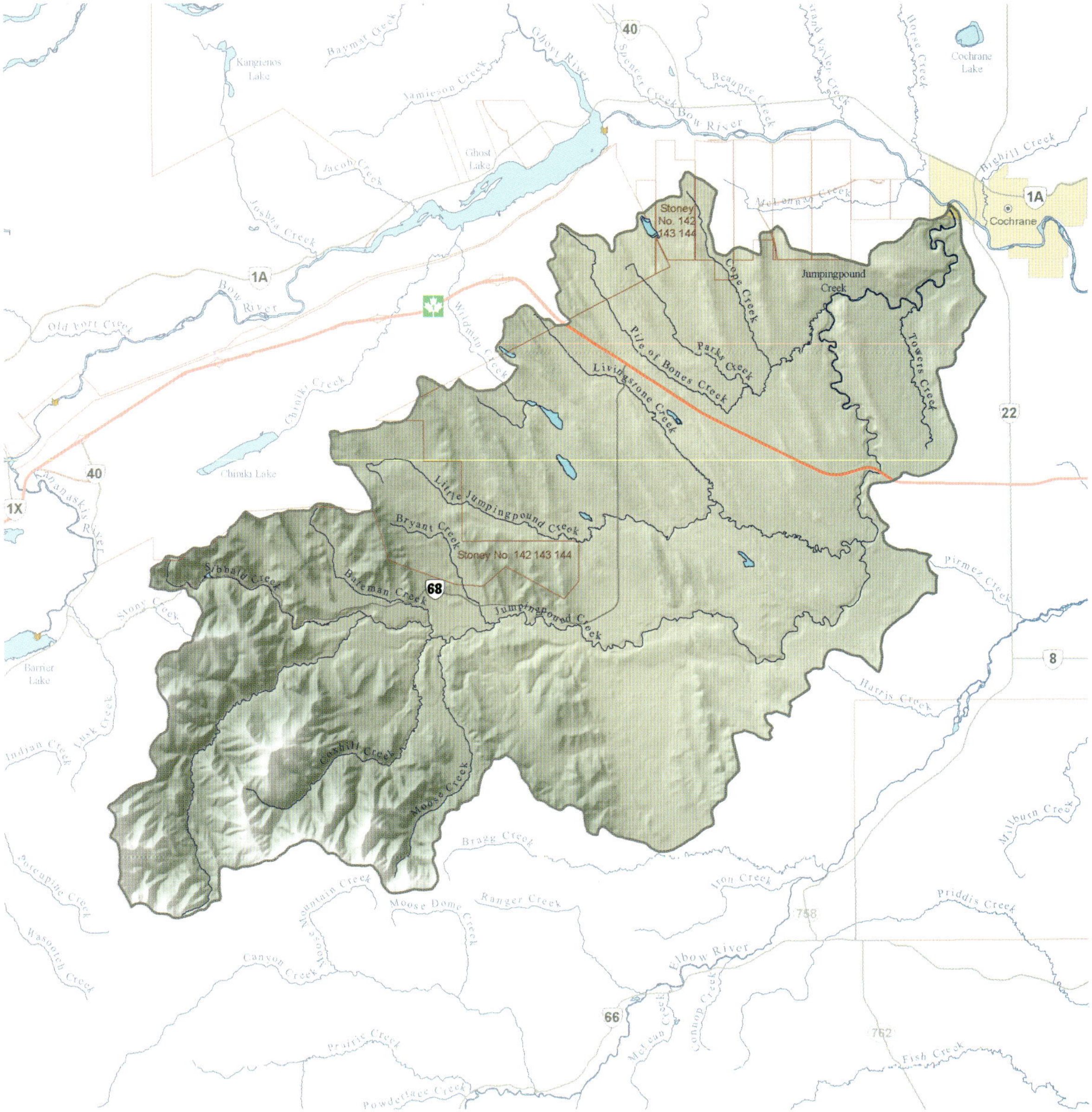
Jumpingpound Creek
Cochrane
Cochrane Lake
Bow River
Ghost River
Ghost Lake
Stoney No. 142 143 144
Cope Creek
Parks Creek
Pile of Bones Creek
Livingstone Creek
Towers Creek
Little Jumpingpound Creek
Bryant Creek
Bateman Creek
Sibbald Creek
Jumpingpound Creek
Coxhill Creek
Moose Creek
Chiniki Lake
Barrier Lake
Bragg Creek
Elbow River
Priddis Creek
Millburn Creek
Harris Creek
Pirmez Creek
Fish Creek
1A
1X
40
22
8
66
68

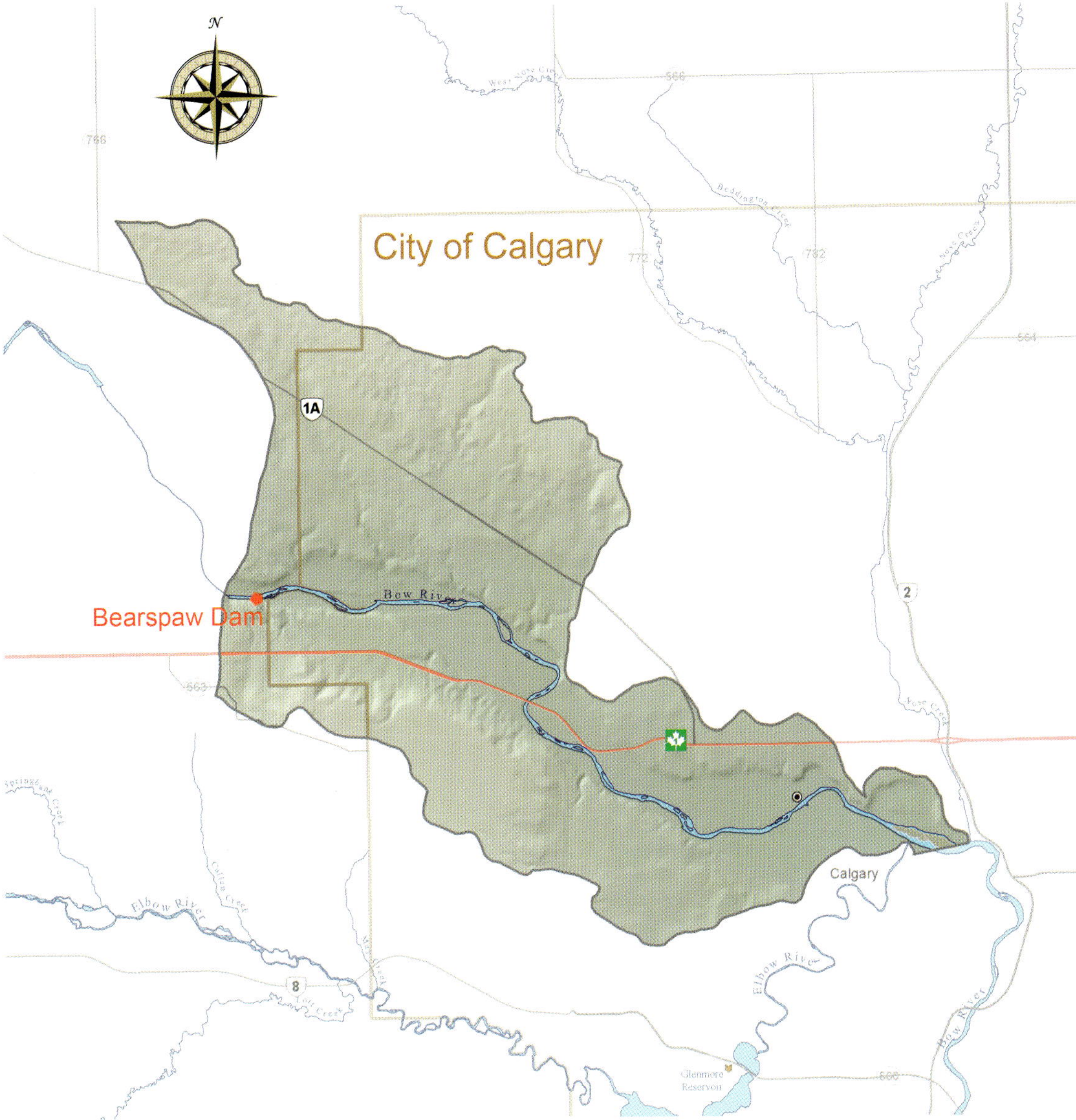
N
City of Calgary
1A
Bow River
Bearspaw Dam
2
Calgary
Elbow River
8
Bow River
Glenmore Reservoir
566
772
782
564
563
766

ELBOW RIVER SUB-BASIN

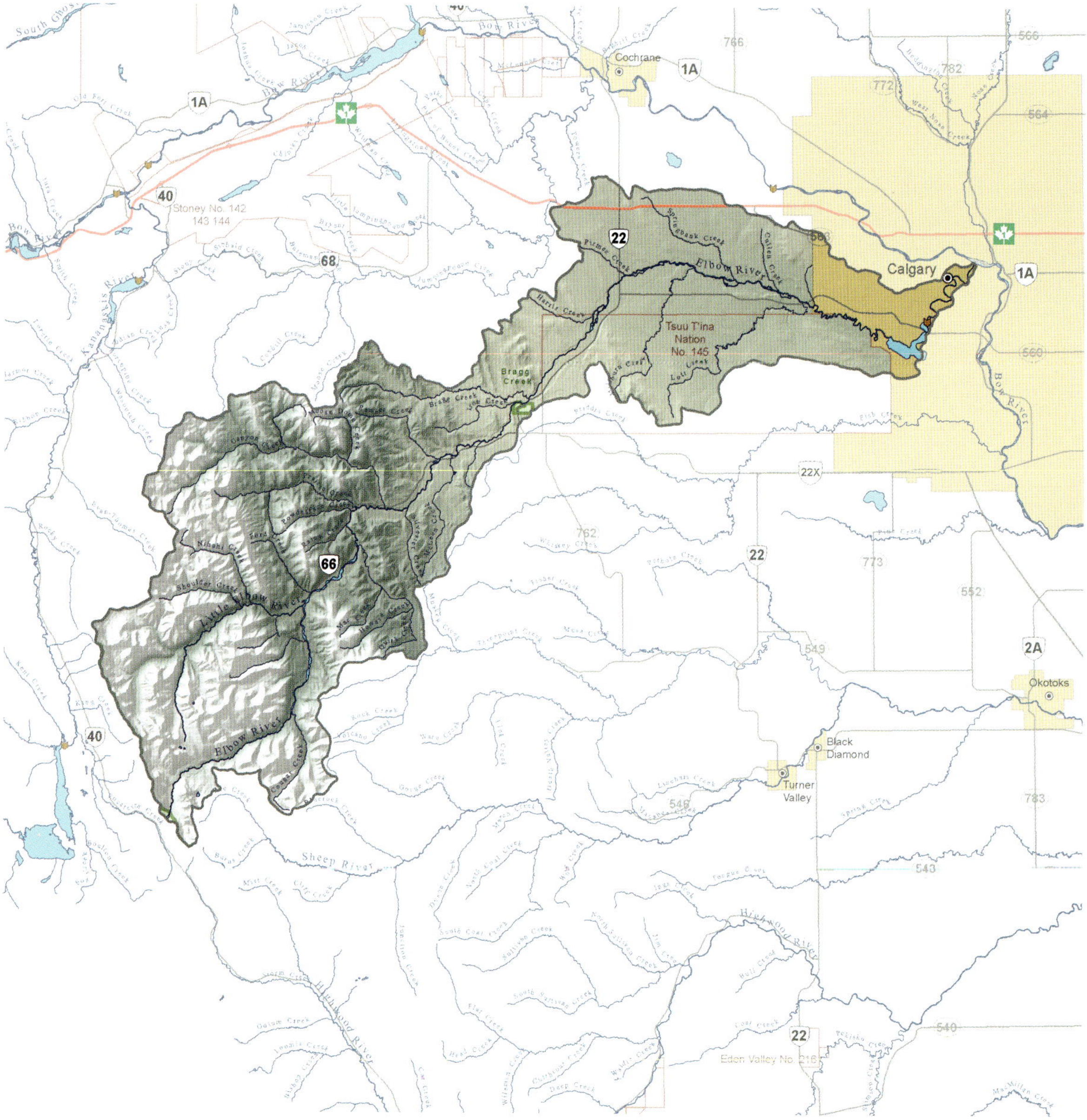

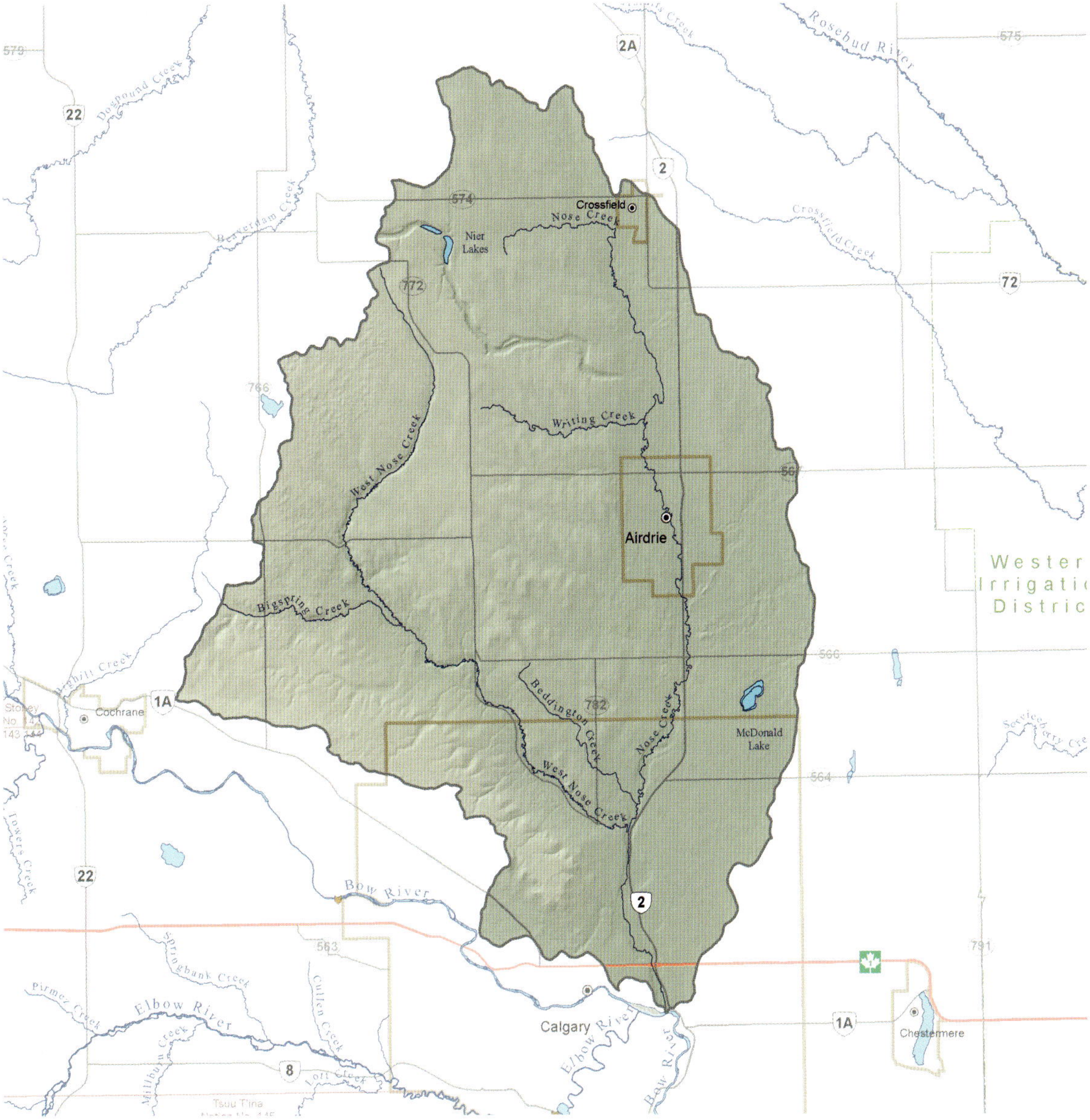
Crossfield
Nose Creek
Nier Lakes
Writing Creek
West Nose Creek
Airdrie
Bigspring Creek
Beddington Creek
McDonald Lake
Cochrane
Bow River
Calgary
Elbow River
Chestermere
Rosebud River
Crossfield Creek
Western Irrigation District
Beaverdam Creek
Jumpingpound Creek
Lott Creek
Cullen Creek
Pirmez Creek
Springbank Creek
Millburn Creek
Jones Creek
Tsuu T'ina
2A
2
22
72
1A
8
574
772
766
567
566
564
563
575
579
782
791

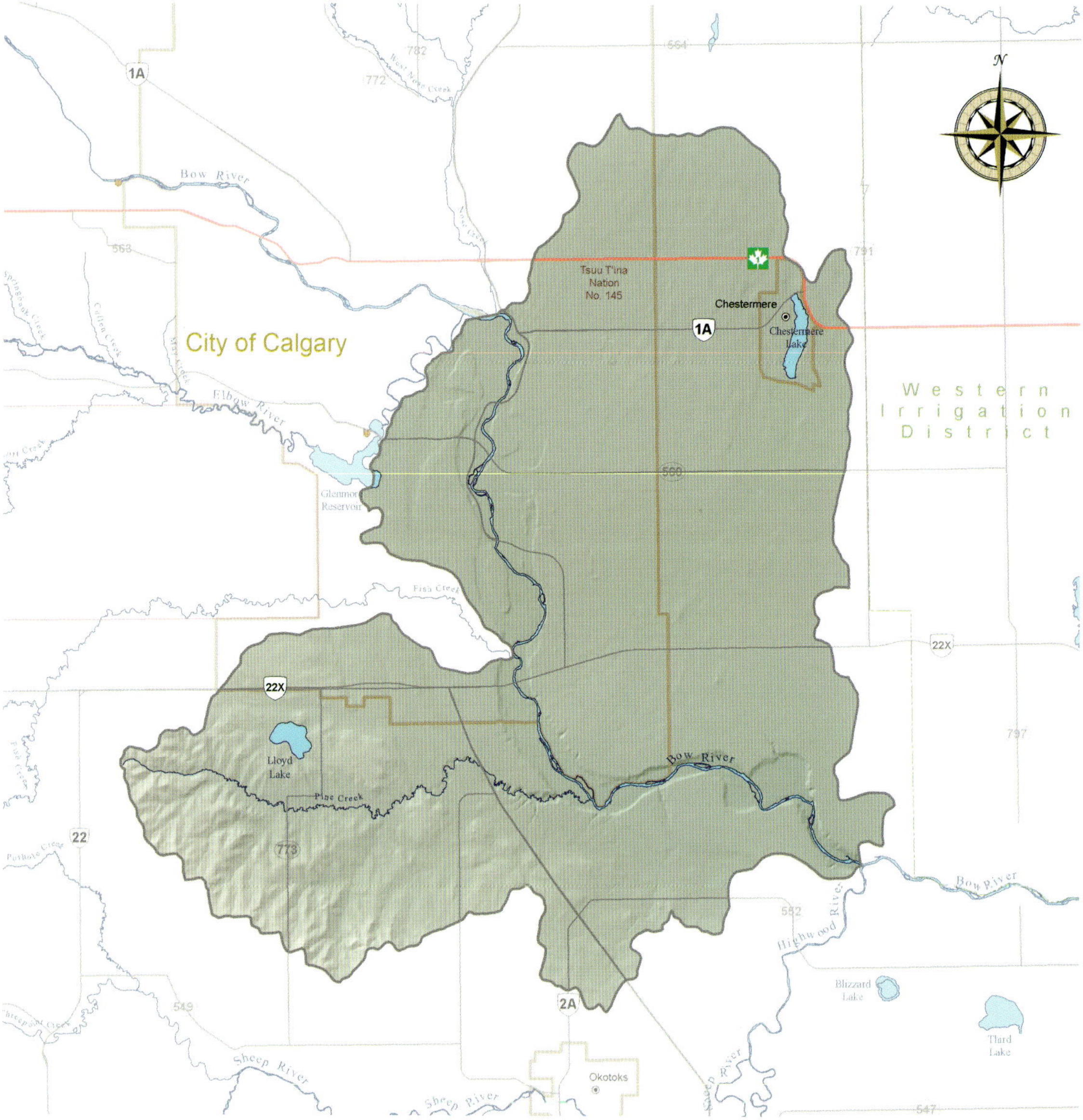
City of Calgary
Tsuu T'ina Nation No. 145
Chestermere
Chestermere Lake
Western Irrigation District
Bow River
Elbow River
Glenmore Reservoir
Fish Creek
Lloyd Lake
Pine Creek
Highwood River
Blizzard Lake
Third Lake
Okotoks
Sheep River
1A
22X
22
2A
773
560
552
549
547
797
791
564
N

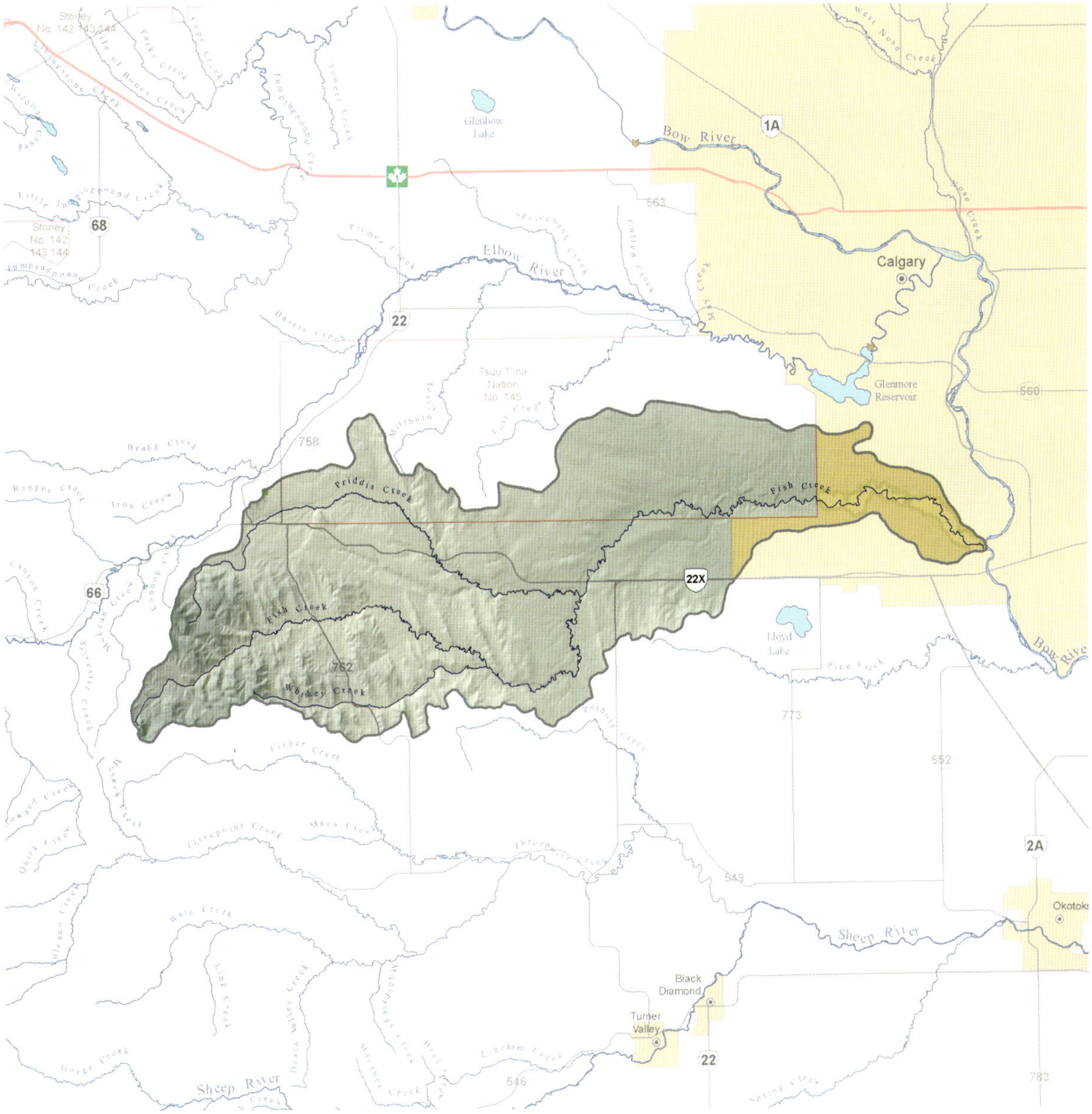
Bow River
1A
Glenbow Lake
Calgary
Elbow River
Glenmore Reservoir
Tsuu T'ina Nation No. 145
Priddis Creek
Fish Creek
Whiskey Creek
22X
22
68
66
758
762
563
560
773
552
549
546
783
2A
Lloyd Lake
Okotoks
Black Diamond
Turner Valley
Sheep River
Stoney No. 142 143 144

SHEEP RIVER SUB-BASIN

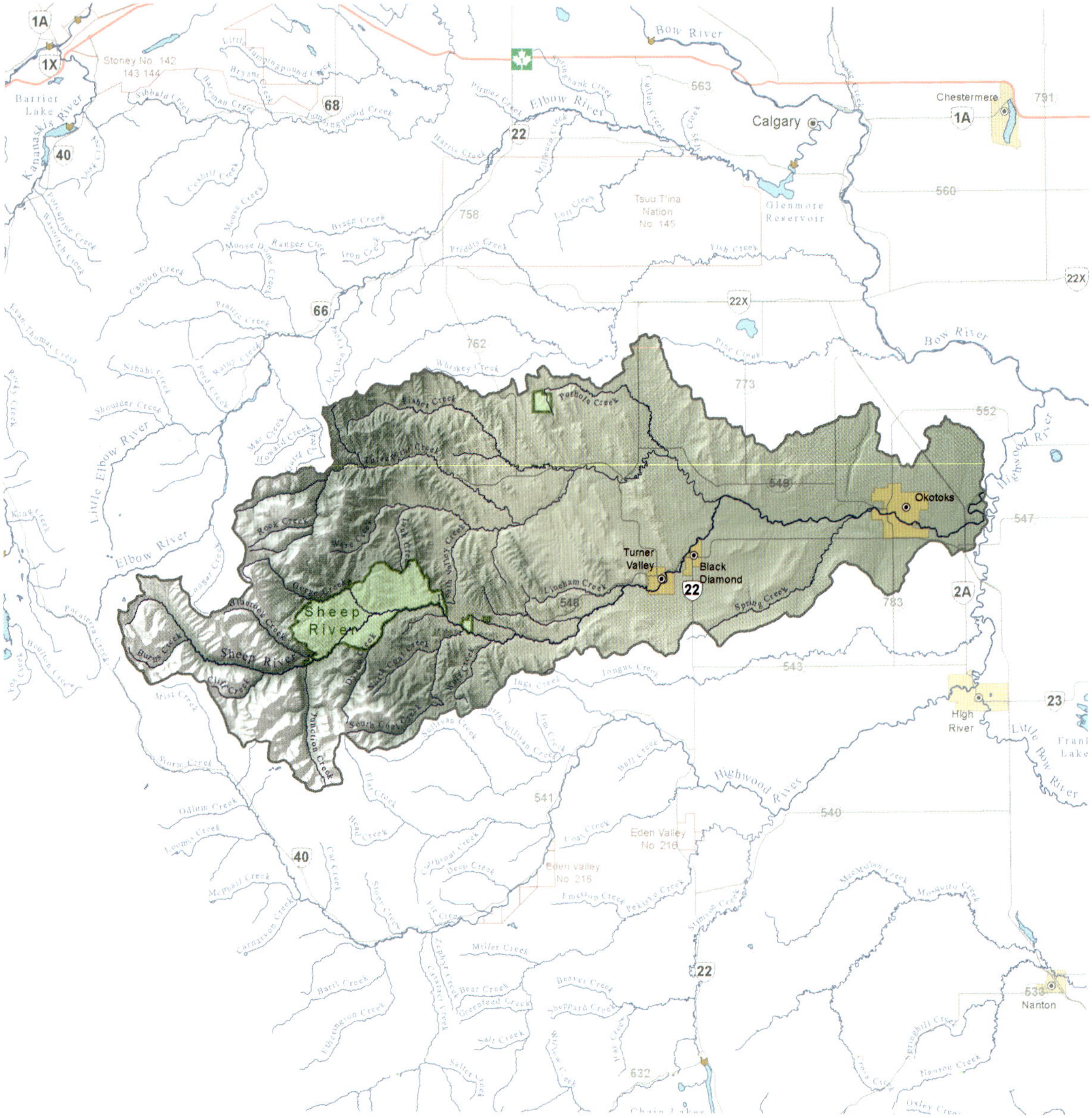

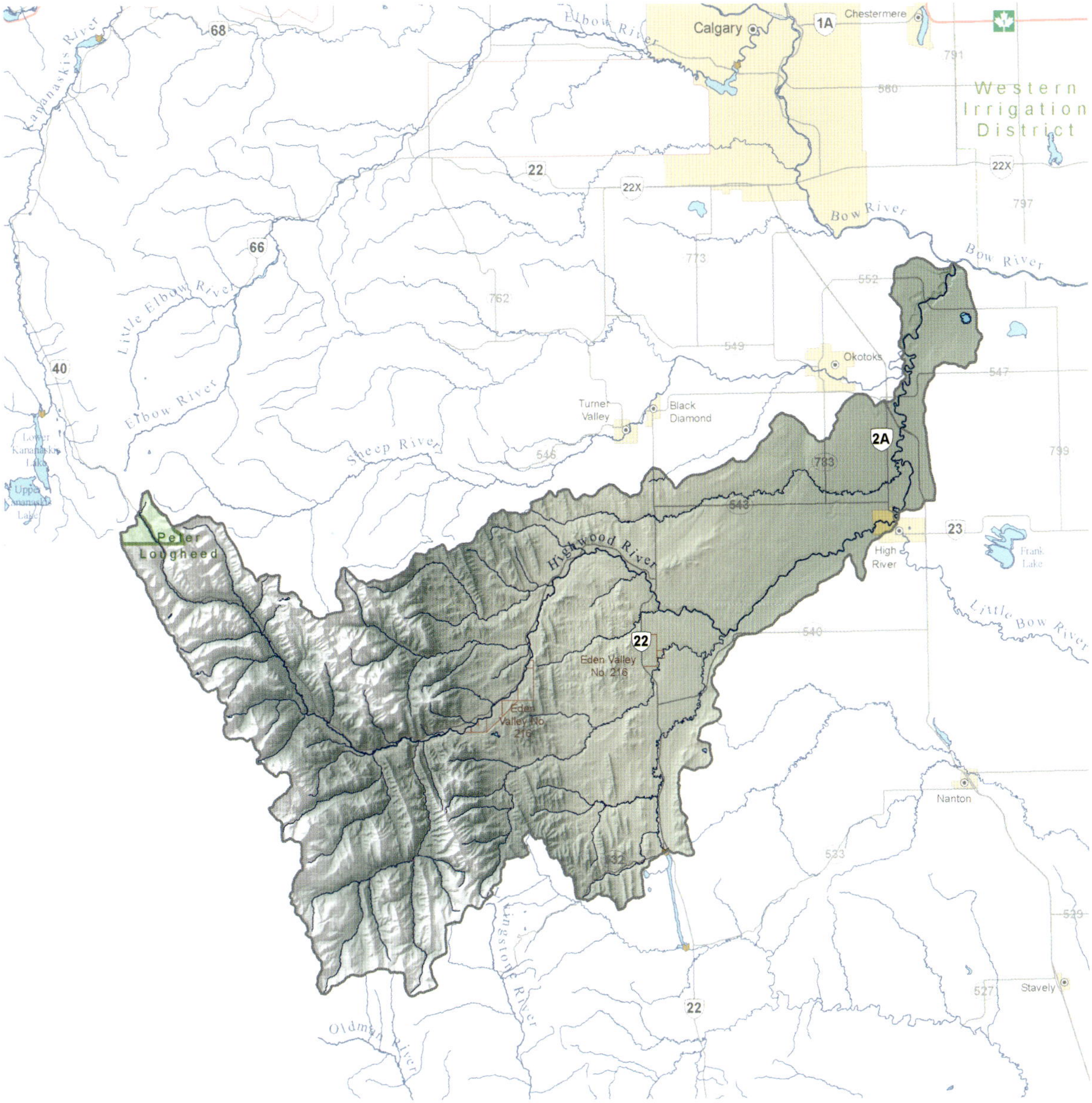
Calgary
Chestermere
Western Irrigation District
Bow River
Elbow River
Okotoks
Turner Valley
Black Diamond
Sheep River
Little Elbow River
Kananaskis River
Peter Lougheed
Highwood River
High River
Frank Lake
Little Bow River
Eden Valley No 216
Nanton
Stavely
Livingstone River
Oldman River

HIGHWOOD CONFLUENCE TO CARSELAND WEIR SUB-BASIN

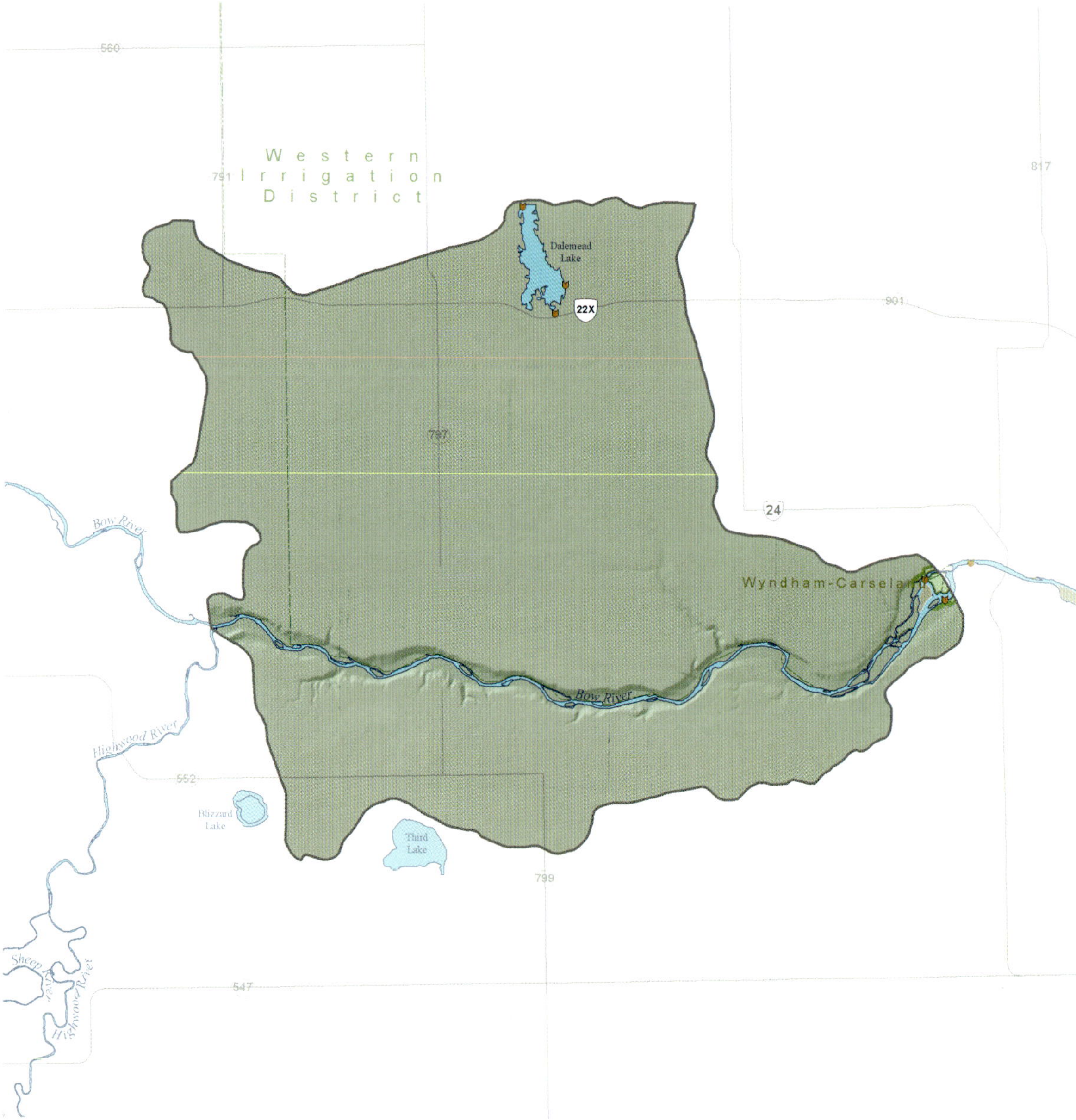

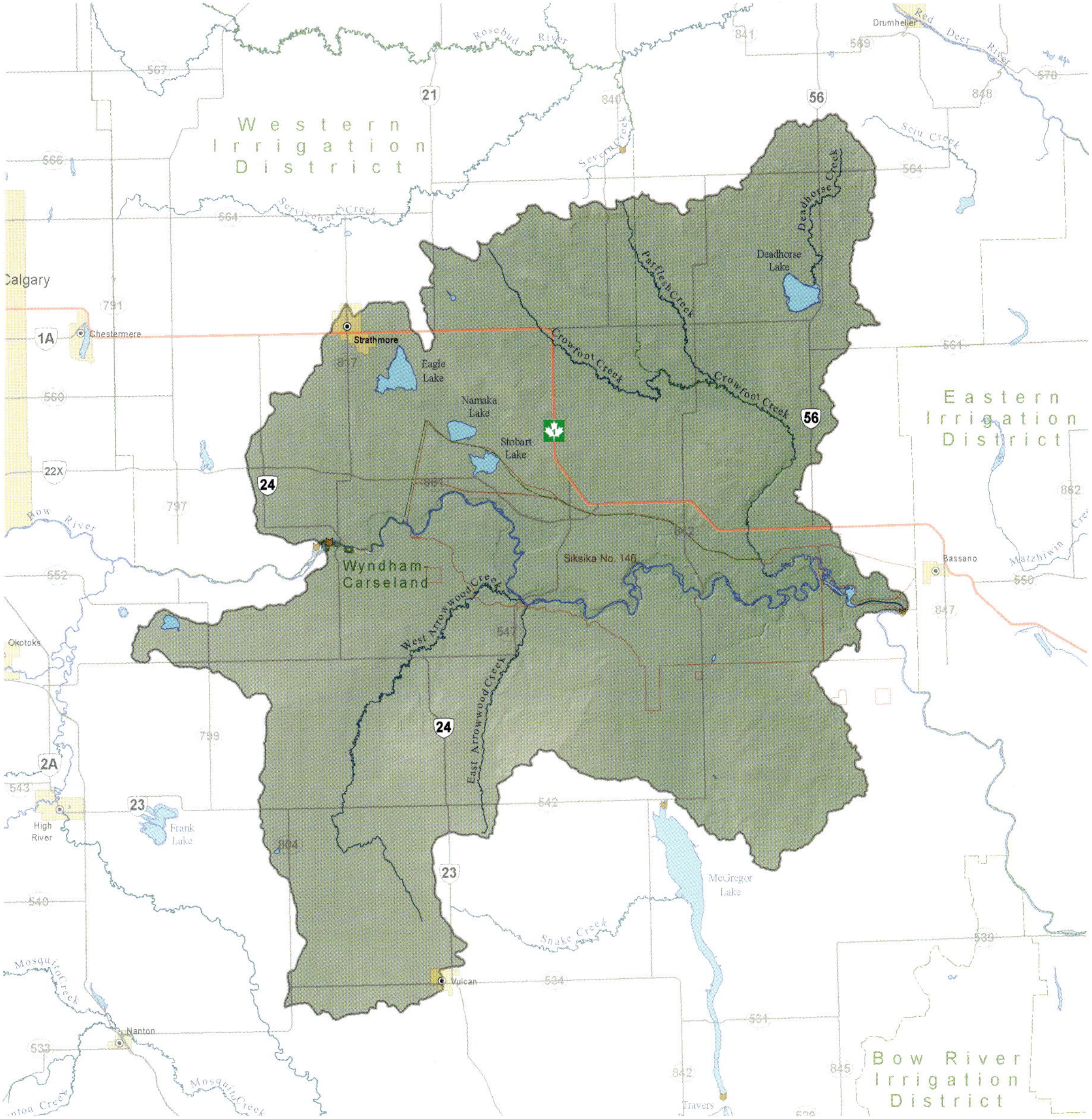
Western Irrigation District
Eastern Irrigation District
Bow River Irrigation District
Calgary
Chestermere
Strathmore
Eagle Lake
Namaka Lake
Stobart Lake
Deadhorse Lake
Deadhorse Creek
Parflesh Creek
Crowfoot Creek
Rosebud River
Severn Creek
Serviceberry Creek
Seiu Creek
Red Deer River
Drumheller
Bow River
Wyndham-Carseland
Siksika No. 146
West Arrowwood Creek
East Arrowwood Creek
Bassano
Matzhiwin Creek
Okotoks
High River
Frank Lake
McGregor Lake
Snake Creek
Vulcan
Nanton
Mosquito Creek
Travers

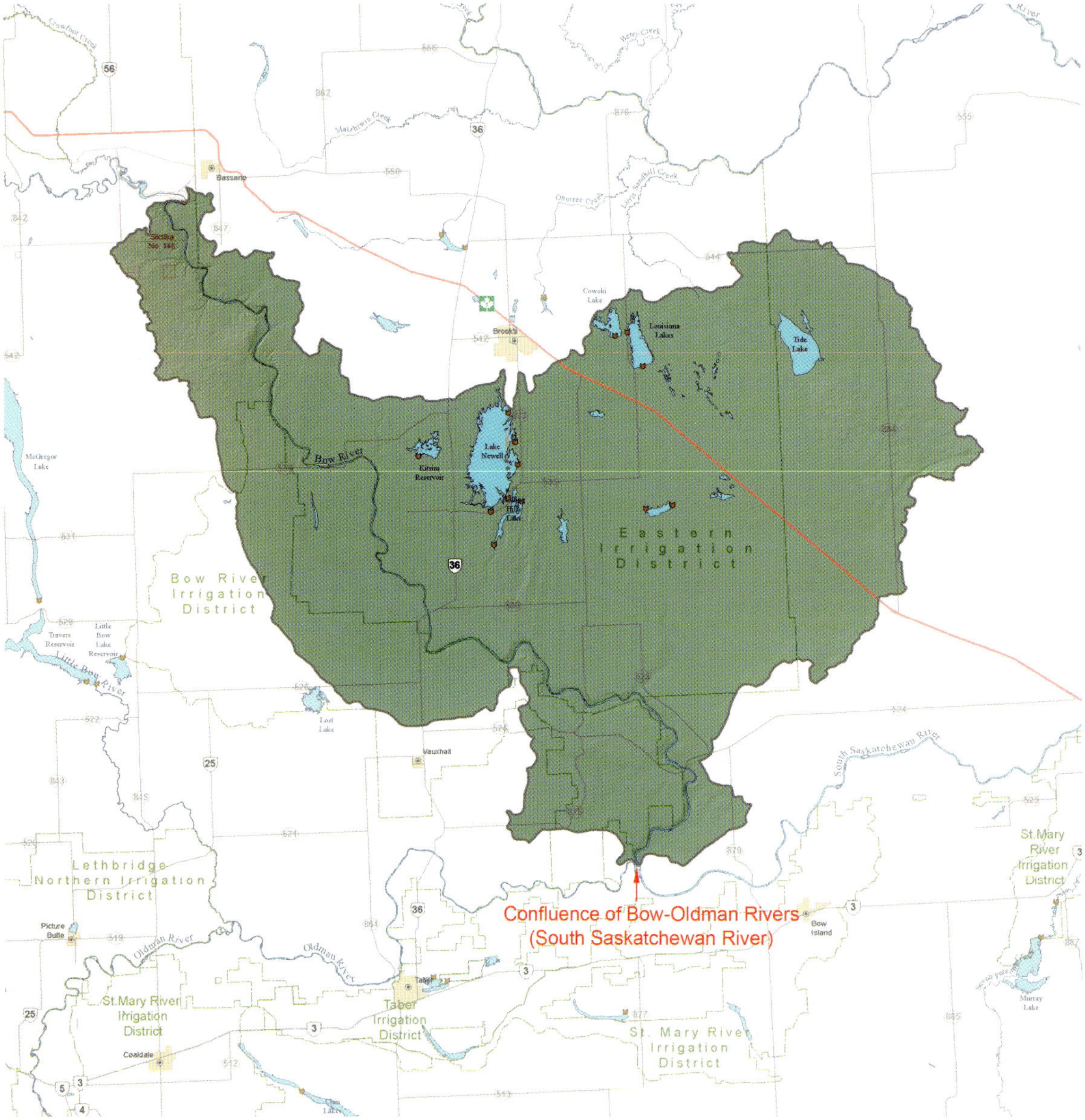
Bassano
Brooks
Bow River
Lake Newell
Kitsim Reservoir
Louisiana Lakes
Tide Lake
Eastern Irrigation District
Bow River Irrigation District
McGregor Lake
Travers Reservoir
Little Bow Lake Reservoir
Little Bow River
Lost Lake
Vauxhall
South Saskatchewan River
Lethbridge Northern Irrigation District
Picture Butte
Oldman River
St.Mary River Irrigation District
Taber
Taber Irrigation District
Coaldale
Bow Island
St. Mary River Irrigation District
Confluence of Bow-Oldman Rivers
(South Saskatchewan River)

My father, Jack Van Tighem, introduced me to these headwater streams from the day I was old enough to join him on long walks into the wild. He had the courage – or perhaps was just sufficiently distracted – to leave me in the company of remote streams for hours at a time. I would never have come to know, love and reflect upon those creeks and their landscapes in the same way if he had been as nervous as too many modern parents have become. With each passing year, my gratitude to that good man grows deeper.

Katherine Govier, Bob Sandford and Don Gorman helped talk me through the logjams that I encountered while trying to figure out how to approach the writing of this book. Bruce Masterman; Bill Hunt; Lorne Fitch; Glenn Webber; my wife, Gail, brother Greg and son and valued collaborator Brian all provided helpful feedback on various chapters. Jim Stelfox and John Pomeroy were kind enough to review drafts of the whole book for errors and inaccuracies, but I may have outfoxed them and retained a few. If so, the blame rests with me, not them. Their assistance was invaluable.

The rivers, streams and watersheds of southern Alberta may face many challenges, but they are also blessed with passionate friends, knowledgeable experts and talented stewards. Many of those admirable people were generous with me, too, agreeing to be interviewed, answering questions and offering insights founded on their own deep experience of the subjects and places in this book. I couldn't have begun to tell these tales without the help of Gordon and Wendy Cartwright, Sarah Cox, Jennifer Earle, Lorne Fitch, Elliot Fox, Wendy Francis, Alan Gardner, Ric Hauer, Glynnis Hood, Bill Hunt, Dave Kay, Daniel Karran, Gord Kelly, Irene Kerr, Gord Lehn, Harvey Locke, Dave Mayhood, Brian Meagher, Ted Morton, Tariq Munir, the late Charlie Pacas, John Pomeroy, Stewart Rood, Uldis Silins, Larry Simpson, Brad Stelfox, Jim Stelfox, Cherie Westbrook and many others.

Thanks to *Alberta Views* magazine and its editor, Evan Osenton, for having published an article that formed the basis for chapter 13. *Alberta Fishing Guide* published an earlier version of the bull trout chapter.

Unless otherwise noted, all photography in this book is by Brian Van Tighem. We appreciate the generosity of Wade Fredenberg, Mike Kelly, Joel Sartore, Gail Van Tighem and Frank Wood for allowing the use of their photographic images. Mark Bennett of the Bow River Basin Council generously granted permission to reproduce their excellent maps. Special thanks are due to Jonathan Ball who drafted the map in Chapter 6 and donated it for use in this book.

The interviews and archival research that went into this work were made possible, in part, by a research grant from the Access Copyright Foundation.

And to the creeks, rivers and green valleys of God's country: thanks for everything. Long may you run.

Alberta Grizzly Bear Recovery Team (Lisa Wilkinson and Gordon Stenhouse, co-chairs). 2008. *Alberta Grizzly Bear Recovery Plan, 2008–2013*. Edmonton: Alberta Sustainable Resource Development, Fish & Wildlife Division.

Allan, J. David. 2004. "Landscapes and Riverscapes: The Influence of Land Use on Stream Ecosystems." *Annual Reviews of Ecological and Evolutionary Systematics* 35: 257–84.

Andrews, Daniel. 2006. "Water Quality Study of Waiparous Creek, Fallentimber Creek and Ghost River." Calgary: Clearwater Environmental Consultants, for Alberta Environment (Project 2005–76).

Annand, Amanda Dawn. 2010. "The 1910 Fires in Alberta's Foothills and Rocky Mountain Regions." Bachelor's thesis, University of Victoria.

Anonymous. 1980. *Alberta Forest Service 50th Anniversary Fact Sheet*. Alberta Provincial Archives.

Armstrong, Christopher, Matthew Evenden and H.V Nelles. 2009. *The River Returns: An Environmental History of the Bow*. Montreal: McGill Queen's University Press.

Armstrong, Christopher, and H.V. Nelles. 2013. *Wilderness and Waterpower: How Banff National Park Became a Hydroelectric Storage Reservoir*. Calgary: University of Calgary Press.

Bow River Basin Council. 2011. *Bow River Basin State of the Watershed Summary: 2010*. Calgary: Bow River Basin Council.

Bow River Project Research Consortium. 2010. *Bow River Project Final Report*. Calgary: Alberta Water Research Institute.

Bradley, Cheryl, Albert A. Einsiedel, Tim Pyrch and Kevin Van Tighem, eds. 1989. *Flowing to the Future*. Proceedings of the Alberta Rivers Conference, Calgary. Edmonton: University of Alberta Press.

Brewin, K., and D.M.A. Monita, eds. 1998. *Land Management Practices Affecting Aquatic Ecosystems*. Proceedings of the Forest-Fish Conference, 1996, Calgary. Ottawa: Natural Resources Canada (Information Report NOR-X-356).

Butler, David R., and George P. Malanson. 2005. "The Geomorphic Influences of Beaver Dams and Failures of Beaver Dams." *Geomorphology* 71: 48–60.

Calgary River Valleys. 2012. "Get to Know the Bow River." Calgary: Calgary River Valleys.

Cochrane and Area Historical Society. 1977. *Big Hill Country: Cochrane and Area*. Cochrane: Cochrane and Area Historical Society.

Costello, Allan B. 2006. "Status of the Westslope Cutthroat Trout (*Oncorhynchus clarkii lewisii*) in Alberta." Edmonton: Alberta Sustainable Resource Development (Wildlife Status Report no. 61).

Craig, John R. 2006. *Ranching with Lords & Commons*. Victoria: Heritage House Books. (Orig. pub. 1903.)

Crerar, A. 1983. "River Basin Management: The Alberta Experience." In Mitchell and Gardner, *River Basin Management: Canadian Experiences*, 271–78.

Daffern, Gillean. 2010–15. *Kananaskis Country Trail Guide*. 4th ed. Calgary: Rocky Mountain Books.

Donald, D.B. 1987. "Assessment of the Outcome of Eight Decades of Trout Stocking in the Mountain National Parks." *North American Journal of Fisheries Management* 7: 545–53

Donald, David B., and David J. Alger. 1993. "Geographic Distribution, Species Displacement and Niche Overlap for Lake Trout and Bull Trout in Mountain Lakes." *Canadian Journal of Zoology* 71: 238–47.

Buckley, Mark, Tom Souhlas, Ernie Niemi and Sarah Reich. 2011. "The Economic Value of Beaver Ecosystem Services, Escalante River Basin, Utah." Seattle: ECONorthwest, for Grand Canyon Trust.

Edworthy, George Edward. 1992. "Exploring the Kananaskis." *Alberta History* 40, no. 2: 16–20.

Enns, Maureen. 2012. *Wild Horses, Wild Wolves: Legends at Risk at the Foot of the Canadian Rockies*. Calgary: Rocky Mountain Books.

Fish and Wildlife Historical Society. 2005. *Fish, Fur and Feathers: Fish and Wildlife Conservation in Alberta, 1905–2005*. Edmonton: Federation of Alberta Naturalists.

Fitch, Lorne. 2014. "Beavers – An Ally or an Inconvenient Species?" *Alberta Water Portal*, August 18.

Popowich, R.P., and J.P. Volpe. 2004. "Troubled Waters: Cumulative Anthropogenic Activity and a Declining Bull Trout Population in the Elbow River Watershed." Paper presented at the Forest Land-Fish Conference II, Edmonton.

Government of Alberta. 1979 (revised 1984). *A Policy for Resource Management on the East Slopes of Alberta*. Edmonton: Alberta Energy and Natural Resources Division, Resource Information Services.

———. 2014. *South Saskatchewan Regional Plan 2014–2024: An Alberta Land-Use Framework Integrated Plan*. Edmonton: Government of Alberta.

Hanson, W.R. 1972. "The Conservation of a Canadian Watershed: A Case Study." Paper presented on behalf of the Eastern Rockies Forest Conservation Board at the United Nations Conference on the Human Environment, Stockholm, 1972. Alberta Provincial Archives.

Hanson, W.R., and G. Tunstell. 1962. "Forest and Water Conservation: Watershed Management on the East Slopes of the Rocky Mountains in Alberta, Canada." Paper presented at the eighth British Commonwealth Forestry Conference, East Africa, 1962. Alberta Provincial Archives.

Hart, E.J. (Ted). 2010. *J.B. Harkin: Father of Canada's National Parks*. Edmonton: University of Alberta Press.

High River Oldtimers Association. 1960. *Leaves from the Medicine Tree: A History of the Area Influenced by the Tree, and Biographies of Pioneers and Old Timers Who Came Under Its Spell Prior to 1900*. Out of print. Holdings of the High River Museum.

Hillman, G.R. 1998. "Flood Wave Attenuation by a Wetland Following a Beaver Dam Failure on a Second-Order Boreal Stream." *Wetlands* 18, no. 1: 21–34.

Hood, Glynnis. 2012. *The Beaver Manifesto*. Calgary: Rocky Mountain Books.

Hunt, Constance, and Verne Huser. 1988. *Down by the River: The Impact of Federal Water Projects and Policies on Biological Diversity*. Washington: Island Press.

Hynes, H.B.N. 1970. *The Ecology of Running Waters*. Liverpool: Liverpool University Press.

Isaak, Daniel J., Clint C. Muhfield, Andrew S. Todd, Robert Al-Chokhachy, James Roberts, Jeffrey L. Kershner, Kurt D. Fausch and Steven W. Hostetler. 2012. "The Past as Prelude to the Future in Understanding 21st-Century Climate Effects on Rocky Mountain Trout." *Fisheries* 37, no. 12: 542–56.

Johnson, E.A., and C.P.S. Larsen. 1991. "Climatically Induced Change in Fire Frequency in the Southern Canadian Rockies." *Ecology* 72, no. 1: 194–201.

Jumpingpound Creek Watershed Partnership. 2009. "Jumpingpound Creek: State of the Watershed Report, 2009." Mossleigh, AB: Palliser Environmental Services.

Kienzle, Stefan W., and Markus Mueller. 2013. "Mapping Alberta's Surface Water Resources for the Period 1971–2000." *The Canadian Geographer* 10, no. 10: 1–13.

Laycock, Arleigh H. 1954. "Water Supply of the Saskatchewan River: Its Source, Use and Conservation." Unpublished report for the Eastern Rockies Forest Conservation Board, Calgary.

MacDonald, G.M. 1982. "Late Quaternary Paleoenvironments of the Morley Flats and Kananaskis Valley of Southwestern Alberta." *Canadian Journal of Earth Sciences* 19: 23–35.

Marshall, S., and E. White. 2010. "Alberta Glacier Inventory and Ice Volume Estimation." *Canadian Water Resources Journal* (in press when consulted).

Masterman, Bruce A., and Jim D. Stelfox. 2009. *Looking Back: An Historical Report of Angler Experiences along the Eastern Slopes of South-Western Alberta.* Edmonton: Alberta Sustainable Resource Development, Fish & Wildlife Division.

McLennan, Jim. 2002. *Blue Ribbon Bow.* Calgary: Johnson Gorman Publishing.

Meredith, Duane, and Don Radford, eds. 2008. *Conservation, Pride and Passion: The Alberta Fish and Game Association, 1908–2008.* Edmonton: *Edmonton Journal.*

Miller, R.B. 1954. "Comparative Survival of Wild and Hatchery-Reared Cutthroat Trout in a Stream." *Transactions of the American Fisheries Society* 83, no. 1: 120–30.

———. 1962. *A Cool Curving World.* Toronto: Longmans Canada, 1962.

———. 1958. "The Role of Competition in the Mortality of Hatchery Trout." J. Fisheries Research Board of Canada. 15, no. 1: 27–45.

Mitchell, Bruce, and James S. Gardner, eds. 1983. *River Basin Management: Canadian Experiences.* University of Waterloo, Department of Geography Publication Series No. 20.

Munir, T.M., B. Xu, M. Perkins and M. Strack. 2014. "Responses of Carbon Dioxide Flux and Plant Biomass to Water Table Drawdown in a Treed Peatland in Northern Alberta: A Climate Change Perspective." *Biogeosciences* 11: 807–80.

Murphy, Peter John. 2006. *The Alberta Forest Service, 1930–2005: Protection and Management of Alberta's Forests.* Edmonton: Alberta Public Affairs Bureau.

Nelson, Joseph S., and Martin Joseph Paetz. 1992. *The Fishes of Alberta.* Edmonton: University of Alberta Press.

Oltmann, Ruth. 1997. *My Valley the Kananaskis.* Calgary: Rocky Mountain Books.

Palmer, Tim. 1986. *Endangered Rivers and the Conservation Movement.* Oakland: University of California Press.

Patterson, Raymond M. 1961. *The Buffalo Head.* Toronto: Macmillan of Canada.

Pollock, Michael M., Morgan Heim and Danielle Werner. 2003. "Hydrologic and Geomorphic Effects of Beaver Dams and Their Influence on Fishes." *American Fisheries Society Symposium* 37: 213–33.

Polvi, Lina E., and Ellen Wohl. 2012. "The Beaver Meadow Complex Revisited – The Role of Beavers in Post-Glacial Floodplain Development." *Earth Surface Processes and Landforms* 37: 332–46.

Pomeroy, John, Ronald E. Stewart and Paul H. Whitfield. 2014 (in prep.). "The 2013 Flood Event in the Bow and Oldman River Basins: Causes, Assessment, and Damages." As prepared for submission to *Canadian Water Resources Journal.*

Pomeroy, John, Phillip Harder, Keith Musselman, Xing Fang and Chad Ellis. 2013. "Marmot Creek Research Basin: Progress and Prospects." Unpublished PowerPoint presentation.

Popowich, R., and G. Eisler. 2007. "An Inventory of Bank Armour and Riparian Disturbance along the Elbow, Sheep and Highwood Rivers, Alberta." Calgary: Applied Aquatic Research, for the Trout Unlimited Canada Riparian Mapping Project (Project AAR06-162).

Rood, Stewart B., Jason Pan, Karen M. Gill, Carmen G. Franks, Glenda M. Samuelson and Anita Shepherd. 2008. "Declining Summer Flows of Rocky Mountain Rivers: Changing Seasonal Hydrology and Probable Impacts on Floodplain Forests." *Journal of Hydrology* 349: 397–410.

Ross, P. Ian, Martin G. Jalkotzy and Marco Festa-Bianchet. 1997. "Cougar Predation on Bighorn Sheep in Southwestern Alberta during Winter." *Canadian Journal of Zoology* 75: 771–75.

Russell, Andy. 1987. *The Life of a River*. Toronto: McClelland & Stewart.

Sandford, Robert William. 2012. *Cold Matters: The State and Fate of Canada's Fresh Water*. Calgary: Rocky Mountain Books.

Schnorbus, M. 2011. "A Synthesis of the Hydrological Consequences of a Large-Scale Mountain Pine Beetle Disturbance." Ottawa: Natural Resources Canada (Mountain Pine Beetle Working Paper 2010–1).

Shaw, Erin Lorraine. 2009. "Lateral Exchange of Water and Nitrogen along a Beaver-Dammed Stream Draining a Rocky Mountain Valley." Master's thesis, University of Saskatchewan.

Sophocleus, Marios. 2002. "Interactions between Groundwater and Surface Water: The State of the Science." *Hydrogeology Journal* 10: 52–67.

Stelfox, Jim D., Dean M. Baayens, Greg R. Eisler, Andrew J. Paul and Georgina E. Shumaker. 2004. "Quirk Creek Brook Trout Suppression Project." Paper presented at the Wild Trout VIII Symposium, Yellowknife (*Symposium Proceedings*, 265–75).

Spry, Irene Mary. 1963. *The Palliser Expedition: An Account of John Palliser's British North American Expedition, 1857–1860*. Toronto: Macmillan of Canada.

Swanson, R.H., R.D. Wynes and R.L. Rothwell. "Estimating the Cumulative Long-Term Effects of Forest Harvests on Annual Water Yield in Alberta. In Brewin and Monita, *Land Management Practices,* 83–94.

Van Tighem, Kevin. 1997. *Coming West: A Natural History of Home*. Calgary: Altitude.

———. 2000. *Home Range: Writings on Conservation and Restoration*. Calgary: Altitude.

Wilcox, Walter. 2008. *The Rockies of Canada*. Calgary: Rocky Mountain Books. (Orig. pub. 1900.)